NEW CLASSICISM

Omnibus Volume

QUINLAN TERRY, STONE SEAT AT DOWER HOUSE, ROYDON, ESSEX, 1978

LEON KRIER, PIAZZA SEDILE, FILADELFIA, CALABRIA, 1983, (WATERCOLOUR BY RITA WOLFF)

EDITED BY
ANDREAS PAPADAKIS & HARRIET WATSON

NEW CLASSICISM
Omnibus Volume
Foreword by Leon Krier

DEMETRI PORPHYRIOS, CHEPSTOW VILLAS, LONDON, 1989

RIZZOLI
NEW YORK

Editorial Note

After many years of promoting new classical architecture by commissioning articles and arranging symposia and exhibitions on New Classicism, I feel the current resurgence of interest in the field makes this a good moment to publish an anthology. In bringing together this volume I have been fortunate to have at my disposal a wealth of material published in *Architectural Design*, which, beginning with the Venice Biennale of 1980, has carefully followed the developments of Classicism's return to strength. This book has been compiled with the help and advise of two invaluable supporters: Leon Krier, whom I would like to thank not only for providing the Foreword, but also for his help and collaboration over many years, and Demetri Porphyrios to whom I am much indebted for his close involvement and for providing many of the illustrations. A number of articles are based on papers presented at the Academy Forum Symposium at London's Tate Gallery, which I organised in conjunction with Richard Humphries in 1988. My thanks go to Sir Alan Bowness, the then director, as well as to Sir John Summerson for joining us in that venture. Other articles have been specially commissioned and full credits are published at the back of the book. Much inspiration has also been taken from the pioneering work of Maurice Culot and the Archives d'Architecture Moderne. I should like to thank the many writers and architects for allowing us to reproduce their work. Thanks are due to members of Academy Editions staff who have helped in compiling this volume, notably Vivian Constantinopoulos, for her general help and for seeing many of the essays through press, and Maggie Toy for helping in the preparation of the pictorial surveys.   *Andreas Papadakis*

FRONT COVER: RITA WOLFF, *ACROPOLIS*, 1987 (WATERCOLOUR)

First published in the United States of America in 1990 by
RIZZOLI INTERNATIONAL PUBLICATIONS, INC
300 Park Avenue South, New York, NY 10010

Published in Great Britain in 1990 by
ACADEMY EDITIONS
an imprint of the Academy Group Ltd, 7 Holland Street, London W8 4NA

ISBN 0-8478-1296-0
LC 90-52754

Printed and Bound in Hong Kong

CONTENTS

LEON KRIER
FOREWORD

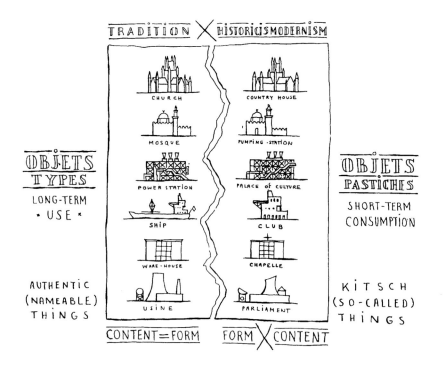

In the last decade of the Millenium, the practice of vernacular building and classical architecture is neither a conventional nor an innocent exercise. It is not taught by schools nor recognised by important institutions; HRH The Prince of Wales, its lone patron, indeed holds an avant-garde position that draws the full blast of enemy fire.

Quinlan Terry and Manuel Manzano-Monis, Abdel Wahed El Wakil and Allan Greenberg are all well-known figures in their respective countries and as such have become the subjects of calumny among their profession and its institutions. Despite claims to be champions of a democratic and pluralist approach, these bodies show very little support towards contemporary classicists. They seem too ready to denounce the classicists' incorruptibility as moral intolerance, and their consistency as dogmatic inflexibility.

In 1990 professional architectural pluralism is indeed years behind political pluralism. The fundamental achievement of the American Revolution was not that convictions have to be sacrificed on the altar of tolerance, but that tolerance as a fundamental attitude allows divergent and even contradictory convictions to live their separate lives peacefully under the rule of law.

Far from being its supporting foundations, 'pluralists' are the flotsam of democratic competition. True democratic plurality embraces both tradition and modernism. The 'pluralist' instead is an enemy of true plurality, for he finds convictions suspicious and dangerous. His dogma is flexibility because he cannot believe in anything for long. He hates to be held responsible because he cannot feel committed, and will excuse or justify his blunders by loading them on the shoulders of family, class or system, of climate, economy and technology – and always of

historic necessity. He will, above all else, defend his holy right to experiment, to remain open, to be unpredictable and even to go wrong without having to feel bad about it.

The 'pluralist' hates nothing more than beliefs: his mass non-conformism fears nothing more than conservative individualism. So it is little wonder that the classicist's detractors will defend almost any arbitrary experiment and the advocates of architectural punk will be highly critical of his mouldings and proportions. They will accuse him of building for the rich and at the same time admire a Hong-Kong bank for exceeding all cost predictions. The radical chic feels annoyed about him sharing invitations to symposia. Although they are perfectly happy to live in Georgian houses, they find it inconsistent of him to use the telephone.

Professional reactions against Terry in England, Barbe in France, Manzano-Monis in Spain, Rob Krier in Austria, Malmquist in Sweden, Blatteau in the US – all are predictably similar. For 40 years, Modernism has been the dominant style of totalitarian regimes of left and right, from Cape Town to Moscow via Chile, Cuba and Romania. Mies was prepared to work for Hitler, and Le Corbusier for Petain. Aalto paid Hitler's sculptor a friendly visit in Berlin in 1942, Terragni worked for Mussolini and Niemeyer for a number of dictators all over the world – and still the bigots continue to quote Herbert Read's disgusting tyrade that 'in the back of every dying civilisation

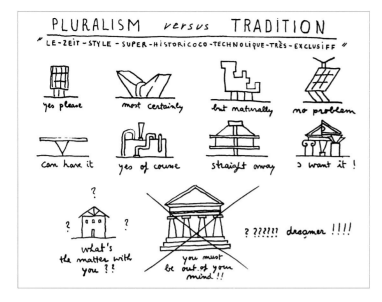

Standardisation, prefabrication, the free plan, the curtain wall, strip window and roof terrace, rolled steel, plate glass and reinforced concrete may all be useful for limited purposes; when raised to the level of exclusive dogmas they lead to the loss of typological order and building hierarchy: to uniformity and arbitrariness.

Historicising the Past
For modernists the present stops arbitrarily somewhere between 1900 and 1914 and all the rest is history. The historicising of the past is their most powerful means yet to ostracise unwelcome traditions and customs. It is a practice which modernist art history and criticism has adopted from revolutionary political theory and practice, ie, that all pre-revolutionary customs and traditions which have not been specifically vetted are reactionary, anti-progressive and anti-revolutionary and therefore must be eradicated or relegated to museums and history books, that all those who do not follow the party line are class-enemies and must be treated as such. This confrontational attitude which is now fast losing credit in politics is still dominating modernist art circles and education.

Struggle to Death? Classicism versus Modernism
Many critics still want to see the competition between Classicism and Modernism as an ideological struggle to death. This clearly reveals a pre-democratic frame of mind because its eradication from professional education and practice had not and will not eliminate the need for classical architecture. It has, however, ensured that for 40 years classical designers had no chance to gain public commissions. It has also secured for at least two generations the practice of the most debased Classicism ever. Furthermore, the brutality of Modernism is at its most extreme when and where it reigns supreme. Not by chance did Modernism produce its best results when it was a minority exercise in the 1920s. The renewed competition is now improving the products of both recent modernism and classicism.

The question can therefore no longer be Tradition versus Modernism but democratic competition, a high level of education and professional practice in all disciplines and non-partisan criticism. The real struggle to death ought solely to be between good and bad design.

Uncertain Fortunes of a Classical Tradition
A classical tradition is never acquired once and for all. It is handed down by individuals, successfully or unsuccessfully, and

sticks a bloody doric column'. Lately they have been expatiating on Ceauscescu's solitary stalinist folly, cynically oblivious of the conducator's 30 year long modernist onslaught on the country's traditional heritage.

Classicism's perennial value, however rationally argued, can have no effect on the reigning professional opportunism, whether it be the nostalgia for an outdated minimalism or for expressionist gobbledegook.

The formalistic uniformity of the late Mies van der Rohe on the one hand and the arbitrary formalism of Hans Scharoun on the other are the foundations of current modernist revivals. *Uniformity* is seen as a necessary expression of mass-society and *arbitrariness* as the artist's revolt against the same phenomenon. The pathological disciplinarian and the unpredictable creator-artist now combine to deconstruct the world. The resulting architectural traumas clearly express the dangerous state which the world is in; that they can become regime-architecture as in France and West-Germany is astonishing. The philosophic sophistries with which such aberrations are justified are truly impregnable to rational argument, common sense and criticism, and hence to serious reform.

For anybody who still had doubts about it, this is the final proof of the architect's singular power and ultimate responsibility in shaping public architecture.

Classicism: A Style?
We do not use the term Classicism as a stylistic classification. In the face of Modernism the old polemic between gothic and classic is largely irrelevant.

Classicism embraces all monumental architecture (of all continents) of traditional construction and conception, fulfilling the vitruvian triad. The work of Albert Speer and that of Hassan Fathy belongs in that classification, as do the Eiffel Tower and the Crystal Palace. The latter are neither anti-historical nor anti-classical or anti-traditional structures; they merely represent new additions to the vast typological and formal repertoire of the vernacular-classical tradition. When however they are elevated to the level of paradigm Architecture is in trouble.

The Philosophic Fallacy of Modernism
Modernism's philosophic fallacy is not its principles, materials and technology, but the fact that these are upheld as a new paradigm, apparently revolutionising, invalidating and replacing all previous architectural traditions and knowledge.

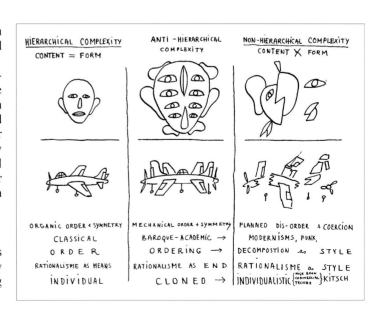

so it may fall suddenly from the highest peaks or rise in a few years from dark confusion. Like every organism, it goes inevitably towards its death and its very maturity contains the grain of senility, but interruption is sometimes a necessary condition for reconstruction.

The great periods of architecture are like different stations in a planet's revolution. The sun of universal ideas illuminates the architecture planet with greater or lesser intensity. It may be that in an extreme elliptical course the planet is attracted by distant celestial bodies. These are the dark days of confusion, of eclecticism and abstraction. If industrial Modernism represents the absolute bottom of our figure we may well have to rise through another hell of eclectic confusion before reaching the warmth of classical inspiration.

The classical is closest to the universal while still being a characteristic of the material world. The true cabinet-maker is inspired by the *idea* of the chair or table, whereas the lesser one is influenced by this particular chair or that particular table. Great cultures imitate universal ideas while lesser ones copy particular cultures.

However admirable his works may be, the typical 19th-century architect was imprisoned in laborious revivalist revolutions around all possible periods of architecture. His immense historical and technical knowledge broke the natural intuition and feeling for proportion and form. His teaching became consequently tyrannical and dogmatic. Instead of inspiring respect of tradition it fostered rebellion.

True traditional teaching instead cares little about the past, it is not historicist, it will not reduce past cultures to catalogues of available form-works, it is not interested in correct dates, names and historic formulae. Instead, it teaches the understanding and practical handling of those timeless principles and techniques which made past works remarkable and speak to our hearts.

What Tradition?

As far as building and architecture go, the evident technical and artistic inferiority of non-traditional building methods, the lack of a rational, that is, transmittable body of knowledge, of common technical and aesthetic principles and foundations, all speak against the establishment of a 'modernist' as opposed to a 'vernacular-classical' tradition.

There is above all no coherent neo-modernist thinking which, like Le Corbusier, would even attempt to build a coherent body of theory unifying town and country planning, architecture and construction. There is linguistically no modernist vocabulary to

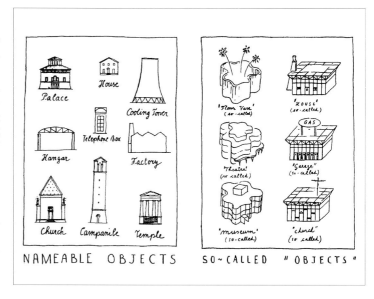

NAMEABLE OBJECTS   SO-CALLED "OBJECTS"

differentiate between civic, domestic, commercial and industrial structures, there is no theory of sign character and symbol, form and content. There is above all the reality of zoning which guarantees the functional deconstruction of settlements and implicitly that of architecture. Zoning makes any authentically differentiated constitution of an urban fabric or even a village impossible by law and principle.

Neo-modernist theory is in fact a shipwreck of collapsed modernist urbanism, of glorified commercial practice ('decorated shed') and various stylistic nostalgias influenced by cubism and Kurt Schwitter's 'Merz', as well as bits of literary theory and fragments of misinterpreted Heidegger; certainly no coherent instrument to rewrite urban planning legislation, or to shape cities and landscapes in a lasting way. Neo-modernist theories are reflections of global disarray rather than visions of a desirable common world. All the reactionary drum-beating cannot alter the fact that there are to be found very few enemies of the idea of traditional urbanism and architecture.

Mass Society and Placelessness

Industrial Modernism has not only proved incapable of building cities and villages, of creating meaningful and beautiful places, it is also incapable of establishing a viable synthesis of man and nature. It merely builds business or industrial zones, suburbs and transport systems, dumping grounds and concentration camps – all forms of mass-employment, mass-transport, mass-communication and mass-elimination. Auschwitz, Birkenau or Soweto, the housing compounds around great cities and even our suburban deserts are all more or less fortunate children of the same Leviathan, reifications of placelessness, of our incapacity to give settlements dignified and enduring human forms. Modernist planning and building concepts are unecological, highly entropical and therefore unstable and transient forms of shelter and settlement.

Traditional Architecture and Town and Country Planning

The renewal of traditional forms of building and architecture only makes sense in a wider context of traditional planning of countryside, towns and villages. The latter fulfill the aspirations of a major part of the democratic citizenry. They have done so in past centuries and will continue to do so in the future. Such buildings and towns can be elegantly and imaginatively adapted to ever new purposes of an advanced industrial society. There is therefore no good practical nor any philosophical reason for imposing modernist solutions where traditional ones have proved

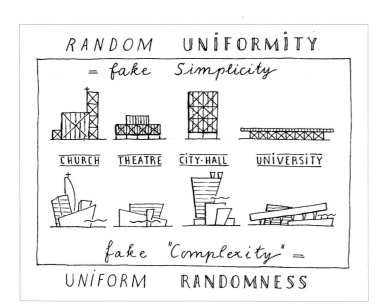

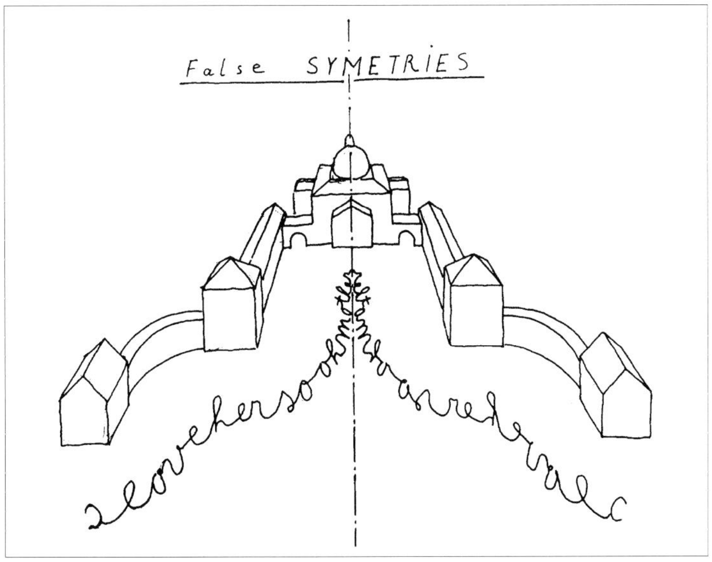

to be superior in environmental, economic and aesthetic terms.

It has been proven beyond the possibility of a doubt that modernist building fashions just don't harmonise with historic and traditional environments and the many New Towns which are uncompromised embodiments of modernist ideals have, despite vast economic resources and total design control, not produced anything nearing the qualities of traditional buildings and towns.

Forcing modernists to design traditional façades in historic centres may be absurd; it is even more absurd to go on pretending that modernist buildings must have a place in historic districts. Many architects and planners still have to learn that also in democracy the basis for creating harmonious cities is good manners, common sense and a sense of propriety. Exacerbating differences is no democratic virtue; democracy does not force political parties to breed ideological opponents within their own ranks, nor does it compel antagonistic religions to merge in a single church.

Modernism and Conservation

Modernists worldwide are extremely keen to have works of their early masters faithfully maintained, restored or rebuilt in their original state. They even militate to have unbuilt projects realised decades after their death. This is an admirable attitude and in the case of the Barcelona pavilion or the Maison Guiette in Antwerp has produced charmingly nostalgic results. Yet equal claims from conservationists to faithfully maintain, restore or integrally reconstruct or build important classical buildings and projects encounters the modernists' scorn and veto. The Charter of Venice even turns the act of maintenance and restoration into an obligatory rape of the fabric of traditional buildings and monuments, no less absurd than handling the restoration of ancient paintings and sculptures according to the manners of Francis Bacon or Marcel Duchamps. It is interesting that the promoters of oblivion should now defend the sanctity and 'historical value' of Modernism's bric-à-brac heritage.

Today the anti-historical stance has been at least semi-officially abandoned. Its heralds have come of age and they paradoxically accuse classicists of being the newest advocates of *tabula rasa*, for their aloof rejection of 60 years of modernist tradition. This time they may even be right, because writing history always implies a great clearing of the table, sorting major and minor events. The great cook, Fernand Point, said that a meal can never be better than the least good of its ingredients. Why then should we spoil cities and landscapes with meaningless crumbs? The purpose of conservation cannot be to save anachronistic and outdated structures because they have been mentioned by Giedion or Pevsner or have received awards.

The Message from Housebuilders

Responding no doubt to housebuyers' tastes, 99% of private housebuilders in Great Britain, France and the USA now build homes of traditional vernacular or classical appearance. While they themselves prefer living, working, holidaying and retiring into traditional environs, modernists blame the public for its reactionary tastes. Yet far from resisting the truly new and unfamiliar, the same housebuyers have no qualms about accepting technical innovations which have revolutionised the domestic environment.

While domestic instruments and appliances have been radically changed by the industrial-scientific revolution, the ancient ideals of domesticity, of domestic comfort and home have not; the experience of modernist mass housing has, if anything, strengthened the demand for their democratisation.

What holds true for domestic ideals is equally true for those of civic beauty. While accepting that modernist town-planning has in general been disastrously wrong, neo-modernists state that traditional patterns of streets and squares must now be realised with modernist construction, composition and aesthetics. This contrasts with the broad public opinion which accepts almost any town plan or building composition as long as its aesthetics are traditional, ie, vernacular or classical.

High Art and Popular Taste

Unlike the case in present day democracies there need be no unbridgeable gulf between high art and popular taste. They ought to differ in quality and refinement, not in type and content. The enduring authority of traditional architectural models cannot be explained away by ignorance, autocratic rule or manipulative tricks; they are proven valid by long-term market trends. Democratic popular taste continues, ironically, to have greater empathy for aristocratic artistic and architectural models than for democratic experimentalism; not because of their aristocratic content but because of their timeless form and substance. No political, artistic or commercial abuse and debasement can for long invalidate them.

Meaning of Universal, Timeless, Eternal, Absolute Values

However 'old' the human race may be in terms of millenia biologically it is able to produce a miraculous variety of 'new'

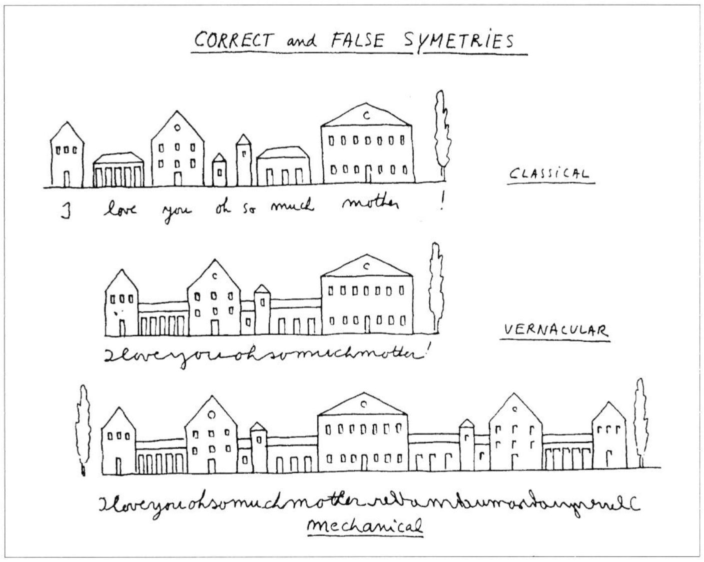

and 'unique' individuals. I believe the timeless and universal principles of classical architecture to have similar inexhaustible capacities. The classical notions of stability and timelessness are clearly related to the life-span of humankind; they are eternal not in relation to an absolute eternity but to the duration of man's earthly existence only. In this context we cannot be interested in how old classical principles are; they are truly not rooted in an historical past but their origin is ever-present. Architecture (Arche-tekton) means literally the form of origin; only this can be the true meaning of a traditional building's timelessness.

'Nameable' versus 'so-called' Artifacts
To the universal plan which inspires, governs and tirelessly reconstructs the universe, man is able to add but few footnotes. Particular cities and particular buildings can always be but imperfect realisations of these quasi-divine addenda. The house, the temple, the campanile, the roof, the column, the architrave, the frieze, the window, the door, the atrium, the street, the square and the city are inventions of man's genius, enriching nature's typological family.

These very names, ideas and objects form man's proper and common world. Hannah Ahrendt claimed that it was their very artificiality that made them so homely for man to live in and use. This continent of man's mind is as limited as the world itself. All the clamorous 'architectural' innovations of the recent past are misapplications of forms and structures belonging to the world of industrial machines and instruments. Through misappropriation forms lose their instrumental and expressive *raison-d'être*.

The inventory of architectural elements and building types is limited and cannot be infinitely extended. They are achievements of human genius surpassing those of the discoveries of the wheel and fire, because for them he found no models but mere hints and analogues in nature.

Names and Nicknames
Buildings aping the appearance of aeroplanes, of ships and trains, of petrochemical plants or containers, lately even of buildings of the past. Virtually one sentence sums up all the confusion and 'creative' sterility of contemporary 'architecture'. The inability to truly innovate is clearly revealed in the modern terminology itself. We know that a 'curtain wall' is neither a curtain nor a wall; the 'Bürolandschaft' is neither an office nor a landscape; the office-park is not a park, the multi-purpose hall is no substitute for either church or theatre, for Odeon or workshop. Hence the unreality and namelessness, the abstractness and

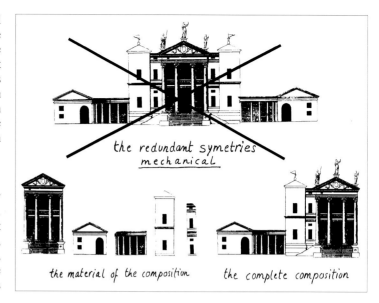

the redundant symetries
mechanical

the material of the composition   the complete composition

placelessness of the industrial world.

'In the language of symbols, there can exist no misunderstanding' (A Pontvik). Mistakes of scale, proportion and size, of form and character, of type and style, are always publicly disqualified by pungent nicknames. Modern 'architecture' is full of such prestigious nicknames: the 'pregnant oyster' (Congress Building in West Berlin); 'Maison du fada' (Unité LC, Marseille); 'the crow' (European Parliament project, Luxembourg); 'the hangar' (Sainsbury Centre); 'the car park' (Queens College residences, Oxford), 'the radiator' (UN New York), and so on. The public only derides what is derisible and false.

Classical buildings, however, are called by their name or purpose: 'the Cathedral', 'the Town Hall', 'the Palace', etc. Symbol and meaning, type and style are not a mere passing convention. A convention in architecture can only be born and have a lasting value when appearance and use establish an evident relationship of truth. A convention in architecture cannot by definition be forced. Modernist 'architecture' has done just that: it has confused the coffee pot and the wine bottle.

It is of course possible to doubt the adequacy of these types of containers for liquids which have, after all, a rather similar 'liquid' quality. A non-conventional person can therefore decide to serve wine in the coffee pot and coffee in the wine bottle. This simple operation, however, complicates life more than the exercise is worth. Such a non-conventional person will need labels if he is not to burn his fingers when pouring coffee out of a wine bottle.

The *random* form and the *uni*-form are the two principal modes of destroying form. Random Uniformity and Uniform randomnes are strictly symmetrical phenomena. The meaningless *uni*-formity of mass-products and the *uni*-form meaninglessness of modernist 'architecture', 'sculpture' or 'painting' are born out of the same Babylonian confusion.

The nickname re-establishes that relation of truth between object and name which a false pretence or an involuntary confusion may have succeeded in clouding temporarily. The nickname is the definitive and devastating form of criticism which a fake or a daub will inevitably earn. The nickname is *language's* revenge in general, and the *name's* revenge in particular for abuse and lack of respect. The nickname is the kitsch object's correct name.

Classicism and Change
One of the tenets of Modernism is that change is the only constant in life, that architecture has to reflect this and be

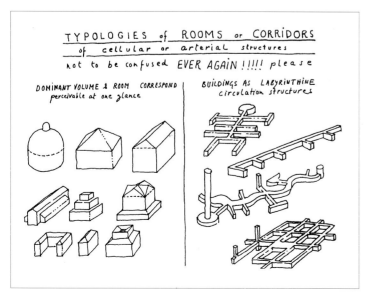

TYPOLOGIES of ROOMS or CORRIDORS
of cellular or arterial structures
not to be confused EVER AGAIN !!!!! please

DOMINANT VOLUME 1 ROOM CORRESPOND perceivable at one glance   BUILDINGS AS LABYRINTHINE circulation structures

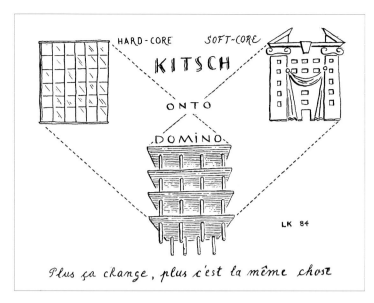

Plus ça change, plus c'est la même chose

architecture has been so vast in the past that only the finest eye can detect an eventual improvement in the classical orders; progressing the art cannot be the concern of everyday architectural practice.

Zeitgeist

The trained eye can not only distinguish styles and periods but can pinpoint a work within a few years and miles of its moment and place of origin. Even the most adept pastiche will not escape intelligent scrutiny. Thus it is impossible not to express in some measure the spirit of one's time, and that is precisely what the notion of *Zeitgeist* describes. *Zeitgeist* is as inescapable as body smell, but it is no guarantee of any kind of quality. It can therefore be of no interest to the artist and craftsman for they naturally long to attain timeless quality, using the best materials and techniques, which are also those that best resist the tests of time, accident and changing tastes. Great architecture does not embody the spirit of our time but the spirit of all time, an element of eternity.

Timeless or Timebound Principles

Buildings ought not to be conceived as objects of *short-term consumption* but of *long-term use*. The principles which guide their design and construction must therefore transcend fashions and whims. Paraphrasing Hannah Ahrendt, without buildings and towns transcending the life-span of its builders, no public realm, no lasting and collective expression as craft or as art, strictly speaking no culture, is possible.

The classical triad of *venustas - firmitas - utilitas* has meaning in a long-term perspective only. There is no more short-term beauty than there is short-term wisdom. Even the most solid and practical structure has a futile destiny if it lacks beauty. Beauty and harmony, utility and commodity, solidity and permanence, are unconditionally interdependent and their links are severed in modernisms. This is the reason why *timeless* or *traditional principles* are in irreconcilable contradiction with *timebound* or *modernist* principles.

On the Power of Classical Architecture

The futile destiny of many contemporary institutions and organisations is clearly revealed in the crude shapes of their buildings. (19th-century architects committed an impropriety when disguising a pump-house as a mosque or temple, but how much more improper it is to design Kindergartens, museums and even churches in the manner of industrial sheds.)

flexible and above all look dynamic; that, conversely, traditional architecture is adverse to growth and change, that it is inflexible, looks static and is therefore outdated and contrary to modern sensibility. On the other hand we find that in nature change is not an end in itself but always has a goal: that organisms grow in order to reach maturity, that in natural evolution change is not gradual and constant but that fossil records lead us to believe that evolution occurs in extremely rapid 'radiations' resulting in bursts of new species followed by 'long-term species stability', ie, tireless reproduction according to type.

Classicism and the Idea of Progress

There are several ways in which classical culture and tradition are understood, and misunderstood. These depend largely on our understanding of the universe and of nature; on whether we believe that progress and evolution have a finality or not, whether their goal has been reached in the past or whether it will be reached in the future; and whether classical ideals can belong to the world of matter at all or only to the world of ideas.

There is little doubt that organic nature has, with the creation of humankind, reached its highest possible, its classical, form. As far as man's biological evolution is concerned, progress is thus a matter of the past; the typological order which shapes the organic world will not suffer any change, for its slightest mutation will mean the instant end of mankind itself.

In our unavoidably anthropocentric conception of time, the typological inventory of organic nature not only seems but is complete. It does not know innovation, but only tireless duplication and reconstruction according to a fixed typological inventory of men, animals, plants, and so on. Typological experiments, genetic idiosyncrasies and crossbreeds cannot reproduce. In nature as it is relevant to man, the principle of life means growth until maturity, reproduction according to type and species stability. Classicism assumes the same to be true for artistic creation. Innovation in Form will occur only with the introduction of a new functional type. This being an extremely rare occurrence, it cannot be of any relevance for day-to-day artistic practice. To elevate it to a principle of life as Modernism has done can only lead to delusions and confusion of categories.

The Perfection of the Orders

Classical architecture reaches its highest expression in the classical orders. A legion of Einsteins and Leonardos could not improve them, any more than they could improve the human figure or its bone structure. As Schinkel put it, progress in

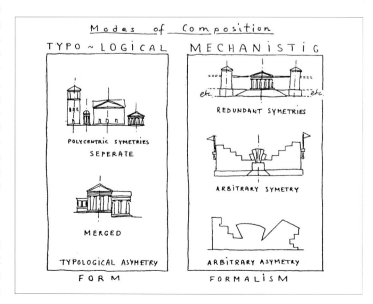

11

All great human institutions are to this day symbolised by classical monuments. In St Peter's in Rome, in the Capitol in Washington and in Westminster Palace in London, institutions and buildings form an indissoluble bond, forever linked as long as men will remember. The dignity of such bodies is made visible in the grandeur of their architecture. On it depends their authority as well as their own self-respect.

Harmony – Firmness – Utility

The universal principles of traditional architecture – harmony, firmness, utility – are concordant with the fundamental goals of all significant human establishments. In great cultures they are the chosen means of wise polity and civilising action. In the whirlwind of all things human they are the guarantors of social bond, stability and peace, the visible realisation of a common moral world.

On the Fragility of Beauty

The beauty of a town or landscape is extremely vulnerable. Just as a false note may spoil the enjoyment of a piece of music, one single ugly building can destroy the harmony of a square, a skyline, a valley. Conversely, even a most beautiful building is unable to seriously improve an ugly place. Whether private or public, small or large, all buildings have a public face, acting positively or negatively on the public realm, making it ugly or beautiful.

On False and True Monuments

The skyscraper and groundscraper are con-monuments. They are private matter in public garb and posture. They are vertical or horizontal *over-concentrations* of utilitarian functions under a single roof or behind one façade. The symbolic emptiness and utilitarian character of their sheer physical bulk humiliates the dignity and station of genuine public structures.

The civic and religious halls and palaces, the arenas, temples, theatres, shrines, libraries, churches, spires, fountains, thermae, terminals and bridges are the *true monumental and symbolic features* of the city. They are the privileged objects of monumental architecture. The public squares and the city's skyline are its inviolable realm and stage, its sacred protectorate.

Whatever the pretensions of its forms, a supermarket is no less or more significant whether wrapped in architectural, nautical or commercial dressing. When situated in a commercial zone its single use and location will forever prevent it from gaining significance beyond its commercial purpose. The reverse is also true: however beautiful and dignified a historical city centre may be, it cannot survive for long its transformation into a shopping, business or leisure zone. In the same way even the largest housing scheme cannot become a city or a public monument, and the addition of more private cells will never invest it with a true civic status. Its functional monotony and uniformity simply do not provide the typological material for significant monumental and urban gestures. The pretentiousness and hollow rhetoric of a Karl Marx Hof, and even of more clamorous recent attempts, reveal only too painfully their domestic substance.

Building Types and Typology

– A building typology is the classification of buildings according to type.

– A building type is the organisational schema of a building in plan and section.

– Building types tend to evolve until they find their most rational, logical and simplest form.

– The complexity of a classical building type is unambiguous and always hierarchical.

– It is composed of essentially simple spaces and volumes.

– Whether symmetrical or a-symmetrical, its composition is always typo-logical and tectonic.

– A classical building type is infinitely replicable, easily recognisable and usable, and therefore it must be non-ambiguous and conventional.

In the age of speed the evolution of new building types seems sometimes inordinately slow despite the appearance of new uses. The fact that airport terminals are in a process of constant reconstruction is a reminder that shelter and function have not matured into an adequate building type. After 20 years of hapless experiments modern commercial malls are now reverting to the 19th-century Galleria type, which itself evolved from the oriental Bazaar and further back from the Roman Basilica type. The 19th-century railway stations have remained virtually unchanged because early on, their use, construction and expression gelled into new and adequate building types.

Buildings are both Expressive and Instrumental

Whether a place of worship, a telephone box or a garden wall, a building expresses the fundamental values of its builders and designers. They are symbols of our state of mind and our self-understanding. Symbols are not mere means of expression and mirrors, they are essential instruments and means to uphold civic and domestic values and give them sustenance. (If we are dressed in rags, our self-confidence suffers as badly as others' confidence in us.)

We cannot design neutral buildings in isolation or away from the world. Buildings of whatever size act upon the world. They must be seen as part of the larger whole.

Industrial versus Artisan Methods of Building

Industrialised building methods are claimed to be faster than traditional ones. This is untrue on two accounts:

a) There are artisan methods of building quickly. After the bombardment of 1692, Brussels, including the spectacular Grand Place as we know it, was designed and rebuilt in *two* years; Catherine the Great had entire cities built in wood within a few months (one of them was not completely ready for her majesty's inspection, hence the legend of Potemkin towns).

b) The *time of construction* must be measured against the lifespan and accumulated maintenance hours of a building; the economic and ecological efficiency of buildings must be measured in a *very long-term* appraisal.

Construction and Appearance

The most important struggle in architecture today is not between Tradition and Modernism, but between true and false traditional building construction. Almost everywhere the building industry has abandoned load-bearing construction in favour of a separation of support-structure and external enclosure, and secondly the replacement of natural materials by industrial substitutes. The reduction of external walls to screens, the tireless differential movements between structure and enclosure, and lastly the substitution of inferior artificial substitutes for natural materials makes even traditional-looking buildings into extremely fragile, vulnerable, high-maintenance structures of extremely limited life expectancy. It also turns most traditionally-styled buildings into authentic fakes, of traditional appearance only, resulting almost unavoidably in 'post-modern' kitsch.

Against the mere *skin depth* of most 'post-modernist' buildings, true vernacular and classical structures are *wall-deep* and *room-deep*. Authentic traditional construction and predominant use of natural materials are essential to ensure the integrity of structure, architectural elements and appearance. A slightly higher initial investment is repaid by a longer life, by less maintenance, better appearances and generally better building.

On Classical ARCHITECTURE and Vernacular BUILDING
All worthy architectural cultures make a fundamental difference between *sacred and public* structures on one hand and *private utilitarian* structures on the other. The former express the dignity, solemnity and grandeur of collective institutions (*res sacra-res publica*), the latter the more modest rank of individual activities and zeal (*res privata-res economica*). All buildings are at once expressive and instrumental for good or for ill.

(A monumental compilation of private cells does not make a monumental building but an empty monumental gesture. An endlessly stretching public hall without proportional height does not make a monumental space.)

(If factories look like cathedrals, housing blocks like royal palaces, and museums like factories, there is something fundamentally wrong about our values and way of life.)

Problems of Classicism
The true causes for the problems now facing classical architecture have been little discussed for the simple reason that after the war it was generally assumed that Classicism was no longer worth a thought. The classical architectural language, we were told, had fatally exhausted itself. This is, of course, untrue, for language does not lose its ability to communicate, even though some men may have lost their will to learn and use it.

The past and present historical crises of classical architectural language have neither polluted nor eroded the language; its rules and meanings have merely been temporarily shrouded in confusion. Its reconstruction can only be undertaken through a clear understanding of what brings about its demise. It is not my intention to condemn historical styles or even historical revivals of whatever taste and period, but I believe that we can only afford the pleasures of style when our house has been given solid foundations.

In the figures I have attempted to clarify the notions of composition of single objects and ensembles, of symmetry, typology and so on.

Classicism is only Human
To claim that the classical principles were overcome by industrial building technology is no less absurd than to declare bread to be old-fashioned. If the vernacular and classical languages are not free of problems it is but an indication that nothing human can be perfect. If there remain unexplored corners, and unexplained contradictions of an art, they are no concern of the professional architect, planner, or committee. They can only be resolved by means of intelligent habit and by secular genius.

This is the true meaning of Classicism. It is of course a belief, and with it man has been able to create his landscapes and cities, his grandest places and monuments. Without it he can but destroy them.

The Artist's Most Precious Tool
It may seem unreasonable to carp about compositional methods and typological habits which reach almost as far back as the origin of architecture itself, and even more bizarre to combine such critiques with the rejection of the dominant planning methods of the last 100 years. Most sensible people will discard such a radical stance as preposterous and could never imagine such a notion becoming influential.

For example, Ruskin and Morris are still disregarded because their philosophy so little influenced events. Yet lack of influence does not mean their philosophy was wrong or that it will always be disregarded: the exploration of a phenomenon and its exploitation may lie years or centuries apart. If you see a beetle lying on his back and struggling with all his legs in the air, will you bother to ask whether he has been lying there for a minute or since time immemorial? The poor bastard may even have forgotten about the use of his feet: he may possibly look in a reproachful way at his rescuer. There is nevertheless little doubt that the good creature may rediscover the advantages of walking about the world and flying in the air once he is back on his feet.

I do not want to join the camp of the sceptics, nor to spoil anyone's pleasure in the grand architectural errors of the past. How could we not admire the Campidoglio, Versailles or even the Grand Palais? Those aberrations are so magnificent that it is sheer pleasure to suspend our philosophic disbelief. Nor am I unduly critical of correct historical revivals; the genius of classical architecture is so pervasive that even the revivals of revivals will be graced with its advantages.

The Critical Faculty
The handful of architects discussed here have all found their way back onto their feet for very different reasons, and in very different contexts. Some speak the language with ease, and others seem not entirely sure whether they are doing the right thing. One thing, however, is certain, as Jacquelin Robertson put it: 'If you start walking that path, there is no return or idle wandering possible, you have to go the whole way.'

When learning a foreign language it is not offensive to have mistakes pointed out. Indeed the critical faculty is the classical architect's most precious gift. The architects presented here share the conviction that we are all still learning. To an old master's eye, these works would seem littered with awkward mistakes and obvious absurdities. Too many still look like nice old buildings recently, but not too well, restored. We have all been brought up to assume that our works should express our age, but, ironically, the best buildings and art works of the past demonstrate that the opposite is true. True artists free themselves from the too obvious moods and spirits of their age. That is why their work is forever young.

On Reprogramming Architectural Developments
Density, *nature* and *location* of modern developments are decided well before they reach the designer. Most development 'packages' or 'briefs' such as housing estates, shopping centres, office parks, industrial estates etc, are defined by zoning and planning guidelines, and by current marketing and financing practices. Many architects are aware of the fact that it is quite impossible to design real cities or villages in such a way; individually they can do little about it if they want to retain the job.

If new developments are to contribute towards the restoration and completion of our cities and villages, architectural programming has to be, so to speak, repackaged before it reaches the designer's table.

———— * ————

TREASURY OF THE ATHENIANS, DELPHI

I

ASPECTS OF CLASSICISM

CLASSICAL ARCHITECTURE
SIR JOHN SUMMERSON

Few people know precisely what they mean when they use the expression 'classical architecture'. It would be very unwise to attempt a definition and I am not going to do so. However, we may perhaps agree that the Tate Gallery (the old building by Sydney Smith, 1897) is classical architecture. It is composed of complex, highly organised elements, transmitted from Antiquity, mainly through North Italian 17th century models, but strongly tinged with the parade and ornamentalism of 19th century France. We may not like it very much: we may find it coarsely modelled and lacking in any fine adjustments of scale. But classical it is: it speaks the language. I presume that it is classical architecture in this liberal sense which is the subject of discussion today.

Not so very long ago it was seriously proposed to demolish the whole front part of this building and substitute for it a modern gallery in a style conceived to be more appropriate to an advanced industrial society with democratic ideals and a true sense of 'fitness for purpose'. I don't know in what grade the Tate is now listed under the Acts but I do know that in this year, 1988, it would be exceedingly difficult to get it demolished.

Times have changed. Since 1939, three things in particular: first, the Modern Movement has been found to contain serious internal flaws, notably a total inability to create a currency of imagery and metaphor. Second, public sentiment about conservation and the environment has turned a somersault; from a general hostility to the pre-war urban environment as obsolete and ugly it has moved to a romantic and nostalgic acceptance of the environment as the 'heritage'. Third, since 1939, the history of architecture has been almost completely re-written. These three issues, interlocking and reacting on each other have landed us in a new climate of architectural thought, one in which it has become possible to talk about modern classical architecture as something with a legitimacy which has long been denied it. I am not concerned whether anybody takes advantage of this new legitimacy, only what is involved on the intellectual plane if they do. In short, I want to bring into sharp focus the principles of classical architecture as exemplified in the Tate Gallery and many thousands of other buildings, some great, many insignificant, all but very few built before the First World War. I am going in at the deep end by asking what future is likely to be in store for the 'Five Orders of Architecture', narrowing the subject down to two questions. One: what, historically, are the orders; when and how did they acquire the mystique which still invests them? Two: what in practice do they mean, ie how do they work? Let me offer some very summary answers.

For the first question Vitruvius is the classic source, and what he tells us is confirmed all the way from Bath to Timgad. Vitruvius makes no mystique of the orders. They are simply the Imperial code of practice for the building of temples. Vitruvius gives only four and of these only two are described in full detail – the Ionic and Doric. The Tuscan earns only a paragraph or two and of the Corinthian he describes only the cap, saying that the other parts are the same as Ionic. He explains the orders as originating in different regions of the Roman world: Greece, Asia Minor, Tuscany. He explains the orders as re-creations in

stone or marble of timber prototypes and he tells his famous story of the invention of the Corinthian cap. He lists the deities to whom the three main orders can be appropriately dedicated. And that is that; all very dispassionate and lucid.

The mystique of the five orders came with the 'canonisation' of Vitruvius a millennium-and-a-half later, with Alberti, Serlio and the architectural theorists who followed. It was Alberti who made the number up to five by adding what he called the 'Italian Order', a late Roman creation which Serlio labelled 'Composita'. Serlio was the first to line up the five like a set of nine-pins, bringing them onto the architectural stage with a theatrical flourish, as a kind of prologue such as that used in Greek plays to explain the action to follow. He gives them a hierarchical sequence from the plain and stubby Tuscan to the over-dressed and lofty Composite. He proposes exact modular ratios for all five. The mystique is established, buttoned up.

The Vitruvian/Albertine/Serlian hierarchy was accepted with variations, elaborations and refinements by all who followed: Vignola, Palladio, Scamozzi in Italy; De l'Orme, Fréart, Perrault in France; Blum, De Vries, Dietterling in Germany and Flanders; Shute, Gibbs, Chambers and dozens of popularisers in England.

The mystique remained intact till the mid-18th century when archaeology began to break the mould. Piranesi, for instance, came up with a host of variant orders found among the ruins of Rome. Robert Adam discovered that the Romans did not use temple columns in their dining rooms. The Greek revivalists formed an alternative mould but it lasted only 30 years. Nevertheless, the five orders still retained their inscrutable magic. The Beaux-Arts discipline, with Guadet and others, conducted it through the 19th century and up to the Second World War. In Britain the Edwardians revived their own Stuart and Georgian Classicism, glancing occasionally across the Channel and, in later years, across the Atlantic but not bothering very much about Vitruvius. Blomfield believed that the British character had produced a uniquely appropriate Classicism of its own, but ended up doing Louis XV. Lutyens had his Wrenaissance, spelt with a 'W'. Cooper went for Beaux Arts, Curtis Green for Italian Mannerism. Burnet was a neo-classicist who exploded into Baroque, and Richardson cultivated CR Cockerell. All these handled the orders with ability, but my feeling is that only Lutyens and Burnet made them come alive. By 1937 the Edwardians were finished. The Modern was ready to take over which, in 1945, it did. It conquered the world and then fell into a dead faint, without, however, actually dying.

Now, the second question. What do the orders mean; how do they work? They have often been compared, to their disadvantage, with a child's box of bricks. That was the reproach which Victorian anti-classicists levelled against them. They were, it was said, ready-made bits of architecture which the architect merely had to pick up and put together to make his design. This, as it happens, is profoundly true, and it is no reproach. The orders are ready made bits and that is what gives them their authority. Speech and language have ready-made grammatical structures and it is tempting to draw analogies with these. But except in the most general sense, such analogies do not work.

Nor do analogies with the diatonic scale and the key system in music. The system is unique to architecture. The basic values of the orders is in two things – their limited plurality and their relative immutability. But before we come to these, what exactly is an architectural order?

An order consists of a temple column, with or without pedestal, and the beam it carries, the latter sub-divided into architrave, frieze and cornice; cornice and architrave being subject to further sub-divisions. The scale of this combination is not fixed because it includes no element inviting contact by the human foot or the human hand, so the order can be diminutive or gigantic, according to the dimensions of the module. Ideally the order controls the entire design. It delegates its authority by transmitting its vertical ratios and some of its profiles to the mass of the building. A secondary order may tangle with the first so that movement on two different scales may be harmonised or counterpointed. An order may announce itself in a portico, continue the conversation in pilasters, detached, half or three-quarter columns or mount a choreographic exposition of all four. It may be present all the time, caging the building in a total embrace; or part of the time; or none of the time, merely hinting at the mood of the building by the loan of some of its attributes. From the orders themselves we move to their relationships, with arches worked out for us by the Romans, while the Vitruvian conventions as to intercolumniation (the spacing of columns) will settle what we may call the tempo of the composition. It is a closed system of infinite internal flexibility. The essence of the game is variety within unity, a totality no part of which can be moved without a chain reaction vibrating the whole design.

In all this, the immutability and the plurality of the orders are essential. Immutability because, like the pieces in a game of chess, the symbols employed must be universally recognisable and their appropriate moves inherent in their shape. Plurality because the mood of the building depends on choice of forms and thus on a recognised, though strictly limited visual vocabulary. Such are the conditions under which the system of 'ready-made bits' makes architecture a medium of communication.

The system can, of course, be undermined by two perfectly sensible questions which are those which the first year student invariably asks. First, why should the orders claim such high authority when they are nothing more that regional types which, by series of historic accidents, crystallised in the Roman world? Second, why five orders? Why not 50 or 500? I see no satisfactory answer to either question except to say that, like the pieces on the chessboard you cannot tamper with their identities by questioning their roots nor can you add to their number. This has been tried. Philibert de l'Orme invented a French Order, James Adam a British Order and there have been others. But so far as I know no 'new' order has been used by anybody except its inventor and then only once. The Vitruvian four plus the Albertine 'Composite' have been around for so long that Western civilisation has come to accept them almost as natural products – part of the natural history of mankind which has grown to maturity and reached a stable condition.

If you think those answers won't do, you can, of course, proceed to the problem of demythologising the orders. Well, you can try. You can play the sort of 'dumb crambo' known as 'stripped classic'. Or you can say 'less is more' and follow Mies to the ultimate classical zero. But what then? You may find yourself in the position of believing that any design on a modular grid is a classical design.

If it comes to a matter of definition I don't think you can eliminate the mystique – the attachment to something of an apparently arbitrary kind which if we are designing a classical building we must accept as an act of faith – in other words the God-given 'ready-made bit'. That, I need hardly say, is something entirely different from the emotive 'bit' or classical reference which finds its way into so much 'Post-Modernism' – the odd Paestum column, the distorted lunette or the split pediment, the evocation of De Chirico or Magritte. In such architecture there may be imagination and wit of a romantic and exciting kind, but it is quite simply not classical architecture. Finally, correct classical architecture is very difficult to design, but if well designed it is not difficult to understand. That perhaps is one of its main claims to a revived legitimacy.

ERECHTHEION, ATHENS

―――――― * ――――――

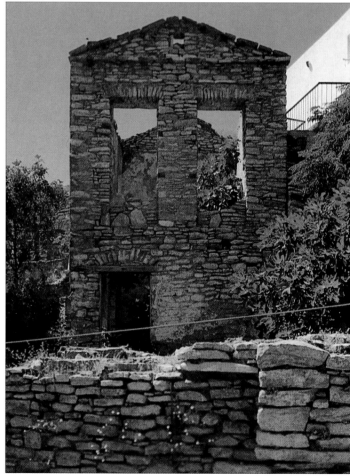

HOUSES AT SYMI c.1800

CLASSICISM IS NOT A STYLE
DEMETRI PORPHYRIOS

FUNERARY MONUMENTS, FIRST CEMETERY OF ATHENS, c.1860-1880

'There can be no social development which excludes all mythological relation to nature . . . and which accordingly claims from the artist an imagination free of mythology.'

Karl Marx, Introduction to the Critique of Political Economy, 1857

It cannot be said with certainty when Modern Eclecticism began – in the 1950s with the late work of Gropius and Wright, with the mature work of Aalto, or still later in the 60s with the early work of Venturi, Moore and Graves. But we know for certain that it is still alive and flourishing today. Its ideological features, however, can hardly be mapped in full without recourse to the ethical dimension of the most pervasive force in our century: orthodox Modernism.

Largely as a result of the cultural sterility we have experienced during the decades following the Second World War, we could now claim that the Modernism of the 20s concerned itself not simply with a wholesale revision of architectural values, but more significantly with the transvaluation of petty-bourgeois values. Uniformity of style and conduct which once – as in the classical world – bore radiant witness to the fact that civilised men spoke the same language and could communicate with urbane ease, now, with Modernism, threatened to become a universal *paradisus artificialis*. By the late 40s, the socialist dreams of the intelligentsia of Modernism were realised – ironically enough – by the Democratic Capitalist State, retaining from the spirit of *Sachlichkeit* only a certain scientificism of vision and a distinct documentary quality. The oracular myth of Modernism, namely that industrial emancipation would lead to social egalitarianism, was given – by the late 40s – a specific content: democracy was to be understood as synonymous with unsolicited distribution of industrial goods. Yet, for the industrial capital, the goals both of distribution of goods and of freedom of choice aimed not so much at

the democratisation of public life as at the creation of vast markets of consumption, which were to behave in a calculated and programmed manner. By the late 1960s – following the contradictory experience, on the one hand of the Welfare State housing programmes, and on the other the exhilarating phantasmagoria of a make-believe, high-tech culture – it had become clear that what in the 20s appeared to have been a global project of democratisation, had suddenly shrunk to a calculated strategy of creating 'circuses of bread and spectacle'.

This socio-economic strategy was parodied in the conspicuous 'consumption of culture' that shaped Modern Eclecticism. In fact, this strategy has been steadily naturalised under the moralising pretext of democratic pluralism. From the middle 60s onward – breeding on relativism, toleration and eclecticism – pluralism emerged as the hegemonical ideology of 20th-century America and Europe. The second half of our century has surely proven to be an age of 'conciliatory culture, widespread, springing out of its own self, visiting the beliefs of all countries and all ages, . . . admitting for observation everything, without fixing any part, since truth is everywhere in bits and nowhere in its entirety, in no country, no period, and no man.'[1] Modernism, having no ontological myth of its own, once appropriated by industrial capital, was turned into an instrument for the ideological production of the very priorities of industrial capital itself. The critical vision of Modernism was lost and the original utopia of social egalitarianism was turned successively into petty-bourgeois humanism in the 50s, into expendable high-tech phantasmagoria in the 60s, and into stylistic eclecticism in the 70s.

Contemporary architecture bathes in the pantheistic limbo of eclecticism. Torn between the dilemma of a frenetic search for novelty and an inherited social mission for a popular language, architecture leafs through history caricaturing remembrances. Who influenced this trend? Virtually everybody; the American shingle style revival, the Arabic tracery of the Middle-East corporate capital, the lyrical neo-Corbusianism, neo-Constructivism, the Queen Anne revival, or the recent Hollywood 'neon'-classicism. The incomprehensibility of designed and non-designed kitsch is reified into culture by the literati of Post-Modernism. Lack of conviction and the ethos of indiscriminate toleration are mistaken for democratic freedom. Collective myth is systematically fractured into countless individualistic trivia, into fastidious and uncompassionate evasions of the human situation.

The tactics of Modern Eclecticism have been explicitly clear. In an effort to recapture culture – for it is only in culture that man can recognise authenticity and freedom – Modern Eclecticism has plunged into history. Utilising the techniques of metaphor and quotation, Modern Eclecticism has undertaken to construct culture overnight. And yet, the 'culture' it inaugurated has been a kind of shorthand, whereby through abbreviation, one caresses the confused multiplicity of stylistic genres, esteeming all, but none in particular, creating, in this way, the illusion of authenticity cherished by the collector of reproductions. Modern Eclecticism started as a quest for the lost 'aura' and has grown into the exemplar of industrial kitsch.

Suffusing the entire sense of Modern Eclecticism has been a readiness to believe that to aestheticise industrial kitsch was to invite its annihilation and to clear the way for a healthy moral growth of ideals. In their attempts to endow industrial kitsch with moral and aesthetic value, the literati of pluralism resorted mainly to two operative techniques: first, that of aestheticising the real; second, that of aestheticising the process of communication. The technique of aestheticising the real was, of course, well known to the Dadaists and Surrealists. For Dada and Surrealism, however, the aesthetisation of reality was fundamentally subversive and infused with a deep moral concern to regain a lost purity. Instead, for Modern Eclecticism the aesthetisation of the real has been an attempt to reify the strategies of an economy which, by its own nature and for its own priorities of profit, has been founded exclusively on the 'production of waste'. In that sense, Modern Eclecticism has attempted to aestheticise the real by moralising infatuation. For 'it is only infatuation . . . that does justice to what exists . . . Something that must be thought beautiful because it exists, is for that very reason ugly.[2]

The second strategy, that of aestheticising the process of communication, is fundamentally linked to the experience of kitsch. For kitsch demands of its users the violent jerkiness of advertisement. We know only too well the source of violence in advertisement: its rhetorical figures of speech are used not in order to please, or to incite us to reflect and thereby gain knowledge of our situation, (as is invariably the case with art) but rather in order to abbreviate a message and send it home by tapping our image of the world. Advertisement is by nature aggressive for when it shocks or tactfully seduces us, we are left with a pervasive feeling of having been cheated; while when due to its boldness or irrelevance it fails to touch us, we are left idiotically embarrassed since we, the interlocutors, have been trivialised.

In a manner similar to advertisement, Modern Eclecticism, by aestheticising the process of communication, links experience to mere anagnosis, reading or decodement. Such an architecture tolerates no aesthetic surplus that would resist consumption and thereby survive as the core of experience. Instead, figurative and syntactic sensuality takes on the quality of nightmare: weightless pediments, 'neon'-classical cornices, emasculated orders, metopes enfeebled by the arrogance of architects in search of fame, engrossed voussoirs, drooping garlands, frenzied volumetric articulations and androgynously historicist plans; in short all sorts of upholstered coteries degenerate into a mere 'style-heap', without essential meaning other than the cult

of 'irony' and the illusion of a make-believe culture. This is an architecture with no discourse; simply quotations, parentheses, brackets, and a kind of disjointed, insidious whisper that spells: advertisement.

It is exactly that quality of advertisement which accounts for Modern Eclecticism's ability to capture the illusion of culture cheaply. The word 'cheaply' should be understood here in its most literal sense. By focusing exclusively on the techniques of communication at the expense of tectonic Logos, Modern Eclecticism did not have to address the fundamental problem that all architecture had to face when confronted with industrial production: namely, that of reconciling construction with style.

Instead, the theoretical and enacted formalisation of the 'decorated shed' has functioned exactly as a strategy for discriminating between shelter and symbolism; between need and myth. The principle of the 'decorated shed' provides for a system of thought which could isolate the budgets to be allocated to shelter and symbolism, exactly at a time when the excesses of Brutalism were stirring a certain disquietude amidst the circles of capital investment. One should be reminded here that Brutalism was an attempt to reinstate an 'aura' to the mute reality of industrial production by aestheticising the latter's abstract emotive possibilities. In that sense Brutalism was doubly suspect: both because of its abstract, non-communicative idiom (as the Eclectics maintained) and because of its dangerous – to the building industry – commitment to individualise the standard unit of industrial prodution.

The principle of the 'decorated shed', however, while encouraging a figurative enrichment of modernist construction, safeguarded against the reorganisation of the building industry that any ontological fusion of construction with style would have necessitated. A reorganisation that would have upset all three levels of the building industry: capital expenditure, skilled labour, and profit distribution. By means of an intuitively resourceful twist, the 'decorated shed' took the modernist precept of 'flexibility' and displaced it from the realm of spatial distribution to that of symbolic attribution. 'Pragmatics, Technics and Semantics' were to be defined by Modern Eclecticism as three independent layers of the architectural experience; as three independent budgets to be shifted around in a game which aimed at delectable fantasy at minimum cost.

The predicament of contemporary architecture, therefore, is our twofold inheritance: a) the semantically mute elements of industrial production – inherited from Modernism, and b) the semantically expendable historicist signs of industrial kitsch – inherited from Modern Eclecticism.

This raises, in my opinion, the crucial problem we face today: if there is a polar opposition between the economic priorities institutionalised by mass industrial society and the yearning for an authentic culture that would sustain individual freedom in public life, under what qualifications is it possible to practise architecture at all? Paradoxically, the only possible critical stance that architecture could assume today is to construct slowly an ontology of building that would contain a mythical representation of itself. To construct, that is, a tectonic discourse which, while addressing the pragmatics of shelter, could at the same time represent its very tectonics as myth.

It is from such a perspective that Classicism should be re-evaluated today: not as a borrowed stylistic finery but as an ontology of building. Renouncing novelty, ephemeral pleasurability, consumable iconographic individualism, and unmediated industrial production, we make an urgent plea for closing architectural discourse towards the constructional logic of vernacular and its mimetic elaboration: Classicism.

The constructional logic of vernacular

Despite the superficial associations with rusticity and nature that the word 'vernacular' brings to mind, the emphasis here is different. It is not stylistics we have in mind, but rather the universal ethos of constructing shelter under the stringent conditions of scarcity of materials and operative constructional techniques. By invoking vernacular, one does not seek the primitivism of pre-industrial cultures.

The temptation to turn one's back on contemporary industrial society in order to return to the security and institutions of some pre-industrial order, when pursued, leaves us suspended amid the reverberations of Plato's ghost: 'what then?' Instead, the essential meaning of vernacular refers to the ethos of straightforward construction, to the rudimentary building of shelter, an activity that exhibits a catholicity of reason, efficiency, economy, durability and pleasure. Certainly, varying materials and techniques attribute regionalist characteristics to vernacular. But beyond sensuous appearances, all vernacular is marked by a number of constructional a prioris which are universal and essentially phenomenological.

To begin with, building – by its very nature – involves the experiences of load-bearing and load-borne, the primary manifestations of which are the column and the lintel. Secondly, it involves the experience of horizontal and vertical enclosure, the primary manifestations of which are the roof and the wall. The floor, since it repeats the original ground, is flat, for it is meant to be walked upon; whereas the roof is inclined for, in addition to its shedding off water, it marks the terminus and should appear as such. Finally, since all construction is construction by means of finite elements, the act of building involves necessarily the experience of demarcating, the primary manifestations of which are the beginning and ending.

When applied to the making of shelter, these constructional a prioris give rise to a set of constructional corollaries which assume a distinct syntactic and figurative status: as for example the gable, which marks the sectional termination of the roof and thus points to the primary experience of entry; or the engaged pilaster, which manifests the confluent experiences of load-bearing and enclosure; or the window and door, which manifest the experience of suspending enclosure locally for purposes of passage; or the colonnade, which demarcates the experience of boundary; and so on.

Classicism: the mimetic elaboration of vernacular
Such constructional a prioris and their ensuing constructional corollaries can be identified – it would appear – beyond fear of interpretative dispute and could therefore serve as the core of a common architectural knowledge.

Yet architecture cannot remain at this 'starting point'. Its vocation is to lift itself above the contingencies of building, by commemorating those very contingencies from which it sprung in the first place. What distinguishes a shed from a temple is the mythopoeic power the temple

possesses: it is a power that transgresses the boundaries of contingent reality and raises construction and shelter to the realm of the 'uselessness of the monument'. In that sense, Classicism – as a sensibility and not as a style – naturalises the constructional a prioris of shelter by turning them into myth: the demarcations of beginning and ending are commemorated as base and capital; the experience of load-bearing is made perceptible through the entasis in the shaft of the column; the chief beam, binding the columns together and imposing on them a common load, becomes the architrave; the syncopation of the transversal beams resting on the architrave is rendered visible in the figures of the triglyphs and metopes of the frieze; the projecting rafters of the roof, supported by the frieze, appear in the shape of the cornice; finally – and most significantly – the whole tectonic assemblage of column, architrave, frieze and cornice become the ultimate object of classical contemplation in the idea of the Order. The Order sets form over the necessities of shelter; it sets the myth of the tectonic over the contingencies of construction. The power of mythical fiction presides. It is the possibility of such an act of mythical fiction that constitutes the prime aesthetic subject-matter of classical thought. Classical architecture constructs a tectonic fiction out of the productive level of building. The artifice of constructing this fictitious world is seen as analogous to the artifice of constructing the human world. In its turn, myth allows for a convergence of the real and the fictive so that the real is redeemed. By rendering construction mythically fictive, classical thought posits reality in a contemplative state, wins over the depredations of petty life and, in a moment of rare disinterestedness, rejoices in the sacramental power it has over contingent life and nature.

Mythical thinking, of course, is not necessarily primitive or prelogical as common opinion might maintain today. It is true thinking for it reduces the world to order. Its truth is no less than that experimentally verified by science. Today, if it appears that the mythopoeic mind cannot achieve Sachlichkeit – objectivity – (and should therefore be doomed as an irrationality that can never attain consensus) this is not because it is incapable of dealing with experiences coolly, but rather because contemporary industrial life has tacitly replaced the objectivity of truth by vulgar positivism and pragmatism. That is why architecture today, under the vulgar tutelage of both modernist and eclecticist objectivity, is systematically denied its mythopoeic power. The vulgarity lies not in the search for objectivity but in the immanence with which consumer culture can boast of being not disinterested contemplation but the mere extension of production.

Notes

1 Théodore Jouffroy, *Le Globe*, 9 April, 1825, 1, p 157, *cf* L Hautecoeur in *Histoire de L'Architecture Classique en France* (Paris: A et J Picard, 1955) Vol VI, p 255.

2 Theodor Adorno, *Minima Moralia*, translated by EFN Jephcott (London: New Left Review Editions, 1974) pp 76-77.

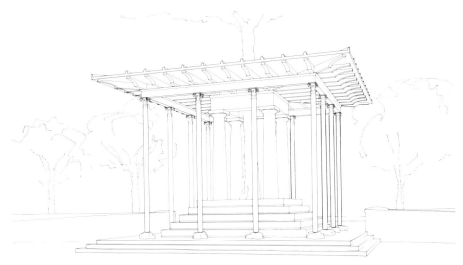

DEMETRI PORPHYRIOS, NORTH PARK PAVILION, BATTERY PARK CITY, N.Y., 1990

THE GREEK ORDER
ALDO ROSSI

PROPYLAIA, ATHENS

In our architectural studies and in our schools, the feeling for the reading of an ancient monument has beenvirtually lost; one may have a repetition of the characteristics of those monuments, a descriptive list of buildings and, at best, the sense of the development of a certain style. This is certainly a lot; but it still does not mean that one can actually stand in front of a monument and grasp its meaning or its essence. In the case

of Greek architecture this has a very particular meaning [. . .] for the Greek temple represents both the order and the exception and, poised between knowledge and the unknowable, it represents above all itself: the Greek temple. Any serious study – of the many on Greek civilisation – tells us that when in Greece the arts reached the highest point of development, they were called precisely 'technique', 'skill' (tecnh) and were regarded purely as a problem of knowledge and production.

One can discern a similar concept in the statements of modern artists like Mies van der Rohe when he writes: '. . . Our real hope is that they (architecture and technology) should grow together, that one day one should be the expression of the other.' That is, he says precisely what the Greek temple proposes and what is the deepest and most lively interpretation of this extraordinary document of antiquity. But this vision of art as experience was already threatened in Greek thought by Platonic speculation, which, going beyond the experiential data, moved toward the metaphysical vision of the temple and its geometrical and mathematical ratios.

Francois Cali [1] stresses a statement by Anaxagoras which is the best explanation of the temple and of its subsequent Platonic abstraction: '. . . What is being shown here is a vision of the invisible, states Anaxagoras of Clazomenae, the last of the physicist-mystics . . . An exile, he died on the day legend gives to the birth of the first great theologian of the beautiful, Plato. The Doric temple then ceased to be the thing of stone on the Acropolis that contained a god within its

confines, that named and honoured him; it became, against the heaven of mathematics, the mortal and visible sign of an immortal and invisible proportion' (pXXVII). As, for Xenophanes, God, mobile and free, represented man's thought, and just as man's thought does not exist in itself outside the thinking man, so the beauty of the temple did not exist outside its *raison d'être,* its being as a temple. But this moment of the history of civilisation having been lost, Plato's trail provided a way to the abstract and numerical relationship with which it was thought that one might translate a perfection which – precisely because it was believed to be *celestial* – ended always being abstract and favouring throughout history an academic position that had little to do with Classicism: the road to the theology of the beautiful was open. In true Classicism, as in Alberti, the classical experience, the normative rules themselves will have life as a model and not an *a priori* position. Cali, by comparing a number of texts, insists on this concept that runs throughout Greek civilisation and on the distortion of this concept brought about by neo-Platonist doctrine; this, in my opinion, is a critical observation of very great interest and goes beyond this single study to a more general conception of history. As he emphasises, in later ages this distortion carries with it the impossibility of translating Greek terms in a concrete fashion. What for us is symmetry was for the Greeks analogy (analogia) or proportion and, already in the Latin world, was taken in as *compositio* and therefore no longer as analogy in contrast to anomaly but as *apta membrorum compositio.*

The Latin translation thus expresses a different concept and Vitruvius indeed found errors of measure in the Doric temples. *Beata culpa!* Never, observes Cali, has such a symbol of measure led so many towards such excess.

At this point Cali's interpretation, his insistence on the living aspect of the temple and, I might add, on the scientific attitude of the technique of the first unknown architects, becomes increasingly convincing. 'The birth of science' wrote Ludovico Geymonat, 'is linked . . . to the production of means with which to sound the marvellous, analysing it into its component parts, compounding it with other material, reproducing it in similar or different circumstances. The most modern philosophy of science has given to these means the name of technique, irrespective of whether they are achieved through empirical or conceptual instruments.' It is in this sense that one should understand the technique of the Greek temple and, in general, this is the starting point for any attempt at grasping the essence of technique in architecture.

Technique can never be understood as abstract speculation or mere instrumentality. And yet classical academicism sought out a certain numerical arrangement in a universal law, transcending Greek architecture in its reality and, in the attempt to reproduce this arrangement, it got lost in fruitless schematic constructions. In this case, to study Greek architecture as such has no meaning. We know that, for the Greeks, art belonged to the broader world of knowledge; the tendency towards art was part of the tendency towards the logical world of speech, of discourse, rather than towards that of images. In this sense, therefore, it is right to speak of the rationality of those monuments, since rationality is built up in its relations and is continually renewed giving rise to ever new techniques.

To conclude, we may sum up the themes which encourage an interest [. . .] in all architectural research which aims at an intelligent, progressive interpretation of monuments. We have said that in our studies and schools this kind of research has often been lost; all that remains, at best, is the awareness of the development of certain relations of architecture. This is also true of the constructive field of architecture, that of building: the lack of interest in history is always marked by a lack of interest in technique. [. . .] Here, in conclusion, one can make only the briefest reference to the fact that the very concept of rationality – which has always belonged to architecture and to the world of building, in so far as it comprises a technical world – is by no means a static concept which, once determined, remains always valid. The tendency today to make modern architecture into a world of established and immutable relations could be but a symptom of its decline. In this sense, the above quotation from Mies is by no means random and not even easily replaceable with quotations from other artists: it refers to the meaning of the work of an architect who has defined a technique and has, therefore, created an architecture. On the contrary, those who consider themselves modern because, for instance, they diligently use certain products of contemporary industry, can discover nothing, let alone infuse the products of that industry with a forward thrust. This is how one should interpret these words of Mies: '. . . The new materials are no necessarily the best. Each material is only what we make it.' Which is to say that new materials are not the ones which are most recent but that they acquire meaning only from the way they are understood: that is, that their modernity is not their novelty but their *raison d'être.* I wanted to conclude with this comparison in order to show that the study of the Greek order and of modern architecture can very well co-exist provided they are not taken as sacred texts. For they may contain a truth and a norm, but they may well equally contain formulae and dogmatism.

Note

1 Rossi refers here to the book by Francois Cali, *L'ordre grec* (Paris 1958), of which the present text was a review.

ALDO ROSSI, MARBURG MUSEUM, DRAWING OF THE INTERIOR COURTYARD

GIORGIO DE CHIRICO, *AUTUMN MELANCHOLY*, 1915

CLASSICAL MELANCHOLIES
MANFREDO TAFURI AND GEORGES TEYSSOT

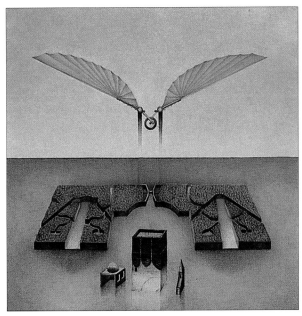

MASSIMO SCOLARI, *THE MACHINE OF OBLIVION*, WATERCOLOUR, 1978 (17.8 X 17.8)

Et voici dans l'air bleu le Décor/tel un somptueux désir d'enfant/réalisé . . .
Paul Valéry, Paradoxe sur l'architecte, *1891*

Classicism is the art of the eternal recommencement, of repetition and of synecdoche. This figure of speech, which is a form of metonymy and which, if we believe the entomologists, corresponds to the way in which ants see things, invests the part with authority to indicate the whole. 'Within the system of Greek architecture' the academician Quatremère de Quincy wrote in 1824 'the least part of an elevation has the ability to make the whole known'. Paul Valery's Eupalinos echoes this rational conception: 'There is no geometry without speech. Without it, figures are accidents . . . By it, each figure is a proposition which can be composed with others . . .' Just as reason governs calculation, so architectural discourse relates back to the unchanging signification and constructs real magnitude by the hard law of numbers.

These neo-classical considerations are well in accordance with the cultural climate before the First World War. German Classicism gives itself up to the drunkenness of the Italian skies, sometimes menacing sometimes pacific; Giorgio de Chirico brings the still fresh traces of the gods back to the heart of the metropolis; finally, Isadora Duncan dances *barefoot*. In the dry shade of the Acropolis, the *gymnopédies* cause the myth of Orpheus to be reborn and announce a nearby era where the geometry of the masses will supersede aristocratic ballet. This sport of the gods will enter all the salons of Europe: in 1912, the great couturier Paul Poiret organises the 'Festivals of Bacchus' in the Butard Pavilion. The highlight of the evening is the interpretation of a theme by Bach which is given by a very lightly veiled Isadora. Her Dionysian art inspires the Apollonian rigour of Auguste Rodin, of Dunoyer de Segonzac and of Antoine Bourdelle. In this geography of classical melancholies, the dialogue between Germany and Italy, portrayed in Overbeck's painting *Germania und Italia* (1828), becomes the emblem of this nostalgia which perpetually attracts the North to the South.

The Silence of the Muses
It is evident that, for Hölderlin as for the painters of Lukasbund, during an epoque of expatriation and exile, the classical offered itself only as the nostalgia of a lost synthesis. For Caspar David Friedrich, faced with the immortality of nature, the development of human works could only be their ruin, since nothing could manage to reconcile nature and figuration any longer; there could only be an inexorable distance of separation. For Arnold Böcklin, inheritor of the 'classico-romantic' dialectic that precipitated during those disquieting nights of Symbolism, man and nature live in a 'sublime' time which is no longer attainable. The image of *absence* pervades Böcklin's *Die Toteninsel* (1880). This absence characterises all research which, in the context of the 'tradition of the new', appeals to the classical sensibility as pure form, the melancholic reverie for an intimate fusion between Idea and Life: the moderns can only discuss the loss of this fusion. In fact, De Chirico, a character whose work illuminates the relationship between Classicism and contemporary art in an exemplary manner, relied on Böcklin's painting. In *La Ronda*, 1920, De Chirico stated that 'classicism is a problem of pruning, of trimming', adding that it is necessary

to 'reduce the phenomenon, the initial apparition, to its skeleton, to its sign, to the symbol of its inexplicable existence'. De Chirico, the 'metaphysical' painter, does not seem to have a notion of time: in his paintings, time is fixed in a petrified space, questioning itself about its own existence. Haunted by the *Muse inquietanti*, the city oscillates between the natural and the artificial: man is reduced to the shape of skittles or of rackets, and the real inhabitants of *Meditazione mattutina* (1912) or of *La melanconia di una bella giornata* (1913) are mythological statues, which have become plaster mouldings, demonstrating their absolute uselessness to the rare humans, miniscule silhouettes, who are still present .

In the *Piazze d'Italia* (1913), the trains, separated from the urban scene by walls, appear on the horizon like symbols of modernity, thus represented in its most banal aspect: that which accentuates the feeling of the immobility of space, by making allusion to infinite, and thus unutterable, events. Existence is inexplicable; the urban universe is inhospitable: it is impossible to inhabit it. Or, to put it more accurately, one could only manage to live in it by observing the spectacle of 'modernity' with a sense of detachment. In a text about Max Klinger, which was published in *Il Convegno* in 1921, De Chirico points out the profound significance of the absences which conceal the German painter's work, in the face of the endurance of traces of an order which insists on lasting despite the fact that it is anachronistic:

> Klinger has revealed, in the most strange and profound manner, the romantic sense of modern life, of the continued development of activities, of machine constructions and buildings and comfort, all due to current progress. What is this romanticism of modern day life? . . . It is the breath of nostalgia which passes over the European metropolis, across the streets black with people, over the great centres buzzing with activity and over the faubourgs opened to the geometry of factories and workshops; over the buildings which, like cubic arches of stone and cement, standing upright amidst the mass of houses and buildings, hide the sorrows and the hopes of insipid daily life in their rigid flanks . . . It is the nostalgia of railway stations, of arrivals and departures; the melancholy of seaports, with the transatlantic steamers which, casting off their moorings, appear in the night on the dark waters, illuminated like a festive city . . .

Nevertheless, De Chirico's cities condense into sacred 'places': by a sadistic process of estrangement, he places the symbols of the community in charred deserts where lithological dialogues are exchanged. Such impossible museums suggest an enigma not so much to those people who live in them as to those who have to impose their laws on them. For it cannot be disputed that we are talking about a law here. Naked, fleshless porticoes, a pyramidal tower, truncated and crowned by a portico of columns which vaguely recalls the classical or 'Tuscan' architecture of Peter Behrens, as in *La nostalgia dell'infinito* (1913-14): the rarefied atmosphere thus evokes a grievous cataclysm, panic-stricken repressions. The law is the law of exclusion; the clocks which seem to have stopped, as in *L'Enigma dell'ora* (1912), accentuate this impression by freezing the flux of all experience. The ghostly world of these canvasses is the world which is described in Nietzsche's Turin letters, which De Chirico had read. But when such abortive existences take the form of manikins, as in *Il filosofo e il poeta* (1916), a scission between the space of representation and the representation of space is irremediably produced. The *Il Grande Metafisico* (1917) and *Le Muse inquietanti* (1925), are placed in front of a classical decor: metamorphosis is presented after it has occurred. It has already taken place, long ago, in a far off and mythological place.

In an article in *Valori plastici* of 1919, De Chirico explained his painting by evoking Jules Verne and the mystery of a city such as London: 'In the construction of the city, in the architectural form of its houses, its squares, its gardens and public landscapes, its ports, its stations, etc, one finds the first foundations of a great metaphysical aesthetic.'

With regard to *Interno metafisico con grande edificio* (1916), one could ask oneself why the urban space is portrayed as a painting within a painting, whilst the canvas is covered with manikins or geometrical objects placed without any logic. De Chirico's manikin is not Heinrich von Kleist's puppet. The elements of its composition evoke here the instruments of classical rationality assembling themselves as 'symbolic form'. The silent perspectives recoil in the face of an oneiric montage which, in turn, deprives the geometric measure of reality and the law of numbers of any sense. The tragedy of 'the inexplicable existence' of the phenomenon is situated in a landscape which refers explicitly to the city of Ferrara, an urban place crossed by the hermetic signs of a new melancholy, there where the tradition of Classicism and of the Renaissance are mingled with ancient secrets, unnameable and unnamed.

In face of the repleteness of Neo-Classicism at the beginning of the century the absence of existance hovers throughout the works of Carlo Carrà, De Chirico or Giorgio Morandi. This same absence is described in the *Chants de la mi-mort*, the poetic drama by Alberto Savinio Giorgio de Chirico's brother, which was published in the *Soirées de Paris*, Apollinaire's review, in July 1914: 'The metallic birds unfold their rigid wings,/the statues advance at a rhythmical pace,/the fountains have dried up'. ('Les oiseaux métalliques déployent leurs ailes rigides,/Les statues avancent au pas cadencé,/les fontaines se sont desséchées'.)

Thus, metaphysical painting was unable to serve as a model for the real town. By taking inspiration from such painting for their project, the Milanese architects, such as Giovanni Muzio or Gigiotti Zanini, attained only some equivocal suggestions. The classical message of the painting of De Chirico or Carrà is rather better perceived, for example in the architecture of reduction of Heinrich Tessenow, in the *rythmic* spaces of the scenographer Adolphe Appia in the ordered sobriety of Scandinavian classicism – that of Edvard Thomsen, Carl Petersen and Ivar Bentsen in Denmark or of Gunnar Asplund in Sweden. In 1935 the Italian critic Edoardo Persico was already writing an article in *Casabella Construzioni:* 'The Neo-Classicism of Swedish architects and their neo-Renaissance style is in no way a reduction to cold formulae: on the contrary, it concerns a very intense reflection on a world impregnated with poetry and hallucinations; it is their way of evoking a terrestrial paradise, an Olympia, and not an archaeological cemetery. Thus, Swedish Neo-Classicism is not the Academy, but an art; it is a strict discipline and not a simple way of creating'. The same desire for spiritual fasting is apparent in all these tendencies: their ultimate objective is to demonstrate that the classical plenitude would not know how to be familiar, that an abyss separates us from it.

The Dialogue of the Dead

Paul Poiret's architect is Louis Süe. Süe and Mare, whose new Orsay perfumery in rue de la Paix was published in *L'Architecture vivante* in 1923, had directed the publication of *Architectures* published by the *NRF* in 1921. It was a very luxurious compilation of interior decoration which had contributed to the formation of the 'French style' since 1914. Engravings by Dunoyer de Segonzac, Roger de la Fresnaye and Jacques Villon accompany a text which is written in the form of a dialogue, Valery's Eupalinos, composed for the occasion. Whereas Picasso, 'the harlequin living in Port Royal' as Jean Cocteau proclaimed, returned to Classicism and the 'Ingresque' style, the slogans of post-war Parisian criticism insisted on the 'new spirit' on 'reconstruction' and on the return to order'. Cocteau, the 'Coq', preferred 'a more Greek art' to Cubism; Andre Gide, at the *NRF*, inclined towards Classicism as the art of renunciation. For Valery, the 'classicist' friend, let us not forget, of Auguste Perret and Pierre Laprade and author of inscriptions on the Palais de Chaillot, 'form is essentially linked to repetition'.[1]

The poet's architectural Classicism is evident in *Charmes*. The 'Cantique des colonnes' (1919) makes the law of numbers sing:

> Our ancient youths/Mat skin and heautiful shadows,/Are proud
> of their qualities/Which are born by numbers.//Daughters of the

golden numbers/Bearers of the laws of heaven,/ . . . ' (Nos antiques jeunesses,/ Chair mate et belles ombres,/Sont fières des finesses/ Qui naissent par les nombres.//Filles des nombres d'or,/Fortes des lois du ciel,/ . . .)

The spirit of the ancient monument inspires the poet in 'Le Cimetière marin' (1920):

. . . This place pleases me, dominated by torches,/Composed of gold, stone and dark trees/Where so much marble trembles on so many shadows; . . . (. . . Ce lieu me plait, dominé de flambeaux,/ Composé d'or, de pierre et d'arbres sombres/Où tant de marbre est tremblant sur tant d'ombres; . . .)

Or (gold) was for Valéry, one of the 'ten most beautiful words in the French language' and Matila Ghyka, author of a famous book on *Le Nombre d'or* (Paris, 1931) underlines in *Sortilèges du verbe* (Paris, 1949) the incantatory charm of words (such as *or, pur, dur, azur* and *marbre*) marking Valéry's verses. Leon-Paul Fargue, in the book's preface, emphasises 'the pleasure one gains in *repeating* the same *melody*', conferring a cabalistic or hieroglyphic value on a word. Mallarme in his *Mots anglais* had already affirmed the existence, outside the 'verbal' or symbolic value of a word, of a secret direction of the phoneme running parallel to the 'pure, sensual sign' of poetry. We again recognise the theme of classical *repetition,* a process which, however, will lose the sense of accomplishment that a ritual respectful of immutable values evokes, in order to transform itself into a *game of chance:* the games of the reiteration and dismantling of the 'signifier', of the duplication and dissemination of 'sense', of the ambiguous impression of the letter and the word, both signs and cryptograms at the same time.

Valéry's Classicism, nevertheless, appears as a certitude which has been undermined at its base.[2] Like Nietzsche he knows that order, the canon of the classical era. has been plucked from hasard: 'What struck [the Ancients] was chance, freedom, caprice . . . ' (II, 563.) 'Order, the fruit of chaos, is the mask of law: in all the arts, and that is why they are arts, the necessity that a happily completed work must suggest can only he engendered by the arbitrary.' (11, 1248.) But the casual element of creation is not the only one which obscures the clarity of the principles, the rules, the laws or canons of the arts in the so called classical periods. Suspicion is also attached to the 'desire for conservation' hidden in the idea of perfection and of the finished form. For chance presides equally at both the transmission of knowledge and the acquisition of learning: 'The glory of the present day gilds the works of the past with the same intelligence with which a fire or a worm in a library destroys this or that.' (II, 632.) The impression of perennial renewal that emanates from Antiquity vacillates before the destruction of the geneology of artistic canons which science and history can no longer guarantee: 'Nothing resembles our present capital of learning our *property* in the subject of history, more than this collection of *accidentally* preserved objects. All our knowledge is, like this [collection] a residue. Our documents are the flotsam which one epoch abandons for another, haphazardly, and in a disordered state'. All this is gathered by the 'wise and pious hands', 'with the arbitrariness which is required'. For a classicist, this is harsh and such melancholic thought is linked to the reflections made by J L Borges and W Benjamin: 'Only lacunae, without doubt . . . But think a little more, and you will soon find that if we were to have *everything*, we would be able *to do absolutely nothing* with it'. (II, 1355-1356.)

Finally, *Eupalinos.* A superficial reading could lead one to believe that it was an Abridgement, a Compendium of the classical and French architectural tradition from J F Blondel to J Guadet, passing via Viollet-le-Duc . . . in short, a sort of improved Gromort. We do find there, it is quite true, numerous common metaphors for the art of building: 'Some buildings are *silent*, others *speak*, and finally others which are more rare, *sing*'. Nevertheless, Valéry reproached his contemporaries for no longer drawing a distinction between a 'work chiselled' (in stone) and a 'work moulded' (in concrete) (II, 1559), an appreciation which is singularly different from the views of the master

of the rue Raynouard.

In posing the 'question of origins', the basis of the idea, in *Eupalinos,* seems to be the order of these subtle analogies which unite the sounds of music to the 'solid art': 'only an Orphic miracle *can* compose dwellings for gods and men'. (II, 98.) We think of Perret's formula; 'everything in an egg', which returns to the Greek oikos, but also the terms of *casket, shrine* and *temple* of which he is fond. Constructing thus becomes a demiurgic act, 'the enemy of similitudes', organising 'inequality'. The builder '*takes the very point where god has stopped as the origin of his act.*' (II, 144.) It must be acknowledged that, in the 20th century, few architects have been presented with such opportunities. The doubt even arises that it is, there too, a game, a mortal simulacrum. Firstly, an initial indication: extracts of *Eupalinos* appeared in the *Nouvelle Revue Francaise* in March 1921, bearing the sub-title 'Dialogue of the Dead'. From that, the sense has become more clear: Socrates, who has met Phaedra beside the Illissus, the river of Time, is a 'dead architect'. (11, 146.) This *dwelling,* this authentic and poetic residence of gods and men exists no longer; it is neither situated in time to come, nor in any privileged 'place'; it is no longer any more than 'a silent ruin, the traces of a lost primordial *form'*.[3] The ghost of Socrates, in concluding the Dialogue, confirms this interpretation: 'There is no *here*, and all that we have just said is as much a natural game of the silence of those infernos as the fantasy of some orator from the other world who has taken us for puppets.' (II, 1947.) Far from bringing reconciliatory myths, *Eupalinos* reveals the *tragic* situation of the architect who, by the repetition of the classical, can only speak infinitely about this death .

In justifying his use of the word infinity, Valéry recalls that '*satisfaction* causes need to be reborn, the response regenerates the request, *presence* engenders absence, and possession engenders *desire'. (II, 1342-3.)* In his theodicy of art, Valery has traced a limit. The Wittgenstein of the *Tractatus (4.115)* has already demonstrated that fixing the limit signifies the unutterable, by clearly representing the speakable. The presence of the classical in modern architecture, by clearly represenhng the absence, the disappearance, the finite, signifies the unutterable and the infinite. A wisdom, at once ancient and modern, teaches us that what remains is not a residue but the departure point from which things can begin to be.

The nostalgia for the 'spiritual abstinence' of the classical still lives. The spirit of Böcklin and of De Chirico is present in the research of Aldo Rossi like two sleeping spectators of a catastrophe which should be confined to a bad dream. The authentic problem for Rossi is to retrieve the *origins* of the architectural sign. The return to primordial forms renews the act of *classical renunciation*: as an ultimate appeal to reason and to memory, the cone, tetrahedron, cylinder, prism and triangle grant an order to those signs which have been devoid of any meaning. Sacred immobility returns to the city. Such is Rossi's genial and moving attempt: to plunge into the familiar alienation of those cruel and tormented structures which can only explore obstinately their own origins and their own formal genealogy. If confronted with a universe of transience and consumption, one wishes to avoid 'the banquet of nausea', it is necessary to return to the metaphysical, to reflection on the origin of being.

But to avoid being washed down on the slope of the dialectic, it is necessary to limit the research to Parmenides. The primordial elements of the world are the natural elements (water, earth, fire, air) forming compounds amongst themselves by attraction and repulsion. Similarly, this is what happens to Aldo Rossi's primordial forms: they can, by turns, be intersected, shattered, composed and decomposed, remaining always with an alchemical or sacred world. The real town – as in De Chirico's *Piazze d'Italia* – is always present as a decor: this effect renders Rossi's 'inactual' world stupefying.

This same stupefaction marks the classical tautologies of Giorgio Grassi, of Miguel Garay and Jose Linazasoro, or of Franco Stella. Others, like Leon Krier (and like the young French architects of the last generation, Bernard Huet, or Christian Portzamparc), try with courage and at times with irony, to acclimatise this surprised tension in an urban . . . or suburban landscape. But neither Tessenow nor Behrens are at the origin of this surreal order. It is an order which does not want to know the violence of the Erinnyes, an order *which knows it has no power*. For the circle closes up again. The unutterable word is once again pronounced. The classical and surreal watercolours of Massimo Scolari bear witness to the continuity of the modern tendencies of the 'anti-avant garde' with the *melancholies* of metaphysical painting.

Ulysses, chained to the mast of his ship and having blocked the ears of his companions, eludes by trickery the seduction of the Sirens, who would have enticed him away to catastrophe and death. As denounced by Adorno and Horkheimer, his heroism is the private act of a seigneur who makes others row for his own benefit: he can neutralise temptation into a pure object of contemplation, in art. In a world henceforth stripped of Form, he who wishes to act will play and replay a fatal and disturbing 'Death in Venice'.

Notes

1 *Owucewa* (in two volumes) jof P Valéry, vol II, Galimard, Paris, 1960, p 554; all our quotations are extracts from this edition.

2 *Cf* the article by Theodor Adorno in *Die Neue Rundschau*, LXXXI, 1960.
3 *Cf* the note by M Cacciari in *Nuova Corrente*, 76-77, Milan, 1978.

FROM LOUIS SÜE AND ANDRÉ MARE, *ARCHITECTURES*, 1921

— * —

THE CLASSICAL TRADITION
MICHAEL GREENHALGH

LEON BATTISTA ALBERTI, SANTA MARIA NOVELLA, FLORENCE, 1456

We must be careful to distinguish between Classicism as simply a style, which is of course open to anyone, and Classicism as part of a broader and hence more pervasive tradition, which arguably requires some range of common values as well. The very word tradition implies more than simple continuity – rather, tradere *means transmission, handing on; or, in the Roman legal sense, handing*

something over for safe keeping. Indeed, any survey of the classical tradition in earlier centuries reveals that Classicism is not restricted simply to art, for the adoption of Classicism can carry a whole series of meanings – political, social, ideological and religious; examples illustrating its longevity can therefore be found in such diverse fields as literature,[1] letter forms,[2] coinage,[3] and administration. The tradition, indeed, has political as well as social and artistic implications; and it is not going too far to say that the Papacy and the Church have been its most avid supporters since late Antiquity, recognising its value and the support it could lend them: 'What is really a tradition is not the institution, but the belief in its value.'[4]

The nature of the classical tradition
The practitioners of Classicism believed that the duty of art is to instruct and improve, rather than merely to entertain; and they first sought their models amongst the famous surviving exemplars of the art of Greece and Rome, because their educational ethos put the whole of Antiquity – letters, laws, deeds as well as art – on a pedestal. In Antiquity artists also looked back to earlier models: they had their *own* classical tradition.[5] Hence Classicism is an approach to art and, indeed, to life, that emphasises the ideal (in form and in content) over the everyday; the power of reason over the often misleading emotions; clarity and simplicity (that is, understatement) over prolixity; measurability (as an

index of beauty) over intuition. Such ideas are as clearly evident in literature as in art,[6] and have led theorists to develop the pendulum theory of artistic sentiment and style, whereby these swing from one extreme to another in cycles – giving us the oppositions Classic and Romantic, objective and subjective, rationalist and emotional, reason and imagination, universal and particular, restraint and abandon, simplicity and complication, ideal and real, Corneille and Hugo, Poussin and Delacroix, and so on. One might say that the classical tradition provides a closely reasoned support for the values of the antique past – the recognised origins of Western civilisation.[7]

The tradition has the following characteristics:
1 It would be misleading to restrict any account of the classical tradition to art alone, for the continuing importance of antique ideals and methods can also be traced through the centuries in areas as distinct as politics, religion, administration, agriculture, social conventions and letter forms as well as the visual arts. Indeed, since at least the time of Constantine, Classicism has been closely linked with an antique-related political and social vision, and for this reason has been of varying strength and consistency throughout the medieval and later periods.[8]
2 The classical tradition is a set of agreed values, rather than just a conglomeration of styles – values which were integral to European society from late Antiquity through to the earlier 19th century. It is dependent for its development, nurture and

survival on prestigious patronage from rulers or the aristocracy – such as that of Augustus, the Papacy, the Medici or Napoleon. From this it is clear that Classicism can be simply a *style*, although it needs more than the slavish copying of earlier works to make a product classical: the best artists are inspired by classical art to create what is essentially a *new* art.[9] Artists who formed part of the classical tradition did so because their clients as well as themselves were part of it – noblemen ordered works from Canova, for example, at least partly because his work rivalled the antiquities they had at home. Indeed, Canova possessed an enormous collection of both antique marbles and terracottas, and it would not be difficult to show that they are *essential* to his work.[10]

3 It is cumulative rather than consistent: that is, the tradition *changes* with each generation, so that – for example – Renaissance art quickly becomes part of the canon, so that artists such Domenichino or Poussin or architects such as Bramante or Palladio are effectively as important as models as the Ancients themselves.

4 Hence, there is little 'purity' about most aspects of the classical tradition, because there is only infrequently (as in the later 18th and then the 19th centuries) the desire to be archaeological or in some way accurate in the way the sources are treated. Because the classical tradition is the accumulation of solutions to artistic problems presented by artists and architects since late Antiquity, it is but rarely that the need is felt to return to the sources and to make (in Rosenblum's phrase) a *tabula rasa*.[11] Hence to reject the Renaissance and Baroque traditions is to reject the classical tradition, and many have indeed done so.

5 The tradition is logically Roman and *not* Greek, because Rome has consistently been at the centre of European consciousness; whereas Greece (except in antique times, during parts of the Middle Ages, and since the 19th century) has been at the periphery.

6 In spite of this, a characteristic of the tradition is that it *is* in general rational, in that it can be expressed as a series of rules (and models) which can easily be explained. Imitation and explication of the accumulated tradition has therefore been the task of many academies – and not just 'art' academies – since their inception in Italy in the 16th century.[12] Just as the tradition itself can be politically oriented, so academies themselves were frequently fuelled by nationalism as well as by artistic theory.[13]

Notes

1 G Highet, *The Classical Tradition: Greek and Roman Influences on Western Literature*, Oxford 1949.

2 F Saxl, 'The Classical Inscription in Renaissance Art and Politics', *JWCI* 4 1941, pp 19-46; S. Morison, *Politics and Script: Aspects of Authority and Freedom in the Development of Graeco-Latin Script*, Oxford 1972; and *cf* Poghio Bracciolini's use of his epigraphical knowledge in his funeral orations: I Kajanto, 'Poggio Bracciolini and Classical Epigraphy', *Arctos (Acta Philologica Fennica)* XIX 1985, pp 19-40.

3 H Wentzel, 'Der Augustalis Friedrichs II und die abendlandische Glyptick des 13. Jahrunderts', *ZfKG* 15 1952, pp 183-7; *ibid* 'Portraits à l'antique' on French Mediaeval Gems and Seals', *JWCI* 16 1953, pp 342-50; *ibid*, 'Italianische Siegelstempel und Siegel all 'antico im 13. und 14. Jahrhundert', *Mitt. KHIF* 17 1955, pp 73-86; *ibid*, 'Antiken-imitationen des 12. und 13. Jahrhunderts in Italien', *ZfKW* 9 1955, pp 29-72; *ibid*, 'Staatskameen' im Mittalalter', *JBuch Berl Museen* 4 1962, pp 42-77.

4 And again: 'a tradition is not a mere observed fact, like an existing custom; it is an idea which expresses a value judgement. A certain way of acting is regarded as right; a certain order or arrangement is held desirable. The maintenance of the tradition is the assertion of this judgement.' Max Radin in *The Encyclopaedia of the Social Sciences*, New York 1959, XV p 63, *qv* tradition.

5 M Pavan, *Antichita classica e pensiero moderno*, Florence 1977, pp 345-59: 'Classicita e classicismo nel guidizio sul mondo antico'.

6 *cf* P Van Tieghem, *Les grandes doctrines litteraires en France*, Paris 1963, pp 29-51.

7 M Greenhalgh, *The Classical Tradition in Art*, London 1978.

8 J. Adhemar, *Influences antiques dans l'art du moyen âge francais; recherches sur les sources et les thèmes d'inspiration*, London 1939; V Bracco, *L'archeologia classica nella cultura occidentale*, Rome 1979; C Ghiri, 'La cultura classica nella coscienza medioevale', *Studi Romani* 2 1954, pp 395-410.

9 M Seidel, 'Studien zur Antikenrezeption Nicola Pisanos', *Mitt KHIF 19* 1975, pp 307-92.

10 M E Micheli, 'Le raccolte di antichita di Antonio Canova', *Riv.It Naz. Archeologia Storia dell'Arte*. VIII-IX, 1985-6, pp 205-322. Canova had some splended Italic terracottas from temple revetments: is he the first artist known to have collected these – or should we imagine people like Ghiberti and Donatello collecting similar material?

11 R Rosenblum, *Transformations in Late Eighteenth-Century Art*, Princeton 1967.

12 N Pevsner, *Academies of Art, Past and Present*, Cambridge 1940; but see the Italian edition of Antonio Pinelli, *Le accademie d'arte*, Turin 1982, with updated bibliography, pp xliii-xlviii.

13 eg P Barocchi, *L'Accademia Etrusca* (exhibition, Cortona, Palazzo Casali), Milan 1985; or M Harari, 'Toscanità = Etruschità. Da modello a mito storiografico: le origini settecentesche', *Xenia* 15 1988, pp 65-72.

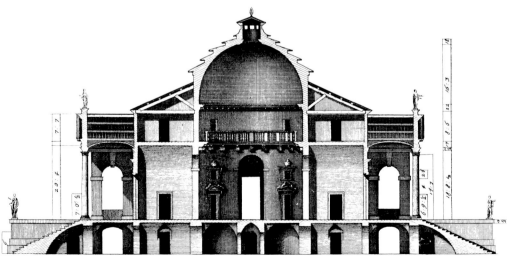

ANDREA PALLADIO, VILLA ROTUNDA, VICENZA, 1550s, DRAWING BY SCAMOZZI, 1778

WHAT THE CLASSICAL CAN DO FOR THE MODERN
ROBERT A M STERN

'No doubt the artist is the child of his time; but woe to him if he is also its disciple, or even its favourite . . . He will indeed take his subject matter from the present age, but his form he will borrow from a nobler time – nay, from beyond all time, from the absolute unchangeable unity of his being . . . But how does the artist secure himself against the corruptions of his time, which everywhere encircle him? By disdaining his opinion. Let him look upwards to his own dignity and to Law, not downwards to fortune and to everyday needs.'[1]

'Live with your century, but do not be its creature; render to your contemporaries what they need, not what they praise.'[2]

I am a modern architect, a product of the continually evolving Western Humanist tradition. As such I do not believe that the present moment is necessarily the best moment or even a particularly important one. Rather, I cast an eye backward to help establish a vantage point, a critical distance to help me define my role in the present and find my way toward the future.

As a Modern, I am convinced of the continuing viability of the classical language of architecture.[3] It is not the only language possible, nor one that should always be used in its pure form. But it is the basic language – the measure, the root, the datum which gives order not only to the lingua franca of the traditional vernaculars of the pre-industrial past, but also to the machine-age vernaculars of mass production. Of all the architectural methodologies yet evolved, I believe Classicism best reconciles the idiosyncracies of the local, the immediate and the expedient with the grand, enobling and enduring values that draw people together in their diversity.

Though possibly once a fixed set of rules, Classicism has been seen as an evolving grammar and vocabulary since the time of its revival in 15th-century Italy. As both a language and a point of view, it represents deep-seated cultural values without sacrificing versatility. The five Orders may be considered by some to have been divinely inspired, but it remains to the individual architect to work out their exact proportional and decorative attributes, to put them to work in the grander, more complex ensemble of buildings and cities. By these individual decisions the architect propels us into a dialogue between an idealised past and an evolving present. The depth of that dialogue is the essence of our Western culture: it not only inspires and guides us but also reminds us who we are, especially as we confront new challenges of building in the context of non-Western cultures.

While in and of itself Classicism embodies no specific political or moral agenda, it is the public language of Western institutions. It reifies the shared experiences that to this day give the wider public a common voice, a common gesture, and a sense of collective identity. It brings the republican spirit of Washington to the county courthouses of the South and Midwest. If, as some have suggested, the memory of slaves mars the Classicism of Jefferson's Monticello, what of Henry Bacon's Lincoln Memorial, whose testament to emancipation draws strength from a particular but nonetheless compelling interpretation of Greek democracy, and is further sanctified by memories of Marian Anderson and Martin Luther King, each of whom chose it as a forum? Classicism is not particular to any one moment or region, or personal to any one architect. Great works of architecture, as surely as those of literature, painting and music, operate on many levels; while they are a product of their social or political situations, they express transcending ideals. To have it otherwise would be to dismiss all art of the past, and indeed the present moment, and idly wait for social conditions to improve.

The perennial vitality of classical grammar, syntax and vocabulary reveals the very most basic meaning of architecture as ordered, intelligible, shared public space. Classicism presents the designer with a codified system of symphonic complexity for relating the smallest detail to the overall structure, for balancing geometry with human measure, and abstract shapes with literal depictions of nature or with verbal ideas. Its synthesis of rational composition, representational details and empathetic form challenges the intellect of the initiate and delights the senses of the layman, as they pause for second and third moments to contemplate the play of light on carved surfaces, the meaning of acanthus leaves, wreathes and garlands, or the literary text of inscriptions. To talk of a forest of columns, indeed to walk among one, is to experience nature in metaphor. The language of Classicism not only embraces such metaphors, it embodies them: it has them built in.

Contrary to the anti-traditional premises of Modernism, the exploration of classical themes has never thwarted architecture's ability to come to terms with either new processes of production or the new types of building required by new programmes. In fact, the opposite is true: by using known models and classical grammar and vocabulary, architects of mass-production technology's first great era were not only able to conceptualise some of the most complex public works ever built, but also able to make those works comprehensible to the public whom they were to benefit. Joseph Paxton's Crystal Palace (1850-51), Henri Labrouste's Bibliothèque Sainte-Geneviève (1843-50) and Bibliothèque Nationale (1862-68), Otto Wagner's Postal Savings Bank (1904-06), McKim, Mead & White's Pennsylvania Station (1906-10; demolished 1963) and various works of Auguste Perret are but some of the classical buildings of the late 19th and early 20th centuries that brilliantly and explicitly incorporate advanced building technology.

Many of us have come to value Classicism anew because of ahistorical Modernism's failure to provide satisfactory built responses to the very critical social, environmental and cultural demands from which its proponents claimed to derive their theories. Modernism emphasised innovation over invention, disruption over continuity, interior monologue over public discourse. In arbitrarily rejecting the time-honoured forms that resonate with a culture we have taken such pains over time to create, it introduced a kind of tyranny of the present (the 'eternal present' was Sigfried Giedion's chilling phrase) that stripped away the rich historic complexities of street ensembles, neighbourhoods and sometimes entire cities, as it revelled in the very personal and self-important thrill of isolated invention. As we turn away from a reductive Modernism and search for more culturally inclusive and more physically satisfying ways to build, Classicism again demonstrates its validity and vitality, enabling architects to carve as well as to extrude, to construct and not merely assemble forms that go beyond the mere exemplification of extra-architectural social or literary ideals.

This renewed invocation of Classicism, and beyond it of

traditional building as a whole, is not intended to substitute one form of cultural absolutism – the imposition of the new – with another, the oppression of the old. Rather, it is intended to affirm the architect's role as a conservator of values; to call for invention rather than the too-easy innovation of 'me-too' shape making; to plea for a 'present-and-future-oriented' materialism infused with the ideal of cultural memory. It is precisely Classicism's timeless otherness that makes it so germane to a culture that simultaneously and contradictorily celebrates explorations in outer space while it searches for its roots in the ethnic cultures of the pre-industrial past.

How an architect approaches Classicism today varies as much as the tradition itself but the intrinsic struggle to protect and project its values is shared by all who recognise artistic creativity as a process of recollection and invention. Why an architect proposes Classicism today is also worth asking: for so long the target of modernist contempt, Classicism was made to serve as a symbol of social and political dysfunction and of a troubled status quo. Is not an adherence to the classical canon – to the discipline of its methods and the richness of its vocabulary – an optimistic undertaking for architects who operate in a culture that in other aspects equally values measure and bravura, computers and rock and roll? Classicism offers the architect a canon, but what a liberal and tolerant canon it is. It proposes models of

excellence in composition and detail. It does not set out on a singular route but points out various ways to participate in a continuum yet contribute to its evolution, to be fresh without resorting to self-indulgent iconoclasm, to celebrate the ideals and the fundamental discourse that bind people together rather than search for the cultural rifts that pull us apart, to reaffirm the communalities amidst the chaos which everywhere all too easily makes its own way without our help. With its deep cultural ties, its innate hierarchy of form and detail, and its capacity for purity and hybridisation, Classicism still seems, after nearly a century's struggle to overthrow it, perhaps not inevitable and certainly not God-given, but surely much more than merely viable: taken in its broad sense, a classical approach to architecture seems to offer a fresh stimulus to modern architects seeking to recapture the act of building as a reconciliation of individuality and community, to reaffirm enduring, even timeless values in a dynamic culture continuously challenged by bold and often disturbing political and technological innovations. Classicism has flexibility and built-in tolerance, but do our architects have the skill and scholarship, the art and wisdom to work within its great canon? Isn't it easier to hide behind the head-lines and profess the hopelessness of a world in holocaust? Or to claim that nothing humanly noble can be done in a world dominated by machines? Isn't it just easier to fling a pot of paint in the public's face?

Notes

1   Friedrich Schiller, *On the Aesthetic Education of Man* (1795), trans by Reginald Snell (London: Routledge & Kegan Paul Ltd, 1954; New York: Frederick Ungar Publishing Co, 1965) p 51-52.
2   Schiller, *On the Aesthetic Education of Man*, p 54.
3   I wish to thank M Lindsay Bierman for his assistance in the preparation of this text. Portions of this discussion grow out of my book *Modern Classicism* (London: Thames & Hudson, 1988; New York: Rizzoli International, 1988), written with the assistance of Raymond Gastil.

OTTO WAGNER, NUSSDORF ADMINISTRATION BLOCK ON THE DANUBE CANAL, WITH THE NUSSDORF DAM TO THE RIGHT, 1894-1908

————— * —————

'THE BLIND SPOT'
LEON KRIER

Never before have so many people, so many professional bodies, institutions, magazines, so many papers concerned themselves with Architecture. Never has there existed such a plethora of schools and professionals who ostentatiously carried 'Architecture' on their coat of arms. Never have there existed so many students, teachers, and historians of architecture, and yet . . . and yet Architecture seems not only something badly defined – far from agreed upon – but most of these people do not know what architecture is, let alone what it was made of. Not being sure what it should be, some pretend it is dead, while others claim it should be dead. If you look for contemporary definitions you will find thousands of books on modern architectural subjects, however only a few would come anywhere near a definition of modern architecture.

In this state of confusion it is only natural that the RIBA's architectural library is selling some of its precious content and, for the past few years, has been more interested in acquiring books on rules governing daylighting and such subjects rather than on architecture. The confusion becomes complete if you look into Pevsner's Dictionary of Architecture[1] only to find out that the term 'architecture' is not even mentioned. Thus, architecture is veiled in a cloud of nonsense: how can a dictionary treat a subject which does not even enter its own intelligence?

Art of Building
We will therefore have to rely on other definitions for enlightenment. Quatremère de Quincy devotes to this subject – Architecture – about 30 pages of his Dictionary,[2] and defines it as an imitative system of building, as the *art* of building, leaving aside its manual aspects. But if architecture is essentially an intellectual discipline it cannot or does not want at any moment to free itself from its subject and origin: building.

Thus, Architecture consists essentially of a body of knowledge concerning the material transformation of nature into buildings and in turn, the translation of an imitative system of Building into an Art of Building.

According to this definition of Architecture, this particular art is not only dead, but it is also etymologically absurd to use the term modern architecture – let alone 'post-modern architecture'. If we look at the architectural schools, at architectural offices, at the statutes of professional bodies, we find that not one is occupied, or even concerned, with the circulation of knowledge about the nature and making of architecture.

Neither architecture nor building
'Architecture depends on function, durability, order, humanity, nature and beauty. Modern architecture has none of these things' (Quinlan Terry).[3] The iconographic and symbolic emptiness of 'modern architecture' can, of course, be explained by the fact that it never belonged to Architecture. Rather, it belongs to packaging and, in its most ambitious examples, it might have been an art of packaging. Modern architecture did not belong to Building. Having its roots in the artisan disciplines, building, as a culture, was circulated through history by collective memory, to be destroyed only by the industrial division of labour and compulsory 'popular' education (or rather re-education). Architecture and building have disappeared as intellectual and artisan cultures. While European cities are mercilessly wrecked by the brutal construction of the new territorial infrastructures of the advanced industrialised state, the architectural profession has entered a crisis which, since 1968, nobody has been able to escape. Only the most retrograde factions of the profession lull themselves with ideals – of the necessity and unavoidability of which they can convince themselves only. The insecurity and cynicism of this generation of operators, who have been in power now for 30 years, is best expressed by a letter of applause which David Watkin received for his book *Morality and Architecture* from a hard core (and probably unrepenting) modernist, (Sir) Denys Lasdun.

Territory and experiment
After the darkest and most destructive period of European urban history – including the two world wars – the building crisis leaves us today to contemplate the damage which has been caused to the cities and the countryside.

If we do not see any major change in the future, it will be because all major political, economical and cultural positions are still occupied by a generation that considered the city and the territory as a field of endless experiments.

Should there be a Nuremberg trial or another Russell Tribunal to investigate the atrocities and slaughter committed to the body of European cities and landscape? The 'prisons' would not be big enough; most architectural schools and the institutions of the profession would fold – their ideas and buildings left (as in 1945), to rot on the rubbish dump of history. However, if this was to occur, there would be little likelihood of such a trial of architecture being any more effective than those at Nuremberg; what I want to say is that a change of style will not suffice this time. We have, after all, to deal here with a generation of people who, in the past 30 or 40 years of their professional life, changed their styles more often than their ties. This wild profusion of manners is being applauded by journalists as Post-Modernism and promoted under the motto of complexity and contradiction.

New interest in architecture
It would be naive to see in the new interest in architecture a necessary sign of its revival. The only characteristic that most recent experiments have in common is their fragmentary nature and provocative eclecticism, which, as never before, juxtaposes styles upon styles in the most vulgar and riotous way; resulting, in most cases, in nothing but Kitsch. And it is Kitsch which must be identified as the most important general cultural phenomenon of the industrial age, as the real zeitgeist of the machine age, pervading all levels of life and culture.

Marginalisation of Architecture
Any revival of Architecture and building culture which is only concerned with the artistic form, and which ignores the necessary manual (as opposed to industrial) culture of architecture's

origin and production, can only trivialise and further marginalise the object which was once man's most important concern. Architecture and building, which once promised the ultimate shelter for man against the afflictions of nature, is reduced to a mere problem of packaging and industrial gadgetry. However, 'to the emptiness of the machine age one has to respond with a soothing and mildly intoxicating decor',[4] and I wouldn't make too much difference between Neo-Rococo or Neo-Cubist.

The Function of Kitsch

Kitsch is no style and it is all styles at once. It is ugly, but the function of Kitsch is not to be beautiful, but to stand for beauty, to replace beauty, to signify a status.

The elusive signification of a social status and the very frustration of what it promises, are the central functions of the Kitsch object. Instead of satisfing the senses, it merely satisfies an instinct, an instinct for beauty and social position. Thus Kitsch is fulfilling its economical function to increase consumption and ease production.

The delaying of satisfaction and the necessary frustration which occurs with the Kitsch object is a necessary basis for these apparently unceasing cycles of industrial production and consumption. The frustration caused by this necessary superficial consumption, is only relieved by a ritualised chain of trivial improvements.

Division of labour and artistic culture

Nothing can be expected of the official institutions. A Reformation of Architecture can only happen slowly, supported by a revival of craftsmanship as part of an anti-industrial resistance. According to Adam Smith 'ignorance is the mother of Industry'.[5] Industrial division of labour results in extreme alienation of the work process. The resulting stultification of the worker has so far prevented, and will continue to prevent in the future, the emergence of any proletarian culture. The existential misery of this class will lead it to resist less and less its total exploitation for production and uncritical consumption. On the other hand, industrial division of labour and the end of the artisan culture of building has degraded architectural work to no more than intellectual speculation. Because craftsmanship is the very basis for any culture, intellectual or manual, the destruction of craftsmanship means effectively the destruction of humanity. Industrial production, far from fulfilling its promise of liberating mankind, is only perpetuating, in a more radical and inescapable form, man's enslavement in stultifying labour.

Permanence and transformation

'If the world is to contain a public place, it cannot be erected for one generation and planned for the living only. It must transcend the life span of mortal man; without this transcendance into a potential earthly immortality, no politics, strictly speaking, no common world and no public realm is possible.'[6]

'The city of stone'[7] became to the prophets of total mobility synonymous with death, inflexibility or even laziness.

A built and protected world which took many generations to build, and which necessarily transcended the lifespan of its builders, was, however solid – or potentially permanent – adapted and transformed according to incidental needs. To destroy such cities and buildings after having used them so successfully and for so long would seem as absurd and superfluous as to destroy a cup after having tasted from it.

In this apocalyptic dawn, crowded with quietly fading meteorites, a reformation of Architecture based on its own rational principles would seem to be a daring enterprise, if it was not of such an excruciating necessity, and if it was not part of a collective striving.

A revival of Architecture

In the light of fast changing fashions, Quinlan Terry's hut reconstruction (after William Chambers) stands out as a heroic, pleasurable and wise restatement of the essential elements of architecture. It is an Encyclopedist vision of what building might have been before it became an art, before the discovery of bronze and before its translation into stone. Now that we are in a period where Architecture and building are vanishing from the face of the earth like an underground stream, this little sturdy structure must be, and should be, a slap in the ideological face of that generation who thought that they had killed architecture once and for all; as such it gives me a great pleasure and I take it as a lesson.

'You cannot plunge in at a deep end; you cannot slap corinthian columns onto reinforced concrete buildings and call it architecture. It is something much more fundamental.'[8]

The intelligence of history

It is this 'something much more fundamental' which a new generation of architects, activists, historians, artisans and artists are fighting for at many different levels.

As this 'something more fundamental' can certainly not be acquired in our absurd educational machinery, nor by scientific investigation, nor in professional offices and institutions, it has to be discovered in the field or in the documents that remain of pre-industrial European civilisation.

The complex social, cultural and economical fabric still leaves enough traces to be investigated – not in an art-historical sense, to classify and store away – but to elaborate the instruments of a new urban, artisan culture.

This cannot be 'news from nowhere' and it is only in an urban society that any large scale resistance to industrialisation is still possible.

Symbol or sign

It is here that we must set out the fundamental differences of a typology of signs and 'decorated sheds' on one hand, and a typology of buildings and urban spaces on the other. A typological order of buildings and public spaces is the organisational core around which society and its institutions build its reality. A typology of signs denies the possibility of creating places of socially different reality. The Coca-Cola or Holiday Inn signs are the same in Los Angeles as they are in Las Vegas. Venturi may plead for a greater diversity of signs, but wherever a merchant society existed, there existed commercial signs. To make a commercial iconography and its dimensional hollowness become the most important carriers of cultural endeavour and expression, is but a thinly-veiled attempt to lift the narrow-minded commercial imperialism onto a badly needed cultural pedestal which its bad consciousness needs more and more after having polluted the world from the Amazons to (ex) Saigon. But the profound crisis which is shaking the imperialist and puritanical righteousness cannot be relieved by hollow cultural pretentions for much longer. 'Complexity is sometimes nothing but simple stupidity, if one opens one's eyes, our times are flooded with it'.[9]

Transformations to come

Virtually all large-scale building operations of the last 30 years will have to be condemned; they are inhuman, inefficient, ugly, badly-built and costly to police. These human deserts will have to become the main concern of future interventions. Not only have they destroyed parts of lively urban centres, but they are also in need of technical and social repair; they need, so to speak, to be de-zoned and reurbanised.

If our attitude to history and culture has to change, it must first of all get away from teaching cultural and political history as a series of apocalyptic breaks, as a series of points of no return.

The blind spot
'What we want is to add to our wealth, without diminishing our pleasure'.[10] Formal education, from having been the pleasurable privilege of a few, has become the tortuous necessity for all. Manual work, which was the basis for human creativity and self-realisation has, through industrial and social division of labour, become a stultifying and socially a degrading exercise.

'All my life I have been waiting for the revival of architecture. I do not think it will happen, but if the right idea could be put out at the right time I think it would happen. How wonderful it would be. The world could be beautiful again. And nothing but a blind spot really stops it.'[11]

Some people are about who keep alive a little awareness, memory and intelligence in an age where under the joint banners of 'education', 'efficiency' and 'security', the memory and faculties of what we know as humanity are systematically drowned in the immensity of entertaining stupidity on one hand, brutality and destruction on the other, where 'without restriction can nowhere be anything produced of importance'.[12]

The last days of humanity
A humanity whose end is no longer the pursuit of pleasure, but the omnipresence of necessity, must find ironically the only pleasure in its own destruction, in the recognition of its ultimate uselessness.

A state of pleasure is also one of contemplation of one's own being and doing.

Narcissus is calm and holds his breath so as not to confuse the reflection of (his own) beauty.

Now if being and doing are but mere necessity, the moment of contemplation has changed from being one of satisfaction, to becoming one of urgency.

In that perspective, the meticulous self-destruction of humanity becomes obviously a moment of relief, a relief from unbearable urgency, ugliness and futile agony.

Notes

1　N Pevsner, J Fleming, H Honour, *The Penguin Dictionary of Architecture*.
2　Quatremère de Quincy, *Encyclopédie Méthodique-Architecture*, Paris, 1788.
3　Quinlan Terry in *Building Design*, 17/9/1976.
4　Le Corbusier, *L'Art Décoratif*, 1925.
5　Adam Smith quoted by Karl Marx in *The Capital: Division of Labour and Manufacturing*.
6　Hannah Ahrendt, *The Human Condition*.
7　Giorgio Grassi, *La Costruzione Logica della Città*, 1966.
8　Quinlan Terry in *Building Design*, 17/9/1976.
9　Leonardo Sciascia interviewed in the *Nouvel Observateur*, 11/1977.
10　William Morris in *Useless Toil*.
11　*Raymond Erith*, Royal Academy Catalogue, 1976.
12　Karl Marx, *The Capital: Division of Labour and Manufacturing*.

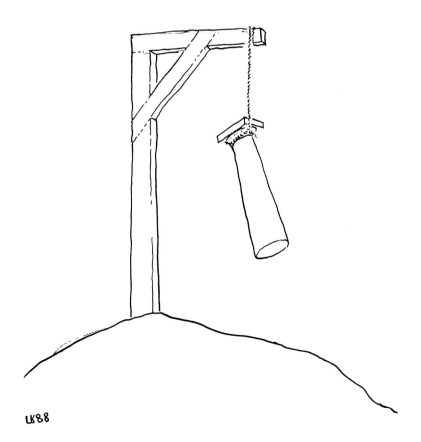

LK88

The Nüremberg-Tribunal of Architecture

THE CONCEPT AND ESSENTIAL FUNCTION OF ARCHITECTURAL DECORATION
LUDWIG LOHDE

The architectural decorations and ornaments that were formerly called 'the architectural elements' are not by any means real or constructive elements of the building, they are merely artistic additions to make the seemingly static members into architectural art forms. The usual division of these so-called 'architectural elements' into straight and curved, decorated and undecorated is a way of explaining them that had resulted from only a superficial knowledge of architectural art forms. Now that Karl Boetticher has opened up for us the concept and essential function of tectonic art forms in his work *Tektonik der Hellenen* (*The Tectonics of the Greeks*), our earlier, very external knowledge of Greek architectural art forms has been replaced by a knowledge of their essence; now we can penetrate to the heart of these phenomena, and only now can we say that we understand them. All who wish to speak or write of architecture and related matters will now have to refer to this work, particularly if, as here, they are concerned with Greek architecture and its forms . . .

Greek building in stone is building in elements; it grows from the combination of free elements, each independent in themselves; when mechanically combined into an architectural whole these enter into a structural relation with each other so that each has to perform a certain architectural function on the basis of its natural qualities. This natural quality in combination with the requirements of its function in the building as a whole determined its practical dimensions, that is, its corporeal relations by length, breadth and height or thickness; moreover, the mechanical combination of the parts or elements with an architectural whole will also determine the *structural* form of each element in the building. The production of the practical, structural forms and their construction will require due attention to the craftsmanship and technique of building, but not, as yet, to the requirements of art. In order to raise the practical, technical form to an *architectural art form*, a special formal language is needed to give expression to its architectural function; only through this formal language does the member proclaim the task which it has to fulfil in its place in the building; only through the artistic form that is allocated to it will it be *individualised*, so to speak, and it can only be used in this specific form in the building in the context and the quality which the architect has designed for it. To give particular examples, the column, once it has been given artistic form, can only serve as a column and not, for instance, as a beam; while the beam, once artistically formed, can only be used as a beam and not as a column. Similarly, the position or placing of each member in the building will seem to be fixed by their artistic form; the column cannot therefore be placed on its head, it can only stand on its foot; the beam cannot be placed with its top or one of its sides facing downwards, it will have to be placed with the side designed by the artist for that purpose facing down.

Now in order to express the function of a member in a building we need images that can make its hidden but active forces evident. If these images are to speak a language understandable to all, they must not be chosen arbitrarily by the artist. If they are to create a generally comprehensible formal language, it will be necessary for them to be taken from man's immediate surroundings. Moreover, what they are to express when applied to the building element will have to be used in the same sense as we are accustomed to in daily life. These images, or symbols, for the expression of the function of an architectural element now appear as the *artistic decoration*, the *ornaments* of the same; they surround the element formed for a constructive purpose as with a casing. So we shall have to differentiate between the basic structural form of an element and its ornamental casing, even if these are, as is generally the case, made of one piece.

The images chosen to express the structural purpose are taken partly from the world of nature, especially plants, and partly from human activity, the crafts. In their artistic use as ornaments, as already mentioned, they are applied in accordance with their use in daily life or the requirements of the worship of the gods. Among the basic models for ornaments taken from the flora are all those that express support and load-bearing in a building, while the images taken from human industries include all those intended to express binding, attaching, linking, a cantilevering projection, a roof or ceiling, or enclosing and separating space. In some cases the ornaments may belong to both spheres, like the bands and strands formed from foliage, those from fruit, and long chains of little ball-like seeds, in the choice of which the trees dedicated to the gods and sacred plants played a particular part as their first and oldest images. In fact we are only concerned here with *hieratic* forms, the temple. For art was almost exclusively concerned with the worthy and characteristic design of the temple and all the forms occurring in it. These hieratic art forms, only created in the service of the gods, were not to be desecrated; they could not be used for ordinary people's dwellings, at least as long as a strict morality and holy usage applied. An old Lycurgean law stated that the ceiling of the common dwelling should only be hewn and its door only be sawed. These tools make the production of a higher art form impossible.

All supporting elements and all those either directly or indirectly bearing parts of the building are given a symbol at the point where they take the load, that is, their upper end, that expresses a burden or pressure. This image is always formed by rows of leaves with their tips drooping down. We call such ornamentation *cyma*; the Greeks call it *cymatia* and the Romans use the same word. The drooping ends or tips of these rows of leaves either do not bend down to their lowest point, and in this case each time only a single row of broad, almost square shaped leaves is used; or the rows of leaves do bend down to their lowest point, and then this ornament usually consists of two rows of leaves of different contrasting form, and positioned so that the spacings of one row are covered by the centres of the leaves of the other.

We shall call the first-named band of leaves *light* and the second *heavy*; the first will indicate a lesser load than the second, which can typify the greatest possible burden. The light row of leaves is characteristic of Doric architecture, and so Vitruvius calls it *cymatium doricum*, the *Doric wave*. The heavy row of leaves is used in all the Greek styles, most frequently Ionic and Corinthian, where it is the only form to appear, and made smaller or larger according to whether it is to indicate a lesser or greater load. The latter is also achieved by increasing the frequency of the *cymatia*; often two ornaments of this kind, but shaped differently, appear one beneath the other, sometimes as many as three or even four. The so-called '*egg-and-dart moulding*' is a cyma used particularly frequently in Ionic architecture. The *Lesbian form* (*Cymatium lesbium* in Vitruvius), with its leaf tips bending over and swinging out again at the base has been given the German name *Herzlaub* from the heart-shaped form of its leaves; it is common to all three Greek architectural styles. In Roman architecture all these occur, as do several other *cymatia* of different shapes and for which we do not have specific names. The profiles of these Roman *cymatia*, although less delicate and charmingly curved and often drawn by the Romans with the compass, are, however, much less different from those of the Greeks than the leaf patterns. In the best age of Roman art these are often copies of natural leaves, they reflect the real world of plants more than the derived shapes of the older Greek architecture, which, copied by the Romans, frequently occur on buildings in a misunderstood and degenerate form. Altogether, only in the depiction of the ornaments that correspond to reality did the Romans, who otherwise only imitated Greek architectural art forms, excel their Greek masters in the best time of their art.

Of the older Greek art forms in Doric and Ionic architecture, which retained the ancient features longest, these cymatia were frequently such that they were only placed before the element in profile, and the leaves seem to have only been painted on these profiles; this was done in such a way that it was not calculated to deceive, nor intended to give the impression of corporeal quality, the leaves were treated purely as surface ornaments, their form only clearly stressed by differences in colouring. So wherever we only see the profiles of such cymatia, but no longer the colour and drawing that have been destroyed by time, we shall have to imagine the ornaments as painted.

Now these drooping leaves are shown to be fixed to the architectural element either with one or several *roll mouldings* (torus), a *string* (astragalus) or a *fillet* (taenia). So immediately below the cymatia we often find profiles that correspond to the shape of these symbols of attachment; they are the so-called *fillets* and *rods* that only project by about the thickness of a belt or girdle, a band or a string. Where the profiles of these images of attachment are missing in Antiquity we have to imagine them as merely painted and represented solely by colour.

The same symbols of attachment on an architectural element are also to be found in the *corona*. The *corona* is the part that forms the upper crowning of the entire building or independent parts of it, that is, elements that do not bear a load but are free and without a load. The corona are understandably characterised by ornaments taken from the royal diadem itself. The ornaments of the antique corona are the so-called *anthemi* (from 'flower') of the Greeks or, as we say, *palmettes*, from the Italian *palmetto*, the fan palm, flowers that spread out in a fan-like shape and often occur alternating with more closed and bud-like shapes. These latter have been called 'lotus cups', although they are no more like these or have been copied from them than the fan-like flowers are like the leaves of the palm. Apart from these anthemia, upright leaves are also depicted in rows, like the cymatia bending over to express a load. However their tips, to express and indicate an element in the building that ends without bearing a load, bend forwards only slightly, as if bending through their own weight; examples are those rows of acanthus leaves on the *cornices* of Roman monuments (the name no doubt comes from the Italian *cornice*, that is, forming a wreath). The name is probably also used to indicate a profile that rises, is contracted below and bends outward at the top, and which Vitruvius calls 'sima', that is, gutter ('sima' is an adjective and so should be supplemented with 'corona', for instance). With

these 'simas', as with the cymatia that are only in profile, we must imagine the characteristic ornament of a corona or a row of upright leaves painted, if these are not chiselled. We see painted anthemia at the top of antique simas or gutters in terra cotta at the bottom, accompanied by bands (meander or bands of leaves), and these should be interpreted as images for attachment or fastening.

The column shaft which rises from the temple podium is shown to be growing from the ground up to the entablature and firmly resisting the load of the latter is represented through art forms, the models for which are to be found in the fluting of hollow plant stalks (stria). All hollow stems that are filled with what is known as pith or medulla are to be found in plants that have very heavy flowers, or umbellas. Examples are elder, castor-oil plant, heracleum and so on. The richly-developed blossom needs good nourishment, and so the stalk of these plants is filled with a loose cellular and tubular tissue, known as pith or medulla, in order to take the moisture sucked up from the earth to the blossom. But since the leaves and blossoms of these plants have to be borne solely by the wooden outside rings of the hollow stem, this has been given strengthening ribs by nature which make it appear fluted or furrowed. This fluting (striae) provided the model for the *channelling* on the columns (from 'canna', the tube). This decoration is known as *rhabdosis* in Greek and *striatura* in Latin. All mechanically joined column drums are linked to form a uniform whole by this fluting, in keeping with the pronouncement by Aristotle. The fluting on the column shafts is of two kinds: either the furrows lie close together, so that virtually nothing remains of the surrounding surface of the rounded shaft, as on the Doric columns, or broad bands are left between the individual furrows as on Ionic and Corinthian columns. Only when the stone of the column shafts was too hard but had a beautiful colour and veining that were to be brought out by polishing, did the shaft remain unfurrowed. Shafts that have a fully-worked fluting at their upper and lower ends, but what is known as a mantle between these finished sections, should be regarded as shafts whose fluting has remained unfinished.

Either the column shafts have no base – it would be better to say they have a common base in the top step or plinth of the substructure of the temple, that is, a common 'stylobate', like the Doric columns, or they have a base, like the Ionic and Corinthian columns, in which the fact that the column cannot be moved, its firm attachment to the substructure, is expressed through ornaments, the models for which are taken from the crafts. These are the circular strings or spirae (cables), which show that the column is firmly attached to the plinth. They are so characteristic of the Ionic column base and so important an ornament by their size that Vitruvius has described this column base simply with the name of the ornament itself, 'spira'. But the Ionic and Corinthian column bases contain a reference to the cylindrical form of the column shaft, which contracts sharply at its beginning and then grows upwards with slight diminution and suddenly spreads outward again shortly before its end. The column shaft has a concave sweep (apophyge) and a projecting cornice (apothesis). Reference is made to this shape on the base with a small cylinder which, like the column shaft, contracts strongly at its beginning and spreads again at the top, or, as Vitruvius says, forms a groove with an overhang, a 'scotia' with 'supercilium'. So like the column shaft it has an apophyge and a projecting cornice. This little cylinder which echoes the contracted column shaft, is called by Vitruvius 'trochilus'. This word is borrowed from the Greek, and the Greeks used it to describe anything that moves around an axis or what one could imagine as being created by such a movement around an axis. On the Ionic column base we often see two grooves, an upper and a lower (trochilus superior et inferior), both joined with threads. So the apophyge and projecting cornice of the column shaft, although joined together, are still indicated separately. These indications or announcements of the architectural form to follow, suggesting an organic link of different parts, are called '*junctures*' by the author of *Tektonik* to differentiate them from those couplings (copulae) that indicate a purely mechanical joint or fastening. These '*junctures*' complete the art form of the structural element by giving what is only mechanically put together and joined the appearance of an organic growth, so making the 'systema' of the building appear an 'organon'.

These junctures therefore appear particularly at the upper ends of the elements, eg. on the capital of the columns and ante, on the ends of the Doric column (epistyle or architrave) and so on. In Doric architecture, in keeping with its severe and simple character, the junctures are generally formed only with fillets that seem to be laid on the upper end of the element, as if placed upon it, This upper fillet or 'abacus' quite generally indicates that another element has been added to the member, and it is actually already a reference to the parallelepiped form of the next element. However an even more precise reference to the architectural form and function of the element is to be found where a characteristic ornament on the following member refers back to the preceding one, so making the juncture and even more marked sign of what is to follow. If, for instance, an ornament on the ceiling like the meander (originally a pattern borrowed from weaving, so describing a band or girdle) is continued on the upper slab of the column capital, this indication of the following part of the building also identifies the architectural function of the column as a *support for the roof*; moreover, an ornament on the cornice, as in the Doric style, may be continued on the juncture of the architrave; this is then characterised by it as a support for the gutter. Similarly, the architrave appears to be characterised as a *support for the roof beams* where it takes up an ornament from the ceiling beams in the juncture, as happens on its inner side.

Finally we must remember the images that are intended to indicate a *cantilevered* or *overhanging projection* and *spreading* or *overspanning elements in suspension*. The suspended projection is indicated through a small body that seems to be hung on to them, like the bobbles weighting the hem of a robe. The so called *drops* or 'guttae', for instance, on the edge of the Doric mutule suggest an ornament attached in rows, and that is probably why Vitruvius has called them 'viae' (*alleys*), which we can only call a designation from the crafts and not a very suitable way to describe them. Attached flower cups as well, the so called rosettes, and cone-like fruit, like the pine cone, are also intended to suggest an element suspended or hanging down, like the hanging rosettes in the hollow mouldings of the Corinthian cornice, which we will probably also find repeated int the coffers of the ceilings. The same applies to the fruit cones on the corners of the so called teeth or tooth marks (denticuli) of the Ionic cornice. The extended or suspended projection of an element is probably also indicated by flowers (anthemia) or leaves placed individually or in several rows like scales starting from the vertical face of the building and stretching forward or growing outward. Such ornaments are occasionally to be found on the lower sides of the mutule.

The *roof* of the Greek *temple* often followed the pattern of a carpet strewn with stars or a starry sky, making the temple the veritable image of the dwelling of a heavenly being. The stars were painted in gold or a colour similar to gold in the hollows of the stone lacunar or soffit, or calymmatia, on a blue ground, and the strengthening ribs of these ceiling plates appear like crossed bands or belts stretched across the space. They are shown to be such (tori) by painted meander patterns or by the so called '*knotted band*', which should properly be called a plaited band. Instead of these ornaments we also find strings, strings of pearls, bands of leaves or strands of leaves, all indicating the same. The starry carpets, borne as it were by these bands, girdles or strands are now supported by the beams suspended over the space, and which are designated supports by the cymatia on their upper edge, where the soffits are resting on them, and as bands or girdles by a pattern of bands or girldes on their lower edge, just as their supports, the columns are designated as such by the appropriate ornaments. So we see in the handling of the ornamentation in the temple ceilings the image of a carpet supported by stretched bands, straps or strands of leaves consistently carried through.

The walls of the temple, that were intended in an antique building merely to *close in space* but not to *support the roof*, are also treated as carpets stretched out between the pilasters in their art form; they are given borders of flowers on their upper and lower ends, which characterise them as carpets enclosing and defining space. The flowers in these borders are turned upwards at the upper end of the walls and downwards at its lower end. This treatment of the walls as a carpet makes the Greek temple a tent construction, since in tents too only the poles support the roof, while the walls only close in the space and support neither the ceiling not the roof. So we see that in the whole as in all the individual parts the art forms of the temple were determined by models that created a formal language, the understanding of which has now been opened to us by the *Die Tektonik der Hellenen*. Accordingly we can close our introductory remarks with the motto which the author of that work placed on the title page of the first edition:

The form of the body is the mirror of its essence!

Understand that – and the seal of the puzzle is opened.

GREEK FIRE
OLIVER TAPLIN

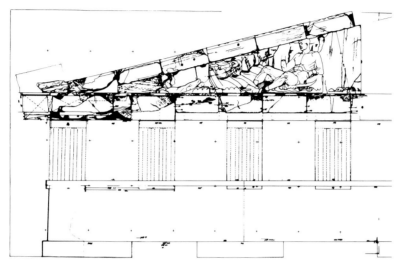

DETAIL OF THE PARTHENON, EAST PEDIMENT, BY M KORRES, ARCHITECT FOR THE RECONSTRUCTION PROJECT

This article is based on extracts from the book and recent television series, Greek Fire. *They are an exploration of 'what has been made out of ancient Greece, and how the modern world has been inspired by, reacted against, imitated, transformed, parodied, recycled and subverted or received Greek culture.'*

'The original Greek Fire was used to destroy enemy ships. It was alleged to stay alight under water, submerged in a contrary element.' In this article, as in the book, it stands as a metaphor for the astonishing resilience of classical Greece: 'it can stay alight submerged in alien cultures, it has the capacity to benefit and to harm, it can be obvious on the surface, or latent below.' Like the Delphic Proverb, γνωθι σεαυτον, the message of ancient Greece – 'its original stones long since fragmented – has meant different things to different ages; and many interpretations have been "right" for different times and places. It is monumental and eternal, yet broken up and open to reformations.'

The following extracts explore the relationship between the individual and the *polis*.

The Self and Society

The individual as a member of the 'democracy' is not the self in opposition to society – the individual against the machine – but an entity which can only fully be an entity in relation to other people. 'The self' only makes sense in relation, not just to immediate family or friends, but to other people in the community as a whole. The classic statement of this priority is Aristotle's 'Man is by nature a political animal'.

This statement needs some expansion. First, the word for 'man' means 'human being' (it is not male). Second, Aristotle is making a quasi-zoological point: as some creatures go round in pairs and some in flocks and so on, so the human animal lives according to nature politically. Finally, political means 'in a *polis*'. *Polis*, often translated as 'city', does not mean 'conurbation', but an entire independent community – the town, sanctuaries, fields, hills, harbours, and everyone who lives there. The usual Greek *polis* was very small, with a population in thousands. Aristotle recommends as a criterion of the optimum size that it should be possible for all the citizens to be addressed by a single herald (without microphone!). Athens, the largest city in classical times (before being overtaken first by Alexandria, then Rome), had in the middle of the 5th century BC about 250,000 inhabitants in all, with perhaps 75,000 of them in the conurbation – about one fortieth of the population of New York City today. It is important to bear in mind this vast difference in human numbers.

The citizens, *politai*, were, as a rule, only the adult males whose fathers were citizens – at Athens (or rather Attica, the whole area of the *polis*, about 2,400 square km) they are reckoned to have been about 40,000 out of the 250,000. It was their privilege to administer their own city, and to fight for her in war, if called for by the majority. It was their citizenship which made them fully human. According to the 'Funeral Speech' of Pericles, which, as given to us by Thucydides, is the finest eulogy of Athenian democracy, if a man does not participate in the *polis*, then, far from being unobtrusive, he is useless. To withdraw yourself from political life in this view – a view endorsed by Aristotle – was to withdraw yourself from being fully human. I F Stone (*The Trial of Socrates*) says, 'I share the Athenian view that a citizen has a duty to take part in the life of the city.' Women, immigrants and slaves had no opportunity to be 'fully human' in this sense.

This Greek view of the place of the citizen in society – of politics – is by no means the standard modern perspective. Moderns tend to define their selves in terms of their own inner beings and perhaps of a small circle of family and friends. Society, the state, is something imposed from outside, something which does not include 'us', which may actually be against us. The starting point of John Stuart Mill's *On Liberty* is a search to find the *minimum* that the state should be allowed to interfere with the private individual. George Steiner puts the contrast with the Greek perspective provocatively: 'we have swung into a very private ideal . . . the belief that the good life is the one which we live in our marriages . . . in our small circles of friendship, that the debts we owe are primarily to those circles and bonds . . . the feeling that the best of us is behind closed doors. This, the Greeks thought, would have been a scandalous failure of human maturity. They clearly foretold our own fate, which is that, when you do this, the mafiosi, the thugs and the third-rate move into the seats of power. And we have very little right, then, to complain.'

The mafiosi, the thugs and the third-rate are presumably the bosses of the multinationals and the people who come under the rough heading 'politicians'. In Athens every citizen was a politician. Plato criticised the amateurism and said that government should be handed over to experts. We have done just that, and relinquished the role to a small number of professionals who are overtly in power and to other small groups who operate behind the scenes. We have thus come to a much more narrow sense of 'political' than in 'man is by nature a political animal'. When a figure such as the Bishop of Durham speaks out, he is told to keep politics out of religion; when sportsmen who have participated in South Africa are threatened with disqualification, we are told that this is muddling sport up with politics. The very idea of religion or sport being divisible from politics would have been incomprehensible to an ancient Greek.

The professional politicians wish to mark off an area as their terrain. This is true of all modern 'democracies', east, west, far east, capitalist and socialist alike. Election is the key to power. But in ancient Greece election was generally regarded as an un-democratic procedure, promoting rule by a few. In ancient Athens *all* qualified citizens were encouraged to participate in the decision-making process in the parliament, indeed they were sometimes literally roped in. All those touched by a red-dyed rope swung around by an official in the civic centre were obliged to attend. The non-politician citizens of modern democracies are not positively encouraged towards open political expression, and have no occasion (like the Athenian assembly) where they can say anything they want without fear of redress. The nearest experience to this now is serving on a jury, perhaps the most truly democratic of our institutions. In British democracy, at least, there is, as Charter 88 points out, discouragement. How often, after all, do we actually participate in a substantive political *decision*? In a representative democracy there are a few seconds every four or five years when the citizens have power over the politicians; and even then we are not voting directly on the issues. Hardly any government in Britain since the war has been put into power by over 50 per cent of those voting (let alone of those qualified to vote), and 42 per cent is constantly called 'an overwhelming popular mandate'. In the last election 75 per cent of the electorate voted; in the US Presidential election of 1988 the proportion was 48 per cent. An ancient Athenian would be totally baffled to hear this called democracy.

The mixed Republic of the Founding Fathers
It is the Greek legacy of *political theory* rather than actual practice which gave birth to the modern kind of democracy. Much Greek political theory was based on the observation that in practice almost all Greek societies from earliest times had three levels of power: a very small number of kings or magistrates; a council of the most powerful men, which generally meant the big landowners; and then a gathering or assembly of all the other citizens. In most places at most times in ancient Greece power lay with the first of these two groups, sometimes in collaboration and sometimes in rivalry, while the third level, the masses, merely rubber-stamped by acclamation. This tripartite analysis is already found in the 5th-century historian Herodotus. In the next century it was more fully explored and theorised by Plato, especially in his *Republic,* and then by Aristotle in his *Politics,* the two foundation works of political science. In their terms, if the 'kings' were dominant you had 'monarchy' or 'tyranny' (the word was not originally derogatory); if the 'knights' dominated, you had 'aristocracy' or 'oligarchy'; if the popular assembly, the many – *hoi polloi* – managed to appropriate the power, then that was 'democracy'. The Greek word actually means 'power in the hands of the common people' (*demos*). Different cities came up with different combinations and emphases. Aristotle's school of political science compiled accounts of 158 different constitutions from all over the Greek world.

Aristotle regarded rule by the many (i.e. democracy) as irresponsibly self-interested and unstable. Characteristically he advocated a compromise, an attempt to have the best of all three types of political system, in other words a *mixed* constitution. When the Greek Polybius was held under house-arrest in Rome for 20 years in the middle of the second century BC, he analysed the Roman constitution in Greek terms and praised the resilience of its mixture. The three levels – consuls, senate and people – regulated each other by having control of certain crucial spheres of influence (though in fact the popular meetings had little power).

There has been much study of how far this Greek political theory actually influenced the Founding Fathers in the United States, who in 1787 drew up the Constitution which has lasted so remarkably well and been so influential in the rest of the world. There can be no doubt of the recourse to ancient precedent; Richard R Johnson finds that 'in retrospect, and judging simply by the frequency of citations made and parallels drawn, the influence of the Greek past reached an unprecedented peak in American political discourse around 1787'. John Corbin said, for example, 'The theory of our constitution derives from Aristotle, and was put into successful practice in Rome . . .' and John Adams that 'it is manifest that the best form of government is that which is compounded of all three forms'.

So the Founding Fathers thought of themselves as establishing a Republic, as in Rome, not a Democracy as in 5th-century Athens. Indeed Athens was a negative model. As Meyer Rein-hold says, 'One of the prime lessons adduced from antiquity by the Founding Fathers was the unsuitability of direct assembly government, because of the instances known of instability and capriciousness of decisions in ancient republics.' The shift to the positive model of Athens was a late 19th-century phenomenon. Earlier in the century the great theorists de Tocqueville and Mill thought that ever-increasing popular participation in the United States would come closer and closer to ancient Athens. The irony is that in our times, when the paradigm of Athens is universally paid lip-service, democracy has moved away from, rather than towards, real participation by the many. The nearest that the *demos* of our era gets to power is a television screen.

'Who wishes to speak?'

Everyone may know that 'the Greeks invented democracy' and that 'Athens was the cradle of democracy', but few have any notion how very different Athenian democracy was from democracy as we know it, or realise that most Greeks, including Plato and Aristotle, strongly disapproved of it. Though many have maintained that it was unstable and short-lived, there was, in fact, democracy at Athens from the great reforms of Cleisthenes in 508 BC, which set up a political organisation that cut across the old clan and local groupings, until 338 BC when Philip of Macedon took over. That timespan is not far short of the time that the American Constitution has lasted. Indeed democratic structures and procedures continued at Athens down into the Roman period, though in a rather empty way. The golden age, however, during which many other Greek cities became democracies under the influence of Athens, lasted roughly from the 460s to the 420s, the period when Pericles was the most influential individual. And this golden age of democracy was also a golden age in many other spheres of activity.

There were, as ever, the three centres of power. There was a small number of state officers, the most important of these being the ten military commanders-in-chief who were elected annually by the citizens. Election was not really a democratic method of choice, but they were subject to rigorous scrutiny after their period in office. The element of the council was supplied by a body of 500. They were appointed for one year from volunteers spread among the groups of community, and the final selection was by an elaborate system of lot. No-one was allowed to serve more than twice in a lifetime, so a large proportion of citizens would serve at some time. It met in a special building on the west side of the Agora, where it prepared all the business for the popular assembly, and was the day-to-day executive government. Every month (there were 10 in a year) 50 of the 500 lived at public expense in the round *tholos* next door, and were on emergency call to deal with urgent business. Their chairman was chosen daily by lot – so the person whose role was nearest to that of the President or the Prime Minister changed *every day*.

Sovereign, finally, was the people's assembly, the *ekklesia*. All matters of principle or substance were settled here by majority vote. Its decisions were final, and there was in effect no party system or opposition. The assembly met in the morning four times a month on the hill called the Pnyx, which was artificially banked to make an auditorium large enough to hold getting on for 10,000 people. The Herald would ask, 'Who wishes to speak?' No doubt a limited number of individuals tended to dominate business, but the fact remains that in principle any citizen whosoever could respond to this call. It has been calculated that at a normal meeting of the *ekklesia* 4,000-5,000, or ten per cent of the citizen body, used to attend, and there was hardly ever more than 20 per cent present. Before taking this to undermine the claims of Athenian democracy, it is worth asking how often ten per cent of a modern community gathers in one place for any occasion, let alone a serious one, let alone 40 times a year. Ten per cent of the adult population of New York City would amount to more than half a million people. Do 10,000 New Yorkers know what is going on in Congress in any given month? Only 50 per cent of the electorate turns out for the one opportunity they have every four years to choose their chief executive.

Athenian democracy actually involved an extraordinarily high proportion of all those qualified in its government. It was truly participatory. Fortunately, the historian Thucydides decided to write out the speech, or his version of the speech, which Pericles delivered in the winter of 430 BC in honour of the Athenians killed in the first year of the Peloponnesian War. Thucydides, writing 15 or 20 years later, was aware that this marked the beginning of the end of the golden age, and that Pericles was himself soon to die of the terrible plague. His 'Funeral Speech' was revolutionary then, and in many ways still is. Students have been arrested in Greece under modern dictatorships for distributing it.

> We are called a democracy, for the administration is in the hands of the many and not of the few. But while the law secures equal justice for all alike in their private disputes, the claim of excellence is also recognised; and when a citizen is in any way distinguished he is preferred to the public service, not as a matter of privilege, but as the reward of merit. Neither is poverty a bar, but a man may benefit his country whatever be the obscurity of his condition. There is no exclusiveness in our public life . . .

Does any modern democracy genuinely aspire to this manifesto?

A city is a reflection on the people who inhabit it. The shaping, the construction, the design – in a (Greek) word, the architecture – express the values and priorities of the society; and in turn they influence that society. Of course there are social and economic forces beyond the reach of architects (there can be little aesthetic coherence in the expansion of Mexico City to contain over 35 million people by the year 2000), but the fact that they are paramount is in its turn a reflection on the society.

Our greater understanding of the political dimension of Greek architecture might not have come too late to affect 20th-century architecture, even though on an intimate scale inapplicable to the commercially-dominated centres of our vast modern conurbations.

Coherent cities would reflect a coherent society. What the Greeks have to offer the city-builders of the next century is not Toytown bits of columns, but the prompting that architecture is worth thinking about, that the placing and grouping of a city centre declares the values of the society which uses it.

---
*

ALLAN GREENBERG, US DEPARTMENT OF STATE, WASHINGTON DC, 1984

II

FIGURATIVE CLASSICISM

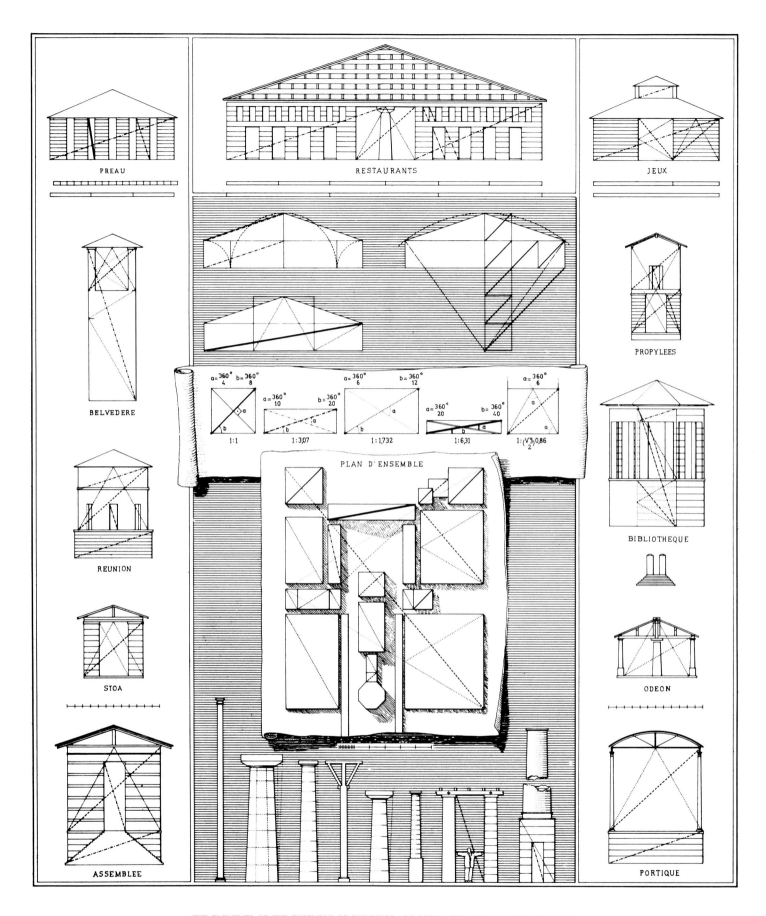

PREAU

RESTAURANTS

JEUX

BELVEDERE

PROPYLEES

$a=\frac{360°}{4}$ $b=\frac{360°}{8}$ $a=\frac{360°}{6}$ $b=\frac{360°}{12}$ $a=\frac{360°}{6}$

$a=\frac{360°}{10}$ $b=\frac{360°}{20}$ $a=\frac{360°}{20}$ $b=\frac{360°}{40}$

1:1 1:3,07 1:1,732 1:6,31 $1:(\frac{\sqrt{3}}{2})0,86$

PLAN D'ENSEMBLE

REUNION

BIBLIOTHEQUE

STOA

ODEON

ASSEMBLEE

PORTIQUE

THE ELEMENTS OF THE ENSEMBLE OF BUILDINGS ARE REGULATED IN PLAN, ELEVATION AND
VOLUME BY A SYSTEM OF PROPORTIONS AND GEOMETRICAL REGULATING LINES. THE REPETITION
OF A LIMITED NUMBER OF FIXED HARMONIC RELATIONS CONFERS BEAUTY BOTH ON THE EN-
SEMBLE AND ON THE DETAILS. THE IS UNDOUBTEDLY THE MAIN JOB OF THE GOOD ARCHITECT, A
CONSIDERABLE AND FACINATING JOB WHICH REQUIRES PRECISION, ATTENTION TO MINUTE DETAIL
AND FANATICISM. THE REWARD TO BE GAINED FROM THE JOB IS NEITHER MORE MYSTERIOUS NOR
LESS ENIGMATIC THAN THE BEAUTY WE ADMIRE IN THE MOST BEAUTIFUL WORKS OF NATURE.

CLASSICAL ARCHITECTURE AND VERNACULAR BUILDING
LEON KRIER

CLASSICAL AND VERNACULAR CULTURE is concerned with producing objects of long-term use as against short-term consumption. CLASSICAL and VERNACULAR contrast the collective and the individual, the monuments and the urban fabric, the palace and the house, the public and the domestic. In classical and vernacular cultures, the discovery, repetition, adaptation and improvement of a limited number of FUNDAMENTAL CONSTRUCTIVE and FUNCTIONAL TYPES become the universal expression of the human activities of collective and individual life. Building and Architecture, as vernacular and classical cultures, can only exist as forms of craft production, where intellectual and manual faculties are exercised in harmony and are not in conflict with each other.

* * *

VERNACULAR BUILDING is the manual-artisan culture of building, based on tectonic logic. As a CRAFT it is concerned with construction of domestic structures, workshops, dwellings, warehouses as well as with engineering works. In general, VERNACULAR BUILDING is concerned with the erection and maintenance of the urban fabric, of the building-blocks forming the streets of the city, its walls and its bridges. BUILDING is a craft culture which consists in the repetition of a limited number of types and in their adaptation to local climates, materials and custom.

* * *

CLASSICAL ARCHITECTURE is the artistic-intellectual culture of vernacular building. As an ART it is concerned with imitating nature in its principles of beauty and permanence by means of a limited number of symbols and analogies. CLASSICAL ARCHITECTURE is a language of construction and tectonic logic, no more no less. It articulates, expresses and adorns construction. Contents other than construction are expressed by other means like architectural sculpture, painting, inscription.

* * *

CLASSICAL ARCHITECTURE and MODERNIST ARCHITECTURE are contradictory, antinomic and incompatible propositions – the former based on artisan artistic productions, the latter on industrial modes of production. The term CLASSICAL denotes the mature, the best; it attains to highest quality and belongs to artistic culture. The term industrial denotes the necessary; it attains to profitable quantity and belongs to material culture. Transcending questions of style, period and culture, CLASSICAL ARCHITECTURE qualifies the totality of monumental architecture based on the fundamental principles of 'venustas, firmitas, utilitas', translated into modern language as harmony/beauty, stability/permanence, and utility/comfort. These terms are unconditionally interdependent and their links are exploded in MODERNISM.

* * *

The condition of ARCHITECTURE to exist as a PUBLIC ART, is to attain material and above all aesthetic permanence. It is concerned solely with the erection of public buildings, halls and monuments, with the construction and decoration of squares and public places.

POLICY STATEMENT
THE FIRST *SOMAI* PROPOSAL
LEON KRIER

Charleston, Williamsburg, Savannah represent ideal models of living. But while our mighty industrial nations erect every day building masses by far exceeding in size and volume any of these towns, we are evidently incapable of equalling them in comfort, harmony and elegance. In the following policy statement I outline how, as a director of SOMAI, I would aim at helping our profession to turn the wheel of fortune again in a propitious direction.

I Global Environmental Problems

1 The Architect's Authority in Democracy

Cities and landscapes are the tangible realisation of our spiritual and material worth. They express and determine how we use or waste our limited resources of *energy*, *time* and *land*.

Town-building and architecture largely define how we live our daily lives and presently these disciplines cause greater long-term problems than our society will be able to solve in the future.

If we are to go by the U S Government 'Global 2000 Report to the President', our present industrial metabolism with nature, of which buildings and towns are an essential part, will, in the near future, lead to a critical collapse of those very conditions which allow man to live on this planet.

However significant the achievements of three industrial revolutions may have been, their combined long-term ecological effects have proved to be catastrophic at a global scale.

Having once been the chosen instruments of creating a desirable human world, building and planning activities are now broadly considered to be a threat. Indeed our common language designates by *unspoiled* not landscapes without buildings, but only those without modern buildings. In that light the public's urge to have greater say in environmental matters is a *de facto* declaration of *no confidence* in the legitimacy of current planning philosophy and building practice.

Whether designing a garden wall or conceiving a regional masterplan, our duty as architects and planners is to work at the realisation of a beautiful *common world*. Wherever we deviate from that calling, we are agents of disorder and instead of being masters of our art we become servants to alien interests. The fact that architectural ideologues and practitioners have, in the last 60 years, been all too eager to follow instructions coming from the industrial, social or political sectors, has not only eroded the fabric of our craft and authority. The effective resignation from our historic leadership has also meant that our abandoned field of authority has been readily invested by other social agents and turned against the interests which we alone can represent and defend. Our individual liabilities for professional failures have, as a result, increased in inverse proportion to our actual loss of power, prestige and income.

2 Problems of Modernism, (a) Architecture & Building

Following the demise of doctrinaire Modernism, many architects are drifting; what they had learned in schools often proved wrong in the real world and as a result many claim the right to decide quite arbitrarily what is architecture; it is therefore quite logical too that the public should just as arbitrarily reject such arrogations. More and more public enquiries, debates and competitions end in a stalemate of apparently irreconcilable positions, dividing the profession, alienating the public and further damaging our dented authority. We are not just facing a temporary crisis but a growing divide which is singularly aggravated by conceptual and linguistic muddles, sometimes opposing or allying factions for the wrong reasons.

The vicious polemics surrounding Graves' Whitney Museum extension, Pei's Louvre Pyramid or the National Gallery extension in London give evidence of the depth of these schisms.

We can indeed no longer speak of *one* architectural profession but instead of various dissenting groups who, while calling themselves architects, hold contradictory views about architecture and aesthetics. Out of Modernism's collapse are clearly born not *one* but *several* constellations. Looking at this worldwide phenomenon in a positive way, we may at long last be witnessing the belated birth-pangs of true architectural pluralism.

Like tyrants, dominant architectural ideologies have so far been ruled by fiat and exclusions, whether in academia, in the public sector or on the building market. Such methods have proven to be unworkable in the long run and while not being necessarily the best form of government, democracy, according to Aristotle, is in every case preferable to tyranny. The one 'architectural' party regimes are clearly not to the taste of democratic custom.

If we are to reclaim a lead in public affairs, the planning and building professions will at last have to recognise the meaning of the democratic revolution.

Freedom of expression and the rule of law are the outstanding virtues of political democracy. A plurality of life-styles, beliefs and hence of architectural and artistic styles are its most natural expression. To rewrite the profession under one ideological banner would be as absurd as uniting Republicans and Democrats in one party or merging antagonistic religions into one single church.

What cannot be united is best divided. What is divided and opposed can only live together in peace by way of a social contract, within some common framework. That is the meaning and basis of democratic competition.

To achieve this should become the goal of *SOMAI*.

3 Problems of Modernism, (b) Town-planning
The ideological heritage and planning principles of three indus-trial revolutions as synthesised in the Charter of Athens have, for the last half-century, constituted the most important directives for the transformation of the natural and man-made environment. They are now part of urban legislations, of prof-essional practice and education in all industrialised countries.

The broad *symbolic*, *formal* and *functional* disorders of our cities and landscapes result directly or indirectly from the application of these directives. Critique without positive com-mitment and hope without operative project are equally powerless to bring about improvements. Present planning fash-ions and legislations are now widely disproved but they continue to cause enormous environmental damage through sheer lack of alternatives. They will be invalidated neither by critical debates nor by optimistic pronouncements. They are now the most serious stumbling blocks in the way of urban, architectural and educational progress, of legislative, artistic and ecological re-form.

It is on this subject that critical opinions are least divided, it is here where radical reforms are most urgent and where consensus is possible.

II Towards a Fourth Industrial Revolution

1 A Magna Carta of the Environment
Rather than going on putting blame and responsibility elsewhere, it is up to urban planners and architects to take again the lead and address ecological and aaesthetic problems in their globality, not in order to raise further critical alarm but to offer bold and realistic solutions.

No other professions possess either the intellectual disci-plines, the practical craft or moral impulse to successfully undertake such a work. It clearly exceeds the means of an individual and naturally falls upon institutions to assume matters of such scope.

It is true that the extent of necessary reforms corresponds to an ecological revolution, in fact to a Fourth Industrial Revolution.

I can think of no organisation better fitted for undertaking such historic a task than *SOMAI*. It is unhampered by ideological and statutory constraints and it is financially independent. It is ideally suited a) to become a constitutional forum for disentan-gling dogmatic conflicts and confusions within the profession; b) to create structures, instruments and a powerful international lobby for reestablishing our professional disciplines and authority on firm ethical and artistic foundations, in short to formulate *The Magna Carta of the Environment* or *The Charter of Chicago.*

2 A Constitutional Document
A Magna Carta of the Environment can only be built upon a long-term political, cultural and ecological consensus. It must be of a fundamental and constitutional nature. To command univer-sal respect, it must transcend partisan interests of political, economical, social, religious and cultural groups.

An environmental charter is a universal *moral* project and as such a necessary complement to the political constitution of peoples. It has therefore to be sanctioned by the most eminent and representative bodies of our society.

3 Different Schools of Thought within one Constitution
It is a propitious omen that at present, the *SOMAI* board is clearly a loose, non-dogmatic group, formed by ambassadors of very different professional convictions, presaging an era of concili-ation, tolerance and true pluralism.

In that spirit *SOMAI* can become an ideal platform not so much for mixing and mingling positions but rather to give th*e major schools of thought* the opportunity for declaring individual objectives and common interests, to clarify theoretical and ethical premises, finally to irrevocably lay down their profes-sional statutes according to which they may be expected, trusted and called upon to act, for the benefit of *individual* and *corporate* clients and for the *common good*.

A three year directorship will be necessary and sufficient time for each of the principal contemporary tendencies to use their best minds in order to
– synthesise their doctrines in clear form and language
– apply them theoretically in exemplary manners and models
– give evidence of their rational and practical intent
– demonstrate their indispensable role in a global ecological, aesthetic and humane construction of the world
– make manifest their legitimacy on constitutional ground within the Magna Carta of the Environment.

III SOMAI and The World Academy of the Environment

The schisms dividing profession and public alike on environ-mental matters bring forth yet again the perennial divergences between 'anciens et modernes' (traditionalist versus modernist; conservative versus progressive; individualist versus collectivist etc ... see addendum A. These fundamental philosophic atti-tudes have divided thinking minds since time immemorial and will predictably continue to do so until the end of time. To suppress one or the other has always been the sign of intolerance in whatever field of endeavour.

I should therefore think it constitutionally pertinent and intellectually stimulating for the directorship of *SOMAI* to alternate between adherents of both convictions. In that way the Institute will run no great risk in granting the director all the independence, freedom of action and association he needs to deploy his abilities in the most fruitful way. It would be a salutory manner for the Institute to avoid inbreeding and smugness and to command in time the widest possible respect.

The Magna Carta of the Environment would naturally have to be formulated by adherents of diverse doctrines i.e. by subsequent *SOMAI* directors, but the final seal of approval would have to rest with a wider *SOMAI* council. This charter would in time become the foundation document of *The World Academy of the Environment* with seat in Washington DC or another World Capital. Modelled on the 300 year old Académie Française, this *non-political* body of the 40 most eminent representatives of major professions would soon take a decisive role in the shaping of the environment and hence in the Construction of the World.

IV First SOMAI Directorship

1 Objectives and Works

Ideas have powerful results when fed in the right form and through the right channels. The ideological heritage of the Charter of Athens shapes our reality not by way of architectural magazines, scholarly treatises and critical histories, but by way of practical manuals, builders' guides, technical primers, By-law handbooks, traffic-planning and zoning fact-sheets etc . . . which architects, authorities, teachers and laymen alike use as matter of course, use in fact as naturally and candidly as ink and pen, telephone-directories or mail-order catalogues.

Most individuals and corporations who are involved in regular building practice, have no patience for abstractions and speculations. They are interested in practical, pleasing and affordable models and solutions. They want advice and guidance for what is buildable in a specific location and with a specific budget, by law, by economic standard, by market-convention, tradition and task. They want normative information in a concise, readable and attractive form.

So far insipid manuals like 'Architectural Graphics Standards', Neufert's 'Architect's Data', 'Time-saving standards for building-types' etc, exert more influence on style, customs and environment than the combined teachings and buildings of past and present masters. They are not neutral conveyors of technical data, but powerful ideological instruments.

If architectural and environmental standards are to be raised in the broadest possible way, then it is in the *quantitative* realm of norms, types and standard practices that *SOMAI* should instigate a *quality* and *media* revolution, namely through the production and publication of Environmental Design Primers in printed and audio-visual form.

2 The Civic Primer'

Should I be entrusted with the first directorship of *SOMAI* I should see my primordial task in directing the production and publication of a comprehensive architectural and urban planning manual entitled *THE CIVIC PRIMER: A Handbook for the ecological renewal of City and Country*. This practical design compendium would be addressed at the largest possible readership, an up-market Readers-Digest for all those who deal with the shaping of the environment, from mayors, public administrators and businessmen down to small developers, house-owners and farmers, equally valuable for professionals and laymen. It would present in a didactic and attractive form traditional alternatives to current planning practices and building types, based on long-term economic, ecologic and aesthetic solutions (see addendum C).

4 Production of The Civic Primer

For the period of my directorship the principal activities of *SOMAI* would be centered on and subordinated to the production of the Civic Primer.

The masterplanning and editing would be assumed by the director helped by a maximum of eight assistants. A scientific committee of top specialists in language, legislation, economy, ecology, politics, administration, finance, business, communications, transport, marketing etc . . . would be appointed as consultants to this project.

Starting out from a radical critique of present planning rationality, ethics and aesthetics (as stated in the addenda A and B), the civic primer would establish a concise and complete panorama, a definitive typological and morphological classification of traditional planning models and techniques as adapted to advanced industrial conditions.

The listing of exemplary models and types would range from large-scale masterplans of cities, districts and parks down to the minute detailing of street-furniture. It will explain the pragmatic use of proportional systems and the correct use of materials, structural systems, color, graphics etc. An exhaustive glossary will purge the semantic gobbledegook of professional jargon and restore architectural and environmental nomenclature in classical clarity.

The illustrations will be of historical and modern examples. They may be designed by the *SOMAI* atelier or be commissioned to outside designers and agencies. They may also be gained through *SOMAI* competitions on specific subjects ranging from 'Hilltown' to 'street-lantern' and from 'Airline-terminal' to 'Motorway-toll-gate' and 'Planting of a marshalling yard' etc...

The Civic Primer would be uncomplicated and practical in tone. It would be crowded with concise and precise notions, packed with three-dimensional images and plans. Particular care would be given to graphic clarity and beauty, precision of scale and consistency. The pleasure of using it would only be matched by its usefulness. The first *SOMAI* Primer could be ready for publicaton by November 1990.

5 Translations of The Civic Primer

The Civic Primer will be specifically aimed at an American and European readership. While other continents, whether foes or friends, continue to dream about and import our outdated models, without sharing their rationale and profits, it is imperative that we put our own house in order before telling others what to do. The Civic Primer's philosophic assumptions will be universal ones, but it will offer no universal style. Although the architectural forms and logic used by different continents are clearly more universal that their forms of speech, their cultural differences are no less significant.

Unlike Neufert's 'Architect's Data', the Civic Primer could not possibly be translated into 25 languages while the illustrations remained unchanged. Eventual translations into languages of other continents will imply conceptual and graphic translations and adaptions to different cultural and material conditions.

6 Extensions of The Civic Primer

A synoptic version of 'The Civic Primer' in form of 12 environmental lessons could be considered for production at a later date designed for secondary school curriculum.

A simplified version of this as children's book/film in the form of a comic strip of high architectural and environmental definition as pioneered by Jacques Martin could be done in cooperation with Walt Disney Productions.

Parallel to such publications, toy-production firms like Revell could market high quality model-kits of all-time architectural and urban favourites like the Republican Forum in Rome, the Williamsburg Capitol, the typical Williamsburg House and Outhouses, Bacon's Lincoln Memorial, Hunt's Chicago Administration Building, the Tower of Winds, the Classical Orders etc, rivalling in youngsters' affections those of military and astronautical hardware. Such ventures are commercially successful in West-Germany and their global educational effects on aesthetic and environmental consciousness could not be overvalued.

7 Further Activities and Publications

As a director of *SOMAI* and as a prelude to the later formation of The World Academy of the Environment, I would in conjunction with other institutions and foundations in Chicago and elsewhere, call meetings of eminent personalities and possible candidates for the future Academy, to debate and pronounce on burning environmental and architectural issues and news items, lobby politicians etc.

THE ARCHITECT'S MORAL IMPERATIVE

Build in such a way that the maxim of your design may
at the same time rate as a principle of
architecture and urbanism.

or

Design buildings in such a way that you yourself and those you love
will take pleasure in using them, look at them, live,
work, spend holidays and retire in them.

LEON KRIER, PLINY'S VILLA, LAURENTUM, 1982, (PAINTING BY RITA WOLFF)

Independently of The Civic Primer the Institute would publish a series of *SOMAI-Pamphlets* highlighting major controversies of the *Traditionalism-Modernism* debate in a lively and polemical tone. These would in the main be edited records of the aforementioned meetings.

Complementing The Civic Primer's Bibliography, I would encourage and support monographical studies and publications on hitherto undervalued architectural subjects and personalities.

V Year 2000 Prospect

I believe that the programme of intentions outlined here could act as a central motor for the overdue restoration of our professional ethics, status and authority. Such a cultural and ecological project, could culminate by the year 2000 AD in the first *World Exhibition of Building and Architecture* where, in Chicago, Washington DC or elsewhere, the construction of separate prototypical urban districts, according to radically different masterplans, would demonstrate different cultural and environmental doctrines as laid down in the Magna Carta of the Environment announcing the dawn of the Fourth Industrial Revolution, The Ecological Revolution.

Similar to Williamsburg, Charleston and Savannah, universally revered as shrines of a nostalgic past, these utterly *new traditionalist* and *modernist* cities within the city could, according to anyone's life-style and philosophy, become the paradigms of a desirable and possible present.

Some Necessary Explanation in the form of Addenda

At present unclarity of vocabulary, confusion of terms, the widespread use of strictly meaningless professional jargon stand in the way of clear architectural and environmental thinking. To help clarify that muddle would be one of my goals as director of *SOMAI*. The terminology used here is in itself sometimes an object of disagreements, for which reason I feel obliged to explain the main notions and concepts.

A I use the terms Tr*aditional* and *Traditionalism* in contra-distinction to *Modernist* and *Modernism.* At present artists, historians, critics and public endemically confuse the terms *modern* and *modernist(ic).* Modern merely indicates time and period whereas modernistic has unequivocal ideological connotations. When historians write of 'The Modern Movement' they clearly mean 'The Modernistic Movements' as opposed to the 'Traditionalist Movements'. Traditional(ist) and modern, Traditionalism and modernity, are non-contradictory notions.

Traditional (artisan) cultures are concerned with the production of OBJECTS for long-term USE. Modernist (industrial) cultures are concerned with the production of OBJECTS for short-term CONSUMPTION. In such antagonistic or complementary philosophies INVENTION, INNOVATION, DISCOVERY have a different status and meaning.

In *Traditional cultures* INVENTION, INNOVATION, DISCOVERY are means to improve handed-down and time-honoured systems of thinking, planning, building, representing, communicating etc in the arts, philosophy, town-building, language, sciences, industries, agriculture etc... They are *means to an end*, namely to conceive, realise and maintain a *solid, lasting, comfortable and beautiful* human world.

Fundamental aesthetic and ethical principles are considered to be of universal value, transcending time and space, climates and civilisations.

In traditional cultures, *industrial* rationale and methods are in a *subservient role.*

In *Modernist cultures* INVENTION, INNOVATION, DISCOVERY are *ends in themselves.* It is claimed that constantly changing socio-economic and political conditions necessarily revolutionise all concepts. There are no universal ethical and aesthetic categories and hence traditional values are accumulations of life-impeding and regressive straight-jackets.

In modernist cultures *industrial* rationale and methods tend towards *dominating* all aspects of life, all polity and politic.

B *Modernist urban planning* essentially works through fragmenting any part of territory (City and Country) into separate *monofunctional zones.* This leads to the effective and habitual mobilisation of society in its entirety (all classes, all species, all ages) in order to perform basic life functions. As a result, CIRCULATION of people, hardware and software becomes the main industrial activity. Artificial ARTERIES and MEANS of circulation become the necessary extensions of human body and mind. Functional *zoning* guarantees the maximum and obligatory consumption of units of hardware and software in the accomplishment of all social activities. Functional zoning is the principal cause for our wastage of TIME, ENERGY and LAND. It is by nature ANTI-ECOLOGICAL.

Traditional urban planning realises man's basic right to reach all habitual urban functions on foot. While making the best use of artificial means of circulation and communication, the good City provides the totality of urban functions within comfortable and pleasant walking distance. Like all mature organisms in nature, it cannot grow by extension in width or height, it can only grow through multiplication. It is a complete and finite urban community, member of a larger family of independent urban quarters, of cities within the city, of cities within the country. The Traditional city is economical in the use of TIME, ENERGY and LAND. It is by nature ECOLOGICAL.

C The *symbolic poverty* of current architecture and townscape is a direct result and expression of functional monotony as legislated by functional *zoning* practices. The principal modern building-types and planning models such as the skyscraper, the Groundscraper, the Central Business District, the commercial strip, the office park, the residential suburb etc are invariably horizontal or vertical over-concentrations of single uses in one urban zone, in one building-programme or under one roof.

Uniformity of use (functional monotony) faces even the best designers with a limited choice between either the expression of true uniformity or that of fake variety. Blandness or Kitsch, artistic cruelty or caricature are the almost inevitable result.

The *symbolic richness* of traditional architecture and city is based on the proximity and dialogue of the greatest possible variety of private and public uses and hence on the expression of true variety as evidenced in the meaningful and truthful articulation of public spaces, urban fabric and skyline.

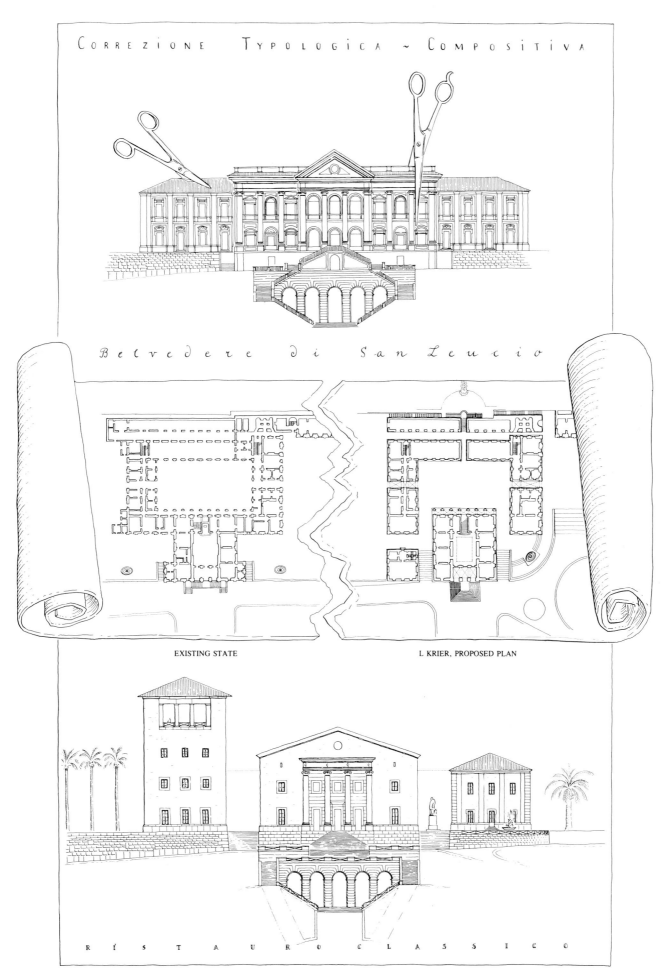

CORREZIONE TYPOLOGICA ~ COMPOSITIVA

Belvedere di San Leucio

EXISTING STATE   L KRIER, PROPOSED PLAN

RISTAURO CLASSICO

TYPOLOGICAL AND COMPOSITIONAL CORRECTIONS TO THE BELVEDERE OF SAN LEUCIO

51

DEMETRI PORPHYRIOS, HOUSE IN CHELSEA SQUARE, LONDON, 1990, (PAINTING BY RITA WOLFF)

THE RELEVANCE OF CLASSICAL ARCHITECTURE
DEMETRI PORPHYRIOS

HOUSE IN SYMI, GREECE, THE ORIGINS OF ARCHITECTURE IN BUILDING

BUILDING AND ARCHITECTURE

Since the early 70s, when the contagious enthusiasm for it broke out in America, Post-Modernism has become a mass phenomenon. From a historical point of view, however, the fact remains that it has contributed to a confusion that has become ubiquitous today and which has halted – at least provisionally – the 'natural' development of modern architecture. The confusion stems from the

difficulty we seem to have today in describing the scope of architecture. We may regard architecture as a focal point of our everyday activities, but nevertheless, when asked to specify what architecture is, we become confused immediately. Our confusion surely arises from our inability or unwillingness to reflect upon the *nature* and *means* of architecture.

Before going into the details of this question we must distinguish between building and architecture. Building (*bâtisse, oikothomiké*) refers to the craft of constructing shelter. It refers to the material techniques of construction, services, structure and functional disposition. Building comprises the knowledge and experience that man accumulates in dealing with the contingencies of providing shelter. Architecture, on the other hand, in the everyday use of the word, refers to the *art* of building (*l'art de bâtir*). Architecture appears to be the product of an artistic intention, not, like building, of necessity. Nevertheless, we feel that architecture is not only an addition, a mere supplement to building. We feel that building and architecture are interrelated experiences, one focusing on the experience of craft, the other on the experience of art. It is exactly this distinction between building as a craft and architecture as an art that has given rise to confusion so often in the history of architecture. What do we really mean when we say that architecture is the 'art of building'? Or in the first place, what do we mean when we say that architecture is an art?

If we compare the first beginnings of the theory of art with its later developments; if, for instance, we compare Aristotle's theory of *Poetics* with Horace's *Ars Poetica* or Quatremère de Quincy's *Dictionnaire,* we find that, in spite of their many differences, they all entertain the view that art can have no other aim than to imitate the world. All the arts, writes Aristotle, are '. . . in their general conception modes of imitation'.[1]

At first sight it may appear as a paradox that so venerated an enterprise as art turns out to be involved with the fabrication of reproductions. But it is precisely this preoccupation with imagery which gives art its distinctive charm and value. 'A work of art is a likeness (*homeioma*) of an original model . . . it is a picture, an image (*phantasma*). . . that reproduces its original not as it is in itself, but as it appears to the senses'.[2] It is clear that this image of the world the work of art fabricates can never be a literal copy of the original model. The organic repetition of nature or the mechanical repetition of industry have nothing to do with artistic imitation 'simply because that which constitutes the primary condition of imitation is wanting; namely the image'.[3]

Art and architecture, therefore, imitate the world by producing resemblances. They do not address abstract reason but sensuous perception. They are concerned with outward appearances and employ illusions, fictitious analogies, reflections, images that are wanting and incomplete. Art and architecture do not copy their models in a servile manner but, by employing genius (*ingenium*), they represent models freely and fashion them anew. The technique of imitation becomes in the hand of the artist a most inventive tool. When art and architecture imitate their models they do not reproduce them mechanically but fabricate a sensuous image which invariably 'awakens' those ideas which are characteristic and essential to the model. Imitation, therefore, should not be understood as aping and mimicry but rather as the free – and therefore wanting and incomplete – production of an analogon.

The identical repetition of the model is similar to mechanical cloning and cannot afford us pleasure. Artistic pleasure proceeds only from comparing the image with the model in order to reflect upon that which has been deemed essential for representation. Imitation, therefore, does not attempt to embody in the image the empirical reality of the things it sets out to represent. Instead, 'the essence of imitation in the arts is to represent reality by means of an image', writes Quatremère de Quincy. And yet, he continues, 'the greatest and commonest of errors consists of confounding resemblance by means of an image with similarity by means of identity'.[4]

features. If there are differences between painting, sculpture, architecture, music and poetry, that is so because each one of these arts imitates reality by means of a limited range of means, materials and techniques. Painting imitates reality by means of line and colour; sculpture by means of relief; architecture by means of tectonics; music by means of sound; and poetry by means of language. Of course, there might be overlaps between the various arts, but what I have in mind here is their essential, specific difference deriving from their medium of execution. A poem could be read aloud but that does not mean that its characteristic medium is sound; similarly, an architectural monument may use polychromy but that does not make it a painting. From this point of view the various arts are but so many 'equal contenders' of reality: each one makes its claim with the weapons it knows best.

This dependence of every art on its specific material leads to the conclusion that the effect of artistic imitation is invariably impaired when there is a tendency to tresspass from one art to another. When sculptural sensuality takes on the quality of nightmare or when painterly acrobatics assume a cardboard imagery we cannot speak of the architectural qualities of a

L TO R: TIMBER CONSTRUCTION OF DORIC TEMPLE, C UHDE, 1903; STONE CONSTRUCTION OF PARTHENON, M LAMBERT, 1877

To illustrate the idea of imitation as resemblance and not identity, I have chosen an example whose ghastly effect cannot be disputed. It is a tomb I saw once in Athens. The form of a tomb has always been a metaphorical statement about the 'house' of the dead. In this example, however, the tomb had been turned into a display of bourgeois cosiness. Its details were rendered in the unmistakable dialect of the products of the housing industry. Here, architecture has become kitsch by proclaiming the stupor of tolerated excess to be the realm of art. Imitation – in the sense of the quintessence of means employed to represent the 'house' of the dead – is replaced by a display of ostentatious realism so typical of the bankrupt.

All arts, therefore, in the first instance, imitate their models in a partial and incomplete way due to the limitations set by their medium of execution. From this specification follow a number of consequences, the most important of which concerns the difference between the various arts. We know that an artist does not choose his medium by accident. When he sets out to work, the material he chooses has a bearing as to whether he produces a painting or a novel, architecture or sculpture. In this sense, the different arts cannot usurp each other's distinctive physical

building. The effect of artistic imitation 'is nullified by the very endeavours that are made to increase or multiply its means; and thus, one art, by trenching on the properties of another, loses its own, and by aiming to be both, becomes neither'.[5]

The problem of the means of imitation is one of the greatest and commonest sources of confusion in both art and architecture today. I cannot enter here into a full description of the history of this confusion. Setting aside any historical considerations, I will discuss the two major contemporary sources responsible for this confusion.

First, let us look at modern architecture. Those who pursued its principles have been very little interested in the theory of imitation. Characteristically of a positivistic frame of mind, modern architects and critics have been openly contemptuous – as a matter of professional ethics – of artistic imitation in general and of the theory of architectural imitation in particular. They divided the history of architecture into a wholly irrational past and a wholly rational future. Questions of representation, figuration and ornament were ruled out as irrational and illegitimate on the assumption that 20th-century man had outgrown such fetishes. Thus, in the aesthetics of modern architecture, the problem of representation assumes a new and different meaning. Figuration is said to have been superceded by abstraction; that is, by a non-figurative 'mapping of essences'.

Putting aside for the moment all reservations concerning the dubious claim that abstraction is totally free of figurative schemata, when we come to examine modern architecture we find that its aesthetics of abstraction have yielded an outright realism. At first this might strike us as a paradox: how is it that an architecture of abstraction could ever be called realistic? And yet, the closer we look at modern architecture (especially its *Sachlichkeit* tradition), the more we realise that the principal aim of its forms consists in confounding abstraction with the raw immediacy and reality of the products of the building industry.

Let me illustrate this by a single characteristic example. Reinforced concrete and the curtain-wall are to modernist Dom-Ino technology what stone, timber and render are to classical technology. But whereas in classical aesthetics render is made to imitate stone and stone to imitate timber, in the aesthetics of modern architecture reinforced concrete and the curtain-wall remain what they are: facts of industrial production. The conception of modern architecture as dealing with *facts and nothing but*

establishes between itself and its model. The result has been a century of realism: the realism of industrial production, of the '*objet trouvé*', and of the misuse of construction and materials; all advanced under the platform of the aesthetics of so-called 'abstraction'.

If the aesthetics of realism of modern architecture led to a loss of symbolic form by underrating the importance of the principle of artistic imitation, by contrast, the aesthetics of multivalence of Post-Modernism lead us today to an even more surprising sterility. This is the sterility that arises from increasing or multiplying the means of imitation.

To counter-balance modern architecture's lack of rhetorical eloquence, Post-Modernism set out to describe 'the idea that an architect must master several styles and codes of communication. . . that he should be trained as a radical schizophrenic. . . (and that he should make) use of the full arsenal of communicational means, leaving out no area of experience, and suppressing no particular code'.[7]

Two fundamental principles soon became apparent: first, the conception that ornament and style are mere clothing; and second, the similar view that building materials and techniques

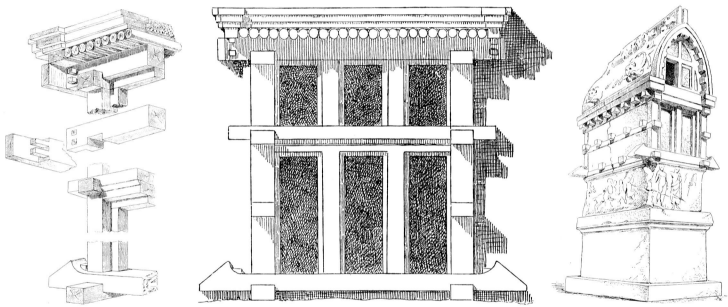

L TO R: ARSACES TOMB, TIMBER CONSTRUCTION; ARSACES TOMB AT MYRA, STONE CONSTRUCTION; LYKIAN TOMB, BRITISH MUSEUM

facts may seem rational enough but has nothing to do with abstraction. If anything, the 'facts' of technology carry an unmistakable realism that is dated and, therefore, not general enough to warrant the use of the term 'abstraction'. Let me not be misunderstood: architecture always works with the 'facts' of technology. But the sympathy that architecture always has with technology is not instanced by the literal adoption of technological 'facts'. Instead, architecture receives from technology facts and returns to the world *forms*. It is in that sense that ornament is said to be the wanting image of 'facts'.

Modern architecture's view of technology, however, is frankly positivistic. Incapable of or unwilling to reflect upon the relationship between building and ornament, modern architecture mistook ornament for mere caprice and crossed it out. *Sachlichkeit* and 'high-tech' modernists alike have maintained (though for different reasons and with various techniques) that 'pure construction is the basis and the characteristic of the new world of forms'.[6]

This constructional puritanism made modern architects blind to the fictitious nature of architecture; it made them forget that the true nature of architecture as art lies in the distance it

are there only for their expressive, associational effect.

The first principle was meant to encourage architects to think 'cheap' and 'flashy': 'The detailing (ought to be) notional and symbolic, quickly conceived for spec builders'.[8] The second principle was meant to 'explode' the code of building techniques and materials; an attitude which, by its rampant inclusivism, endorsed the whole wretched empirical reality encouraging the building industry towards the frenetic manufacture of waste products. 'Wood is warm. . . and full of knots and grain and so it is used domestically. . . (whereas) nylon. . . (and) the inflatable system is naturally pudgy, squashy, cuddly, sexual, and pleasant to touch. . . (and so they are used) in entertainment areas and other unmentionable places'.[9]

The post-modern pleas for utilising the 'full arsenal of communicational means' are being answered today by a *Style Macaronique* where anything goes. The sterility of the angst-ridden, emasculated parodies that fill the magazines is a direct consequence of the proliferation of communicational means. To paraphrase Adorno, 'superfluous jettisoning of meaning like ballast'[10] turns Post-Modernism into an exercise of sterile inventiveness. The post-modern mind invents so that things appear changing; and things change so that the mind appears to be inventive.

We are now in a better position to judge the nature of imitation and its relationship to modern and post-modern architecture. The foregoing discussion can be summarised in five points:

1 The scope of artistic imitation is to represent reality by means of an image that is wanting and incomplete. Imitation has, therefore, nothing to do with aping or the production of facsimile copies. Imitation represents its models freely and becomes in the hand of the artist a most inventive tool.

2 The particular way in which the image is wanting and incomplete distinguishes one art from the other. Consequently, each art imitates reality by means of a limited range of means, materials and techniques. Painting imitates reality by means of colour and line, sculpture by means of relief, architecture by means of tectonics, and so on.

3 Since the wanting image of artistic imitation is directly linked to the specific means of each art, it follows that whenever the means of an art are increased by trenching on the properties of another, the effect of artistic imitation is annulled.

4 Modern architecture discarded imitation altogether. As a result, its forms were the raw 'facts' of the industrial technology and materials it utilised. Thus extreme realism short-circuited any possibility for the emergence of symbolic form.

5 Post-Modernism assumed 'saturated' imagery would enhance architecture's meaning. By trenching on the properties of other branches like scenography and graphics, it lost sight of tectonics: architecture's distinguishing feature. Its indulgence in superfluous meaning has led to a travesty of architecture.

All along I have been speaking of the specific means of imitation proper to each one of the arts, but I have not as yet described the means proper to architecture. What are the means of architectural imitation? What are the particular tools and techniques of architectural imitation and how have they developed? Have they been the intuition of one man – perhaps a genius – or have they come into existence by natural habit and the accumulation of experience?

All historical, literary and formal evidence lead us to believe that the origins of the means of architectural imitation are to be found in the craft of building. Repetition and empirical judgement led builders to develop a habit of 'seeing' and 'judging' the constructional soundness and functional convenience of a particular solution. Over the years and centuries, a few chosen building solutions acquired a natural authority as truths. Such is the power of habit and consensus that soon this select number of building solutions became universal laws. They shed their marks of particularity and stressed their typicality (eg, the gable of my house as opposed to the idea of 'gable').

A select number of building solutions – like that of the gable – are responsible, in the first instance, for the invention of form. Man, in contemplating these forms, recognises in them the cumulative knowledge, experience and genius of his species and thereby wishes to commemorate them. At that very moment, those select building solutions drop their use value and assume an aesthetic, symbolic value. The necessities of shelter are superceded by the aesthetics of tectonics; necessity is commemorated by means of symbolic form; building becomes architecture. 'It is not for pleasure but out of necessity that our temples have *gables*', wrote Cicero. 'The need of discharging rainwater has suggested their form. And yet, such is the beauty of their form . . . that if one were to build a temple on Mount Olympus – where I am told it never rains – one would still feel obliged to crown it with a *pediment*'[11] (emphasis mine).

It is in that sense that architecture is meant to imitate the constructional origins of its building craft. Its etymology (*archetectoniké* means origins of building), historical development, and formal preoccupations confirm the fact that architecture celebrates construction and shelter by means of *tectonic order*.

In the tectonics of classical architecture the experience of load-bearing is represented by the entasis of the column; the chief beam binding the columns together and imposing on them a common load becomes the architrave; the syncopation of the transversal beams resting on the architrave is represented by the triglyphs and metopes of the frieze (one recalls here the literary evidence of *Iphigenia in Tauris* where Pylades advises Orestes that if he wants to get into the temple of Diana unnoticed, he should slip through the voids of the metopes); the projecting rafters of the roof supported by the frieze appear in the shape of the cornice; similarly the mutules, dentils, guttae, echinus, abacus, volutes, etc, all are images that imitate their respective constructional models.

It is not simply the tectonics of classical architecture that give evidence in support of this argument. All classic architecture – that is, all architecture we speak of as enduring – has derived its forms by means of imitating its building techniques.

The Sumerian temple retains memories of the reed construction with which houses were built. The rock-cut tomb of Arsaces in Myra imitates the constructional principles of indigenous timber framing. The Lykian tomb, now in the British Museum, is a representation in stone of the contemporary elements of building construction. The Egyptian tectonic order is an imitative representation both of constructional principles and of the lotus figure, the remembrance of which the columns commemorated. The half-engaged columns of early Romanesque architecture that subdivide the wall do not represent the constructional principles of classical antiquity but instead formalise in stone the round timber pales used in the construction of Norwegian stave churches, like that at Borgund. Finally, the applied order of the portico in the Forum Holitorium, Rome, shows the way by which Hellenistic and Roman architecture celebrates the constructional principles of both post-and-lintel and arcuated tectonics.

This list is only indicative and could draw its examples from primitive architecture, the architecture of early civilisations, of the Far East or of our own Western tradition.

We should stress yet again that the forms of all classic architecture are not realistic copies but rather imitations of their respective constructional models; the idea of imitation having the sense of a wanting and incomplete image.

Here a clarification should be made. It concerns the way in which a realistic 'fact' of construction becomes mythical 'form'. We know that the architectural form, say that of a pediment, does not celebrate the experience of this or that particular gable. Nevertheless, the form of a pediment is not a mere fairy tale. It has a fundamental reality. This reality is neither physical (in the sense that this pediment is made out of marble) nor historical (in the sense that this pediment is a fair cross-section of all the pediments known to history). The fundamental reality of the pediment is *mythical*. The images of construction and shelter that imitation gives us are myths. That is, they are figurative objectifications of man's building experience. In architecture, the challenge of construction, building and shelter over nature is turned into a mythical image. As such these myths are remote from empirical reality – in the sense that they do not objectify a particular, individual building experience. But at the same time they are part of empirical reality – in the sense that they objectify a common, universal building experience .

We can understand now why architectural form is not a matter of individual fancy or invention. Its peculiarity as mythical form is that its formal refinement and social authority cannot be fully developed in the lifetime of a single individual. Those who think otherwise have to pay the price of seeing their buildings being all the more readily confused with waste products.

I began by considering the way by which building is at the root of all architectural imitation. Constructional technique and the commodious disposition of shelter are the first guides. Sound building shows the way to typical solutions, the formal characteristics of which acquire over the years a symbolic value. Such symbolic forms go through a long process of stylisation or refinement, the purpose of which is to objectify them in their typicality. Architecture is born. Architecture objectifies its own origins; it looks at its past as building and through a process of mythical imagination it assigns to all its time-honoured building solutions a special physiognomy. In this respect architecture is neither an arbitrary adornment nor the inevitable causal outcome of building technique; it is the mythical form that man gives to his building craft by means of the principle of imitation.

Architecture makes us see the building craft from which it is born, from which it detaches itself as art, and to which it alludes.

DEMETRI PORPHYRIOS. PROPYLON. SURREY. 1985

———— * ————

57

THE ERECHTHEION, PORTICO OF THE CARYATIDS, DETAIL

PROPYLAIA AND ATHENA NIKE, ATHENS

IMITATION AND CONVENTION

Whenever we visit or look at a building, we find our attention moving in two directions at once. One is pragmatic, and concerned with how the building functions. The other has to do with the nature of the building we see the building as something that has been made. This is so since in human fabrication, in general, significance lies not in the utility or beauty that may accompany the artefact

but in the recognition of ourselves as the makers of that artefact.

This recognition is essentially a contemplative experience and, when viewed like this, the building – though it may be useful – refuses to be used in any way. Architecture begins precisely here; it speaks of the usefulness which produced it in the first place, from which it detaches itself as art and to which it always alludes.

We may therefore ask: what is the nature and purpose of this detachment and what are the means by which it is achieved? In other words, in what sense can we say that architecture detaches itself from the contingencies of shelter and construction and, if so, why and how does it do that?

The conception of architecture (and art in general) as having a relationship to contingent reality which is not direct but potential, can be traced back to Greek antiquity. In his *Poetics*, Aristotle discusses poetry and art as a form of truth liberated from experience: a response awakened in the observer by the transformation of experience and contingent reality into fictitious play. The central principle of Aristotelian aesthetics is that art is the imitation of nature. But what exactly are we to understand by the expression 'imitation of nature'?

The term 'imitation' has been so much used and misused in literary and popular discussion that its original Aristotelian meaning has been virtually lost. Already by the Hellenistic and Roman periods, the *Poetics* was not widely known and the major

commentary which had taken its place was Horace's *Ars Poetica*. Working within a Hellenistic framework of thought that favoured the art of rhetoric, Horace distinguished between style and content and emphasised the former at the expense of the latter. The preservation of Aristotle's text was ultimately due to the literary cultures of Islam and Byzantium. The first printed edition of the *Poetics* appeared in Venice in 1508, and from then on a number of translations and commentaries were published during the Renaissance. Later, Neo-Classicism turned the *Poetics* into codified, normative principles, at the same time elevating art into an idealised, metaphysical realm. With the advent of 19th-century romantic theories of genius, imagination and subjectivity, the *Poetics* lost its appeal, and by the time Brecht contrasted Dramatic and Epic theatre most of Aristotle's original ideas were forgotten. In fact Brecht did what was expected of him by this time: he associated the *Poetics* with naturalistic, outmoded ideology and thereby dismissed it without being prepared to understand it.

In a certain sense Brecht was right in suspecting the *Poetics* of outmoded clichés – Aristotle's text had been so often associated with the generalisation 'art imitates nature' or other similar statements found in Renaissance treatises on poetry, art and architecture. In fact, similar commonplaces are still current today and I suspect that is why in everyday language the word imitation brings to mind cloned replicas. Given our century's preoccupation with modern art, one can understand how such a naturalistic theory of art might appear suspect.

It is true that in his *Poetics* Aristotle writes that 'art imitates nature' (*e techne mimeitai ten phusin*). But this could not possibly have the sense that art is a reproduction of natural objects, since nature for Aristotle is not the physical world that surrounds us but rather the active force of the universe. Indeed the inadequacy of the English translation 'imitation' for the Aristotelian *mimesis* can be shown by a passage in the *Poetics* where it is mentioned that the artist 'imitates things as they ought to be' (*oia einai thei*). This passage shows clearly that imitation (mimesis) does *not* refer to a literal transcription of the world. It does *not* denote the servile duplication of the model; it is neither a copy nor a simulation of the physical world that surrounds us.

To imitate things as they *ought to be* means to represent something in a way that allows us to come closer to knowing it. Artistic imitation, in the Aristotelian sense, reveals the artist's (and our own as observers) preoccupations, concerns and criteria of evaluation. In that sense an imitation of the world is always a transformation of the world, since what we select to represent through the work of art is necessarily what we have deemed to be relevant for representation.

An etymological nuance throws further light on the Aristotelian concept of mimesis. We read in the *Poetics* that the artist imitates '*things* as they ought to be' (the italics are mine). Surely Aristotle does not have in mind here 'things' as mere physical objects. Heidegger has pointed out that the old German word for *thing* 'becomes the name for an affair or matter of pertinence. In fact, the meaning of the Greek word for thing (*pragma*, from *prattein*, that which has been acted upon and therefore rendered pertinent) is still preserved in the English word as when we say, "he knows how to handle things" – he knows how to deal with what matters.'

The meaning of Aristotle is clear. The artist imitates things as they ought to be (and therefore not necessarily as they are in the real world). What is more, he imitates no physical objects as such but rather 'things' in so far as they are the vehicles of an essential significance to him. It is in this sense that we can say that the Aristotelian concept of mimesis shows the way in which the world is true for us.

Consider for a moment Hume, who writes that 'the rules of architecture require that the top of a pillar should be more slender than its base . . . because such a figure conveys to us the idea of security . . .' (*A Treatise on Human Nature*, II, I, iii). The entasis of a column does not follow the exact profile of the tree trunk. It comprises an image of nature's visual statics.

Consider also Le Corbusier: 'Let us reflect for a moment on the fact that there is nothing in nature that . . . approaches the pure perfection of the humblest machine: the tree trunk is not straight . . . If we say with certainty that nature is geometrical it is not that we have seen it; it is rather that we have interpreted it in accordance with our own framework' ('The Lesson of the Machine' in *L'Art décoratif d'aujourd'hui*). The Corbusian *pilotis* comprise an image of nature's geometricity by analogy with the machine.

In these examples, both Hume and Le Corbusier speak of the way the column imitates the tree. Neither of the two speak of actually imitating a tree. Hume discovers in nature's workings an anthropomorphic image. Le Corbusier, on the other hand, discovers in nature a geometricity which is made pertinent by his admiration for the precision and exactitude of the machine. The classical imagination looks at the tree trunk and sees in it an image of stability, which it commemorates in the form of the

L TO R: SHED IN TUSCANY; SHED IN THE ENVIRONS OF BOLOGNA

entasis of the column. Le Corbusier, aspiring to the attainment of mechanical geometricity, sees the tree trunk as a precise cylindrical form.

In both cases the artist imitates no physical objects as such, but rather 'things' in so far as they have an essential significance for him. From one artist to another (or between different historical periods) the significance brought forward might vary and indeed it does; yet all art is imitation in the sense of representing the relevance that some-'thing' has for us. It is in this sense that we should understand the Aristotelian concept of imitation. Mimesis (imitation) discloses the way by which the world is true for us.

In what fashion does art speak to us? What are the means by which artistic imitation discloses the truth of the world for us? Does the work of art appeal to reason? Does it describe the world with concepts and discursive language? Aristotle reminds us here that a work of art is neither science nor philosophy but a likeness (*homeioma*) of some-'thing' found in the world.

Of the issues arising from the notion of artistic likeness, three demand special attention. In the first place, the notion of likeness points out that the work of art is always rendered in a sensuous medium (for example, paint, marble, sound, etc) and therefore speaks to us through the senses and not through the intellect. Art and architecture do not reach us by means of abstract reason but through our senses. Their medium is not discursive thought but sensuous form.

Secondly, in so far as the artistic medium is materially different from that in which its model is fashioned in the first place, we can say that a work of art is a likeness of the model. A painting of a landscape does not use leaves and shrubbery but simply paint. A sculpture of a maiden does not use the maiden in flesh, nor does it attempt to render the folds of her dress in real cloth. Similarly in architecture, a column does not render the bark of the tree with the moss growing on it. This is an obvious point and yet, so often, we tend to forget the necessary 'distance' that artistic likeness demands. I am reminded here of a postcard I once saw in Spain, a colour photograph depicting two flamenco dancers. Its author must have found the photographic impression wanting and, eager to 'enrich' it, he added real lace for the lady's skirt and silk for her blouse. Somewhere there must be an 'improvement' of this postcard where the castanets can be heard aloud and the aroma of the Sevillian dusk touches our nostrils.

We know of course that this is kitsch. For what is kitsch if not

thereby discloses the way in which the world is true for him. If, or when, we find such truth relevant to ourselves, we rejoice and call the work beautiful.

The third aspect of the notion of aesthetic likeness concerns the common understanding of likeness as *trompe-l'oeil* illusionism. In naturalistic theories of art it is assumed that the excellence of a painting corresponds to the faithfulness with which a painted representation matches the reality. Pliny, for example, records the story of the contest between Parrhasius and Zeuxis. The latter painted a bunch of grapes and birds flocked to peck them. Parrhasius then painted a curtain so realistically that he deceived Zeuxis, who asked for it to be drawn so that he might see the picture behind. Similarly Vasari tells the story of the young Giotto who painted a fly on to a picture by his master Cimabue so convincingly that Cimabue was deceived and made a gesture to drive the fly away.

Imitation – in the classical Aristotelian sense – has nothing to do with this idea of illusionistic likeness. From the outset artistic imitation abjures the satisfaction of merely naturalistic depiction. It does not aim at deception. Not for a moment does artistic imitation leave us in doubt about the fact that it intends to portray

L TO R: SHED IN THE ENVIRONS OF BOLOGNA; BREMO HOUSE, VIRGINIA

a hallucinatory promise of the world in flesh 'inducing a hedonistic relaxation as a compensatory strategy' (Adorno). The difference between kitsch and art is that kitsch simulates as a compensation for that which is not; art imitates in order to distance itself from that which is and thereby throw new light on to it. This distancing is not a sign of ineptitude on the part of the artist but, rather, a crucial characteristic of artistic production as such. By distancing himself from his model, the artist forces us to see what we have never seen before, pointing out a relevance that might otherwise have gone unnoticed. What the work shows is elicited from contingent reality and is brought forward for our contemplation. There is enough resemblance with the model for us to understand what the work refers to; the rest is all 'truth'. To continue with our previous examples: the entasis of a classical column makes us see, in the diminishing girth of a tree trunk, nature's law of stability; on the other hand, the cylindrical form of the Corbusian column makes us see a projected geometricity of nature and thereby the machine as *bella natura*. Art and architecture construct a new world by both preserving and cancelling out the contingent world of our everyday life. The artist imitates the world by distancing himself from it and

what is essential, not merely what is naturalistic. Imitation (the likeness of) does not involve the false belief that we are in the actual presence of what an image represents. Instead, we approach the work of art as an image (*phantasma*, likeness) of the world which the artist has judged to be especially worth commemorating.

The work of art exists as a bridge between the example and the precept. It represents a universal truth (*ta katholou*) by imitating particular examples chosen for their typicality (*ta kath' ekaston*). This is not to say that a general idea is embodied in a particular example, but that the particular case is generalised by artistic treatment. No doubt this is the meaning of Goethe when he writes that 'a special case requires nothing but the treatment of a poet to become universal'.

The classical architrave generalises the otherwise particular and contingent experience of post and lintel construction. The aim here is not to reproduce the lintel itself as a structural member with its sectional dimensions and material properties specified by the engineer, for that would be a symbolically mute gesture. Instead, the form of the classical architrave makes us see the structural members which produced it in the first place, from which it has detached itself as art and to which it always alludes. The form of the classical architrave makes us recognise the universal law of gravity and stability. In fact, recognising some-'thing' means knowing what is universal and essential. Recognition is the experience of familiarity with the world, not simply as a collection of contingent objects and events, but as an intelligible narrative. 'The reason why men enjoy seeing a likeness', writes Aristotle, 'is that in contemplating it they find themselves learning or inferring and saying perhaps, "Ah, that is he"'.

It is this emotional delight accompanying the pleasure of recognition of what is true for us that becomes the chief factor in the enjoyment of the arts. The theory of imitation (mimesis) seems to suggest, therefore, that art and architecture are a form of knowledge that serves to deepen our understanding of ourselves and thus our familiarity with the world. Let me pause for a moment and take stock of what we have said thus far:

1 Artistic imitation does *not* denote the servile duplication of the model; it is neither a copy nor a simulation.
2 The artist imitates things as they ought to be; that is, he represents what he has deemed relevant for representation. Artistic imitation, therefore, is a transformation of the world.

The artist shows us, in sensuous form, a representation of some-'thing' found in the world. This always involves establishing a distance from the model. It is exactly this distance which gives significance and truth to the work of art.

It is the distance which separates the timber shed from the temple that gives classical architecture its significance as a commemoration of shelter, construction and the laws of nature. It is the distance which separates the real cow from that painted by Van Doesburg that makes the painting a canonic statement of the primacy of objective, abstract essences. The theory of imitation is at the core of both traditional and modern art.

I have spoken of the relations that artistic imitation establishes between the work of art and the world. But what about the relations between one work of art and another? It is obvious that like a painting, a statue, a sonata or a poem, a building is one of a class of similar forms. To understand what classical architecture is, therefore, takes us beyond the discussion of the imitative relations that bind the timber shed to the temple. We have to ask the question of the relations of one classical building to another and with this idea two considerations become important: *convention* and *originality*.

 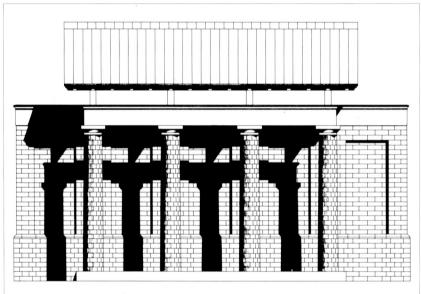

DEMETRI PORPHYRIOS, HIGHGATE PAVILION, LONDON: GAZEBO, 1981

3 The artist imitates no physical objects as such but rather 'things' in so far as they have a significance for him. In that sense, artistic imitation discloses the way in which the world is true for us.
4 The work of art is always a likeness of some-'thing' found in the world.
  a A work of art is a likeness in so far as it always uses sensuous form as its medium and never employs intellectual or discursive language.
  b A work of art is a likeness insofar as it is rendered in a medium that is materially different from that in which the model is fashioned in the first place. This introduces a necessary and telling distance from the model.
  c A work of art is a likeness not in the sense of *trompe-l'oeil* illusionism but of a categorical order. The work of art exists as a bridge between the example and the precept. The work of art represents a universal truth by imitating particular examples.
5 The aim (purpose) of art and architecture is to afford an emotional delight that accompanies the pleasure of recognition of what is true for us.

The study of conventions is based on analogies of form. It is clear that any classical building (and this applies equally to all classic architecture we speak of as enduring) may be studied not only as an imitation of the world and construction, but as an imitation of other classical buildings as well. Virgil discovered, Pope reminds us, that imitating nature was ultimately the same thing as imitating Homer. Once we think of a classical building in relation to other classical buildings, we can see that a great part of creative design addresses the formation and transformation of conventions.

All art and architecture is equally conventionalised, but we do not notice this as such conventions are always meant to appear natural and universal, otherwise their authority and role as the binding 'cement' of society would be undermined. In fact, conventions can best be studied when one travels, for unless we are unaccustomed to the conventions of a country they do not stand out. The same is true with the conventions of art and architecture.

Today, however, the conventional element in architecture is elaborately disguised; first by the modernist slogan 'down with conventions; long live the free spirit of experimentation'. Though such slogans were useful to the movement in the 1920s, they became meaningless once modern architecture had established itself. There have been, of course, a few for whom modernity had meant a permanent state of crisis. According to this view architecture is always *in extremis*. But even when we examine the recent deconstructionist mood of transgression and de-simulation of excremental culture, we come across numerous conventions which, while admittedly perhaps short-lived, are necessary for the production of any work. In fact, deconstruction does not deny the conventional element; it cannot, by its very own definition. It simply suspends the view that conventions are meaningful in order to see what happens when the tacit assumptions of convention no longer run.

In that sense today's neo-modernists are no different from the post-modernists. They both thrive on convention: the first by dismembering conventions in the name of deconstructionist critique; the second by saturating the market with 'instant conventions' in the name of pluralism. I have never understood why Jencks has kept the neo-modernists at a distance, denying them a slice of the post-modern cake. Very soon he will realise this and by 'discovering' them he will give to Post-Modernism a few

and the aristocracy that had sustained him for centuries, and found himself confronted with an anonymous and frequently uneducated public. This new client, we are told, he openly despised. At the same time the artist demanded the public's approval even when it could not understand his art. This 19th-century romantic attitude had much to do with the modernist slogan of 'down with conventions' and is still with us today, especially among those neo-modern aesthetes of a deconstructionist persuasion.

But it is hardly possible to accept a view which imagines that a creative architect stares at a white board and designs *ex nihilo*. Human beings do *not* create in that way. Architecture may employ technology and it may be implicated with social and economic parameters; architects might read philosophy and novels – that is all OK and human. But architecture is not made out of these things. Buildings can only be made out of other buildings. Architecture shapes itself. Its forms can no more exist outside architecture than the form of a sonata can exist outside music.

Any serious study of architecture (and art in general) soon shows that the real difference between the great and the lesser

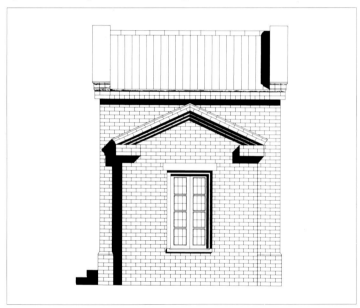

DEMETRI PORPHYRIOS, HIGHGATE PAVILION, LONDON: GARDENER'S PAVILION, 1981

more years of life.

Copyright laws – another factor that disguises the importance of the conventional element in architecture – would make it difficult to appraise an architecture which includes, say, Palladio, much of whose architecture is paraphrased from others, or Schinkel whose buildings sometimes follow their sources almost verbatim. If for a moment we move to poetry, I am reminded of Milton who asked for nothing better than to borrow the whole of the Bible.

The distance between a new work and the model that has inspired it is indeed always the hallmark of creative talent, pointing out the contemporaneity of the work. But at the same time we have to realise that the conception of a great architect entrusted with a heritage must be as elementary to us as it was to Alberti. And yet such an attitude would seem to violate the prejudices about 'creation *ex nihilo*' that most of us are educated in today.

Historically, of course, we have been told to believe that this 'fall from grace' was triggered by the profound change in the social position of the artist/architect after the middle of the 18th century. He gradually lost the patronage of the Church, the State

architect is that the former imitates the principles of a great heritage, unlike the latter who copies the mannerisms of his predecessors or his contemporaries. That is the true meaning of creativity and originality. Whereas, if creativity is to be understood as production *ex nihilo*, there would soon be no place for competence and intelligence and we should then not be surprised if schools and professional bodies set up 'creativity tests'!

The subject of imitation and convention raises the question of how architecture can be meaningful. Architecture as one of the aspects of civilisation is concerned with recurrent images that afford recognition of the world. The roof, the portico, the column, the white-washed wall, the brick pergola opening up to the garden, all connect one building with another and help make intelligible our architectural experience of the world. Through the technique of imitation architecture raises itself above the mere contingencies of building and sets symbols for recognition. By means of convention these symbols are composed, varied and recomposed in an ever-changing chain of variations. Yet always the aim is to make man come to terms with the world. The role of imitation and convention in architecture is to elicit that which is lasting and true for us from the transient.[12]

VAN PELT AND THOMPSON, THE GENNADIUS LIBRARY, ATHENS, 1923-25, DETAIL OF FRONT PORTICO

VILLA TRISSINO AT CRICOLI, 1538

THE RELEVANCE OF CLASSICAL ARCHITECTURE

In the last 25 years architects have articulated a devastating critique of the ideological assumptions of modern architecture. The critique concerns both the aesthetics of architecture and the organisation of the city. For the modernists, the ideal of reductive purity was ideologically charged and in this sense modernist buildings were seen not only as things of beauty but also as anticipations of the

radiant universal city of the future; in other words, of a city that would stand as a symbol of a liberated and non-hierarchic society. In that sense, Modernism has been the only avant-garde movement of our century. This avant-garde commitment to such a goal of an emancipatory social liberation required, among other things, a refusal to look back to the various architectural traditions, all of which were supposed to have connotations of authoritarian domination. The old stylistic differences, whether regional, historical or attributable to class distinctions, were soon to dissolve. Style meant ornament, it meant decoration and since it symbolised status seeking, conspicuous consumption and display it was bound to be socially and morally objectionable, intellectually indefensible and aesthetically corrupt.

As regards urban design, we know that the modernist approach was a radically rationalist *tabula rasa,* a clean slate: zoning, the city in the park, the free-standing building, the disappearance of the street, and the square, the destruction of the urban block. In short, it meant the destruction of the urban fabric of the city. All that was systematically hailed by the modernists as an ingenious advance in urban social engineering. Take, for example, Hilbersheimer who claimed that 'every exception and every nuance must be cancelled out; abstract, mathematical order must reign so that it may constrain chaos to become form'. Hilbersheimer was neither the first nor the last modernist planner. In the mid-19th century, Jules Borie had spoken of similar crystalline

palaces for the brave new world and, I suppose, as late as 1969 designers like Superstudio still believed that their 'landscrapers' could be socially regenerative.

In my book on Alvar Aalto I have stressed this double objectivism of modern architecture: the objectivism that aimed on the one hand at the mathematical abstraction of the city and on the other at the extinction of symbolic meaning. I discussed how Alvar Aalto emerged as a significant figure in the 50s and 60s exactly because he adopted strategies which appeared to undermine this double objectivism. In that sense, Aalto was the first modern eclectic and by extension the first post-modernist. In fact, Aalto had a catalytic effect in the debates which took place in the mid-60s between the Whites and Greys. Out of these debates two major concerns emerged: the importance of the rhetoric of style and the primacy of context. The whole post-modernist culture was indeed founded on these two concerns. Architectural thinking slowly moved away from modernist planning towards contextual strategies and eventually towards a rekindled interest in traditional urbanism.

The reorientation which took place in the 60s and which later developed into Post-Modernism was and still remains based on an eclectic attitude. Much like 19th-century Eclecticism, the aim of modern Eclecticism has been to look at historical styles merely as communicative devices, as labels and clothing. Style itself was seen as having no natural relationship to the tectonics of building. Since this eclectic mood had nothing to do with the values of revivalism, it soon became clear that there could be no common criteria of aesthetic evaluation. Hence a pluralism that sprung out of 'an age of conciliatory culture, widespread, visiting the beliefs of all countries and all ages, accepting everything without fixing any part, since truth is everywhere in bits and nowhere in its entirety'.

Many, including myself, have discussed the architecture of the last 25 years as historicism, contextualism, relativism or the aesthetics of accommodation. I don't want to take issue here with any of these interpretations. In a sense, all these accounts are accurate evaluations of our contemporary mood. If we are to understand, however, the phenomenon of post-modern architecture we must look at the distinctive use of its stylistic devices and conventions.

Modernism as an avant-garde made us familiar with the idea of showing rather than concealing the conventions and devices which are used in constructing a work of art. I refer here to what the Russian Formalists called the foregrounding of the device; an idea found in the alienation effect, for example, of Brecht. This idea of estrangement and foregrounding the device so character-istic of Modernism is maintained by Post-Modernism. Post-modernist works show themselves for the contrivance they are, but in doing so they also state that everything else in life is a contrivance and that simply there is no escape from this. Hence the self-referential circularity of the post-modern quotation and the extreme fascination with parody and meta-linguistic com-mentary. Let me look now at the three major meta-linguistic idioms of Post-Modernism today: Post-Modern High-Tech, Post-Modern Classical and Post-Modern Deconstructionist.

The engineer's language of the 19th century had a direct relationship to the contingencies of construction and shelter. The social vision of the Polytechnicians gave it a futuristic aura which was to be exploited ever after by the so-called high-tech architects. But as we know, Ferdinand Dutert's Palais des Machines was indeed a high-tech building in the sense that it pushed the engineering skill of its time to its limits for a socially purposeful brief. On the contrary, contemporary so-called high-tech buildings are only make-believe simulations of high-tech imagery. It is in this sense that we can say that High-Tech acts today as a meta-language. The device, namely technologism, is shown here for the contrivance it is. In a culture where the frontiers of technology have moved away from building towards space and genetics, the idea of a high-tech building can only be either wishful thinking or a make-believe.

The second idiom of Post-Modernism today is that of the Post-Modern Classical. Hansen's 19th-century Academy in Athens was a reworking of the classical language where the principles of commodity, firmness, and delight were all respected. On the contrary, post-modern classicists use the device of parody. They favour playful distortion, citation, deliberate anachronism, dimi-nution, oxymoron, etc. Ultimately, this is yet another make-believe cardboard architecture.

Finally, Deconstruction today is marketed as a recent avant-garde. But it is neither recent nor an avant-garde. It is but another version of the post-modern movement. The language adopted is that of the constructivist avant-garde. But whereas the aesthetics of the Constructivist, say Chernikhov, were ultimately grounded in the social vision of an emancipated urban proletariat and in the hoped-for technology of the new industrial state, post-modern deconstructionists today exploit the graphics of the avant-garde so that they may benefit by association and promote themselves as a new critical wave. They loudly reject such ideas as order, intelligibility and tradition. Architecture is supposed to become an experience of failure and crisis. And if crisis is not there, well then it must be created. In this respect, post-modern deconstruc-

tivists lack a socially-grounded critical platform. If anything, Deconstruction today is a version of aestheticism. And let me add: those who claim amnesia have systematically resorted to historicism.

These three versions of the Post-Modern – Post-Modern High-Tech, Post-Modern Classical and Post-Modern Deconstruction – differ widely in their stylistic preferences, symbolic content and social constituencies but they share a similar scenographic view of architecture. This view of architecture as scenography can be summarised in Venturi's principle of the 'decorated shed': construction (firmness), shelter (commodity) and symbolism (delight) are distinct and unrelated concerns. They do not influence each other. Construction, shelter and symbolism are each governed by their own rules and they share no common aim. This scenographic attitude in the production of a building coupled with the fascination with parody I mentioned earlier are the two fundamental characteristics of the Post-Modern. Confronted with post-modern architecture one has a feeling somehow that all values have been researched and rejected. We are of this or that opinion just for the fun of it.

I have great respect for the inventive ingenuity of the post-modernists but I have repeatedly in the past criticised them as regards exactly these two points: the principle of the 'deco-rated shed' and the aesthetics of parody. The self-paralysing parodies they thrive on, when unwrapped from their intellectual-ist idiom, are but dispirited commonplaces. If my view has been that of a classicist, it has been so not because of a transcendental belief in the immutable nature of the orders but because I have come to realise that *Classicism is not a style*.

Let me clarify what I mean here. The critique launched by contemporary classicists starts, quite significantly, not with the aesthetics of architecture but with the strategies of urban design. In other words, the critique addresses the destruction of the traditional urban fabric, the progressive abstraction of the city through zoning and the excremental experience of the Las Vegas Strip. The 20th-century city, argue the classicists, works well from the sewers up to the sky-scrapers as long as one considers the wastage in human and natural resources as a concommittant to the sustaining of the overall edifice.

Instead, the classicists propose the wisdom of the traditional city: English, European, American or otherwise. The issue here is not one of stylistics but of ecological balance: to control the sprawl of our cities, to reconsider the scale and measure of the urban block, to emphasise the typological significance of design, to establish hierarchies between public and private realms, and to rethink the constitution of the open spaces of the city.

As regards the aesthetics of architecture, the classicists adopt the theory of imitation. Art, it is argued, imitates the real world by turning selected significant aspects of it into mythical repre-sentations. Consider the following comparison. A documentary record of the atrocities of civil war can be contrasted with Goya's or Ruben's 'Atrocities of War' that depict Saturn devour-ing his children. The documentary record can only provoke disgust. Goya's imitative representation of the real world, however, does afford us aesthetic pleasure. This is so exactly because it establishes a distance from reality which allows us to contemplate our universal human predicament.

Similarly, a classicist would argue, architecture is the imitative celebration of construction and shelter qualified by the myths and ideas of a given culture. Such myths might have to do with life, nature or the mode of production of a given society. Ultimately, architecture speaks of these myths and ideas but always through the language of construction and shelter. celebrating construction and shelter by means of tectonic order.

Surely, many modernists have spoken about 'honest construc-tion'. But I want to stress here that classical imitation has nothing in common with the structural functionalism of modern architecture. Modernism makes no distinction between building and architecture. Modernism does *not* imitate construction and shelter; it simply uses raw building material without any imitative mediation. In that sense, Modernism has produced buildings but, as yet, no architecture. The result has been a century of mute realism in the name of industrial production. On the contrary what makes classical architecture possible is the dialogic relationship it establishes between the craft of building and the art of architecture. Our imagination traverses this dialogic space between, say, a pergola and a colonnade, and establishes hierarchies, levels of propriety and communicable systems of evaluation.

Classical architecture needs also another dialogic relationship: this time the relationship between one building and another. This point is very important. Today the market ethic of the original and authentic is based on the pretence that every work of art is an invention singular enough to be patented. As a consequence of this frame of mind, demonstrating the debt of, say, Giulio Romano to Bramante is today called scholarship but it would have been denounced as plagiarism were Giulio Romano still alive. I think it is unfortunate that it is not only the inexperienced modern architect who looks for a residual originality as a hallmark of talent. Most of us today tend to think of an architect's real achievement as having nothing to do with the achievement present in what he borrows. Since we have been educated as modernists we tend to think that our contribution comprises solely in that which is different. We therefore tend to concentrate on peripheral issues of stylistics.

What I am suggesting here is that the real contribution of an architect lies in what he/she chooses to borrow. Let us think for a moment of the greatness, say, of Alberti. His greatness lies in the fact that he gave a new life to the humanist theme itself which he passed on to the 15th century from the sources of antiquity. The world of Alberti was very different from that of antiquity; the technology was different, the politics were different, the *haute couture* had changed, but the great humanist theme of commodity – firmness – delight was still alive and will stay alive.

Let me finish by saying that architecture has nothing to do with 'novelty-mania' and intellectual sophistries. Architecture has nothing to do with transgression, boredom or parody. It has nothing to do with parasitic life, excremental culture or the cynical fascination with the bad luck of others. Architecture has to do with decisions that concern the good, the decent, the proper. Decisions about what Aristotle called the *EU ZEIN*, the good and proper life. Surely, what constitutes proper life varies from one historical period to another. But it is our responsibility to define it anew all the time. If we choose to embrace the tradition of the classical we will find no recipes but we will encounter again and again a kind of genius for practical life, a kind of genius that is actually less of a gift than a constant task of adjustment to present contingencies. It is in this sense that we can speak of the classical as that which endures; but this defiance of time is always experienced as a sort of historical present.

Notes

1 Aristotle's *Poetics*, MSS. Parisinus 2038, 1 1447a. English translation here taken from S H Butler, *Aristotle's Theory of Poetry and Fine Art*, St.Martin's Press, 1894.

2 S H Butler, *Ibid*, pp 124, 125, 127.

3 Quatremère de Quincy, *An Essay on the Nature, the End, and the Means of Imitation in the Fine Arts*, trans by J C Kent, Smith Elder and Son Co, London, 1837, p 13.

4 *ibid*, p 17.

5 *ibid*, p 28.

6 Hannes Meyer, 'Building', 1928, in Ulrich Conrads, ed, *Programmes and Manifestoes on 20th-century Architecture*, Lund Humphries, London, 1970.

7 Charles Jencks, *The Language of Post-Modern Architecture*, Academy Editions, London, first edition, 1977, pp 7 and 97.

8 *ibid*, p 78.

9 *ibid*, p 82.

10 Theodor Adorno, *Minima Moralia*, trans by E F N Jephcott, Verso Edition, 1978, p 141.

11 Cicero, *De Oratore*, L3, c 46, The LOEB Classical Library, Harvard and Heinemann.

12 All quotations from Aristotle are from his *Poetics*, MSS Parisinus 2038, English translation by S H Butler, *Aristotle's Theory of Poetry and Fine Art*.

L TO R: C H HANSEN, UNIVERSITY OF ATHENS; T H JEFFERSON, UNIVERSITY OF VIRGINIA

ALLAN GREENBERG, TREATY ROOM, DEPARTMENT OF STATE BUILDING, WASHINGTON DC, 1986-87

THE ARCHITECTURE OF DEMOCRACY
ALLAN GREENBERG

THE CAPITOL, WASHINGTON D C, 1824 AND 1850

Ancient Greece is the birthplace of humanism, democracy and classical architecture. These ideals are all founded on the belief that the individual is the measure of worldly endeavour and that intellectual life, government, and architecture should be built around the communal and private needs of people. In architecture, this anthropocentrism focuses on planning buildings to balance harmoniously the

physical needs related to commodity, firmness and delight. It also encompasses the spiritual dimensions of beauty, relation to place and expression of meaning. Greek anthropocentrism led, miraculously and perhaps uniquely, to anthropomorphism: the quality by which buildings embody human attributes and qualities. For example, the classicial column, the basis of the Orders of architecture, has both gender and character. The doric column is male, strong and heavy: the ionic is matronly, thinner and more elegant; and the corinthian is maidenly, even more slender, and the most elaborate and ornate. Thus, the rows of columns supporting the roof of a Greek temple, or any truly classical building, are also people. This fact was so real for the ancient Greeks that columns and people were interchangeable. At the Erechtheion the columns are women sculpted in stone.

Anthropocentrism focuses the architect's attention on designing buildings that satisfy the need we humans have for physical comfort and psychological well-being. Through our innate perception of balance, gravity and structure within our own frames, we empathise with buildings and, reciprocally, building can reinforce a sense of physical order within ourselves. For the architect, physical comfort has two different aspects: first, adjusting the design of the building to suit the human frame, and second, ensuring that the design not only accommodates our need to feel a sense of stability and structural solidity, but even reinforces that sense. For example, the crucial keystone which

secures an arch in place, or the column capital which spreads out to receive more easily the load of the lintel, gives us a visceral sense of stability.

Psychological comfort in architecture is achieved through aesthetic satisfaction, easy orientation within the building, and a logical relationship between rooms, corridors and all parts of the programme. It also involves dividing the exterior into base, mid-section, and top, so as to correspond to a person's legs, torso and head. The principle also applies to the design of walls within rooms. A wainscot, or chair rail, defines the lower part of the wall and separates it from the mid-section or waist; a cornice forms the top or head. Such anthropomorphic correspondences are important factors in providing orientation within our environment. The concept of psychological comfort also encompasses our need to embody in architecture significant social experiences, political ideals, and religious beliefs. Thus classical architecture depends on the impress of regional, geographical, and cultural characteristics. These forces are synthesised by the skill of individual architects, and used to forge the unique qualities that make up the architecture of each nation, region and period.

The history of classical architecture over the past three millenia may be likened to a great river which flows into the future from the past. Each of its many tributaries represents various nations and cultures. These, in turn, are fed by a multiplicity of smaller rivers and streams representing the architecture of different regions and cities within each nation. The smallest brooks and rills are works by individual architects. The fine degree of difference between the architecture of different nations, or individuals, is easily read because the formal language of classical architecture is so highly developed that it is possible to tell the hand of a great architect even in small details like mouldings.

The uniqueness of classical architecture in the United States rests on its role in the forging of a new nation which was also the first federal democratic republic in history. Architecture both expressed and reinforced the nation's highest ideals. For the country's founding fathers it was imperative that city plans and the architecture of public buildings express the authority vested in 'We the people', who constitute the government. Elected presidents and representatives merely serve the citizenry. This concept is quite different from a government that uses architecture to project the power and prerogatives of a king, who rules by divine right. Such a government serves its royal master rather than his subjects.

The United States is fortunate that its founding fathers not

the plan a symbolic representation of the nation. They also stress the importance of communication to help bind together what was previously 13 independent states into one nation.

The earliest public buildings in Washington reinforced the meanings that are implicit in the city's plan. The Capitol, like its namesake in ancient Rome, was set on a hill and is the plan's major focus. From its great Rotunda, still the tallest building in the city, 12 avenues radiate out and extend, by implication, to the nation's borders. This place is the conceptual centre of the nation. The Rotunda is an empty space which is dedicated to the sacred right of citizens to assemble freely for political, or any other, purpose. This right is so important that the chambers of the Senate and the House of Representatives are literally moved sideways, off the main axis, and onto the building's minor axis. Neither is the Rotunda used by the President, who occupies a separate building, the White House. Thomas Jefferson called the Rotunda 'the first temple dedicated to the sovereignty of the people, embellishing with Athenian taste the cause of a nation looking far beyond the range of Athenian destinies.'

The dome of the Capitol was first designed by Benjamin Henry Latrobe and Charles Bulfinch and later, in its present

THOMAS JEFFERSON, MONTICELLO, CHARLOTTESVILLE, VIRGINIA, 1771-82

only wrote the legal documents establishing the nation, but were also interested in architecture. For these men, it was important that architecture embody the noblest ideals and aspirations of the society it served. Architecture was a didactic enterprise and its spiritual purpose was to teach civility to citizens. This goal becomes realised when city plans and architecture are able to represent the meaning and significance of the nation's ideals in the design and ornament of the buildings housing its institutions.

Their first important step toward realising this purpose was to create a new capital city, Washington D C, at the geographical centre of the new nation. The brilliant city plan of 1791 by Peter Charles L'Enfant embodies key democratic ideas in its iconography. The Mall is the spine of the plan and represents the Constitution which binds the nation together.The White House and Capitol are located so as to explicitly express the separation of powers. 15 public squares in different parts of the city are dedicated to the 13 founding states and the first two new states to join the union. These squares, along with the sites of major public buildings, are tied together by a system of diagonal avenues overlaid upon the city's grid plan. The avenues, named after individual states, combine with all these elements to make

form, by Thomas U Walter. Their designs grew out of the great domes of the Roman Pantheon, St Peter's in Rome, and St Paul's in London. In Washington, the meaning is transformed to express democratic ideals. This transformation of European forms to serve democratic needs started early in the colonial period as settlers established new lives in the American wilderness. Within the space of a few years they transformed their English architectural heritage to suit different construction materials, building techniques and climate. This new architecture also expressed their growing sense of social and political independence, as is clearly seen in the New England saltbox, a house type which evolved out of the English yeoman's cottage.

The house had a special significance in early American architecture. It was during this period that the small single family dwelling became a work of architecture in its own right, perhaps for the first time. Its simplicity and austerity infused both the form and meaning of the best works of American architecture, including public buildings. Thus, buildings for state government became known as *statehouses*. Just as the private house shelters a family, so state government represents a larger unit of human families. The domestic connotation also suggests openness and is an invitation to visit and to participate in developing legislation to improve the quality of life in the state. Similarly, the English Law Court building became the courthouse and schoolhouses were for free public education.

The rediscovery of the architectural heritage of ancient Greece in the late 18th and early 19th centuries expanded the range and vocabulary of American architecture. Greek as well as Roman sources were used because of their associations with early forms of democratic and republican government. This use was a logical extension of colonial design, which had been influenced by England's 'Glorious Revolution' and the architecture of the mercantile cities of Italy and Holland.

The United States industrialised during the 19th century and its economy expanded at a rapid rate, a transformation that affected almost every aspect of life and dramatically improved the overall standard of living. A whole range of new utilitarian building types came into being. These were often treated as significant structures and given what I call a utilitarian monumentality. The regard in which they were held grew out of the public awareness of how important these buildings were to the economy and to improving the quality of daily life.

buggy, and railroad from farms, villages, and cities. They returned home inspired with a vision of a new urban America. Over the next decade thousands of local civic associations were organised to promote plans for improving the quality of life in cities and towns. The plans encouraged economic growth and called for rebuilding slums; creating metropolitan parks, transportation, water supply and sewer systems; and improving housing, schools, and universities. The work of these civic associations became known as the City Beautiful Movement. They were driven by a belief that a beautiful and healthy environment improved every citizen's well-being.

The City Beautiful was a grass-roots movement. An important component of its programme was a preoccupation with local communities that used democratic means and the resources of both philanthropy and taxation to achieve their goals. The movement's local emphasis may be related to the fact that the architecture of the White City germinated in the 1876 Centennial Exposition in Philadelphia. This celebration of the anniversary of the Revolution, and of the political values it stood for, also occasioned a renewal of interest in the classical architecture, both colonial and federal, of the nation's founding era. It was

FREDERICK GRAFF, THE FAIRMOUNT WATER WORKS, PHILADELPHIA, PENN, 1819-22

A critical date in the history of American architecture is 1893, the year of the World's Columbian Exposition in Chicago. Known as the White City, the exposition's architecture and grounds were planned by Daniel Burnham, Charles McKim, Augustus St Gaudens, and Frederick Law Olmsted, assisted by a group of architects from New York and Chicago. Their great achievement was to present the public with a new vision of urban architecture, an image of what cities and towns throughout the nation could be like with the application of proper planning principles, good architecture, and the balm of abundant gardens and parks. The vision was timely, for by 1893 urban areas were overwhelmed with problems related to the massive growth of population and the uncoordinated expansion of industry and commerce. Slums abounded, together with the social problems endemic to such environments. Ugliness was pervasive, city government corrupt, and improving the quality of life in cities seemed to be almost beyond reach. No one doubted that the means were available. What was lacking was a blueprint to focus the energy of reformers and planners. This was one of the achievements of the White City.

People travelled great distances on foot, by horse, horse and

also an occasion to examine their roots in the architecture and city planning of England, Holland, Italy, and ancient Rome. This process is described in the State of Virginia's Bill of Rights as a 'frequent recurrence of first principles'. Our towns and cities were reinfused with the spirit of its democratic birth, seeking further inspiration from its sources.

Another direct outgrowth of the White City was the McMillan Commission Plan of 1902 for the growth and development of Washington D C. This plan created the modern city of Washington. The planners were, again, Burnham, McKim, St Gaudens, and Olmsted. In the late 19th century Washington was a very different city from the one we know today. A Smithsonian Institution forest preserve shared much of the Mall with a railroad station and its marshalling yard. The absence of building or zoning controls permitted the same chaotic patterns of development found in other cities, together with attendant slums, congestion and ugliness. Following the guideline proposed by the McMillan Commission, the city was dramatically rebuilt and expanded during the next 30 years. The Mall was restored and lined with buildings in accordance with L'Enfant's plan; the railroad was removed and a new terminal, the present Union

Station, erected; the Lincoln and Jefferson memorials were built; the south portion of the Mall's cross axis was expanded with a lagoon and landfill park; a major system of local and regional parks was created, together with one of the earliest parkways; the White House was restored; the complex of government buildings known as the Federal Triangle was built; the Capitol expansion, including a complex of office buildings for House and Senate and a new Supreme Court, was completed; and new schools, housing, and commercial facilities were planned.

The McMillan Plan had a second and equally important function: it served as a handbook for civic associations nationwide to use as a model on which to base their own plans. Its broad scope galvanised hundreds of similar plans for cities and towns. The *Comprehensive Plan for New Haven* of 1904 by Frederick Law Olmsted Jr and Cass Gilbert and the *Plan of Minneapolis* of 1917 by Edward H Bennett are examples of plans for small cities. The best known, however, are the 1909 *Plan for Chicago* by Daniel Burnham and Edward H Bennett and the 1931 Regional *Plan of New York and its Environs* by Thomas Adams. These proposals were vastly expanded encompassing metropolitan regions. The generation of urban development plans created by the City Beautiful Movement used the services of the finest architects, engineers, planners, landscape architects, and artists. Many recommendations of plans were implemented and, today, constitute the finest parts of our cities. It is not unusual to find small towns like Naugatuck, Connecticut, possessing five buildings by McKim Mead and White, or Pasadena, California, with important buildings by Arthur Brown and Myron Hunt.

To assess the scope of these changes, we must imagine Chicago or New York as they were in the 1880s: cities of low buildings, a handful of which were more than four or five storeys high. Yet in the space of three decades, both cities were almost completely rebuilt and had majestic groups of tall masonry buildings of uniform height grouped around the tower of the Board of Trade. New York became the city of skyscrapers, the very symbol of the 20th century.

The vast legacy of the City Beautiful Movement is as yet largely undocumented. It includes elaborate systems of local, regional, and national parks; metropolitan water and sewer systems; a new generation of buildings for federal, state, and local government; the rediscovery of regional styles of architecture in the United States; the construction of public libraries in almost every city and town; the first programmes of federal subsidised housing which, unlike the modernistic public housing 'projects' that would isolate and stigmatise the poor, simply reflected the fact that the poor aspire to the same qualities in a home that are sought after by everyone else; skyscrapers, shopping centres, and other new building types; new and expanded schools, colleges and universities; and resort, recreation and sports facilities. Buildings for industry became the province of architecture. Power stations were designed with a new utilitarian monumentality, like Roman aqueducts. The new factories and warehouses were simple, but they were also powerful architectural statements whose eloquence dignified work. The great bridges of the time, including the suspension bridges across the rivers of New York, were designed by architects and engineers who also contributed to the design of highways such as the Merritt Parkway, and to related gasoline stations and rest stops. In short, the framework of buildings and structures encompassing our everyday life became architecture.

As the new century began, technology transformed the building site. In skyscrapers like the Singer Tower of 1908 or the Woolworth Building of 1913, almost every modern technological invention is used: frame construction employing steel or reinforced concrete, metal and glass curtain walls, elevators, heating, ventilation, and air conditioning systems, electricity,

running water and plumbing, and building techniques involving prefabrication, the use of machine tools, mass production, and diverse forms of industrial technology. Though Modernism claims to have brought technology to architecture, in fact it had been fully absorbed into the fabric of American classical architecture before the end of the 19th century. Classical architecture forged a new synthesis between the building industry and technology that revolutionised both the fabrication of materials and construction technology; it has always responded to the needs of architecture, current and future, at the same time reinterpreting the past and drawing it into the present.

The goal of the City Beautiful Movement was to transform the environment of our everyday lives into architecture. No aspect of life was too insignificant to warrant the attention of the architect, landscape architect, planner, or industrial designer. The era's new objects – telephones, typewriters, and office furniture – became the particular focus of attention for these industrial designers and architects who understood the anthropocentric principles of classical architecture. For example, the early Underwood typewriter has a cavetto moulding at its base which is a classical building plinth designed in miniature. Anthropomorphism was an integral part of the process of architectural and industrial design.

The extraordinary success of the City Beautiful Movement, like the parallel development in England to improve city and country life and create Letchworth and Hampstead Garden Suburb, stands in poignant contrast to the catastrophic failures of modernistic housing, urban renewal, and highway programmes. Looking at the Interstate Highway programme in the United States, for example, one of the costliest public works projects in history, one is hard-pressed to find anything of architectural or even human interest. For the contrast is not only architectural. It is also social and political. The City Beautiful did not require massive state subsidies or oppressive and authoritarian legislation to implement its plans.

It is both ironic and sad that the City Beautiful, with its comprehensive range of concerns, is the unacknowledged source and the inspiration for the manifestos of the Congrès International d'Architecture Moderne as well as the urban renewal and housing programmes they generated in the United States. The extraordinary success of the City Beautiful also provided the courage and the confidence which the modernistic architect and planner needed to propose and to implement the plans which wreaked havoc on millions of lives. By demolishing entire neighbourhoods and rebuilding them according to completely speculative and anti-urban principles, they destroyed urban social and economic structures and created the cruellest urban buildings and spaces in history, spaces which Norman Mailer has defined as 'landscapes of psychosis'. But what could be expected of modernistic architecture? It eschewed the past as irrelevant and espoused authoritarian political principles that were antithetical to individual freedom and the democratic process. The forms of the new buildings and urban spaces expressed Modernism's ideology, just as did the architecture of democracy its own values and ideals.

The missing elements in modernistic design and planning are the humanism and anthropocentrism which are the core of classical architecture. The very mechanism by which we sense our bodies' resistance to gravity and perceive ourselves in relation to the environment, is incorporated into its language of architecture. This is why classical architecture is both timeless and tied to a particular time and place. It is these qualities, together with those of democracy, urbanity, and continuity with the past, that continue to identify classical architecture as the appropriate language of architecture in the United States for the 20th as well as the 21st centuries.

CLASSICAL AMERICAN URBANISM
CARROLL WILLIAM WESTFALL

Architecture has one primary purpose which is to serve the political life. From this it follows that as the forms of political life are changed and improved, so too must the way buildings serve it be changed. This improvement, whether in politics or building, means it is always possible to improve the fit between the pattern of nature and our own imitation of that in our own knowledge. Because this improvement is possible, it is the responsibility of people to seek that improvement. To avoid that responsibility either by avoiding politics or by using cities for purposes that do not hold the improvement of knowledge as their primary purpose is to be less than human.

To respond to that responsibility, the client, the architect, and the critic or historian must ask: how will this building serve the individuals for whose use it is intended by assisting them in finding their happiness? This is primarily and fundamentally a political question when politics is understood in its classical sense, namely, the means by which the individual perfects his nature.

Except in Modernism, the term *city* has a concretely political meaning. A city is any polity, large or small in size and reach, existing as the locus of politics, and existing because and when politics exists. Because politics is the art of living together, the political forms of cities will differ according to the different forms of the art of living together, and so too will the architectural and urban forms serving that politics. Thus, it is the case that the most important way in which buildings differ from one another is not according to their style, their structural system, their specific functions, or the identity of their designer but according to the political purposes they serve in the city they help form.

Cities differ according to the political purposes they are to serve. The ways these purposes are reached differ according to the circumstances of the place in which the city's citizens pursue the art of living together in politics. Different places necessarily have different circumstances — of climate, materials, and the wherewithal to build, of habits, traditions, and customs. These will colour the form given the purpose of the political life. The United States is the product of the first formulation of a political form in pursuit of an explicit purpose: governments are instituted among men in order to secure the individual's inalienable natural rights. Individual rights precede the authority of government. The citizen is the basis of the polity. This is the fundamental lesson of the American Revolution.

This lesson stands in sharp contrast to the modernist alternative invented during the French Revolution which holds that the polity defines citizenship. A polity that defines citizenship is a top-down structure. In it, the lesser, smaller unit may do that which the higher, larger unit allows. The medieval church and Holy Roman Empire are the clear examples. Currently, this model survives in the planning ideology of Le Corbusier and in various aspects of urban renewal and planning practices which hitch the expertise of specialists to the power of centralised government to impose a plan on a site the experts find unwholesome. In a top-down structure, regions, provinces, and towns, and a range of specialised agencies, are given authority and tasks by the central regime. Universities and other institutions are organs of that regime. And the citizen has only those political and property rights given by the regime.

The American polity is a mixed top-down and bottom-up system. Its bottom-up component recognises that government originates at the smallest, least unit which is the individual. The individual's way of life, or regime, is the base upon which any larger polity or regime is formed. There will always be such larger entities because no one can avoid living with others; even during his time at Walden Pond, David Henry Thoreau regularly enjoyed the society of visitors there and in the nearby town of Concord. The parts of the regime in which the individuals participate multiply according to their inclinations and energies to form a graded hierarchy rising upward and expanding outward from bicycle club or condominium association at one end to the largest unit, the federal government defined in the Constitution, at the other.

A review of United States history reveals a wide array of different relationships between the bottom-up rights and the top-down powers that change over time and according to regional traditions. The best buildings and urban settings have always manifested an active interchange between the two extremes with the individual giving something up to a larger entity and receiving something in return that only that larger entity could supply. People willingly taxed themselves to build inspiring public buildings and bound themselves to restrictive land covenants to assure handsome street frontages, often within a clearheaded understanding of how the smaller unit fitted into the larger whole. The courthouse town was characterised by something that was unmistakably the courthouse. A university town was crowned by a place that looked like a university, although the particular university might be as different in time, place and appearance as the University of Virginia is from the University of California. And in Chicago, the vision of what a coherent city looked like was found in forms as diverse as the Burnham and Bennett Plan published in 1909, the controls already imposed on houses fronting on West Side boulevards planned in 1869, and the restrictions their builders imposed on the commercial buildings planned for the post-World War I Michigan Boulevard.

Occasionally, circumstances are propitious to producing architectural and urban complexes dynamically balancing the contending top-down and bottom-up claims that animate our polity. The recent past has not produced them, but a more distant past has. To see them and thereby learn from them, we need to look at them with traditional eyes which recognise that cities are built to serve purposes that governments can fulfill and which buildings must serve. Simply put: no purpose, no government; no government, no city. Or, to put it positively, from people to purpose, purpose to government, and government to city. That is the order necessary for good city building in America.

A useful place to look in order to learn what the character of good city building is in America would be the same place we look for instruction in the political basis of our country, to the work of the founding fathers. Among them no one was more

73

articulate, in both words and architectural and urban design, than Thomas Jefferson. Jefferson designed three distinctive American cities of three different sizes – the federal capital of Washington which was built according to someone else's design, the state capital of Virginia in Richmond where his state house was built while his ideas about the larger city plan were only partially carried out, and the smallest and best of the group which was completed in its entirety at the University of Virginia. Among these, the University is Jefferson's best model of what the characteristics are of a distinctive American linking of purpose, government, and urban form.

Jefferson intended that the example of his village be considered a model. We may take his meaning to be that a model contains what is true and an example embodies it. In examining an example we seek to see the model. The true things it exemplifies are still valid because if something is true once, it is always true. Truth does not change from time to time and from place to place. Jefferson held that it is a self-evident truth that all men are created equal and are endowed by their creator with certain inalienable rights. That was true then, and it is true now. In the same manner, then as now, it is true that in the normative situation, a people's purpose is embodied in its government which is in turn embodied in its city. Our problem, then, is to find the physical characteristics of the academical village that make it a good, normative model for a city and are to be imitated in making a city patterned after its model because those characteristics are true no matter the circumstances of time or place of their appearance.

The academical village contains the model for an American city even though it is a mere village and is less than a city, less than a state, and less than a nation. This is so because whether the model be exemplified in an action, a law, or an urban setting, in the American system something that is merely smaller may not settle for a lesser justice in its administration of authority, a lesser order in its arrangement of affairs, or a lesser beauty in its parts and whole. The academical village was lesser and smaller only because it was more specialised. Because it is smaller it can more easily reveal the model than a larger and more complex example.

The purpose for which the university was founded was clearly stated: it was to raise citizens who could exercise the authority of government to assure the fruits and benefits of liberty. That purpose was translated into a clear programme for the form of the instruction, the content of the curriculum, and the design of the buildings and their assemblage into what the founder called his academical village. Jefferson saw it as a place where the authority of knowledge in the form of a way of life and a place for living that life governed the place's citizens who in this case were teachers and students.

In looking at the example we must seek the characteristics of the model and not of the example. The example is in the classical style characterised by columns, piers, arches, lintels, load bearing masonry walls, cornices, and other aspects of building that are characteristic of the circumstances prevailing when the example was built. The role those elements play in embodying the character of the model must be present in some form in all circumstances, but this is not the place to take up the issue of how these elements vary in different circumstances. Our concern now is another level of architectural and urban design, one that is more abstract and therefore less easy to extract from the visual appearance of things. But even though it is abstract, it deals first and foremost with the physical characteristics of the academical village including both its buildings and the things that are not buildings, that is, its roads, paths, and open spaces.

What the model illustrates may be organised in any number of ways. What follows is one concatenation of nine characteristics

intended as a coherent and complete whole which must all be present in some form in any entity that claims civic status within the American polity, be it precinct, village, town, city, state, or nation. This is said with a recognition that while this concatenation can be coherent, it cannot be complete, for the same reason that a narration of an action that is indubitably just or noble can convey a coherent understanding of the action but cannot convey the full justice or nobility it embodies.

In the architectural and urban design, there must be:

1 A clear separation of the parts into discrete units.

   One assurance that such a separation is present is found in the ability to name the parts, for without coherent identities, there cannot be a coherent assemblage. At the University, the names are clear and familiar after even the briefest introduction by a native: that is the Rotunda, that is the Lawn, those are the pavilions and the colonnades, ranges, paths, walls, gardens, and roadways, and that was the anatomical theatre.

2 A clear representation of the functional role each part plays.

   This, too, requires an introduction but not a full explanation of every part: if the Rotunda is a library and a pavilion is a professor's house, then anyone can figure out where the students live and where they eat.

3 A hierarchical distinction between the parts revealing which are more important and which are less important in fulfilling the purpose of the whole.

   Imagine this: if Jefferson had been designing an institution for a top-down polity, he might have put a rector in the Rotunda (in his foundation it was administered by a faculty committee) and distributed the books among the professors' pavilions.

4 An appearance for each part that allows it to be distinct while also allowing it to appear as a part of the larger whole to which it belongs.

   Each of the more important parts is a separate and distinctly designed unit, all interchangeable with one another but clearly part of this whole and not an alien from elsewhere, with a variety of different examples of the same class of thing (eg, columns, entablatures, tabernacle windows) pervading the whole. Meanwhile there is an even larger whole of which this is a lesser entity: it is in Rome, in Washington, and in Richmond, as well as at Monticello and in the Massachusetts State House in Boston.

5 A clear geometric scheme controlling the disposition of the parts and their relationships to one another and to the whole. The geometry does not necessarily carry a content by being based on various traditional proportions or by possessing putative symbolic meanings. The geometry gives evidence of a coherence in design and reveals that the design is based on forethought and can be justified – there are this many rooms of this size, in this sequence in this length of Lawn because . . .

6 A clear gradation of spaces and uses ranging from public to private.

   The physical configuration must both accommodate and represent the character of the bottom-up basis for the polity by making thresholds available for privacy. But it must also provide for the top-down authority by making public places available for the assembly or simply mingling of those who consent to the form that authority takes. The Lawn and Rotunda are totally public, the student rooms and the upper floors of the pavilions which were intended for the professors' families are totally private.

7 A clear demarcation between what belongs to it and what does not – in this case, between the civilised space of the university and the expansive wilderness surrounding it.

   Now effaced, the original design revealed a clear sequence from the uncut wilderness through the gardens to the Lawn.

The edge made clear the limit of the village's authority, and the Lawn presented with absolute clarity the normative condition of the civil landscape that the wilderness would become.

8   The exclusion from the form of the design of those things that are needed but are not capable of being included with decorum.

This requires a sense of decorum; not everything is allowed. It also acknowledges that some things that are required must be excluded from the civil realm they serve. (After Romanticism converted wilderness from uncivilised landscape where undecorous things could be placed into a positive alternative to an urban setting, there was nowhere to put these things.) Current knowledge and experience allowed Jefferson to include privies within the academical village, but the anatomical theatre had to be exiled just beyond the edge. It was a unique thing whose danger to health was known but where the remedy to that threat was not.

9   And, finally, as Jaquelin Robertson has observed, residences dominate and establish the primary character of the place.

The design of both the buildings and their dependent landscaped areas begins with the form required for the individual pavilions and student rooms. They predominate in the design as a whole. And their assemblage into larger wholes dictates the circulation routes.

Each of these nine characteristics flows from the purpose the physical complex is to serve which in turn dictates the form given the organisation of the authority that governs the activities of those seeking to fulfill that purpose. Simply put once again: from purpose to government and from government to city, in this case Jefferson's academical village. What one finds here one finds also in any well-built American city, any of which could be used to exemplify the model of what is distinctly American in classical urbanism.

But haven't the gifts of modern science – the miracles of technology, the sophistication of the social sciences, the freedom from former ignorance about how the physical world works – made it clear that a city is merely the reflection of the ever changing, new demands of the present? Is it not so that because times change, so too must cities? Is it not the case that whatever the academical village exemplifies, it is obsolete because in these changed circumstances, we cannot or should not build that way any more?

My claim is not about the primacy of circumstances but about the primacy of something that does not change. It is that purpose begets government and that government builds cities. When we forget that, when we forget that liberty requires a government that blends bottom-up and top-down principles, we let our governments, whether they be the ones that govern a university or the nation or any of the larger and lesser units in between, serve less than the best purposes and fall into disarray. The condition of American architecture and urbanism suggests we have fallen into the thought that the authority we possess as independent individuals is superior in all instances to the authority we possess in common and vest in government. Can we expect better if we no longer honour the cardinal principle of good urban form, that those who live in the city build it, and those who build the city live in it? In thinking that individual liberty is opposed to government and that individual rights can be secured with some means other than the authority of government, we have made it impossible to continue to build the classical American city which is the only distinctly American city.

RICHMOND, VIRGINIA, c 1846; STATE PENITENTIARY, CITY HALL, CAPITOL, GOVERNOR'S MANSION.

———— * ————

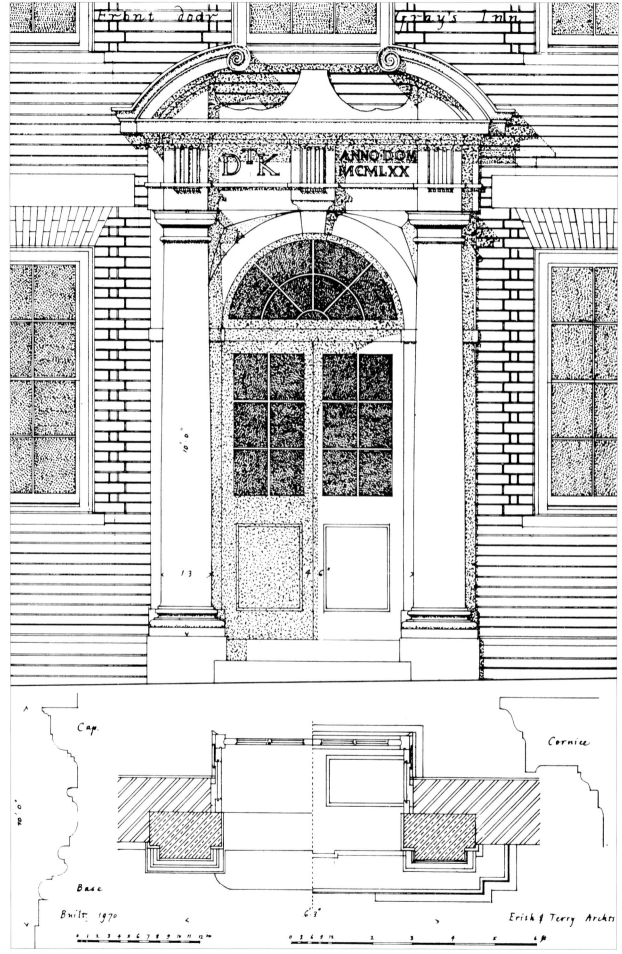

Front door   Gray's Inn

D K   ANNO DOM
           MCMLXX

Cap.   Cornice

Base

Built 1970   6'3"   Erith & Terry Archts

ERITH AND TERRY, 10 SOUTH SQUARE, GRAY'S INN, LONDON, 1970

THE AUTHORITY FOR ARCHITECTURE
QUINLAN TERRY

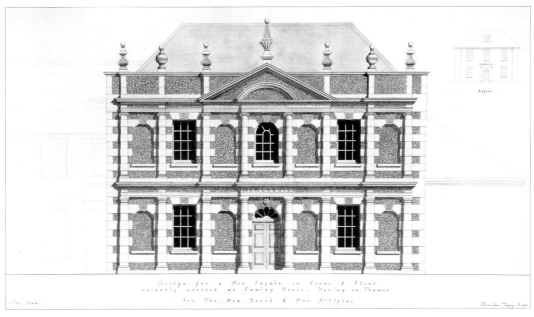

QUINLAN TERRY, FAWLEY HOUSE, HENLEY-ON-THAMES, 1989

ONE WONDERS WHY . . .
THE SEVEN WONDERS OF THE MODERN WORLD

1
Do you ever wonder why old buildings were symmetrically planned with the front door in the middle, whereas modern buildings are not?

2
Do you ever wonder why Georgian windows are right in size and proportion, whereas modern windows are not?

3
Do you ever wonder why old buildings do not have *expansion joints*, whereas modern buildings crack without them?

4
Do you ever wonder why old materials last for hundreds of years, whereas modern materials do not?

5
Do you ever wonder why old buildings are genuine and express their structure (be it brick, timber or stone) whereas modern buildings are usually clad in a veneer?

6
Do you ever wonder why old buildings in cities were arranged in terraces and squares, whereas most modern schemes need point blocks to achieve the same plot ratio?

7
Do you ever wonder why old buildings are so easy on the eye, whereas modern buildings are not?

In short, do you ever wonder why all the buildings of the past (particularly those in the 17th and 18th centuries) are so good in function and appearance, whereas all the buildings of this age are not? The answer is simple. There has been a revolution in architecture, the old order has been killed and the pigs have taken over. As in *Animal Farm*, the time was ripe for revolution, because the classical tradition had become so degraded and weak; but we are now feeding on the husks that the pigs have left behind, and the time is now right for a counter-revolution.

QUINLAN TERRY, THE ORIGIN OF THE DORIC, IONIC AND CORINTHIAN ORDERS

THE AUTHORITY FOR ARCHITECTURE
AND HOW IT SHOULD DEVELOP IN THE FUTURE

Until recently it was felt that the modern style had come to stay and that architecture should continue to develop along modernist and technological lines. However, in the last few years more and more people have become disenchanted with the appearance and durability of modern buildings and unconvinced by the intellectual arguments which support them. They have therefore tended to look back to see how people made buildings in the past and have suggested that traditional architecture in some form should be a viable alternative to what we see being built all around us today. The argument between Modernism and Traditionalism is debated more and more vehemently and has now become the main issue in the architectural scene. I come to you as a convinced traditionalist having spent all my working life erecting classical buildings and I hope to show you, not only that it is possible to build this way today, but that it is better than the modern approach. I therefore give you eight important authoritative principles from which to look at this subject.

1 Materials

The traditional materials are brick, lime mortar, stone, stucco, slate and timber. The modern materials are cement, steel, reinforced concrete, glass, aluminium, plastics, asphalt, roofing felt and asbestos.

From a technological point of view the traditional materials have one overriding advantage to all the modern materials which is that they remain virtually inert with daily and seasonal changes in temperature. Technically speaking, the coefficient of thermal expansion on stone and brickwork in lime mortar is so minor that it is absorbed within the mass and flexibility of the wall. But the coefficient of thermal expansion on reinforced concrete and steel is considerable, and the figure for aluminium and laminated plastics is about double that of reinforced concrete. In practical terms this means that a modern structure will move with changes of temperature to such an extent that it will crack unless expansion joints are designed into the fabric at regular intervals (about 20ft centred vertically and horizontally). This expansion joint must be filled with a pliable material such as mastic in order to keep the structure weathertight. All mastics break down under ultra-violet light and will fail in ten years. In most European countries driving rain beats upon the walls horizontally and enters the structure at the weakest point: the expansion joint. This sets up corrosion to the reinforcement and other adjacent materials, out of sight, and is the chief cause of decay and ultimate collapse of modern buildings. For this reason modern structures have a very limited life. Traditional structures, on the other hand, need no expansion joints and have none of these problems. That is why they last for hundreds of years and can be repaired and reused indefinitely.

One also ought to consider the cost in terms of high consumption of fossil fuels in the production of traditional and modern materials. Stone and sand only needs to be quarried. Bricks need to be fired in a kiln, but many bricks, like Flettons, are made of a shale that burns by itself through the brick. On the other hand the temperatures required for making cement, steel and large sheets of glass require a very high consumption of the earth's resources and are seriously damaging to the environment.

2 Construction

Following on from materials is modern and traditional construction. Modern construction for large buildings is invariably a steel or concrete frame to which is attached a veneer of walling, be it glass, brick, stone or plastic. These panels are held back to the frame with cramps (again out of sight for inspection).

Traditional construction for large buildings was invariably a solid thick loadbearing wall made of masonry with openings in the wall for windows and doors. The advantage of modern construction is primarily financial in that it can achieve a thin wall and a very high building which is of great advantage to the developer by cramming more space on to a limited site. Whereas a traditional building can only really be raised about six floors because the thickness in the brick wall becomes excessive at the lower levels if the number of floors is increased further. Traditionally, buildings were only raised to six storeys because, before the days of electric lifts, people would not wish to climb any higher. But too many people living and working on too small an area of land causes problems in our inner cities that are insoluble. These towers of Babel inevitably lead to confusion.

3 Windows

A traditional window was designed in such a way that it lit the space inside the room comfortably; that is, it was not too large or too small to make the room either too hot in summer or too cold in winter. Our forefathers found that a little over one tenth of the floor area was about right for reception rooms and slightly smaller for bedrooms. The windows were therefore arranged in the external wall in such a way that the rooms were well lit and could be easily furnished.

On the other hand, the modern window is normally vastly in excess of ten percent; sometimes it runs from wall to wall and from floor to ceiling. In this way the space inside can be very uncomfortable, hard to furnish and expensive to keep warm in winter and cool in summer.

4 Span of Rooms

Traditional buildings generally have a span of 20 feet from the window to the spine wall, making the complete span of the building 40ft with windows on either side. If you put your scale on the plans of 18th-century cities you will find that all the buildings, whether they are offices or houses, generally have a total span of about 40ft. This is because they found, by experience, that there was enough daylight to make rooms comfortable up to that span and it would be unreasonable to expect people to work more than 20ft from the external wall for light and air. The modern building has no discipline of this sort and often plans vast chasms of space away from the external walls, putting people in working conditions where they can only survive like broiler chickens with artificial air and artificial light. Not only is this not socially desirable for the people who are unfortunate enough not to work near an openable window, but it requires great expense in servicing, burning up the resources of the earth to keep people lit and ventilated in reasonable comfort. Of course, all this high consumption contributes to global warming.

5 Roofs
Traditional buildings always had a pitched roof which was covered with slate or tile and, on very flat pitches, lead. All pitched roofs, if correctly detailed, last for hundreds of years and provide the best protection to the rain. In order to pitch a roof properly one needs a simple plan underneath because of the geometry imposed by the pitches at the hips and valleys. Traditional buildings therefore generally have simple geometrical plans.

Modern buildings generally have flat roofs covered in asphalt or roofing felt. The life of these materials is very short indeed and is generally regarded as being 20 years maximum before major repair is required. The advantage of a flat roof is that it imposes no discipline on the architect: he does not have to consider solid geometry as he works on the arrangement of the plan and section so his untidy mind can conceive a building in any way he likes and simply cover it with a flat roof.

6 Symmetry
Symmetrical design is a characteristic of natural objects and is so obvious that it hardly needs to be described; everything that is beautiful is symmetrical. I do not mean that buildings must be identical about the centre line; and in fact, when you study human anatomy you will see that certain organs like the heart and liver are arranged on different sides, but the general physique of a building should strive at balance and symmetry. It is normal to have the entrance hall of a house (or large building) in the centre with the front door in the middle. In modern architecture all these natural principles are rejected under the specious pretence that it restricts the freedom in design. In fact it imposes a necessary discipline. So many modern plans are really a diagram worked out from the client's brief without being modified and assimilated into a consistent arrangement.

7 Beauty: The Orders
My last two points concern beauty. I have left this to the last because a building that does not have the other ingredients I have just described will never be beautiful. But having achieved these fundamental necessities it is also essential to express them in a way that is easy on the eye. In the past, beautiful forms in architecture have invariably found their expression in the five classical Orders: Tuscan, Doric, Ionic, Composite and Corinthian. I cannot tell you why they are so beautiful nor really when they originated, except to say that they are much older than Greece and probably go back to the dawn of history. I do not think it is necessary for one to believe that they were given to Moses when he built the Tabernacle in the wilderness or to Solomon when he built the Temple in Jerusalem, but it is necessary to believe in their intrinsic merit. They have an order and consistency of beauty which has always satisfied the taste of civilised men and societies.

Perhaps, for this reason, the Modern Movement has rejected all the Orders on principle. There is not one modern building which employs them. The raison d'être of modern design seems to be the rejection of all familiar classical principles and forms.

8 Beauty: Mouldings
Beauty in architecture is not simply these Orders but the mouldings that go on them. Not only have mouldings of this sort been developed over thousands of years as a combination of construction and weathering but also the shapes have been devised by the minds of men who notice the effect of light and shade and the casting of shadows on simple geometrical solids. Thus the cyma recta casts a hard shadow at the top and a softer shadow at the bottom, the corona casts a shadow right across the bed moulds but these can be penetrated by the modillions under the corona. It is this contemplative pleasure of light and shade which strikes a chord of appreciation in the minds of those who have eyes to see.

I think we are very poor judges of how our work will look in a hundred years time. It is important for us to realise that Palladio did not try to express his age when he built the Villa Rotunda but thought in terms of a Roman house; and yet, to us, it looks the epitome of the Quattrocento. Similarly Lord Burlington built Mereworth Castle in Kent which was the closest copy he could get to Palladio's Villa Rotunda. And yet, Mereworth does not look like Italy or the 15th-century but the epitome of 18th-century England. Somehow or another, whether it is the materials, the brief from the client or the way we detail our mouldings and weatherings, the age and the national characteristics always find their way into the end result. I have no doubt at all that my work will look like late 20th-century English Classicism.

QUINLAN TERRY, TROMPE-L'OEIL NYMPHAEUM AT WEST GREEN HOUSE, HAMPSHIRE, 1974

THAT THIS HOUSE WOULD BUILD TRADITIONAL BUILDINGS

I fear that we architects tend to think that the built environment is really the sole preserve of the architectural profession, whereas in fact it is of equal, if not greater concern to all those involved in the building industry and particularly the general public who use these buildings. The questions that this debate raises are not new; in fact almost every time I am invited to speak it is on a variation of this same theme. At a recent Architecture Club meeting the motion before us was this: Vitruvius, art thou sleeping here below? Is there a role for Classicism *today*?

When I debated with Richard Rogers at the Oxford Union in 1987 it was on the theme of 'How should Architecture be *developing*'. At Bath recently the theme was 'How can new buildings be erected in historic cities'. One could go on and on. But the reason the same theme keeps reoccuring is that ordinary people are *not happy* with the new buildings they see around them. It all seems to belie some deep-rooted and perhaps subconscious distrust of all things unnatural which have been thrust upon us by this brave new world of technological achievement. In the last year or two these feelings have been justified by a new awareness of environmental issues. . . Far more important than any whim of fashion is the question of which way of building is least harmful to our fast disintegrating planet.

I am sure we have all been involved in discussions on this theme on many occasions. Sometimes, lest I should seem too fanatical, I find myself trying to reassure my hearer by saying 'of course, I make *compromises*, I don't write with a quill; or I don't go to my office on horseback,' and then I wonder why I try so hard to curry favour with the opposition. For if you seek perfection you must study from the past; if you want to perfect your calligraphy you *must* use a quill; and if you are seriously concerned about the environment and the cumulative effect of high energy consumption, you will *long* for the day when you can walk to work.

The time is now overdue for us to ask: is it wise to use all the technology we have at our disposal?

We *can* now design hermetically sealed buildings, totally dependent on lifts and artificial light and air conditioning; (full of refrigerants and CFC's, and costing the earth to maintain) but what of the cost in global warming and human comfort? We *can* build 200 storeys high, but what about the infra-structure, the roads and railways, and crime at street level? We *can* erect structures in stainless steel and reinforced concrete and cover them in a veneer of plastic or curtain walling, but do we consider how to recycle these unfriendly materials when the buildings are worn out. . .

New materials! That's what is always being quoted against traditionalists. I've heard it all before. . . *ad nauseam*. They say: 'Why not move with the times? Why not experiment with new materials and the new methods of construction now at our disposal?' The answer is very simple: these new materials don't last, and the new methods of construction don't produce a permanent or waterproof structure – thus making nonsense of the first and foremost purpose of any building, which is to keep out the rain!

In Cambridge we all know of the plight of the History Faculty Building, and the number of recent buildings which have had to be re-roofed – just a few of the list of casualties of these new, ambitious, hitherto untried methods of building. They call it High-Tech, and it receives high praise and Gold medals from the RIBA but it never ceases to amaze me that an assortment of plastic and steel tubing clipped together around a perspex-clad frame and leaking at every joint can pose as a great technological achievement. How pathetically all this compares with any genuine traditional building, with thick masonry walls, properly proportioned windows and a slate roof; or like the Pantheon in Rome with its great brick dome and monolithic marble columns heaved into position 2000 years ago and still in daily use. That is the technology that should be our guide; and the first point it makes is that only natural materials can withstand the test of time . . . clay bricks, clay tiles, lime mortar, stone and slate. Incidentally, these materials cost a fraction of modern materials in terms of energy consumption – compare a stone quarry to a steel furnace. And they can always be reused – even lime mortar can be put on the land.

The great thing about traditional building is that it leads inevitably to architecture. If you allow yourself to design within the constraints imposed by traditional materials and construction (and if you are not frightened of the criticism you will undoubtedly receive) you will very soon discover the wisdom of the historic styles, be they classical or gothic. Thus we have, in this city, pendicular gothic at Kings College Chapel; Gibbs indulging in Italian pastiche at the Senate House; William Wilkins building Greek revival at Downing; and, a few years later, Gothic revival in the screen at King's Parade. For Classicism is a search for a universally valid form of architecture, and, of course, if something is universally valid, it is valid at all times. In that sense you are always doing something that has been done before.

So much for the intellectual arguments; but the general public don't need arguments – they use their eyes, and like the child in the Emperor's New Clothes, they state the obvious: don't we all know what we mean by an unspoilt village? It is not a village without any traditional buildings but one without any *modern* buildings.

As I see it, the choice is this. Are we to satisfy the short-lived lusts of a throw-away society with their glossy space-age structures, which suck out the earth's resources and leave behind a scrap heap of unrecyclable rubbish? Or do we return to sanity and build slowly and traditionally, like our forefathers; *preserving* our God given resources for the generations that are to come? If we want a future for our grandchildren, I propose that we build traditional buildings.

(*Note* 'Would': subjunctive mood and is the expression of a wish rather than an actual fact. It is the mood of doubtful assertion.)

THE RADIANCE OF THE PAST
ROBERT ADAM

ROBERT ADAM, STOKE PARK, STOKE POGES, HERTFORDSHIRE, 1990

After the darkness has been dispelled, our grandsons will be able to walk back into the pure radiance of the past. **Petrarch, Africa IX.**

Ten years of new classical architecture have given the revival an unavoidable historical significance. This significance was confidently denied classical architects by the modernist establishment at the start of the decade. Architectural practice and education have, nonetheless, continued to be dominated by the Modern Movement and New Classicism has been forced to grow up in the unique anti-historical atmosphere created by Modernism.

Belief in progress through revolution and the creative irrelevance of the past has made serious historical study a largely academic activity. The art of the past is considered to be of no practical interest and a contemporary artist would only benefit from social or spiritual observations of historical works. This has led to a misunderstanding both of the process of revival and of past revivals. It is a misunderstanding that is often shared by exponents of New Classicism.

New Classicism is only the latest of a continuing series of revivals that stretch back through history. Some, such as the Renaissance and Neo-Classicism, are well known; others, such as the Attic revival of the first century BC and the 12th-century Latin revival, are less familiar. The importance of these revivals in cultural history cannot be denied and it will be of some benefit to examine the historical phenomenon of revival in relation to the latest attempts to draw inspiration directly from the past.

To examine revivals it is necessary to define a revival: An architectural revival is the physical expression of an architect's desire to demonstrate to his public that he wishes to remind them of an historic building form specifically because it existed in the past and which, for some subsequent period of time, fell out of general use. This revival could occur several times or once, it could be done wholly or partially, it could be done accurately or inaccurately; it is still a revival.

Mimicry

The idea of revivalism as imitation or mimicry lies at the foundation of current critical attitudes to New Classicism. Even a cursory examination of these three acknowledged periods of revival does, however, reveal a much more complex picture than could be used to characterise anything that could be simply described as mimicry.

The Carolingian revival or *renovatio* is described by Richard Krautheimer, the leading historian of this period: 'the idea of *renovatio* was bound to include the most heterogeneous concepts: a "Golden Age" of undetermined antiquity; a pre-Byzantine Rome in which the church had been more independent; a fictitious Constantinian Rome in which Imperial power had been conferred on the Pope; the Rome of the Emperors . . ; and last but not least the Rome of the first Christian centuries where so many martyrs had died . . . All these different images of a Rome of the past were blended into one; and the ardent desire to revive the past was vital and compelling in the philosophy of policy of the eighth and ninth centuries. It is only natural that this idea of a return to the past should manifest itself in architecture.'[1] And, indeed, as surviving buildings such as the Lorsch Abbey gateway demonstrate, this manifestation seems as far from our image of direct copying as their understanding of classical Rome is from our own.

The idea that Italian Renaissance respect for Roman antiquity went so far as to include simple copying does not originate from either 15th-century buildings or 15th-century theorists, but from 16th-century mannerist authors. Both Brunelleschi's[2] and Bramante's[3] work, for example, contain Romanesque and proto-Romanesque elements and in 1542 Alberti considered that ancient architects 'do not . . . tie us down to follow them too closely, as to transcribe their very designs into this work of ours; but stir us up by their instructions to produce something of our own invention.'[4]

In the late 18th century and in the 19th century revivalist movements coincided with and were influenced by an increasing and scientific interest in archaeology and history. There is, as a result, a much greater accuracy in form and detail which can be mistaken for pedantic copying.

The distinction between revival and copying was, however, apparent to contemporary architects of both the classical and gothic schools. Lord Aberdeen's promotion of Greek revival warned against simple imitation 'such as would evince the frigid pedantry of the mechanic',[5] and Ruskin was careful to state that 'it is no sign of deadness in present art that it borrows or imitates, but only if it borrows without taking interest, or if it imitates without choice.'[6]

Contemporary descriptions of buildings often concentrated more on their originality than their revivalist qualities, and closer examination of many revivalist buildings reveals a preoccupation with functional and structural problems. It may be hard for us to reconcile high Gothic revival with Pugin's dictum that 'all really beautiful forms in architecture are based on the soundest principles of utility',[7] or to see, with Thomas Hope, an English building in the Greek style as being absolutely unique,[8] but this is how they were seen at the time.

This brief examination of these periods of revival raises some important issues. The Carolingian revival demonstrates that an erroneous or corrupted vision of the past can produce revivalist architecture. The Renaissance and 19th century show that our own view of revival as mimicry clouds our understanding both of the intentions of designers and of the formal content of their buildings. The definition of revival, given above, combined with these findings raises a further question: if the designer's intention to communicate is the basis of the definition of revival, and if we acknowedge that both an erroneous vision of the past can produce revivalist architecture and that our own vision of revivalist buildings can disguise the designer's intentions, are there more revivals than we realise?

In architecture and the other arts further revivals have, indeed, been identified. In sculpture a neo-Attic school drawing on earlier 'classical' models is known to have existed in the Hellenistic period. In the late Roman Empire a revival of earlier Roman architecture was recognised as long ago as 1764.[9] A 12th-century revival of sculpture and literature was established in 1927.[10] Burlington's Palladian revival in the early 18th century in Britain is well known but, due to the problems of distinguishing revival from survival, is rarely acknowledged as such.

It is clear that the principal periods of revival cannot be dismissed merely as periods of architectural mimicry. It is also clear that the phenomenon of revival is probably more widespread than is conventionally admitted. Before examining past revivals in more depth it is important to consider the problems and pitfalls which will be encountered in attempting to identify architectural movements as having a revivalist content.

The Identification of Revivals
Visual Evidence

From the 15th century onwards the mass of literary evidence for the motives of architects and the interpretation of architecture increases dramatically. It can, therefore, be a relatively straightforward task to demonstrate whether or not an architect intended to make a reference to an historic building form. As we go back into the Middle Ages and beyond the problem becomes greater as, not only do we have less and less first hand accounts of buildings, but the concept men had of their own past becomes harder to identify. Under these circumstances there is a tendency to rely increasingly on largely visual evidence.

The problem of visual evidence can be demonstrated by two modern views of the motives of the sculpture of the 13th-century Visitation Group on the front of Reims Cathedral. This very classical group is considered by Walter Oakshott,[11] on the basis of technical and comparative studies, to be inspired by revivalist motives. Henri Focillon, on the other hand, committed to the non-classical independence of gothic art, considers that the classical appearance is due to an unconscious 'natural correspondence of profound affinity'.[12]

This problem can be further complicated by the primarily archaeological discipline of stylistic dating, which, as it relies on the concept of continual stylistic development, tends to ignore the possibility of revivals (or at least stylistically accurate revivals) and copying. This has caused problems with the dating of Roman, Greek[13] and Egyptian[14] sculpture.

On the other hand, on visual evidence it is just as easy to create relationships between buildings of different periods that do not exist. Buildings by their function and construction have many common characteristics and humans seem to have a universal fascination with geometry.

Survival and Revival

Even if a relationship between the built form of two periods can be clearly demonstrated by something more than visual evidence, in order to be sure that it is a revival it is necessary to demonstrate that it is not a survival by estabishing that there has been an intervening period when this type of design fell out of general use. The distinction between survival and revival can be surprisingly difficult to establish.

In the first place, due either to accidental preservation or to our own partial view of history, we can hold a distorted view of what was significant at the time. A revival can pass undetected or a survival can be given less significance than is appropriate.

In the second place, in establishing whether a design feature is a survival or a revival the most important consideration is just how short a period of time can be said to constitute the necessary discontinuation of the use of that form. It is just such short periods of time that are most easily disguised by historical perspective and archaeological accident.

The current architectural climate can be used as an example. It is generally acknowledged that the present architectural revival began in about 1975. Classical architecture was being taught and practised widely until about 1955. In spite of the the short period of Modern Movement domination of architecture and the continuing trickle of neo-Georgian and surviving practitioners, no-one calls the present classical revival, in any of its forms, a survival.

This example highlights two important facts: relatively short periods of time can be sufficient to establish a suspension in the practice of an architectural type (although the frequency and speed of building must also be considered); the dominant architectural type or types must be considered.

Influence, Copying and Documentary Evidence
The few years that seem to be required to establish a sufficient break in usage to indicate a revival, complicated by some continuing practice throughout this break, raises the possibility of what seems to be a revival being no more than an unselfconscious stylistic influence uncoloured by any intention to refer to an historic style.

The common phenomenon of verbatim copying raises similar problems. While direct copying can be very important in revivals, some types of reproduction do not relate to historical aspects of the original but solely to its symbolic value in some other way, generally as an aspect of religious devotion. The reproduction of archaic religious images throughout antiquity and the continual construction of versions of the Gesú all over the world are examples of verbatim copying without intention to revive a style.

The only way out of these problems is by reference to contemporary documentary evidence. The most conclusie evidence is from the architect or a contemporary observer. In an attempt to understand or even establish the existence of any revival, and most particularly where there is little or no conclusive evidence, it is most important to attempt to understand the

tion of history and the changes brought about by differing ideas of history – the history of historiography – and yet examples of visual anachronism persist. When attitudes to history differed anachronisms not only increased but could become so pronounced as to almost disguise the original historic vision to modern historians.

Awareness of the process of historical change has a commensurate effect on the awareness of anachronism. After the destruction of the civilised political continuity of antiquity, the concept of history it fostered was also destroyed. In *Historians of the Middle Ages,* Beryl Smalley describes this attitude as it became a specific medieval outlook: 'The student of medieval art learns to accept flatness as a convention: it does not spoil his appreciation of the picture. In the same way the student of medieval historiography must learn to do without written perspective in historical presentation. A medieval writer could distinguish stages in the history of salvation, but they were religious stages. He did not discern change or development in temporal history. . . Past and present interlock: ancient precedents imposed themselves on the present; the past resembled the present as the historian saw it. He had no sense of anachronism.'[16]

REINTERPRETATIONS, *L TO R*: T HANSEN, ATHENS ACADEMY, 1859; ANDREA PALLADIO, VILLA EMO, FANZOLA, c 1567

particular vision of the relevant era, that is, the understanding men had of themselves and their past and how they related to their past both ideologically and visually.

Historical Vision
The vision each age has of its past is central to an appreciation of revivalism. As Herbert Butterfield says: 'Over and again we discover to what degree . . . men do their thinking and form their attitudes by reference to some presumed picture of a procession of the centuries. The framework which people give to their general history – the notion they have of man in time and of the process of time – may do much to determine the rest of their outlook.'[15]

Anachronism
Differing attitudes to the past, and in particular their relationship to the arts, are often represented by the changing perception of anachronism. As all ages are locked in their own particular appreciation of their surroundings, the past is always to some extent represented in contemporary terms. Since the 19th century Western society has had a strongly developed apprecia-

The rise of Humanism and the early Renaissance is famous for Lorenzo Valla's exposure of the forgery of the Donation of Constantine in 1439. This was based on the evidence of both historical and philological change and is a classic example of the new sense of history.[17] Only a few years later Filarete wrote in his *Treatise on Architecture*: 'if you have to represent antiquity do not dress them in modern dress. Do not do as many I have already seen who alter the suitability of clothing. Frequently they have given modern dress to ancients.'[18]

Reinterpretation
The gradual development of an analytical and archaeological attitude to history since the Renaissance has presented a clear, if not always accurate, picture of the differences between past societies and their works of art. With this knowledge history has been viewed critically and from time to time some periods have come into favour, others have passed out of favour and artistic revivals have reflected these changes.

Reinterpretation is not, however, limited to this familiar phenomenon of changing attitudes to architectural styles. It can also be found in the adaptation of specific aspects of past styles to new buildings. This is most apparent in the adjustment of the meaning of classical architecture and particular classical details, derived from pagan temples, to Christian churches.

This issue preoccupied renaissance architects who were aware of the fact that, by reviving Roman architecture, they were creating a distinction between contemporary gothic architecture and a different architecture which was known to be associated with paganism.[19]

Such an awareness, if it existed, was not so clearly defined in the Middle Ages. Attitudes to history, already described, limited the concept of literal reconstruction. Classical themes do, nonetheless, appear in a religious context.[20]

Changing attitudes to an historical period can alter the meaning of buildings and details. This changing or progressive reinterpretation of the same historic information gave both mannerist and baroque architects the oppurtunity to distance themselves from the High Renaissance, while maintaining their interest in the revival of antiquity, by turning their attention to different features, such as large scale and rich decoration, on the same surviving buildings that had been studied by Brunelleschi and Bramante.[21]

At its most extreme the symbol can be reduced to no more than the plan form. In medieval architecture the plan can be one of the few recognisable references to the past.

Revivals of Revivals
As history is reinterpreted by successive generations, so the same period can fall out of favour and come back to prominence for a second and even a third time. Equally, a past epoch can be architecturally represented by a revival which can be revived in its own right. Furthermore, these two types of revival of revivals can be combined so that a revival can be revived and simultaneously lead the reviving architect to examine the period first revived. This type of progressive reinterpretation can lead from the revival of a revival to the revival of revival of a revival and beyond.

This confusing phenomenon finally demonstrates the complexity of the historical vision that can lie behind the apparently simple desire to revive a past architectural style. All architectural revivals will be based on a more or less incomplete understanding of the period which is being revived, will of necessity be founded on a contemporary reinterpretation of that period and

L TO R: SCHINKEL, CHARLOTTENHOFF, POSTDAM, 1829-36; OTTO WAGNER, FIRST VILLA, VIENNA, 1886-88

Symbolic Revival
In practice, very few buildings go so far as to literally recreate past buildings. Features of old buildings are copied, modified and assimilated to suit the functional, constructional or visual requirements of the period. Many of the details so adapted are more symbolic than directly representative of the architecture they seek to revive. In the 1960s, for example, the inclusion of a double pitched roof in any material symbolised traditional, and hence historic, building. The pitched roof has had extraordinarily powerful negative associations for modernists and its omission was the only stylistic condition that Mies van der Rohe placed on his chosen contributors to the 1927 Stuttgart Exhibition.

A number of building elements have had a simiiar effect. In the early gothic revival the presence of a pointed window in an otherwise classical building was sufficient to signify the style[22] and, by contrast, in the early Renaissance the round arch symbolised Classicism – for Filarete it was one of the hallmarks of the 'ancient manner of building'.[23]

Most reviving architects rely on symbolic revival to a greater or lesser degree, either deliberately or out of ignorance, and the symbol itself can be highly abstracted.

will be expressed with elements which symbolically represent the past.

Motivation
Now that the identification and background to revivals can be clearly understood, it is possible to return to the definition of an architectural revival and the intentions of the architect. To understand a revival it is essential to understand the motives of the architect. Although there is a tendency to assume that revivals are no more than nostalgic yearnings for a past age that can never be recovered, reviving architects have been just as aggressive in claims for originality, functionalism or morality as were the exponents of the Modern Movement.

Reverence and Romanticism
One underlying motive can be said to constitute the prime motive for revival. A wholehearted revival is unlikely to exist without a deep-rooted reverence or respect for the revived style. The effort involved in introducing what will, at some time, be a new representation of an historic building type, must, if it is to be executed with any conviction or merit, be undertaken with some

reverence for the historic sources.

There is consistent expression of just this kind of reverence and respect to be found where accounts of motivation have been recorded. In antiquity the only surviving architectural treatise is by Vitruvius who considered that the ancients 'reached perfection, approving only those things which if challenged, can be explained on the grounds of truth.'[25] Palladio states that it is always his opinion 'that the ancient Romans, as in many other things, so in building well, vastly excelled all those who had been since their time.'[26] Alberti can discount a critic by saying: 'I for my part have more faith in the men who built the Baths and the Pantheon and all those noble edifices than I have in him.'[27] Equally characteristic is Inigo Jones' view that 'who follows the best of the ancients cannot much err'[28] and Winkelmann's declaration that 'the only way for us to become great . . . lies in the imitation of the Greeks.'[29] The most extreme examples of this attitude occur when architectural reverence is combined with religious zeal. Pugin, for example, claims of Gothic that 'as the faith itself is perfect, so are the principles on which it was founded.'[30] This is in contrast to Nicholas Biddle of Philadelphia who, in 1806, announced that 'the two great truths in the world are the Bible and Greek architecture.'[31]

This reverence for the past can, in its more extreme forms, become romantic. Romanticism displays an anachronistic awe for the past. The past is transferred into a fictional world which, as it is viewed from a safe distance, commands an unreal respect for idealised characteristics which, at best, existed as a harsher reality. It seems to be an intensification of reverence into a passionate and distorting enthusiasm. While all visions of the past are to some extent distorted, reverence can exist without the extreme distortion of Romanticism, but Romanticism cannot exist without a kind of reverence. Romanticism is then a species or aspect of reverence; the aspect of reverence which is at the root of some kinds of anachronism.

Politics, Morality and Function

Reverence for the past alone rarely stimulates an architectural revival. It is necessary to look deeper but, as the past is searched for evidence of other motives, we find that the finer details of human intentions are lost and we are left with only the cruder impulses that can be seen to have changed history.

In the absence of other information, the tendency to see revivals as political expressions of broad historical movements is as irresistible as the tendency to see only the most broadly recognisable revivals. There is no reason to believe that this is not, at least broadly, correct and there is ample evidence for political attitudes to revival in well documented periods.[32]

Nationalism has been a consistent motive for revival. Pugin considered classical architecture to be essentially foreign and gothic, notwithstanding its French ancestry, to be essentially English.[33] Colin Campbell, on the other hand, when he wished to discredit English Baroque for being under the influence of 'things that are foreign' sought to revive the sterner Classicism of Inigo Jones, in spite of the Venetian origins of his architecture.[34] Ironically this same national baroque was revived in order to associate Edwardian nationalist ebullience with a 'time when architecture in England was on the progressive wane.[35]

The convictions that underlie political beliefs are closely associated with and are often expressed as moral obligations. The exhortation to moral action is the most powerful weapon in the political armoury. So too architecture and architectural revival have long been associated with exhortation to moral action in design. The earlier quotation from Vitruvius demonstrates that the moralising architectural concept of adhering to a truth displayed by an assumed set of natural laws existed in antiquity. This idea of truth to human proportions reappeared in the Renaissance under the influence of Vitruvius' surviving works and possibly from a neo-Platonic search for the physical expression of an ideal.

In the 19th century the new pragmatism of science and a moral revival were brought together in the gothic revival. In as much as the moral revival was a religious revival, so the use of morality as an essential architectural principle was associated with the revival of gothic architecture as an essentially Christian architecture.[36] At the same time gothic was promoted as both structurally and functionally correct.[37]

Although this relationship between morality and function remains unique to the gothic revival and its successor, the Modern Movement, the claim of Functionalism has not been limited to these movements. Palladio set out his reconstructions of ancient buildings not only for 'delight' but also so that 'lovers of architecture may thence receive great utility' and so that 'it may be very manifest how good the method was which the ancients observed in building.'[38] Even when the Counter Reformation called into question the church's whole classical legacy from the early Renaissance, Saint Charles Borromeo could still permit the use of the classical Orders in church building 'for the sake of structural durability.'[39] When any structural motives for revival were negated by the advance of engineering science in the 19th century, classical revivalists turned against the gothic revival later in the century on the basis of constructional practicability, claiming that Gothic was 'totally unsuited to modern requirements.'[40] The repetitive nature of classical detail was thought to be most suitable for industrialised building production.[41]

Originality, Primitivism and Eclecticism

The motive for revival which is at once most obvious and most unexpected is the desire to be original. It is obvious in the sense that any revival must occur after a sufficient break in the use of the revived style and, as a new architectural movement, must be seen to be different to the contemporary style it seeks to displace. Originality is only surprising if revivalism is regarded as mimicry, and we have now established that this is an inaccurate and misleading view. Even the most reverent attitude to the past would not preclude the possibility of a desire to be original. Revival as a means of achieving originality can take a number of different forms.

The most characteristic route to originality in revival is through discovery. In 15th-century Italy, for example, the discovery of the classical past after, what they considered to be, a millennium of barbarism was so dramatic a revelation as to make the adoption of classical forms a startling innovation.

The visual impact of a newly revived style can be such that the motive for originality becomes the intention to surprise or shock by stylistic contrast. This is well expressed by Lord de la Warr's reaction to Stuart's Greek revival work for Lord Nuneham: 'God damn by blood, my lord, is this your Grecian architecture? What villany! What absurdity! If this be Grecian, give me Chinese, give me Gothick! Anything is better than this!'[42] Of course, when Greek became the fashion it lost its capacity to shock and, as James Elmes shows, the time became right for surprises of a different nature: 'we had converted Greek architecture into the most humdrum sort of design. nay it seems to have paralysed our powers of design and composition altogether, so that the only alternative left was to escape from it by plunging *headlong* into Gothic and Italian styles.'[43]

The choice of style in itself can be a means of achieving an original result. If a style is revived because that style has a reputation for novelty, originality can be sought by association with it. The revival of baroque architecture at the end of the 19th century was partly motivated by the freedom of interpretation of classical themes peculiar to that style.

Running through these particular aspects of the search for originality in revival is the simple desire to be original for its own sake. This does not seem to have been hindered by the knowledge that a revival is always something derived to a greater or lesser extent from the work of others.

The consequences of the pursuit of originality when coupled with revivalist intentions can have diverse consequences. The search for new and relevant aspects of our architectural past has, from time to time, led the designer and theorist into an imaginary world of innocent and primitive architecture. This not only had the advantage of apparently allowing the accretions of civilised perception to be removed to reveal a more truthful and direct conception of architecture but also had the benefit of producing some very unusual forms. Primitivist ideas of this kind influenced both the gothic revival and Neo-Classicism.

The Greek revival was faced with the task of establishing the validity of primitive forms in the face of the 18th-century concept of progressive betterment which saw classical architecture gradually improving since antiquity. The idea that a return to Greek architecture was a return to purer form was met with derision: 'They might with equal success oppose a Hottentot and a baboon to the Apollo and the Gladiators as set up Grecian architecture against the Roman.'[44]

Classical architecture in particular offers the opportunity of mixing revivals by the selection of details and forms from different periods. It is questionable whether eclecticism of this type constitutes a revival, in as much as the intention of the designer may not be to remind the observer of some specific period of the past. Eclecticism can, however, be regarded as a series of symbolic revivals gathered together on a single building. As classical architecture, and to a lesser extent gothic architecture, have developed over several centuries within a continuing tradition, the eclectic use of elements from different periods within this tradition can be used to advantage to create distinctive and original designs which have complex associations with the past.

The analysis of revivalism involves much of the history of Western architecture with all the complexity and variety that this would imply. We can now see New Classicism not only as the continuation of the traditional development of Western architecture but also the act of revival itseif as the rebirth of one of the underlying motive forces in architectural progress.

It should no longer be possible to see revivals in terms of the pejorative caricatures of Modern Movement historians. These were based on the naive belief that Modernism was a revolution that had eliminated artistic development through the medium of its own history. The survival and even the success of New Classicism has demonstrated that the promised 20th-century artistic revolution, like so many of this century's revolutions, ended in the 1980s. With the burden of modernist history cast off, New Classicism can breathe freer and more invigorating air.

Notes

1 Richard Krautheimer, 'The Carolingian Revival of Early Christian Architecture', *Art Bulletin* Vol XXIV 1942.
2 Peter Murray, *Architecture of the Italian Renaissance*, ch 2.
3 *ibid*, ch 5.
4 Leon Battista Alberti, *Ten Books on Architecture*, 1485. Leoni edn 1755, bk I, ch IX.
5 Earl of Aberdeen, Introduction to Gwilt's edn of Vitruvius, 1823.
6 John Ruskin, *The Seven Lamps of Architecture*, 1849, ch V para IV.
7 A Welby Pugin, *The True Principles of Pointed or Christian Architecture*, London 1841, p 12.
8 Thomas Hope, *Observations on the Plans and Elevations* designed by James Wyatt for Downing College Cambridge, 1804.
9 Robert Adam, *Introduction to Ruins of the Palace of the Emperor Diocletian at Spalato*, 1764.
10 C H Haskins, *Renaissance of the Twelfth Century*, 1927.
11 Walter Oakshott, *Classical Inspiration in Medieval Art*, London, 1979.
12 Henri Focillon, *Art d'Occident*, 1938. Phaidon English edn 1963.
13 In particular by Prof Brunhilde Sismondo Ridgway of Bryn Mawr College, Philadelphia.
14 W Stevenson Smith, *Art and architecture of Ancient Egypt*, London 1958.
15 Herbert Butterfield, *Man on his Past*, 1955, ch 1.
16 Beryl Smalley, *Historians in the Middle Ages*, 1974.
17 Valla exposed the Donation of Constantine, the claim that Constantine had given temporal power in the West to the Pope forged in the Middle Ages, on the basis of that period's lack of historical perspective.
18 A Filarete, *Treatise on Architecture*, 1465.
19 In particular the substitution of pagan symbols of sacrifice with Christian symbols.
20 Also the adaption of ancient relics for Christian use, for example, the 11th-century Cross of Lothair contains pagan cameos and Abbot Suger of St Denis had an antique bowl converted into a chalice.
21 For example, Sansovino's Biblioteca Marciana was intended to achieve correct classical regularity and detail, and Sangallo's Porta S Spirito was said by Vasari to 'equal the works of the ancients'.
22 As Pugin said: 'Many architects apply the details and minor features of the pointed style to *classic* masses and arrangements.'
23 A Filarete, *op cit*.
24 This plan form was only represented by four examples in the early Christian era up to 400. They were all important buildings but did not establish a tradition until they were revived in the late eighth century.
25 Vitruvius, *The Ten Books on Architecture*, bk IV ch II. Trans W H Morgan, 1914.
26 Andrea Palladio, *The Four Books on Architecture* 1570, Isaac Ware edn 1738. Author's preface.
27 In a letter to Matteo de' Pasti, his site architect at Rimini *circa* 1450. The 'him' is a critic, Manetto.
28 From his notes. Quoted by James Lees-Milne, *Tudor Renaissance*, 1951.
29 J J Winkelmann, *Reflections on the Imitation of Greek Works in Painting and Sculpture*, 1755.
30 Pugin, *op cit*. Footnote p 10.
31 Said after a trip to Greece. The result was the Doric Columns on Philadelphia's Biddle Bank.
32 From 1888 lecture, *The Revival of Architecture*.
33 Pugin, *op cit*. p 66.
34 Quoted by Kerry Downes, Hawksmoor, 1969.
35 Speaker at the AA in 1898.
36 So Pugin *op cit*: 'Let the beautiful and the True be our watchword for future exertions in the overthrow of modern paltry taste and paganism, and the revival of Catholic art and dignity.'
37 See Violet-le-Duc and also the Church Building Act of 1818.
38 Palladio *op cit*. bk III Preface.
39 Anthony Blunt, *Artistic Theory in Italy 1450-1600*, 1940. The council of Trent and Religious Art.
40 Philip Webb, quoted by W R Lethaby, *Philip Webb and his Work*, 1935. Also comments of Goodhart-Rendell on the demise of the Arts and Crafts Movement.
41 Lionell Budden, *Town Planning Review*. Vol VI 1916-16.
42 Quoted by J Mordaunt Crook, *The Greek Revival*, 1972, part 1.
43 *ibid*.
44 Quoted by Mordaunt Crook, *op cit*.

———— * ————

JOHN BLATTEAU ASSOCIATES, RIGGS BANK, WASHINGTON DC, 1986

PICTORIAL SURVEY
FIGURATIVE CLASSICISM

JOHN BLATTEAU ASSOCIATES, THE BENJAMIN FRANKLIN DINING ROOM, US DEPARTMENT OF STATE, WASHINGTON DC, 1984

JOHN SIMPSON, *ABOVE*: PATERNOSTER SQUARE, LONDON, 1988; *BELOW*: VIEW FROM THE TOWER, PROPOSAL FOR LONDON BRIDGE CITY, 1989 (PAINTINGS BY CARL LAUBIN)

ALLAN GREENBERG, FARMHOUSE IN CONNECTICUT, 1979-83, *ABOVE*: LIBRARY; *BELOW*: ENTRANCE FACADE

ALLAN GREENBERG. *ABOVE*: OFFICES FOR BRENT PUBLICATIONS, NEW YORK CITY, 1985; *BELOW*: US DEPARTMENT OF STATE, WASHINGTON DC, 1984

LEON KRIER. BELVEDERE HOUSE. SEASIDE, MIAMI, FLORIDA. 1988 (PHOTOGRAPH BY STEVEN BROOKE)

LEON KRIER, HOUSE IN CORFU, 1988 (PAINTINGS BY RITA WOLFF)

LEON KRIER, *OPENING DAY*, ATLANTIS, TENERIFE, 1987, (PAINTING BY CARL LAUBIN)

CHARLES SHOUP, HOUSE IN KORONI, GREECE, *ABOVE*: DOOR DETAIL, *BELOW*: OVERALL VIEW

ROBERT ADAM, *ABOVE*: CROOKED PIGHTLE HOUSE, HAMPSHIRE, 1990; *BELOW*: DOGMERSFIELD PARK, HAMPSHIRE, 1986

DEMETRI PORPHYRIOS, HOUSE IN KENSINGTON, LONDON, 1987, VIEW OF HALL FROM LANDING

DEMETRI PORPHYRIOS, HOUSE IN CHEPSTOW VILLAS, LONDON, 1988, VIEW FROM THE STREET

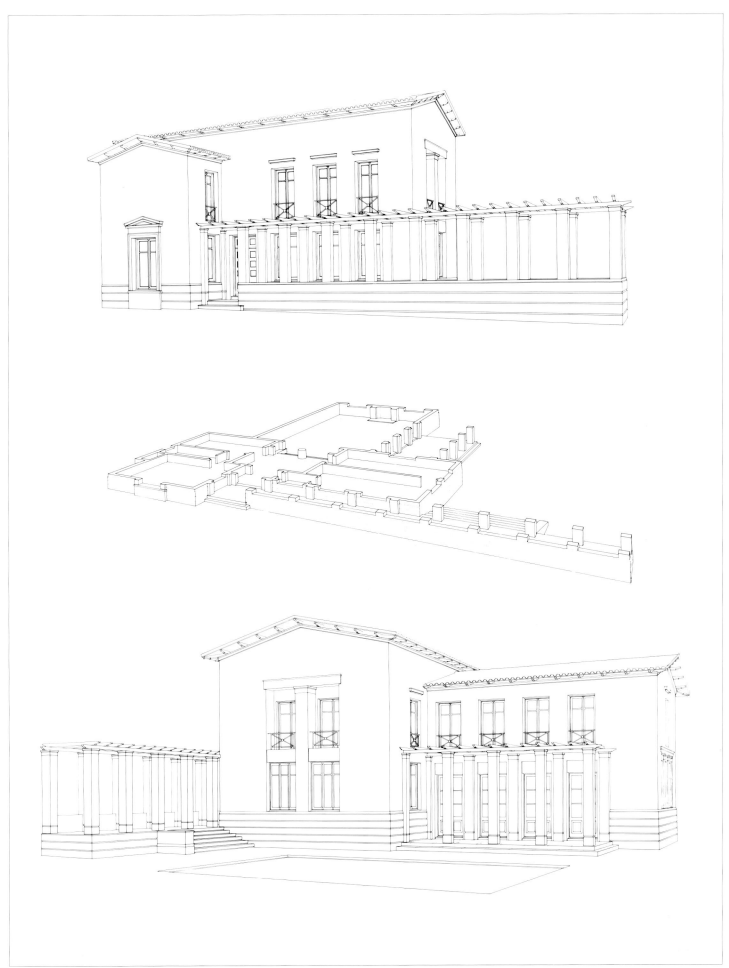

DEMETRI PORPHYRIOS, HOUSE IN ATHENS, 1990, *ABOVE*: VIEW FROM THE STREET; *CENTRE*: GROUND FLOOR; *BELOW*: VIEW FROM THE GARDEN

QUINLAN TERRY, HOWARD BUILDING, DOWNING COLLEGE, CAMBRIDGE, 1986, ENTRANCE ELEVATION

QUINLAN TERRY, RICHMOND RIVERSIDE, LONDON, 1988, DETAIL OF RIVERSIDE FRONTAGE

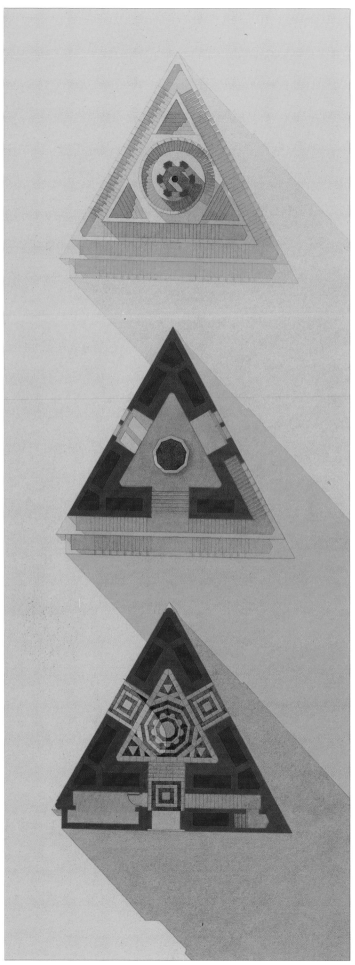

ABDEL WAHED EL-WAKIL, MIQAT MOSQUE MINARET, MEDINA, 1990

HAMMOND BEEBY & BABKA INC, *ABOVE*: THE HAROLD WASHINGTON LIBRARY CENTER, CHICAGO, ILLINOIS, COMPLETION 1991;
BELOW L TO R: THE DANIEL & ADA RICE BUILDING, THE ART INSTITUTE OF CHICAGO, ILLINOIS 1989; HOLE-IN-THE-WALL GANG CAMP, CONNECTICUT, 1988

COOPER, ROBERTSON & PARTNERS, PRIVATE RESIDENCE, EAST HAMPTON, NEW YORK, 1988, DETAIL OF WEST FACADE

COOPER, ROBERTSON & PARTNERS, *ABOVE*: ERTEGUN VILLA, EASTERN LONG ISLAND, NEW YORK, 1990; *BELOW*: REED GARDEN, KATANAH, NEW YORK, 1985

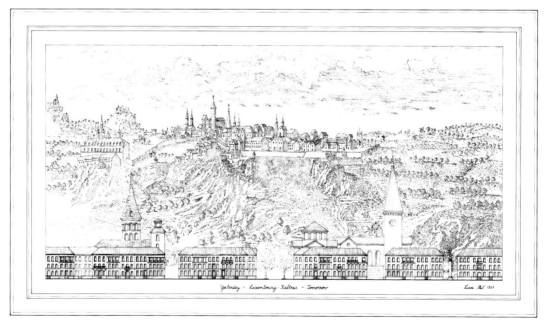

ARCHIVES D'ARCHITECTURE MODERNE, COMPETITION FOR THE RECONSTRUCTION OF RUE DE LAEKEN, BRUSSELS, 1989, *ABOVE*: LIAM O'CONNOR AND JOHN ROBINS, *CENTRE L TO R*:
JEAN-PHILIPE GARRIC & VALERIE NEGRE, JANUSZ P MACIAG. *BELOW*: LUCIEN STEIL, *YESTERDAY-LUXEMBOURG – KALTRIES-TOMORROW*, 1987

PIERRE BARBE, QUINTA DO VINAGRE, PORTUGAL, 1965-75, *ABOVE*: THE NEW WING; *CENTRE*: CORNER OF FARM; *BELOW*: STABLES

ABOVE: JULIAN BICKNELL, HENBURY ROTUNDA, CHESHIRE 1984; *BELOW*: CHARLES WARREN, LEVINE HOUSE, NEW YORK, 1990

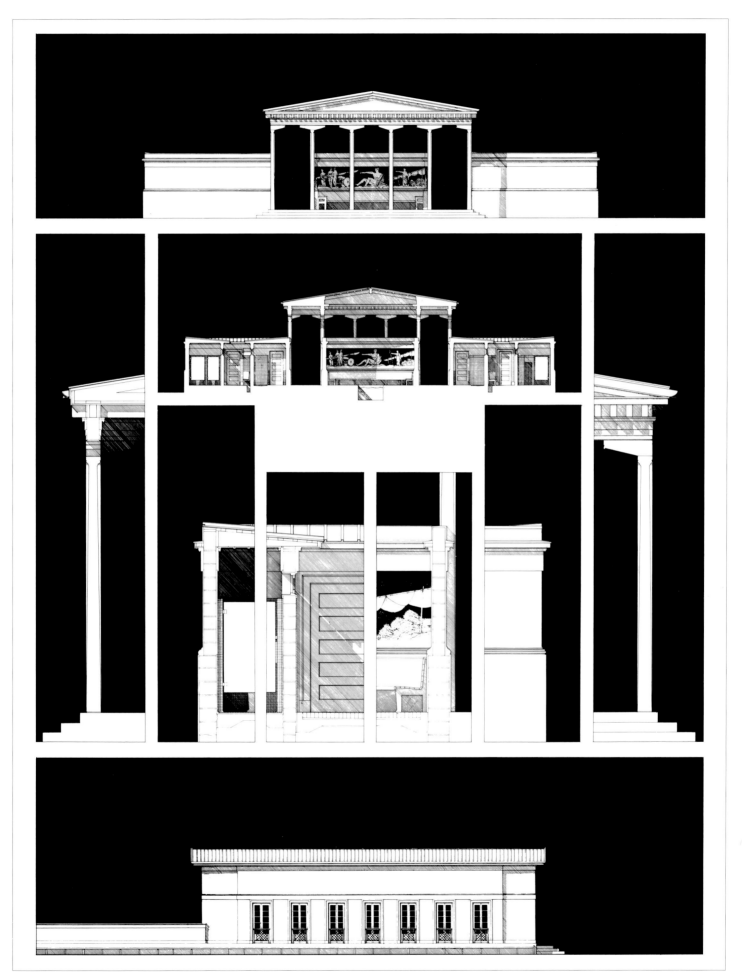

CHARLES BARRETT, BATH HOUSE PROJECT FOR SEASIDE, MIAMI, FLORIDA, 1990

ABOVE: CHAPMAN TAYLOR PARTNERS, BESSBOROUGH GARDENS, LONDON, 1988; *BELOW*: JAMES GORST & ASSOCIATES, HOUSE AT PIE CORNER, BEDMOND, HERTFORDSHIRE, 1990

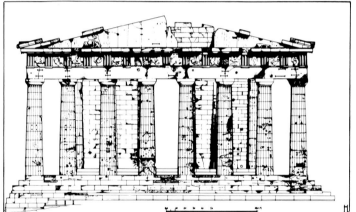
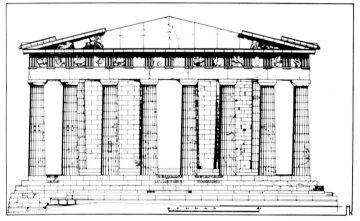

THE RECONSTRUCTION OF THE ACROPOLIS, ATHENS, *ABOVE*: THE ERECTHEION; *CENTRE*: M KORRES, PARTHENON, EAST AND WEST FACADES, ACTUAL STATE IN 1983 AND PROPOSED
RECONSTRUCTION; *BELOW*: DETAIL OF RECONSTRUCTION OF THE ERECTHEION

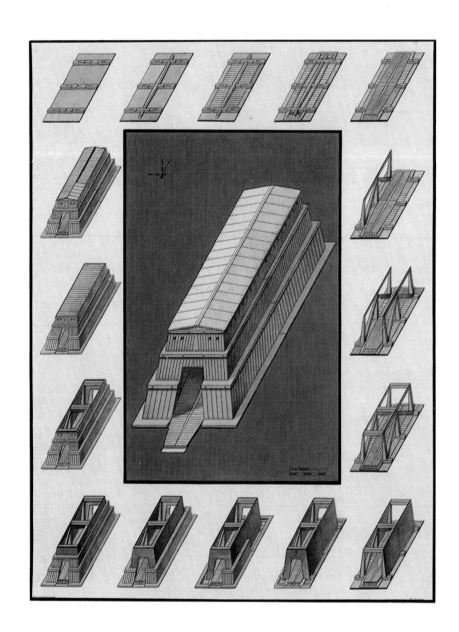

MASSIMO SCOLARI, MONTAGE SEQUENCE OF THE ARK, 1986

III

ABSTRACT CLASSICISM

FREART DE CHAMBRAY, *PARALLÈLE DE L'ARCHITECTURE ANTIQUE AVEC LA MODERNE*, PARIS, 1650

ON THE TYPOLOGY OF ARCHITECTURE
GIULIO CARLO ARGAN

Most modern critics who depend ultimately on some form of idealistic philosophy would deny that an architectural typology could in any way be valid. They are right in so far as it would be absurd to maintain that the formal value of a circular temple is increased as it approaches an ideal 'type' of circular temple. Such an ideal 'type' is only an abstraction; so it is inconceivable that an architectural 'type' could be proposed as a standard by which the individual work of art could be valued. On the other hand it cannot be denied that architectural typologies have been formulated and passed down in theoretical treatises and the work of famous architects. It is therefore legitimate to postulate the question of typology as a function both of the historical process of architecture and also of the thinking and working processes of individual architects.

There is an obvious analogy between architectural typology and iconography: typology may not be a determining factor of the creative process, but it is always in evidence much as iconography is in figurative arts, though its presence is not always obvious. How does an architectural 'type' appear? Those critics who would admit that 'types' have a certain importance are those who explain architectural forms in relation to a symbolism or to a ritual pattern connected with them. This kind of criticism has not resolved (and cannot resolve) a crucial problem: does symbolic content exist before the creation of the 'type' and determine it – or is it just a subsequent deduction? This question of precedence is, however, not decisive where it is considered in the context of an historical process; when symbolic content precedes the 'type' and determines it, this content is only transmitted in connection with certain architectural forms; in the same way when the reverse happens, the succession of forms transmits the symbolic content in a more or less conscious manner. There are cases in which symbolic content is sought for consciously as a link to an ancient formal tradition; such a procedure may become an important consideration by virtue of its historical and aesthetic function. Two test cases of a conscious linking of architectural form with ideological content are those of the symbolism of centralised religious building of the Renaissance studied by Wittkower; and that of a Baroque architectural allegory studied by Sedlmayr.

Quatremère de Quincy gives a precise definition of an architectural 'type' in his historical dictionary. The word 'type', he says, does not present so much an image of something to be copied or imitated exactly as the idea of an element which should itself serve as a rule for the model . . . 'the model understood as part of the practical execution of art is an object which should be imitated for what it is; the "type" on the other hand is something in relation to which different people may conceive works of art having no obvious resemblance to each other. All is exact and defined in the model; in the "type" everything is more or less vague. The imitation of "types" therefore has nothing about it which defies the operation of sentiment and intelligence . . .'

The notion of the vagueness or generality of the 'type' – which cannot therefore directly affect the design of buildings or their formal quality – also explains its generation, the way in which a 'type' is formed. It is never formulated *a priori* but always deduced from a series of instances. So the 'type' of a circular temple is never identifiable with this or that circular temple (even if one definite building, in this case the Pantheon, may have had and continues to have a particular importance) but is always the result of the confrontation and fusion of all circular temples. The birth of a 'type' is therefore dependent on the existence of a series of buildings having between them an obvious formal and functional analogy. In other words, when a 'type' is determined in the practice or theory of architecture, it already has an existence as an answer to a complex of ideological, religious or practical demands which arise in a given historical condition of whatever culture.

In the process of comparing and superimposing individual forms so as to determine the 'type', particular characteristics of each individual building are eliminated and only those remain which are common to every unit of the series. The 'type' therefore, is formed through a process of reducing a complex of formal variants to a common root form. If the 'type' is produced through such a process of regression, the root form which is then found cannot be taken as an analogue to something as neutral as a structural grid. It has to be understood as the interior structure of a form or as a principle which contains the possibility of infinite formal variation and further structural modification of the 'type' itself. It is not, in fact, necessary to demonstrate that if the final form of a building is a variant of a 'type' deduced from a preceding formal series, the addition of another variant to the series will necessarily determine a more or less considerable change of the whole 'type'.

Two salient facts show that the formative process of a typology is not just a classifying or statistical process but one carried out for definite formal ends. Firstly, typological series do not arise only in relation to the physical functions of buildings but are tied to their configuration. The fundamental 'type' of the circular shrine for instance, is independent of the functions, sometimes complex, which such buildings must fulfil. It was only in the second half of the 19th century that an attempt was made to set up a typology based on the order of physical functions (typical plans for hospitals, hotels, schools, banks, etc) which, however, has not produced any important formal results. Historical 'types', such as centrally planned or longitudinal temples, or those resulting from a combination of the two plans, are not intended to satisfy contingent, practical requirements; they are meant to deal with more profound problems which – at least within the limits of any given society – are thought fundamental and constant; it is, therefore, essential to lay claim to all the experience matured in the past in order to be able to conceive forms in such a way that they will continue to be thought valid in the future. However much a 'type' may allow of variation, the ideological content of forms has a constant base, though this may – indeed should – assume a particular accent or character at any particular time. Secondly, although an infinite number of classes and sub-classes of 'types' may be formulated, formal architectural typologies will always fall into three main categories; the first concerned with a complete configuration of buildings, the second with major structural elements and the third with decorative elements. Examples of the first category are centrally or longitudinally planned buildings; of the second, flat or domed roofs, traviated or arcuated systems; and of the third, orders of columns, ornamental details, etc. Now, it is clear that a classification so constituted follows the succession of the architect's working process (plan, structural system, surface treatment) and that it is intended to provide a typological guide for the architect to follow in the process of conceiving a building. So that the working out of every architectural project has this typological aspect; whether the architect consciously follows the 'type' or wants to depart from it; or even in the sense that every building is an attempt to produce another 'type'.

But if the 'type' is a schema or grid and the schema inevitably embodies a moment of rigidity or inertia, the presence of such a schema needs to be explained in the context of an artist's creative process. This leads one back naturally to the general problem of the relation between artistic creation and historical experience, since it is from historical experience that the 'type' is always deduced. What requires further explanation, however, is the proposition that at least a part of that historical experience presents itself to an architect who is designing a building in the form of a typological grid. The 'type', so Quatremère de Quincy has said, is an 'object' but 'vague or indistinct'; it is not definite form but a schema or the outline of a form; it also carries a residue of the experience of forms already accomplished in projects, but all that makes for their specific formal and artistic value is discarded. More precisely in the 'type' they are deprived of their character and of their true quality as forms; by sublimation into a 'type' they assume the indefinite value of an image or a sign. Through this reduction of preceding works of art to a 'type', the artist frees himself from being conditioned by a definite historical form, and neutralises the past. He assumes what is past is absolute and so no longer capable of developing. Accepting Quatremère de Quincy's definition, one might say the 'type' arises at the moment when the art of the past no longer appears to an artist as a conditioning model.

The choice of a model implies a value judgement: a recognition that a certain definite work of art is perfect and has to be imitated. When such a work of art reassumes the schematic and indistinct nature of a 'type', the individual action of the artist is no longer bound to a value judgement; the 'type is accepted but not 'imitated' which means that the repetition of the 'type' excludes the operation of that kind of creative process which is known as mimesis. In fact, the acceptance of the 'type' implies the suspension of historical judgement and is therefore negative; although also 'intentioned', directed to the formulation of a new kind of value in as much as it demands of the artist – in its very negativity – a new formal determination.

It is true that the assumption of a 'type' as a starting point for the architect's working process does not exhaust his involvement with historical data: it does not stop him from assuming or rejecting definite buildings as models.

Bramante's Tempietto of San Pietro in Montorio is a classic instance of such a process; it obviously depends on a 'type': the peripteral circular temple described by Vitruvius (Book IV, Chapter 8) which integrates the abstraction of the 'type' through historical 'models' (for instance, the temple of the Sybil at Tivoli), and so appears to claim for itself the status of both model and 'type'. Indeed it seems characteristic of Bramantesque Classicism to aspire to a syncretic union of ideal antiquity (which is essentially 'typical') and of historical antiquity which has a status of a formal model. An instance of a diametrically opposed attitude is that of neo-classical architects who assume classical architectural typology, not classical architectures, as a model; so that the movement produces works which are merely three-dimensional transcriptions of 'types'. If the concept of typology could in some way be brought back to that of 'tectonics' as defined by Cesare Brandi (*Eliante o della architettura*, 1956), one might say that typology is a notional base on which formal development of the artist must inevitably rest.

It will, therefore, be clear that the position of the artist vis-à-vis history has two aspects, the aspect of typology and that of formal definition. That of typology is not problematic: the artist assumes certain data, taking as a premise of all his work a group of common notions, or a heritage of images, with all their more or less explicit content and their ideological overtones. This aspect may be compared to the iconographic and compositional treatment of themes in figurative art. The aspect of formal definition, on the other hand, implies a reference to definite formal values of the past on which the artist explicitly arrives at a judgement. This judgement, however, must itself imply a typology since, whenever a value judgement on given works of art is passed, a judgement must also be passed about the way in which the artist, in creating them, has dealt with the relevant typological scheme.

The question of the value of architectural typology has recently been examined by Sergio Bettini (*Zodiac*, No 5) and by G K König (*Lezioni del Corso di Plastica*; Editrice Universitaria, Florence, 1961). In these writings the opinion prevails that an architectural 'type' must be treated as a schema of spatial articulation which has been formed in response to a totality of practical and ideological demands. From this one might deduce that the formal invention which overcomes the 'types' is a response to immediate demands in reference to which the 'type' had lost any real value. A recourse to the 'type' would therefore occur when the immediate demand which the artist is called to answer has its roots in the past. A significant instance is provided by the comparison between modern religious and industrial architecture. Industrial architecture which deals with new demands has created new 'types' which often have great importance for the later development of architecture. Religious architecture which answers demands rooted in the past has resulted in typological repetition (artistically valueless) or in attempts at freeing the artist of all typological precedent (as, for instance, Le Corbusier at Ronchamp). These have led to the proposing of counter-types, mostly ephemeral or unacceptable – there are few instances of modern developments of historical 'types'.

The conclusion must be that the typological and the inventive aspect of the creative process are continuous and interlaced – the inventive aspect being that of dealing with the demands of the actual historical situation by criticising and overcoming past solutions deposited and synthesised schematically in the 'type'.

———— * ————

VERNACULAR CLASSICISM
ALAN COLQUHOUN

S SERLIO, *SCENA RUSTICA*, OR *SCENA SATIRICA*

The theories of architecture put forward in a given period often consist of transformations and recombinations of earlier theories. Moreover, it sometimes happens that a later theory reverses an earlier one and that two concepts previously antithetical may become allies. The phrase 'vernacular Classicism' seems to be an example of this type of transformation. To all appearances it is an

oxymoron. Throughout the self-consciously classical periods – both Hellenistic and post-Renaissance – 'classic' stands to 'vernacular' as high art stands to low art, though the actual words 'classic' and 'vernacular' were not used until after the Romantic movement. In Romanticism, ideas associated with the vernacular were given a value independent of the place which they had held in the classical hierarchy of artistic styles. The 'low mimetic' style now became the model for art in general and was used to express the kinds of serious ideas previously reserved for the 'high mimetic' style.[1] But in Romantic thought, the meanings carried by the two terms remained antithetical.

The word 'classical' or 'classic' was not used generally in connection with architecture or the visual arts until after the German Romantic movement, when the opposition Classic/Romantic was first coined.[2] Previously, when critics or historians wished to refer to the art of Greece or Rome, they usually spoke of the 'antique'. Nonetheless, in poetics the word 'classical' was used as early as the second century AD when the grammarian Aulus Gellius used it to distinguish between the *scriptor classicus* and the *scriptor proletarius*. The words 'classicus' and 'proletarius' were borrowed from Roman tax law, 'classicus' referring to the first of the four social orders supposedly founded by Servius Tullius. In this metaphorical translation to literature, the *scriptor classicus* was he who wrote for the few, and the *scriptor proletarius* for the many.

The word 'classicus' was revived in the Renaissance, first in Italy, then in France and England, when it meant either texts used for instruction in schools, or standard Greek and Roman texts worthy of imitation by modern authors. In this context, 'classical' had the connotation of 'highest class', and it entailed the stylistic transformation of the various vernaculars of post-medieval Europe in conformity with Greek or Roman models. It need hardly be said that this is one of the senses in which the word is still used today, though its normative implications are no longer taken for granted.

It seems quite legitimate to use 'classical' in this sense to describe the architecture of antiquity as well as the literature. The connection was indeed made in the Renaissance, and in the following three centuries during which classical theory dominated all aspects of European culture. The post-Renaissance period not only revived many of the artistic practices of the ancients, but also their artistic theory: that of Vitruvius in architecture and those of Aristotle's *Poetics* and Horace's *Art of Poetry* in literature and painting. It is chiefly from these sources that academic Classicism derived such fundamental ideas as *imitation* and *decorum*.

Thus, both in a certain phase of antiquity itself and in the Renaissance, 'classical' signified practices codified in a system of canonic rules which claimed superiority over all other practices, whether these were taken as 'grammatical' in a narrow sense, or more broadly 'artistic'. A similar process had taken place in India in about the fourth century BC when the ancient language of the Vedas was codified by the grammarians and was called *Sanskrit* (from the roots *sam* = together and Kr = make).

The word 'vernacular' is equally derived from social and economic concepts. *Verna* meant slave, and 'vernacular' signified a person residing in the house of his master. Hence the later meaning, applied first to language and then to the arts, of indigenous and lowly forms.

Within the context of European history, then, the word 'vernacular' can be taken to apply to practices of *making* (linguistic, constructional, etc) which are either anterior to, or untouched by, classical theory and practice. Such practices, continuing in parallel with those of 'high art', were recognised by classical theory and were placed by it at the lowest level of the artistic hierarchy. (In Serlio's representation of Comedy, for example, where the *fabrique* consists of 'vernacular' buildings arranged without symmetry, in contrast to the classical symmetry of the noble style more appropriate for Tragedy.)

After the break-up of the classical canon at the end of the 18th century, however, these non-classical vernacular forms of art began to be studied in and for themselves. They began to be thought of, not as 'styles' within a larger system, but as forms of art possessing their own significance, challenging the universalist claims of the classical system. Art and literary criticism, after the onset of Romanticism and Historicism, attempted to reverse the values of the classical and the non-classical (eg to establish medieval art as superior to classical art) or to relativise all systems according to some theory of historical development.

Eric Auerbach's seminal literary study *Mimesis* of 1946 is an outstanding example of the latter tradition. Auerbach distinguished between the typology of classical literature and that of various non-classical texts, notably the Bible and medieval literature. Whereas classical literature was characterised by '. . . an abundant display of connectives . . . a precise gradation of temporal, comparative and concessive hypotaxes . . . and participle construction', the Bible and the writings of the medieval period had a tendency to 'string different pictures together like beads' and to 'divide the course of events into a mosaic of parcelled pictures'.[3] He saw these and other related features as belonging to a specifically Christian tradition whose ideas could not have been expressed in terms of classical decorum, since they demanded a mixture of styles: the treating of noble subjects in an ignoble setting.

Whether or not it would be legitimate to identify this kind of paratactic literary structure with 'vernacular' art in general, it seems evident that Auerbach is describing a general non-classical tradition which flourished in the early period of Christian culture, and which owed a great deal to local traditions. Clearly there are problems in trying to apply this paradigm to *all* medieval art. The gothic cathedral, for instance, is by no means a 'vernacular' building. It is a codified representational system, and, as Panofsky showed, was organised with a logic which was analogous to scholastic thought. It can therefore be claimed that High Gothic art had many of the underlying characteristics of Classicism. Indeed it was itself based on antique architecture, in the form in which it had survived the Dark Ages, and as modified by northern vernacular habits. But medieval 'imitation' of building allows for a greater degree of paratactic freedom than is permitted in the predominantly hypotactic structures of classical architecture. The acceptance of the unequal towers of Chartres and other cathedrals, and the additive and pragmatic arrangement of monastic complexes are cases in point. In contrast to this, a classical building was conceived as a body whose parts, perfectly distinct in themselves, were related to each other in a co-ordinated and self-sufficient hierarchy, on the analogy of the human body.

The concept of 'order' which this exemplifies, and which characterised classical thought, was summed up in the Pythagorean epigram, 'order and measure (*taxis* and *symmetria*) are pleasing, disorder and excess (*ataxia* and *asymmetria*) are ugly and baneful'.[4] Whatever logic the gothic cathedral may have possessed, it did not represent this kind of order. It may have been intended to lead the faithful to a vision of perfection, but it did not in itself constitute a bodily image of such perfection.

What appealed to the Romantics about medieval art was its mixture of styles and its parataxis. As evidence of the former we can quote Ruskin in *The Stones of Venice*. 'Everything in nature', he says, 'has good and evil in it, and artists, considered as searchers after truth are. . . to be divided into three great classes. . . Those on the right perceive and pursue the good and leave the evil; those in the centre, *the greatest,* perceive and pursue the good and the evil together and the whole thing verily as it is; those on the left perceive and pursue the evil and leave the good'[5] [my emphasis]. Ruskin's 'three great classes' are, of course, the same as those mentioned by Aristotle in the *Poetics;* he simply inverts them. As for the Romantics' love of parataxis, we find it in both literary and architectural criticism. In one of his 'Fragments', Novalis describes the ideal modern poetry thus: 'Disconnected, incoherent narratives that nonetheless have associations, like dreams. Simply poems that are perfectly harmonious, but also without coherence or any meaning. . . which must be like pure fragments of the most disparate ideas.'[6] A similar attraction for the irrational and incomprehensible is found in the young Goethe's remarks about Strasbourg Cathedral: 'With what unlooked for emotions did the sight surprise me . . . a sensation of wholeness, greatness, filled my soul, which, composed of a thousand harmonious details, I could savour and enjoy, yet by no means understand or explain.'[7] Friedrich Schlegel's descriptions of Gothic are couched in similar terms.

The notion of parataxis, or 'laying things side by side' might seem, at first sight, incompatible with that other crucial concept of Romantic aesthetics: organic wholeness. But for the Romantics the fragmentary and apparently disordered surface of a work of art, far from indicating a lack of organic unity, was in fact a sign of a more profound unity, which escaped analysis because it sprang from the depths of the artist's unconscious mind.

The 'primitivism' which we find in the Enlightenment is very different from this Romantic approach to vernacular architecture. The 'return' is not to a particular, idiosyncratic culture, based on local craft traditions; it is to the sources of architecture as a universal language obeying the necessities of natural law.

Neo-Classicism looked back to a 'natural' architecture which must have existed before society became corrupted, or before architecture became fragmented into all those 'dialects' which historical research and travel had disclosed. The postulation of a common, primitive culture, which Laugier shares to some extent with Rousseau, does not involve the empirical discovery of an actual vernacular; it is an hypothesis based on what logically should have been the case, conflating what is logically with what is chronologically anterior.

We do not know a great deal about the pre-monumental architecture of Ancient Greece, but what we do know leads us to believe that it had no relation to Laugier's primitive hut. Nor is it certain what the sources of Greek monumental architecture were.[8] Laugier was no more concerned with the 'real' Mediterranean vernacular than was Rousseau with an actual, historically primitive society. He was concerned with a distillation of classical doctrine. He was not seeking to return to the earliest hours of man, but to the pure sources of classical architecture. This process entailed, not the discovery of vernacular building, but the *re-vernacularisation* of Classicism with which to substantiate a myth of origins.

Therefore, when we define 'vernacular' in terms of the 18th century notion of the primitive, we are involved in an argument which is characteristically classical. The myth of origins, as recorded by Vitruvius, was an integral part of classical doctrine and was necessary to the establishment of Classicism as a universal system based on nature. But to 'understand' a particular belief in historical terms is not necessarily to subscribe to it. Today we can hardly fail to see the attempt of the 18th century to create an architectural ontology as having been bounded by 18th-century epistemology. The belief in the essential being of architecture, and of its origins, is consistent with, and inextricable from the ideas of the 18th-century grammarians. Like language, architecture is a universal form of knowlege, but not thoroughly worked out. It has come about through the rough-and-ready ordering of our representations. The history and practice of both language and architecture present us with the elements of truth; it is up to us to unravel the skein that has been wound up through the centuries without system, and to put its threads into the right order.[9] It is only in terms of such a linguistics that we can understand what the 18th century meant by ontological truth, and how it was applied in architectural discourse.

When, therefore, we use the expression 'vernacular Classicism' we are describing a process by which Classicism, within the terms of its own theory of language, recreates its own origins. It is a movement backwards within a closed *épistemè*. In all attempts to discover an ontology of architecture within Classicism (just as in all those cases where the classical system filtered down to local builders – from Italian farms to English provincial buildings), we are likely to find traces of those elements of high style which originally belonged to a sophisticated and highly developed architecture of monuments – the very antithesis of vernacular building.

Notes

1   For a definition of high and low mimetic styles see Northrop Frye, *Anatomy of Criticism*, Princeton, 1971.
2   By Friedrich Schlegel, cf René Wellek, *History of Modern Criticism*, Cambridge, 1981, vol 2, p 14.
3   Eric Auerbach, *Mimesis*, Chapter 5 'Roland against Ganelon', also chapter 7 'Adam and Eve', Princeton, 1968.
4   Timpanaro-Cardini, *Pitagorici, Testimonianze e Frammenti*, Florence, 1958, p 299, quoted in David Summers, *Michelangelo and the Language* of *Art*, Princeton, 1981, p 314.
5   John Ruskin, *The Stones* of *Venice*, Vol II, chapter 6 '*The nature of Gothic*', George Allen, 1886, p 187.
6   Novalis, *Oeuvres Complètes*, ed A Guerue, Paris, 1975, quoted in Tzvetan Todorov, *Theories* of *the Symbol*, Cornell, 1982, p 176.
7   Wolfgang von Goethe, *Von deutscher Baukunst*, 1773.
8   Cf J J Coulton, *Greek Architects at Work*, Granada, 1982, Chapter 3 'The Problem of Beginning'.
9   Cf Michel Foucault, *The Order* of *Things*, Panther Books, 1970, Chapter 4 'Speaking'.

S SERLIO, *SCENA CLASSICA*, OR *SCENA TRAGICA*, AND *SCENA GOTICA*, OR *SCENA COMICA*

*

ORNAMENT AND CLASSICAL ORDER
JOSÉ-IGNACIO LINAZASORO

J-I LINAZASORO, MAIN SQUARE AT AZCOITA, 1982

Each architecture moves forward towards a deeper understanding of the total experience of architecture itself. In that sense, the concept of historical development points to a process of typification that constitutes new experiences which, regarding their fundamental characteristics, could be glimpsed in former historical stages. The renewal of classical order proposed by 20th-

century classicists has as its point of departure the realisation of a crisis in 'language' as a mechanism for the expression of architectural content. This crisis had already become apparent in the forsaking of the Orders which post-Enlightenment treatises and above all Eclecticism advocated. The source of the problem lay in the fact that Eclecticism put toward a theory of equivalence of historical forms. Contents and conventional stylistic formulations were thought to be the outcome of their correspondence with determinate historical periods. This came to mean that a good deal of these formal contents had already become obsolete. For this reason it seemed meaningless to revive the Orders simply by means of a stylistic renewal.

Neo-classical treatises and the classical tendencies within Eclecticism could be founded, therefore, only on a process of typification that aimed at a deeper understanding of the 'elements' of architecture; an understanding that lay outside all stylistic formulations. The loss of style was to become, ultimately, the inescapable destiny of the classical project.

This search, however, should be compared with that of the modernist avant-gardes, which, contrary to the reductivism of the classical project, offered the alternative of stylistic renewal. It is important to point out Adolf Loos' criticism of the Viennese Secession, the representatives of which he demotes to mere decorators.[1] Similarly, one should be reminded that others – like Tessenow[2] or the Scandinavian Doricists – had consciously with-

drawn from the stylistic positions of the modernist avant-gardes.

With such qualifications, the only possible answer by the classicists was silence (what Kraus called *Totschweigentaktik*), a voluntary retreat in the face of a debate that was *not* a debate and which did not pertain at all to classical thought.

If we actually compare the polemics employed by the defenders of Classicism with those of the avant-garde, the former appear victorious. At the same time and in spite of what has often been stated by historians, it is the classical position that made an opening towards the technological and functional advances of the 20th century. Tessenow, for exmple, replying to Poelzig regarding the 'modernity' or 'antiquity' of certain forms, wrote with a certain irony: 'Maybe Poelzig is right when he asks himself why he kept on designing windows that were already old–fashioned, vertical and with small panes instead of horizontal and long ones. Basically the question is: why should that be wrong and this right? Why? I ask myself, really, in all seriousness.'[4] In the face of Poelzig's evident superficiality, Tessenow's answer underlines in its wisdom, his indifference to an inaccurately stated problem.

The Problem of Ornamentation
The most important contribution of 19th-century treatises had been the typological and systemic analysis of composition. One of the central questions raised by the treatises following the

eclectic phase was the isolation and study of ornamental forms.

Unlike the old debate, the *Querelle des Anciens et Modernes,* this was not a matter of eliminating traditional forms but rather of reducing those forms to a precise and clearly legible architectural repertoire. Two tendencies are characteristic of the period: first, a progressive 'essentialisation' of architectural forms and second, a sporadic but significant use of ornamental forms. It is important to point out that both these tendencies of 'essentialisation' and 'sparse ornamentation' are intimately related: they do explain each other.

Lukács, a contemporary thinker who examined extensively the problem of ornamentation, considers it as a self-referential aesthetic operation; one that is orientated towards evocation and which has a clear preference towards abstract thought: 'Ornamentation lacks in "reality" because it ignores empirical objectivity and the connections with the real world deliberately; because it puts in the place of the real world abstract constructions of a purely geometric nature.'[5] The expression 'lacks reality' implies a sense of 'gratuitousness', that which is 'superfluous' as distinct from the 'necessary' or essential. These reflections remind us of further comments made by Tessenow on the subject: 'The best qualification one can apply to ornament is abstration. The unconscious, the inexplicable ornament always lacks determination, it is something which divorces it to a great extent from the work. . . if we remove form from ornament there is nothing left. . .'[6]

This is an important though not a substantial appreciation of ornament. One must consider that ornament – particularly in architecture where Lukács' suggested 'lack of reality' gives to it an autonomous significance – can highlight the articulation of architectural elements by reinforcing their formal content.

But there exists another consideration: that of ornament as an evocative element which may acquire an importance in itself. Lukács observes that the borders between purely ornamental art and evocative art often overlap, whilst Tessenow recognises the force of 'habit' as a basis of ornamentation: 'We only do it' wrote Tessenow, 'because it was done in the past, it is not spontaneous.'[7] Tessenow's perception of ornament comes remarkably close to that of Loos. Despite the fact that Loos' *Ornament and Crime* is concerned more with the problems of 'formal essentialisation' than with ornament itself, he nonetheless wrote: 'I have never stated, as purists maintain to the point of absurdity, that ornamentation should be systematically suppressed. Only that, when is disappears due to a contingent necessity, it can no longer be employed again.'[8] For Loos, as for Tessenow, ornament is only one among many indispensable architectural elements; it is a 'residue', a reference, a group of forms which, after becoming obsolete and devoid of meaning, still linger in the mind as a habitual reference to the past.

'Our education', wrote Loos, 'is based on classical culture. . . From the moment humanity understood the greatness of classical Antiquity, a single mode of thought linked the great architects through the ages. . . And each time that architecture moves away from its models due to mediocre and mere decorators, there appears a great architect who once again refers it back to Antiquity.'[9] In an explicit restatement of this 'profession of faith', Loos introduced references to the classical Orders in some of his buildings, demonstrating in this way that ornament emerges out of its own 'formal essentialisation'. In the otherwise 'naked' facade of Michaelerplatz there appears the classical Order of the columns and in the Rufer house a classical cornice crowns the composition. Loos' use of ornament has an intentionally sporadic and polemical character: hence, the contrast between 'essentialised' and ornamented forms seems abrupt and violent. On the other hand, Tessenow's use of ornament seems natural and obvious. The organisational schemes of classical

Order are seen more clearly in his 'essentialised forms' and ornament is employed in a more traditional manner.

In the work of all 20th-century classicists there always appears a reference to the past and to forms already obsolete. Gunnar Asplund, for example, used ornament in a manner similar to Loos and Tessenow, though on occasion with greater subtlety. The big decorated panels of his Göteborg City Hall are similar to the ornamental panels of Loos' Rufer House; that is, they appear as explicit *references.* Asplund, however, employed these forms in two ways: whilst constrasting them with the essentialised forms of the facade, he also established a 'bridge' which, acting both as an evocative and compositional device, related the new facade to the adjacent neo-classical Old City Hall. Asplund's ornamental forms reappear in his detailing, as for example in the Stockholm Library. In this case, ornament seems to act as 'furniture', reinforcing the building's significant form.

Ornament and 20th-century Classicism, therefore, raise a similar question: how can 'obsolete forms' help us understand the very nature of ornament itself? In the case of the Modern Movement, the formalism masked behind its spurious 'functionalism' denied altogether the legitimacy of ornament. Instead, 20th-century classicists reaffirmed the importance of ornament and conceived of it as a process of 'essentialisation' of form.

'Essentialisation' of Forms

The problem of 'essentialisation' of forms (the problem of arriving at a basic structural composition devoid of superfluous additions) has very little to do with the modernist conception of 'pure' forms, as, for example, the 'flat facade'. The modernist conception of 'pure' form ignores deliberately the distinction between form and ornament by turning form into ornament.[10] The modernist flat facade is not the outcome of a reductive process. 'Essentialisation', properly speaking, results only when emphasis is given to the elements of composition. The flat facade should be understood as an undifferentiated formalist gesture: a strip window could be understood as a pictorial gesture but it can never be the outcome of a process of 'essentialisation'. To understand this process, we may recall Loos' Nihilismus Cafe[11], a project which, by exposing the 'linguistic chaos' proclaimed by Kraus, served as a critique of the decorativism of the Viennese Secession. The Nihilismus Cafe was not so much a manifesto against ornament as a clarification of what are the elements of composition.

The Michaelerplatz facade, however, is Loos' most expressive example of 'essentialisation'. It is important to remember that certain critics – Benevolo for example – have considered this work to be the canonic precedent of the 'flat facade' of the Modern Movement. But if we study the building we recognise, first of all, that Loos placed himself between the 'Ancients and the Moderns', convinced that he was following the fundamental procedures of the old Viennese masters: 'I have chosen real marble,' wrote Loos, 'because any imitation disgusts me, and I have made the plaster as simple as I could because the Viennese bourgeois would also build simply. . . I always had the illusion of having resolved the building in accordance with the criteria of the old Viennese masters. This illusion was reinforced when a modern artist, an antagonist of mine, said: he pretends to be a modern architect and builds a house like the old Viennese houses!'[12]

What Loos intended to reveal was the facade's essential compositional structure; and this is what is expressed by the Michaelerplatz building: windows, base, cornice, roof, etc, are precise compositional elements. Loos' building thus seems traditional because it sets out and resolves eternal problems; inasmuch as it addresses fundamental architectural principles, it is a classical building. 'Each time that architecture moves away from its models due to mediocre and mere decorators, there appears a great architect who once again refers it back to Antiquity.'

We have considered the process of 'essentialisation' of forms from the perspective of the history of official architectural styles. And yet, rural architecture – less subject to change or fashion – may illuminate further the development of 20th-century Classicism, particularly the Classicism of Tessenow and the Scandinavians. The re-evaluation of rural architecture started with the Enlightenment via the Picturesque. Later on, William Morris, though ideologically a romantic, understood popular architecture not simply as a formal repertoire but above all as the product of an artisanal culture that was opposed to industrialisation. The designs inspired by Morris' writings were an important influence on architecture's 'loss of canonic style'. Consequently they encouraged a reductivist ethic in that they proposed an architecture that was rooted in construction and the forms directly derived from it. In Tessenow's early drawings one may easily recognise a position which continues that of Morris, probably through Muthesius.

With Tessenow and the Scandinavians we witness a phenomenon that had a distant precedent in Palladio: classical forms are mixed with others of a rural character. This is not a case of mere combination; instead, classical forms recover their essential, immediate character and are thereby freed of all stylistic niceties. In Tessenow's Hellerau Institute the rural pediment combines with the slender order of the pillars: vernacular and classical architecture are no longer separated by stylistic barriers. In fact, 20th-century Classico-Vernacular suffered both from the irretrievable loss of the meaning of the Orders and from the degeneration of Morris' ideas into 'cottage style' and 'vernacular regionalism'. Instead, in Tessenow's Hellerau Institute both rural and classical elements recover their essential raison d'être.

Tessenow's rapprochement of elements, as for example in the Klotzsche School, is matched by the masterly work of the 'Scandinavian Doricists'. Demetri Porphyrios, in a recent article, described the convergence of rural and classical elements of these architects and their similarity to Tessenow's work. Discussing Asplund's vernacular Woodland Chapel and Lewerentz's classical Resurrection Chapel, Porphyrios writes: 'Asplund's vernacular and Lewerentz's Classicism feature a universal primitiveness that is diffused in the primordial porticoed entry, in the unaffected singularity of the rectangular or circular aula, in the coarseness of texture or in the severity of the elevational composition. . .'[13]

Asplund, like Tessenow, began working under the influence of Morris' Romanticism. Already in his 1918 Woodland Chapel, however, he had set foot in a universe where the classical forms and those of rural origin were tending to converge. The Woodland Chapel stands as the point of departure for all his subsequent work; later, the loss of 'style' that he initiated by means of 'essentialisation' was to mark his most influential buildings like the Stockholm Library, the Göteborg City Hall or the Enskede Crematorium. Asplund – as was the case also with his contemporaries Lewerentz, Bergsten or Thomsen – advances towards the construction of a classicism 'without style', a Classicism determined primarily by the composition of 'essentialised forms'. In the reading room of Stockholm Library he repeats, typifies and essentialises the conventional reading room of late 19th-century libraries; and yet in so doing he manages to free the primary elements of architecture from their stylistic burden. The dome,

for example, stands as the 'essentialised' form of all previous 'stylistic domes'. It essentialises the different historical solutions of domical form. Ornament – as exemplified by the large base of the building, the Hellenistic quotations of the frieze and the different bas-reliefs – plays a disquieting role exactly because of its contrast to the vast unadorned surfaces of the building. The result is a building which, like the Michaelerplatz, is both conservative and radical. A building that is 'essentialised' but not purist.

Asplund's Göteborg City Hall is likewise of great interest. Apart from being an 'essentialist' exercise in which compositional order relates to the order of the building's construction and structure, it also relates to the formal order of the adjacent neoclassical City Hall. The phases of its design development are indeed revealing. Asplund set out designing this building with stylistic conceptions similar to those of the Secession. Later on he chose an eclectic interpretation. In the course of the design, the problems of composition and ornamentation became pressing. The final solution, 'essentialist' in character and stripped of stylistic references, opens up a new line of investigation concerning the relation between old and new buildings. With certainty similar only to that of Loos in Michaelerplatz, Asplund disregards questions of style and espouses the lessons of the classical tradition.

In the Enskede Crematorium, the classical colonnade merges with the almost atavistic idea of the house – the impluvium. This idea does not arise from a return to sources; it is the totality of the classical experience that from this point on imprints itself as dramatically as the Greek temples, next to Nature and in contemplation of it. Asplund's wisdom brings forth the idea of the monument, its perennial and essential problems.

Tessenow, on the contrary, addressed the idea of the monument only through the house and the utilitarian public building. Indeed, one of Tessenow's major preoccupations was with the one-family house which derived from the Siedlungen of Garden Cities. Tessenow explored the subject in great depth; he essentialised the one-family house with such precision that apart from the specific quality of some details one could almost talk of an architecture 'without an architect'. The entire history of the German house is analysed exhaustively: a history exemplified by the gothic houses the Fuggerei,[14] or Goethe's little house in Weimar,[15] experiences that Tessenow could understand as different examples of one sole project and for which he himself advanced the most essentialist solution possible.

Tessenow's apparent naiveté can only be considered as the result of an attempt, almost unique in an architect, to approximate the old master builders of the past. It is in his mature works – eg the Klotzsche School – that his role as a master builder is clearly discernible. The Klotzsche School is an 'urban building' in a way similar to Jefferson's University of Virginia or Durand's *Ensembles formes par la combinaison de plusieurs edifices*.[16] And yet Tessenow's Classicism does not refer to these precedents, literally; rather it alludes to them by means of an eminently 'essentialist' choice which identifies and clarifies the compositional elements of these buildings. In a sense, Tessenow understands construction in a way similar to Mies van der Rohe. The support stands out from the wall to signify the Order: no longer in the sense of Summerson's 'simplification' of the classical Orders but in the profound sense of the Order as compositional element, that is, as an element that transcends its mere constructional function.

Notes

1 A Loos, *Ornamento y Delito y otros Escritos*, Gustavo Gili, Barcelona, 1972. Also see the periodical *El Carrer de la Cuitat*, Nos 9 and 10, Barcelona, 1979.

2 On Tessenow, see H Tessenow, *Osservazioni elementari sul costruire*, Franco Angeli, Milan, 1974. This book includes a list of Tessenow's writings and those about him. Also see G Wangerin/G Weiss, *H Tessenow, ein Baumeister, 1876-1950*, Verlag Bacht Gurb, Essen, 1976.

3 On the Scandinavian Doricists see especially Demetri Porphyrios' article. 'Reversible Faces: Danish and Swedish Architecture, 1905-1930' in *Lotus* 16, Milan 1977. Also B Zevi, *E Gunnar Asplund*, Ediciones Infinito, Buenos Aires, 1957.

4 Quoted by G Grassi in *Osservazioni elementari sul costruire, op cit.*

5 G Lukács, *Ästhetik*, 1963, here taken from the Spanish translation *Estética*, chaps I and II.

6 H Tessenow, *Osservazioni elementari sul costruire, op cit.*

7 *Ibid.*

8 A Loos, *Ornamento y Delito y otros Escritos, op cit.*

9 A Rossi, *Para una arquitectura de tendencia. Escritos 1956-72*, Gili, Barcelona, 1977, chap 1.

10 The flat facade, essentially, is an invention of the visual arts. One could understand how it could have consequences in architecture but it should be stressed that its preoccupations are not strictly speaking architectonic. It should be pointed out that even the photographs of modernist buildings of the time sought to emphasise the essentially 'flat' character and by extension, therefore, their pictorial value. See for example, the photographs of Gropius' Törten taken by Moholy Nagy.

11 An extensive discussion of A Loos' Nihilismus Cafe can be found in F Amendolagie and M Cacciari, *Oikos: de Loos a Wittgenstein*, Officina Edizione, Roma, 1975.

12 A Loos, *Ornamento y Delito y otros Escritos, op cit.*

13 D Porphyrios, *op cit.*

14 L Benevolo *Storia dell'Architettura del Rinascimento*, translated in English as *The Architecture of the Renaissance*, Routledge and Kegan Paul, London 1978.

15 I refer here to the Frauenplan of Weimar, where Goethe died in 1832 . This building is described in *Der Baumeister*, No 1, 1934. Though this is a country house characteristic of the lower aristocracy or upper bourgeoisie of that time, it nonetheless corresponds to the typical traditional German country house.

16 I refer to some of the models for hospitals proposed in *Précis de Leçons*.

H TESSENOW, ONE-FAMILY HOUSE FOR THE RUHR VALLEY

H TESSENOW, ONE-FAMILY HOUSE

ON THE QUESTION OF DECORATION
GIORGIO GRASSI

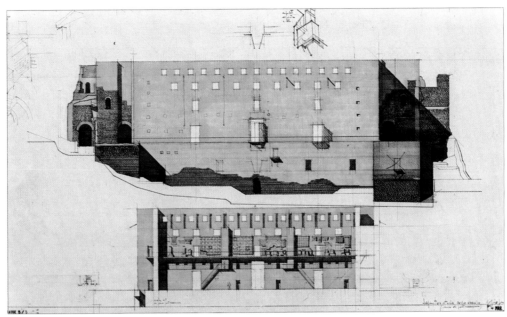

GIORGIO GRASSI, ROMAN THEATRE AT SAGUNTO, 1985, BASIC PROJECT

Given the analytical character of architecture, one could speak separately of its structure, building elements, techniques and materials, distribution, dimensional relationships, etc. What remains, therefore, outside the description of any architecture, is that part of its composition which, in the words of Le Corbusier, is pure création de l'esprit: *that part, that is, which has nothing to do with*

purpose, technique, and so on. Decoration is precisely this: formal invention, the plastic fact par excellence, which finds in itself its own raison d'être.

In general, everyone who within the experience of the European Modern Movement has posed the question of style in a responsible fashion – that is, everyone who has posed the problem of a common and unified language for architecture – has had to grapple also with the problem of decoration. That is the case with the main avant-garde movements and all those significant personalities, such as Loos or Tessenow, Oud or Le Corbusier. Despite this, the official line of the Modern Movement (which is invariably the line laid down by Gropius and by official critics whom Gropius had accredited himself) has always been an intransigent denial of the problem as such: a true and protracted exorcism. But the problem of decoration, a constitutive feature of architecture, has nonetheless recurred at every step and in every single work, irrespective of programmatic declaration.

In a famous series of remarks in defence of the 1951 Shell Building, Oud raised again this important problem: 'Purists as we are, we may well call Wright fanciful, romantic, unrealistic and so on, but what a great architect he is, what an artist! Gropius, on the other hand, so reasonable and honest, is too bogged down by ethical, technical and social problems. His mind is involved intensely in everyday life, and the informing prin-

ciple of his work is to provide a good, solid, built form for this life; but is that enough? Can we be content with this cold intellect? This is not enough for an architect who aspires to a new architectural culture. The architect must revert to being an artist. If we wish to save architecture from the levelling tendency of our times, from the mortal influence of a functionalism which has raised itself from being a means to being an end, we must be far more fully committed than we are. An architect without architectural ideals is not an architect.'

Oud's line of argument is very clear: the pursuit of a new architecture is first and foremost a process of reappropriating all the elements which define it as such. In this sense – and this is true for Oud and also for Loos, Tessenow and Le Corbusier – the problem of decoration becomes a particular moment in the process of design, a phase defined by the enquiry into the language of architecture, a phase in the enrichment and completion of that language itself.

This choice, then, has a particular significance vis-à-vis the official position of the Modern Movement, already obstinately stiffened into the role of a new academy. It is a choice of standing firm in the face of one's own responsibilities, of not masking one's own uncertainties. In this sense, Oud's Shell building is a manifesto. At the time of the Shell Headquarters, Oud was a recognised master, his best-known housing districts were among the loveliest things that Modern architecture had produced. Oud was, therefore, an inevitable point of reference in any discussion of the Modern Movement. At a certain point in his career, he realised a work, the Shell Headquarters, which was berated as a 'scandal'. With this project he demonstrated his readiness to cast out past successes and privileges and rethink anew his views on architecture. In the Shell Headquarters Oud set himself all the themes of traditional architecture, from classical composition right down to the question of decoration. For this reason he had all the critics against him, and there was talk of betrayal.

Oud passionately defended his project: 'The Shell Headquarters is for me an attempt to rediscover architecture as an expression of the soul. As a consequence, you will find in it elements which have proved good conductors of feelings through the ages and which have been founded on universal understanding: they concern geometry, symmetry, harmony, proportion and also, here and there, hierarchy. Furthermore, I have addressed issues such as the idea of exemplar, ornament and so on . . . Ornament is not used here to conceal compositional defects. The building could quite well do without it, but its function is to emphasise the building's meaning. The decorative parts – for instance the balustrades on the staircase – do not distort the materials or methods of construction; if anything, they are tailored to the constructional nature of the materials. The ornament of the attic storey is not random: it allows the light to play through the gaps. It is conceived for light itself, not for the shadow of its moulding. The same is true for the decorative solution above the entrance: light and life come into play through ornament. Life is illuminated, not determined, by the ornament. It is not just an ornament to be looked at; it gives joyous shape to the necessities of life. Similarly, the plan of the building has conquered its form: it is not a dead academic figure, as my American friends have suggested, but has grown out of an aesthetic rather than a functional need . . . The Shell building is my favorite creation.'

The clarity of Oud's moral position in front of the regressive involution of his fellow travellers – those implacable defenders of the slogans of the Modern Movement – is fairly evident from this impassioned indictment. Here was a man who, having achieved indisputable results, had the courage at the height of his career as an artist to risk everything anew, even the mastery he had gained, in the hope of reaffirming a principle which he felt he had lost along the way.

Irrespective of the results achieved in this project, this choice of Oud's is fundamental for the future development of architecture; it is a choice which we ourselves must reckon with. It should also be regarded as one of the most worthy and stimulating events in the history of Modern architecture – generally so unedifying.

In classical architecture decoration was the plastic, ornamental resolution of the architectural and constructional detail. With time, decoration became increasingly detached from the facts of necessity; it became a self-centred exercise, a question of exquisite form, until finally it annulled its functional origins.

It is in this context that one should judge the arguments of Loos regarding his famous but equally disconcerting entry for the Chicago Tribune competition, a discussion that was both logical and rigorous but one that was taken to the limits of the paradoxical by the author of the most famous essay in modern architecture: *Ornament and Crime*. Here too, as with Oud, we encounter the immediate rejection of false dogma and again dissent from the illusory search for a *new style*. An answer which, regarding the question of ornament, was in many ways definitive.

In *Vers une architecture*, Le Corbusier, speaking of the Parthenon, dwells upon the meaning of the moulding in classical architecture. His aim is to seek corroboration and his argument becomes interesting as well as overtly tendentious when it reaches the conclusion: the Parthenon is not the work of Ictinos and Callicrates – its official architects – but of Phidias, who sculpted its reliefs and mouldings. Insofar as the Doric temple is constructed of elements that are entirely fixed in their form as well as in the meaning that custom attributes to them, Le Corbusier continues, there exist various examples of Doric temples made by Ictinos and Callicrates, but only one Parthenon. Only here does the whole freedom of its execution and thus its uniqueness and beauty lie in the precision of the relation between entirely predetermined elements and their perfect realisation, that is, in the work of the sculptor, in the decoration.

Three architects, three very different ways of tackling the same question, but one single choice: that of freedom, consistency and responsibility vis-à-vis one's work; and of intolerance and rejection of everything which emerges as reductive of one's own premises and tradition – including, here, the arguments of one's own personal polemic. Without false modesty: as *masters*, in fact.

How could a unified image of the experience and statements of the Modern Movement have held out as long as today? Though *Ornament and Crime* served as programmatic declaration of the Modern Movement on the question of ornament, Loos himself was the first one to denounce the narrow-mindedness and ambiguity of the polemics against ornament. With his Chicago Tribune competition he showed that polemical arguments are just that: they exist to be superceded. *Ornament and Crime* and his Chicago Tribune competition – both tendentious to the limit of the paradoxical – are in reality two faces of a single question, open and problematical.

Perhaps the main reason why ornament has been attacked, first of all by Loos himself, lies ultimately in its main characteristic: that is to say that ornament is of its own being, self-sufficient, something apparently without purpose. As regards the *gratuitousness* of ornament – that is, the gratuitousness in relation to form as defined by use and need – I shall here quote two revealing passages, one by Le Corbusier, the other by Heinrich Tessenow; both are positive arguments.

'Profile and contour (*Modénature*)' writes Le Corbusier,'have entered in, and they are free of all constraint; they are a pure invention which makes the outward aspect radiant or dulls it. It is in his contours that we can trace the plastic artist; the engineer is effaced and the sculptor comes to life. Contours are the touchstone of the architect; in dealing with them he is forced to decide whether he will be a plastic artist or not. Architecture is the skilful, accurate and magnificent play of masses seen in light; and contours are also and exclusively the skilful, accurate and magnificent play of volumes seen in light. Contours go beyond the scope of the practical man, the daring man, the ingenious man; they call for the plastic artist.'

Further on and in connection with the Parthenon Le Corbusier writes: 'The mouldings of the Parthenon are infallible and implacable. In severity they go far beyond our practice, or man's normal capabilities. Here, the purest witness to the physiology of sensation, and to the mathematical speculation attached to it, is fixed and determined: we are riveted by our senses; we are ravished in our minds; we touch the axis of harmony. No question of religious dogma enters in; no symbolical description, no naturalistic representation; there is nothing but pure forms in precise relationships.'

Le Corbusier's line of argument is extremely clear; one can only either agree or disagree with it. Its aim is to stress the enormous distance which separates the technical, utilitarian, everyday features of architecture from decoration as a synthetic element, representative of architecture and of its long process of

GIORGIO GRASSI, ELEMENTARY SCHOOL AT BERGORO, 1977

maturation. A perfect marrying of theory and practice of design.

The passage from Tessenow is somewhat singular. Tessenow was an architect who, according to the official critics of the Modern Movement, ranges among German academics, that is, an adversary. He taught at the school of architecture in Berlin and held a course parallel to that of Hans Poelzig, who was the tutelary deity of the expressionist current in Germany. Thus, on the one hand, there was Poelzig (who made his students draw in charcoal and wanted them to express themselves with imagination and a spirit of freedom) and on the other Tessenow, who had them design small single-family houses in ink, and with maniacal precision. This rigorous attitude to work, to the *métier*, was one of Tessenow's most characteristic traits. Furthermore, in spite of not being acknowledged by official architectural criticism, Tessenow was a very interesting writer and a most perceptive essayist. I shall therefore here quote an excerpt from his book, *Hausbau und Dergleichen*, written in 1916:

'Technique' writes Tessenow in his chapter on 'Technical Form', 'always tries to obtain the simplest possible form and the greatest possible energy; it accepts form only insofar as it is inevitable; otherwise, technique turns its back on form . . . technical work is basically the enemy of form; apart from the fact that in every application we inevitably try also to answer an aesthetic need, that is, apart from the fact that even when designing a machine we tend towards beauty, the machine and technique as such have nothing to do with beauty . . . If we think of a complicated, showy and particularly meaningless ornament, and at the same time we think of a copper wire with a strong current running through it, we are faced with two possible and antithetical forms. In the first case we have a prevalence of form without anything essential hidden behind it; in the second case have an almost total absence of form, with a very clear content. In our work as architects we can accept neither the one nor the other of these attitudes. We seek a form which can fully express everything which is alive. . . The purest technical form is unlikely to fascinate us or to appeal to us; that is why we try to avoid it, though we ought to be appreciative of it, especially today. But technical form cannot be an objective for us in any way, because it means the sway of the rational. Unlike creative work, technical form does not have that 50 percent of necessary stupidity. Technical form believes too much in what we already know and not enough in what we cannot yet know but feel and intuit; or it believes too little in form as such.'

Tessenow's line of argument, and in particular his surprising allusion to that 50 percent of necessary stupidity, is of extraordinary interest. It is of relevance, of course, to the specific character of ornament I have mentioned, namely its gratuitousness. Insofar as it is indeed gratuitous, ornament is self-centred, that is, it reflects only itself. In that sense its origins come second when compared to the form itself: the column no longer has the primary meaning of support, it has meaning in itself by correspondence to the various Orders in the form of which a column can in fact be rendered. ('It is no accident', recalls Adolf Loos, 'that the Romans were not in a position to invent a new Order or a new ornament. They were already too advanced to do so.') The result is that the relationship with the original practical aim is weakened to the point of non-existence.

If we were to exclude the *symbolic* kind of decoration (which is always extraneous or marginal to the historical experience of architecture and its process of stylisation and which is also, according Le Corbusier, the negation of ornament as *pure creation of the mind*) then we realise that the choices of which we have spoken are the only two possible regarding the question of decoration. Both answer the theoretical needs of rationalist thought; one is that expressed by Le Corbusier, the other is the position adopted by Loos and Tessenow.

But a great divide lies between them. Le Corbusier's position betrays all the tension of experimentalism (of the avant-garde, in a canonical sense). This position needs always to recast architecture as a language that is renewed continually, always defining a *new decoration.*

Loos and Tessenow support the opposite position: although they develop their arguments differently, both look for confirmation in the past, in the history of forms. They do *not* believe in a new kind of ornament. In any event, they do not believe in the *new:* their interest revolves around tradition. They do not pose the problem of their direct participation in the resolution of this question. According to Loos and Tessenow, decoration is in reality reduced to a question of *quotation.* Once again we have Loos' great Doric column, or the pediments affixed to the bare facades of the houses by Tessenow. These are surely two different answers to the question of ornament, but they both indicate a similar attitude and a responsible choice regarding the history and meaning of forms.

Loos imposes a certain form – the column – on a determined place; a form which is immediately recognisable by reference to history and which cannot be modified in its internal relationships. Loos abandons any hope of seeking an explanation for it – *the column as inevitable fact* – and he seems to place it before himself and to run an admiring look over its lines, its measurements, its fateful ratios. That is, he runs his eye over something which has been formed in our own past and which, therefore, belongs to us; something we seem to know almost everything about, but whose innermost meaning has been lost.

Tessenow's attitude is perhaps more problematical, more open and, one is tempted to say, more practical. Tessenow seems to have found the key to the interpretation of the classical forms of decoration in the link which unites them with everyday life, as in a sort of direct comparison with forms dictated by use. The process is always the same: as he completes the composition of a building – for instance a house – Tessenow introduces, almost unexpectedly, the silhouette of two columns and a pediment. This is a precise reference to the experience of the past, which breaks sharply with the problem of decoration in current terms. This addition to the composition, however, instead of introducing an element of pomposity, restores the composition to a natural and familiar condition. This process has something in common with the compositional ethos of rural architecture.

The new architecture of the Modern Movement (at least its declarations, programmes and manifestos) always posed the question of form in global terms. It established no hierarchies of a practical order, but only value judgements of a *moral* order: that is, it launched slogans (like its sworn anti-historicism or the battle for the flat roof). According to the official positions of the Modern Movement, the technical element, the functional element, the constructional element, and so on, are to be virtually indistinguishable one from another, let alone the decorative element! Everything is blurred. It is for this reason that, in reality, the denial of decoration as such is turned into the claim that *everything is decoration.* For Le Corbusier, for instance, a plan, a moulding or a window are all to be resolved in the same way: that is, *plastically.*

If we look at a completely new type of architecture, for instance that of Michelangelo's Laurentian Library, it is possible to describe its architectural structure, its spatial distribution, the definition of its volumes, and finally one may talk exclusively of its constructional and decorative details. This is mainly because, for every detail, Michelangelo gives an authentic, completely new solution though always based on the elements of classical architecture. His 'new solution' *is not* to be understood in the sense of a formal experimentation, as an end in itself, but rather as a thorough investigation of those inherited elements.

At this point one might well ask whether the question of decoration can still be posed today in general and objective terms, after so many years of ideological terrorism by the Modern Movement. The theoretical hypothesis of rational architecture seems to come closest to a sensible approach to this problem. Rationalist thought believes in the historical continuity of architecture and in the fixed and immutable laws that historical experience offers to design. Rationalist thought applauds the repetition and the cognitive character of design. It focuses on the syntactic aspects of architecture and studies the relationships which link architectures remote in time one to the other.

Let us look, for example, at an operational choice which is inseparable from the architectural experience of Rationalism, that is, the choice of *simplification.* Simplification is an operation carried out on the elements of architecture and stresses precisely the sense of *generality* which emerges from the analysis of architecture in time. This sense of generality is what causes us to say (for instance, with regard to the reference made to Michelangelo) that those completely *new* forms were in reality the very forms which Michelangelo had before him; that is, the concrete experience he had to deal with.

Simplification is applied to forms, but it does not make choices in this field except in the sense of constructing a rational and suitable discourse vis-à-vis the present. The question of simplification is closely linked to what I have said about decoration because simplification pertains to ornament and does so precisely through a process of typological investigation, even though disengaged from issues of function or use.

I could give two examples: one is the Rufer house by Loos, the other is the Oldenburg exhibition by Behrens. In the Rufer house a smooth cornice at the top of the outer walls echoes the design of a cyma found in a textbook. Here the moulding, the ornament, has been simplified. On the front of the building, rigorously plain and simple, three classical metopes are introduced.

The other example concerns one of the first architectural experiments by Behrens, namely the buildings for the Oldenburg exhibition of 1906. When Behrens alludes to the structural and architectural motifs of the Renaissance (thus stressing the simple geometrical forms of the pavilions through the use of colour alone) 'he makes decoration' in the strictest sense of the word. I mean he makes decoration in the *classical sense.* The elements of classical decoration have undergone a process of simplification: that is, a process of archetypal reduction and of stylisation (the theory on the origins of triglyphs, antefixae, etc, is well-known). If it is true that some classical ornaments represent the simplification of technical and constructional elements, it is also true that from the start the techniques involved must have been largely superceded. The aim, however, always was to refer to this very technique for reasons which, though now forgotten, are not completely incomprehensible.

With their exemplary quotations, both Loos and Tessenow put forward what they consider the insuperable points in the history of architecture, those fixed points which are no longer open to further advancement and progress and which, as a consequence, are unsuitable for any further experimentation: that is, the Orders. In Loos' case a necessary element such as the column becomes a decorative element exactly because the long course of architecture needs to be explained and because one ought to indicate the limits of architecture itself. For Loos, the use of the column as a decorative element stands as a recognition of the unchanging primacy of this particular form. In this sense the columns of the Michaelerplatz house and those of the Chicago Tribune, though sharing a similar raison d'être, are in fact different but complementary responses to the same manifesto.

As I have already mentioned, this research into forms addresses the question of decoration and corresponds to a design procedure which goes back a long way in the history of architecture. This procedure has special relevance to the nature of architecture insofar as it is a practical activity; it concerns the very elements of the *métier.* And it assumes particular importance in connection with notions like that of *imitation* as it was understood differently over the centuries.

If we consider, for example, the studies by Raphael and his pupils of the Domus Aurea, we can get an idea of the meaning these terms had in the Renaissance: the literal sense of the uncovering of an unknown but paradoxically familiar figurative world, capable of answering pressing and contemporary questions. The sense of responsibility and involvement implicit in the relationship which had grown up with antiquity at that time was also felt in the secret nature of these investigations. *Imitation* was primarily a discovery on the craft level: it went well beyond mere copying, because it no longer represented a shared language but a technique, even if that also had been abandoned. *Imitation was primarily a representation of technique*; that is, it was the *metiér.* This is true of the relationship, for instance between the *villa dei misteri* and early 20th-century painting. The same is also true for Masaccio and Piero della Francesca, who had a similar relationship of great immediacy. Such is the extraordinary relationship that exists between forms remote from one another in time: a fateful closed circle, a world which extraordinarily repeats itself because of an incredible identity of means and ends; of expressive means, that is, technique, and of expressive ends, that is, the *métier* in the most human and noble sense of the term. Such is the meaning of constant modernity.

Such are the relevant issues to an architecture which sees itself as patient research, as work of an exquisitely material and craftsman-like nature. It is not a cause of alarm, however, to see these issues being mediated through personal or individual choices as in the examples of the Modern Movement mentioned here. This mediation is not at odds with Rationalism's aim at generality; indeed it is Rationalism's necessary precondition since architecture is here understood as *collective work.*

This attitude often privileges certain forms in what we may somewhat ambiguously call an *architecture of reference:* an architecture, the fixed points of which already mentioned seem to play the role of definitive and complete answers regarding architectural form. This attitude makes it possible for people – even if different and remote from one another in time – to recognise one another and to work together, so to speak, united by common aims and by a common idea of research in the realm of form. This is a choice that makes it possible for an agreement which needs no declarations and slogans, but which is born and develops by means of different works which in themselves, however, remain singular and unique.

By now it is obvious that everything mentioned here in the form of observations and linked to one another through the theme of decoration, is in fact an example: the question of decoration becomes here an excuse for a conclusive reconsideration of certain significant facts in the recent history of architecture. A similar analysis could be done starting from other specific questions: for instance, the question of *style,* of *métier,* or of ideas like that of *monumentality, the classic* and so on.

In every case, as long as one always starts from questions that are specific to architecture, one encounters the same issues. I believe that the primary aim of such studies is to give a more plausible understanding to the questions themselves, as they relate both to the Modern Movement and to the traditions that have been handed down to us. Furthermore, such studies have a practical aim as well: that of familiarising ourselves with the specific and constitutive quest of our work; with those questions and issues which have been outlawed, exorcised and replaced by ephemeral opportunist and inadequate fads.

ALDO ROSSI, *THE ANALAGOUS CITY*, 1976

AN ANALOGICAL ARCHITECTURE
ALDO ROSSI

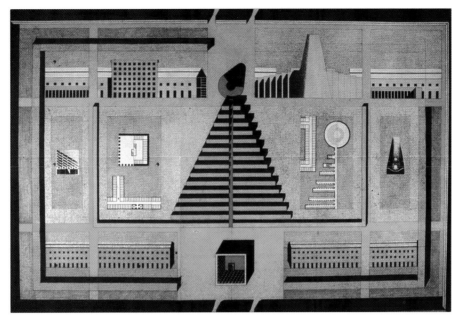

ALDO ROSSI, MODENA CEMETERY, ITALY, 1971-84

Although in my architecture things are seen in a fixed way, I realise that in recent projects certain characteristics, memories, and above all associations have proliferated or become clearer, often yielding unforeseen results. Each of these designs has been due increasingly to that concept of the 'analogical city' about which I wrote some time ago; meanwhile that concept has developed in the

spirit of analogy. Writing on that subject, I stated that it was mainly a matter of a logical-formal operation that could be translated as a design method.

In order to illustrate this concept, I cited the example of the view of Venice by Canaletto in the Parma Museum, in which Palladio's project for the Rialto Bridge, the Basilica, and the Palazzo Chiericati are arranged and depicted as if the painter had reproduced an actual townscape. The three monuments, of which one is only a project, constitute an analogue of the real Venice composed of definite elements related to both the history of architecture and that of the city itself. The geographical transposition of the two existing monuments[1] to the site of the intended bridge, forms a city recognisably constructed as a locus of purely architectonic values. This concept of the analogical city has been further elaborated in the spirit of analogy toward the conception of an analogical architecture.

In the correspondence between Freud and Jung, the latter defines the concept of analogy in the following way:

'I have explained that "logical" thought is what is expressed in words directed to the outside world in the form of discourse. "Analogical" thought is sensed yet unreal, imagined yet silent; it is not a discourse but rather a meditation on themes of the past, an interior monologue. Logical thought is "thinking in words". Analogical thought is archaic, unexpressed, and practically inexpressible in words.'

I believe I have found in this definition a different sense of history, conceived of not simply as fact, but as a series of things, of affective objects to be used by the memory or in a design. Thus, I believe I have also discovered the fascination of the picture by Canaletto in which the various works of architecture by Palladio and their removal in space constitute an analogical representation that could not have been expressed in words.

Today I see my architecture within the context and limits of a wide range of associations, correspondences and analogies. Whether in the purism of my first works or the present investigation of more complex resonances, I have always regarded the object, the product, the project, as being endowed with its own individuality that is related to the theme of human and material evolution. In reality, research into architectural problems signifies little more to me than research of a more general nature, whether it be personal or collective, applied to a specific field.

My associates and I are striving to create new interests and alternatives. The quotation from Walter Benjamin: 'I am unquestionably deformed by relationships with everything that surrounds me', might be said to contain the thought underlying this essay. It also accompanies my architecture today.

There is a continuity in this, even though in the most recent projects general and personal tensions emerge with greater clarity, and in various drawings the uneasiness of different parts and elements can be felt to have superimposed itself on the geometrical order of the composition.

The deformation of the relationships between those elements surrounding, as it were, the main theme, draws me toward an increasing rarefication of parts in favour of more complex compositional methods. This deformation affects the materials themselves and destroys their static image, stressing instead their elementality and superimposed quality. The question of things themselves, whether as compositions or components – drawings, buildings, models or descriptions – appears to me increasingly more suggestive and convincing. But this is not to be interpreted in the sense of *vers une architecture* nor as a *new* architecture. I am referring rather to familiar objects, whose form and position are already fixed, but whose meanings may be changed: barns, stables, sheds, workshops, etc – archetypal objects whose common emotional appeal reveals timeless concerns.

Such objects are situated between inventory and memory. Regarding the question of memory, architecture is also transformed into autobiographical experience; places and things change with the superimposition of new meanings. Rationalism seems almost reduced to an objective logic, the operation of a reductive process which in time produces characteristic features.

In that respect I consider one of the studies realised in the course of work on the Modena Cemetery competition as especially important. In redrawing this design and in the very process of rendering the various elements and applying the colours to parts that required emphasis, the drawing itself acquired a complete autonomy vis-à-vis the original design, so much so that the original conception might be said to be only an analogue of the finished project. It suggested a new idea based on the labyrinth and the contradictory notion of the distance travelled. In formal terms this composition is like the game *Il gioco dell'oca*.[2] In fact, I believe this resemblance explains its fascination and the reason why we produced several variations of the same form. Afterwards, it occured to me that the 'death' square is particularly noticeable, as if it contained some profound automatic mechanism quite apart from the painted space itself.

No work, other than by its own technical means, can entirely resolve or liberate the motives that inspired it; for this reason, a more or less conscious repetition is produced in the work of anyone who works continuously as an artist. In the best of cases, this can lead to a process of perfection but it can also produce total silence. That is the repetition of objects themselves.

In my design for the residential block in the Gallaratese district of Milan there is an analogical relationship with certain engineering works that mix freely with both the corridor typology and a related feeling I have always experienced in the architecture of the traditional Milanese tenements, where the corridor signifies a life-style bathed in everyday occurrences, domestic intimacy, and varied personal relationships. However, another aspect of this design was made clear to me by Fabio Reinhart driving through the San Bernardino Pass, as we often did, in order to reach Zurich from the Ticino Valley; Reinhart noticed the repetitive element in the system of open-sided tunnels, and therefore the inherent pattern. I understood on another occasion how I must have been conscious of that particular structure – and not only of the forms – of the gallery, or covered passage, without necessarily intending to express it in a work of architecture.

In like fashion I could put together an album relating to my designs and consisting only of things already seen in other places: galleries, silos, old houses, factories, farmhouses in the Lombard countryside or near Berlin, and many more – something between memory and an inventory. I do not believe that these designs are leading away from the rationalist position that I have always upheld; perhaps it is only that I see certain problems in a more comprehensive way now.

In any case I am increasingly convinced of what I wrote several years ago in the *Introduction to Boullée*:[3] that in order to study the irrational it is necessary somehow to take up a rational position as observer. Otherwise, observation and, eventually, participation give way to disorder.

The motto of my entry in the competition for the Trieste Regional Office was taken from the title of a collection of poems by Umberto Saba: *Trieste e una Donna*.[4] By this reference to one of the greatest modern European poets I attempted to suggest both the autobiographical quality of Saba's poetry and my own childhood associations of Trieste and Venice, as well as the singular character of the city that brings together Italian, Slav, and Austrian traditions.

My two years in Zurich had a great influence upon this project in terms of precise architectonic images: the idea of a great glazed cupola (*Lichthof*) such as the one at Zurich University by Moser, or that of the *Kunsthaus*. I have combined the concept of a public building with this idea of a large, centrally illuminated space; the public building, like the Roman bath or gymnasium, is represented by a central space; here, in fact, three large central spaces related to one another, above which are the corridors of the upper storeys that lead to the offices.

The large spaces can either be divided or used as a single area for general assemblies; they are indoor plazas. Each is lit through large panes of glass recalling those I referred to in Zurich. An important feature is the raised stone platform. This actually exists and represents the foundations of the old Austrian railway depots. It has been modified only by the openings through which one is able to enter a series of spaces occupying the lower level of the building.

I retained this basement level as a good way of expressing the physical continuity between old and new: by the texture of the stone; its colour; and the perspective of the street running along the sea. This project is closely related to that for the students' hostel made at about the same time, which represents a link between the design for Casa Bay[5], and the Gallaratese block.

From Gallaratese it borrows the typology of rectilinear volumes with outside corridors, containing the students' living quarters, while with Casa Bay it shares the relationship with a sharply sloping site. The blocks of students' rooms are enclosed within an open framework of steel galleries linked at various points, and the whole building may be seen as an elevated construction anchored to the ground. The factory-like blocks are joined to a social services building, also developed on a centralised plan, the focus of which is a large open space with various rooms arranged above; the central room functions as the dining and assembly hall. It, too, is lit from above like the Regional Office Building. This steeply pitched roof of glass points toward the foot of the hill and, as can be seen from the drawings, is the focal point of the entire complex.

The use of light materials and, in particular, the contrast between steel and glass – combined in a way that emphasises their technological or engineering qualities – and other materials suggestive of masonry (stone, plaster, and reinforced concrete) is expressed with clarity, and the design is restated by means of its specific relation with nature. The preference for light materials and open structural work corresponds to the space over the slope, like a bridge in other words, while the heavy part reposes directly on solid ground.

In a way, this sort of contrast was already introduced in the design for a pedestrian bridge at the *XIIIth Triennale* (1963), in which the metal bridge enclosed in transparent steel netting contrasted with the static mass of the piers echoing the arcade behind. This same netting reappears in the housing at Gallaratese. The project for a bridge at Bellinzona in Switzerland followed a similar development; this was part of the overall scheme for the restoration of the castle, carried out by Reichlin and Reinhart, and the bridge was intended to connect the upper part of the fortifications with the part situated near the river passing over the via Sempione. In that design the two concrete supports, that would probably have been varnished, were supposed to resemble the grey stone of the castle walls, and the bridge was once more covered in metallic netting. By means of such examples, I hope to be able to illustrate the problem of new building in historic town centres and the relationship between old and new architecture in general. I believe that this relation, or bond as it can be understood in the broader sense, is most satisfactorily expressed through the careful use of contrasting materials and forms, and not through adaptation or imitation. But the same principles serve as an introduction to the contrasting relationship with nature pursued in the villa at Borgo Ticino (Casa Bay).

I have a special fondness for this design because it seems to express a fortunate condition. Perhaps it is the fact of living suspended in mid-air among the trees of the forest, or the similarity to those riverbank constructions, including even fish-ermen's shacks, which for functional reasons – but also owing to the basic repetition of their form – remind us of prehistoric lake dwellings.

The typological image of the building is of elements growing along the slope, but forming an independent horizontal line above it, the relationship to the earth being shown only by the varying height of the supports.

The architectural elements are like bridges suspended in space. The suspension or aerial construction allows the house an existence within the forest at its most secret and unattainable point – amongst the branches of the trees.

The windows in each room open at the same level as the branches themselves, and viewed from certain parts of the house (the entry, the hall, and the bedrooms) the relation between earth, sky and trees is unique.

The positioning of the building in the natural environment operates in this unusual fashion not because the building imitates or mimics nature, but rather by the fact of being superimposed, almost as an addition to nature itself . . . trees, earth, sky, meadow.

Notes

1 Actually situated in Vicenza.
2 The playing board consists of 63 divisions painted in a spiral, each ninth space depicting a goose.
3 *Architettura saggio sull-arte* by Etienne-Louis Boullée, translated by Aldo Rossi (Padua, 1967).
4 *Trieste and a Woman.*
5 Project for a villa in Borgio Ticino (with G. Braghieri), 1973.

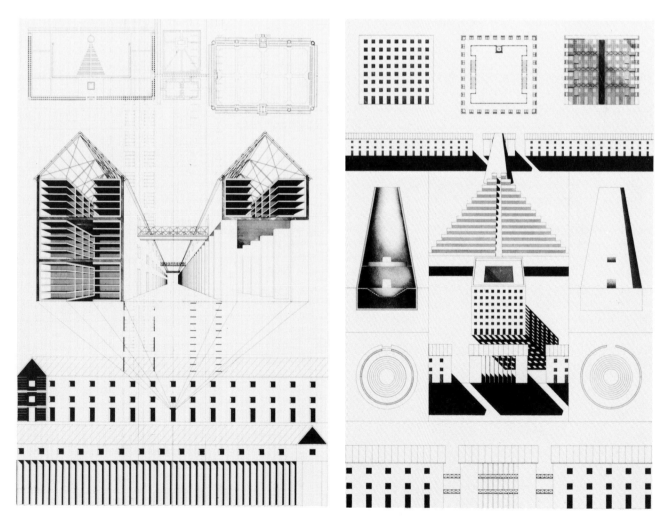

ALDO ROSSI, MODENA CEMETERY, ITALY, MASTER DRAWINGS, 1971-84

NEO-RATIONALISM AND FIGURATION
IGNASI SOLÁ-MORALES

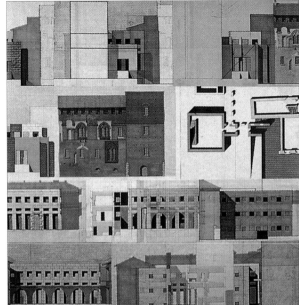

L TO R: ALDO ROSSI, IL TEATRINO SCIENTIFICO, DETAIL, 1978; GIORGIO GRASSI, CASTELLO DI ABBIATEGRASSO, 1970

In Italy the term Rationalism acquired renewed prestige during the 60s. A body of doctrines and a repertoire of works matured exactly during the years when the dissolution of modern architecture – whose origins lay precisely in the Rationalism of the historical avant-garde of the 20s – became abundantly clear.[1] By 1973, when Aldo Rossi organised the architectural section of the Milan

Triennale, the neo-rationalist doctrine had been fully formulated. The movement had an expressly public status not simply as regards cultural politics but moreover in connection to its theoretical position.[2]

The intellectual milieu that nurtured those ideas was to be found in three circles. Of these, the Milanese circle was the most clearly formulated, no doubt due to the irrefutable presence of Ernesto N Rogers and the group around *Casabella-Continuità*. The second circle was that of the Venice School of Architecture: under the guidance of Giuseppe Samonà the school stressed the importance of relating architecture to the city. The third was the circle of Ludovico Quaroni whose compromise with the architecture of the Modern Movement did not make him lose sight of the limitations of modern architecture and of the need for its revision.

Rogers, Samonà, Quaroni and their respective circles in the cities of Milan, Venice and Rome formed the framework within which it was possible to find young architects who had not taken part in the struggle for the institutionalisation of the Modern Movement. Such young architects had not been involved in the chaotic race of the 50s for economic development nor had they witnessed the gradual decline of the principles of the Modern Movement as they were turned into instruments of property speculation and of the destruction of the city. Moreover, since the 60s represented a definitive trivialisation of the functional, technological and social principles of the Modern Movement, it

was left to a group of young architects to demand that such principles be reappraised. They had both a yearning for the purity of the Modern Movement and an interest in restating the theoretical foundations of architectural design. This deliberate self-criticism that young architects made of their own tradition generated a voluminous critical literature: the history of the Modern Movement itself was now the object of a relentless debate aiming at reinterpreting Modern Architecture's ultimate significance. Furthermore they set out to formulate theoretically both the specific tools of architectural discourse and those general, logical and rational methods that would support architectural design practice.

Ultimately the task of re-establishing foundations began in the 60s with Aldo Rossi, Carlo Aymonino, Guido Canella, Manfredo Tafuri, Emilio Bonfanti, Giorgio Grassi, Giorgio Polesello, Luciano Semerani, Nino Dardi, Vittorio Gregotti, and others, and was marked at its core by a moral drive. The majority of these architects drew their criticism of Christian Democratic policies of architecture and urbanism from the political positions of the left which they occupied. They rejected conventional professionalism because of the commercial vulgarity to which it had reduced Italian architecture and design (for though acclaimed worldwide, Italian design had reduced the images of the Modern Movement into *kitsch*) and the immorality of its urban policies which were based on consumerism and destruction.[3]

Historical Standpoint

The neo-rationalists began their critical revision of modern architecture with a historical reading. That was a task they could not and did not want to avoid; their masters had bequeathed them a taste for history. That was contrary to the mainstream of the Modern Movement which had shed away its interest for architectural history. In Italy, however, the love for architectural history had never ceased; if anything it had gained impetus from the studies of the work of the protagonists of the Modern Movement. The issues of *Casabella* on Wright, Loos, Oud, and those analysing contemporary work carried out by architects in their home towns were very popular at the time. In this way *Casabella* contributed to the discovery of secondary modernist architects and thus to the formulation of a dialectically conceived history of the Modern Movement. The Modern Movement was no longer to be thought of as the monolithic tradition set out by the Giedion-Pevsner-Zevi line, but as an interplay of tendencies in face of which it became necessary to be critical and discerning.

To reconsider modern history meant, at the time, to propose as models certain names against others – Oud against De Stijl, Terragni against Futurism, Asplund against Nordic Organicism. But all these 'discoveries', the polemical value of which was accompanied by a hesitant definition of a new taste, were but the first step in an investigation of the historical origins of Rationalism. The historical reappraisal of architecture, beyond the narrow limits of the modernist avant-gardes, became necessary. Tafuri looked for the origins of the modern architect in Brunelleschi's Renaissance, while Aldo Rossi became fascinated with the architecture of the Enlightenment as the most genuine manifestation of the rationality with which modern culture built its cities.[4]

The appeal that the architecture of the Enlightenment exerted on the young neo-rationalists was not grounded simply on its historical aura. Rather, it was a real source of theoretical, ideological and formal inspiration. Kaufmann's influence was decisive in this respect.[5] To understand the formal innovations of the modernist avant-garde as a continuation of the 'break' that Enlightenment architecture had initiated was to add to the latter's figurative values certain ethical resonances. By analogy, therefore, neo-rationalist 'genuine avant-garde' was to stand against the trivialised versions of 50s' and 60s' Modernism as neo-classical purism had stood against the trivialisations of 19th-century historicism.

Italian neo-rationalists also showed renewed interest in the treatises and manuals of architectural history, thus illustrating a salient tendency to find models and references in the past that would be capable of clarifying present problems. Giorgio Grassi showed special interest in Le Muet, Viollet-le-Duc, Tessenow, Hilberseimer, while Aldo Rossi focused on Boullée, Palladio and Loos. Yet another common development in such historical studies was Rossi's restatement of the universal principles of architecture. At the time Rossi had an interest in the architecture and urbanism of the socialist countries. Since the mid-60s, the influence of Aymonino in the University of Venice and its *Gruppo Architettura,* as well as the knowledge and publication of works from the German Democratic Republic, the Soviet Union, Czechoslovakia, Yugoslavia and Poland had the great value of challenging the dominant architectural and urban models of European capitalism. This European socialist model – itself an offspring of the Modern Movement – was influenced by socialist policies and saw the ideal of collective values as the main objective in the construction of the city.[6]

Critique of Architecture

The comprehensive critique launched by the neo-rationalists did not stop itself simply in historical reappraisal but moved on to formulating methods of analysis and design which were to have a powerful influence on the development of architecture. The design process itself was to be subjected to rigorous analysis so that whimsical architectural forms would be eliminated. In years past, too much personal licence and calls to creativity and inventiveness had dominated the architectural panorama. Such an approach had undermined the confidence in general principles. The 'international picturesque', as Nino Dardi has called it,[7] was no longer acceptable and against its intuitionist whims the solidity of a general method would have to be opposed. The will to avoid the pitfalls of idealism and a renewed interest in the social sciences were procedures used against voluntarism or ideological constructions.

The neo-rationalists of the 60s found in structuralism the necessary theoretical tools for their own method of architectural analysis. Structuralism (as for example in the work of Lévi-Strauss) studies social facts – say kinship relations – both as independent objects and as systems of differential relationships. 'Object' and 'difference' are the key notions in structuralism; its descriptive and analytical categories are supported by the nexus of relationships that the researcher can find in the material he studies.[8] The neo-rationalists, distancing themselves from semioticist temptations, felt the need to act in a similar way within the field of architecture. There is certainly a parallel between the structuralist methodology of the social sciences of that period and the analytical tools developed by Italian neo-rationalists in their search for the objective foundations of design.[9] From this point of view, the recognition of the autonomous architectural object entailed a fundamental epistemological change. The notion of environment, so characteristic of the picturesque tradition, was now of no interest: the city as 'constructed fact' was the referent from which analysis should proceed. Aldo Rossi's seminal text of these years, *L'architettura della città,* put forward a 'théorie d'ensemble' which established the analytical methods of Neo-Rationalism.'[10] The physical reality of the city became the point of departure, the material datum of every analysis, and the context within which any architectural work was to be judged irrespective of its scale, functional or stylistic characteristics. To recognise the city as the fundamental architectural reference meant to efface all boundaries between architecture and urban design. Every physical intervention was now to be measured against the physical and constructed reality of the city.

This realisation that the city is a necessary referential datum entailed a break with the Taylorist logic of the production line that characterised the Modern Movement. Against the linear design process of the Modern Movement (ie, from the industrial element, to the building, to the city) Neo-Rationalism proposed the techniques of topography/cartography and typification.

With the techniques of topography/cartography one can describe the actual condition of the city or its parts, and it is possible to carry out analytical operations based on the objective data and accurate dimensions provided. Topography describes the site and the physical structure of the settlements upon which the city is founded. It tells us about the material conditions upon which architecture operates. Cartography describes the intervention – the architectural activity – upon the physical site, showing us the form created from the moment these interventions take place. The morphological analysis of the city and its architecture cannot be explained by conditions other than those of its own form. No reference, therefore, is necessary to the 'life of its inhabitants, to its 'society', to its 'style' or 'culture', to all those phenomena which do not have a material counterpart discernible through topography and cartography.

Furthermore, due to the importance of description, it would now be necessary to develop a discourse which would be, above all, about the differences of forms: thus a renewed interest in taxonomy and formal typification is established. Description would now mean the description of relationships; above all the description of a structure of *formal* relationships.

The same line of enquiry leads to the typological understanding of architecture. By using the notion of type (taken from the academic tradition) Rossi found a way to describe architecture in relation to its physical conditions and by means of descriptive categories that do not depend on the 'idealist' concepts of style and character. Building types are formal constants that permit the classification recognition and description of buildings of all periods and places. These formal constants act as containers that reduce the complexity of architectural appearances to their most outstanding physical characteristics.

Through the notion of type one is able to understand architectural form as a system that describes the logic of its own formation; a system that describes the transformations of the elements of a certain formal repertoire. The notion of type permits also the study of the city's relations of production as well as its formal developments or ruptures. Ultimately, the city's physical structure and that of its buildings can be related in an analytical whole.

Reductivism

The architecture that evolves from such theoretical premises has evident reductivist characteristics. The Modern Movement perpetrated a romantic conception of art, and for Gropius, Benhe or Corbusier, modern architecture had to unite the whole human environment into one organised and poetic impulse.

By contrast, an almost puritanical austerity characterised neo-rationalist architectural theory. Interest lay only in the physical and structural expression of architectural and urban forms. Architecture was to emerge out of a highly intellectualised and abstract procedure. In the search for a new foundation, rational architecture resorted neither to criteria of other practical fields, nor to the images found in the technical and artificial world of the modern city.[13] An enormous difficulty now became apparent: how does one make the transition from analysis to design? How can analytical procedures provide something more than information about the site, the urban structure or the possible formal repertoire; how can something more than factual information be found? Analysis seems to offer only a clear and orderly description according to certain dominant criteria but it gives no clues as to the process of design.

Though loathe to admit it, neo-rationalists encounter at the project state the need to take a step into the unknown. This is an intuitive moment for which the analytical process cannot generate an intentionality: this cannot arise from the repertoire of urban typologies. Due to the reductivism of its morphological repertoires, the analytical method, no doubt, tends to reduce the available alternatives to a minimum. The city and its architecture are seen as the articulation of a few permanent and immutable elements – certainly with an almost metaphysical sense – which offer a complete compositional range of design possibilities. But even so, the moment of free choice, the moment of decision that guides from the analytical stage to the project cannot be eliminated. Perhaps in an attempt to minimise subjective risks, neo-rationalist theory does not deal with this stage in a conscious way. In my opinion, this point of crucial ambiguity surreptitiously introduces a component of freedom or chance into an otherwise rigorous intellectual method.

If the avant-garde of modern architecture aspired to individual freedom that was manifested in subjectivism and experimentalism,[14] Neo-Rationalism chooses to operate within the field of necessity. The debate between necessity and innovation reintroduces an old dispute: the dispute between a theory of

imitation versus a theory of invention. Neo-Rationalism seeks to defend itself from the formal arbitrariness of the modern avant-garde by resorting to the imitation that architecture necessarily makes of itself. A traditionalist component – or, if one prefers – a self-reflective one is thus introduced. Architecture does not invent since its repertoire has always existed. Its elements have always been the same and they appear always inside the peculiar 'nature' which is the tradition of architecture. In a manner similar to the academic tradition but with a more radical and elemental procedure, Neo-Rationalism defines its design possibilities within the discipline of Architecture. It is this body of accumulated knowledge that defines its rules and the repertoire of its possible references, establishing, in this way, a framework for all design decisions.[15]

Perhaps the connection between academicism and Neo-Rationalism might seem at first paradoxical. And yet, the Neo-Rationalism of the 60s and 70s cannot be understood without reference to its most conspicuous predecessors: the rationalists of the Enlightenment and the tradition of the mimetic conception of architecture during the 19th century.

In its purest expression the notion of imitation considers that the contents of architecture cannot be invented by the architect in each project; such content is viable only insofar as it refers to architecture itself, to its tradition, so that it can be construed as a metalanguage, a self-referring operation whereby architecture speaks of itself, presents itself anew and in this renewed representation performs the basic aesthetic action of imitating its own doings. It is no longer nature, generically considered, which is the object of imitation but rather a pre-existing sector of the real world which serves as a reference for architectural discourse. Consequently, the foundations of Neo-Rationalism lie in its conception of the architectural project, the limits of which are already established by architectural tradition and whose field of action is logically framed by the constant return of types, plans, and basic elements: all synchronically understood as permanent and immutable, rooted in tradition and history.

Figuration

One must now analyse how it is that the neo-rationalist problem of formal figuration (which lacks a general and explicit solution) is resolved in specific cases.

The comparison of the work of two architects – Aldo Rossi and Giorgio Grassi – may indicate two radically different solutions to the problem of figuration. These two architects (who collaborated for some years and who had much in common) clearly exemplify the positions analysed in this essay. In both cases their work shows the reductivism previously referred to. The influence of Structuralism is clear in both cases, and their interest in history can be interpreted as a form of remembrance of a permanent architectural heritage, the diversity and fundamental logical unity of which constitutes the precise context within which architecture had, is, and will continue to manifest itself. But though they share a common position on several theoretical points, their architecture is different.

Aldo Rossi, in addressing the problem of figuration, proposes a subjective criterion. Analysis and the systematic and rational method do not encompass the design process in its totality. There is a final point in this process which is governed by subjective intuition. 'There is no art that is not autobiographical', writes Rossi in his 'Introduction to Boullée'.[16] To propose an autobiographical condition of architecture might appear to contradict what has gone before. But this is not the case.

Rossi's architecture mediates the break between the objective and the poetic discourse inherent in modern culture. Between reason and desire there exists a gap that can be bridged only by means of analogy: an analogy that is hesitant, painful and fragile to the extent that it is personal, mythical and contingent. [17] It should not surprise us that recently Rossi explained his work as an autobiography. Putting aside the *esprit de système* of his projects and writings of previous years, he decided to stress the most subjective aspects that ultimately make up the figures of his work.[18] In his drawings, relationships and displacements are established surrealistically, no longer explicable by reference to a logical system but intelligible only to a Freudian consciousness, for it is in the uncontrolled interaction of biographical events that the net of associations which structures our behaviour is built up. If the memory of a coffee pot or the recollection of the landscapes of childhood could be brought forward at the time of designing a theatre or a students' residence, Rossi's methodological discourse ends up by becoming a celibate machine, not unlike the way in which surrealism conceives of the confrontation between desire and impotence.[19]

The surreal and therefore illogical component, dreamed rather than materially manifested, is for Rossi the plausible explanation for his figurative options. The solution might appear surprising; but not if we remember that it was precisely the surrealist tradition which maintained the most committed critical stance against the Modern Movement and that it is surrealism that has given the best expression to the futility of modern reason. With this leap into the unknown Aldo Rossi, with the greatest anguish but also lucidity, points simultaneously to the necessity and impossibility of the neo-rationalist project.

By contrast, in Giorgio Grassi the problem of figuration addresses different issues. Grassi refuses the subjective approach and his becomes a spirited research for an objective foundation of his formal decisions. Perhaps it is Grassi who sets out the problem of figuration with the greatest rigour precisely due to the lack of an objective solution which he does not want to relinquish in any case.

There are two approaches in Grassi: that of anonymous architecture and that of the objectivity of construction. In the last 30 or 40 years, Grassi has written the most salient and inspired texts on the lessons to be learned from anonymous architecture. His analysis of rural buildings, of the Gothic one-family house, of the housing schemes of the Modern Movement, all seem to point towards the same end: the encounter between an objectively defined, socially acceptable figuration and the architecture of the house. In Grassi's work the collective social condition of architecture is not simply reaffirmed but becomes instead the very foundation of his convictions. Only through their social legitimacy can architectural forms become plausible.[20] Building types and compositional elements – few and schematically reduced to their most essential features – are acceptable only if one can find in them a verification of their efficacy and social acceptance. These types and elements have material validity only in their constructive logic and in the historical experience that legitimises their functions. Grassi's figuration, which reflects his demanding social ethics, tends towards anonymity, towards a dissolution of the subject in a collectivity that is more willed than existing, and which assures the authenticity of his references.

Where Rossi dwelt on contradiction and duality and even employed a personal poetic which freed him from the requirements he had imposed upon himself, Grassi, on the contrary, espouses a millenial tendency, a utopian projection towards a socially and technically coherent space which, though in reality exists only in fragments, is now made absolute and becomes eventually the basis of his work.

Contradiction and utopia, dualism and monism are, in the end, the opposite attitudes that guide these two architects in their search for solutions to the obscure problem of figuration. The problem of realism again reappears as an open, unresolved question. At the same time, the experience of both architects demonstrates in different ways but with equal intensity that the neo-rationalist project is an insoluble question.

Notes

1 Cf *Teoria della progetazzione architettonica*, Dedalo, Bari, 1968. Also see texts by Canella, Coppa, Gregotti, Rossi, A Samonà, Scimemi, Semerani and Tafuri in a publication bearing the same title and comprising of lectures delivered in a symposium in 1966. Formerly published under the title A*spetti e problemi della tipologia edilizia*, Venice. During the academic year 1963-64, the neo-rationalist methodology had already been initiated in a systematic way.

2 The book Ar*chitettura razionale*, Franco Angeli, Milan, 1973, constitutes the catalogue of the architectural sections of the Milan Triennale. The term *Tendenza* was then coined by Massimo Scolari. The connection that exists between Italian Neo-Rationalim and that of the 'New York Five' marks both the moment of the movement's consolidation and of its eclectic diffusion in the 70s.

3 The Italian design boom is exemplified by the exhibition organised by the MOMA of New York, 1972, entitled Italy: Th*e New Domestic Landscape*. From the 50s onwards it is the socially committed Italian cinema that deals with the themes of urban devastation and property speculation.

4 See Manfredo Tafuri, *Teorie e storie dell'architettura*, Laterza, Bari, 1968. Also, Aldo Rossi, 'Introduzzione a Boullée' in *Saggio sul'arte*, Padua, 1967.

5 See Aldo Rossi, Emil Kaufmann e l'architettura del'illuminismo' in *Casabella-Continuità*, No 222, 1958.

6 See 'Gruppo Architettura' Q*uaderni di Documentazioni*, Nos 1 and 2, Venice, 1971 and 1973, including texts by Aymonino, Babri, Lena, Polesello, Semerani, Burelli, Billa and others. Also the references to the architecture of socialist countries in the book *Architettura razionale, op cit*, note 2.

7 See Constantino Dardi, *Il gioco sapiente*, Marsilio, Padua, 1971.

8 See Gilles Deleuze, *L'écriture et la différence*, Ed Minuit, Paris, 1967.

9 The references by Aldo Rossi to the work of Lévi-Strauss are frequent and explicit in many of his writings.

10 See Also Rossi, *L'Architettura della città*, Marsilio, Padua, 1966.

11 See Massimo Scolari, ' Un contributo per la fondazione della scienza urbana', in *Controspazio*, Nos 7-8, Rome, 1971.

12 These ideas are first encountered in Aldo Rossi's 'Considerazioni sulla morfologia urbana e la tipologia edilizia' published in Venice, 1964, as part of *Aspetti e problemi della tipologia edilizia, op cit* note 1, later included in the book *L 'Archittetura della città, op cit*, note 10.

13 See Xavier Rubet de Ventós 'El funcionamiento como puritanismo' in the book *La estética y sus herejias*, Anagrama, Barcelona, 1974.

14 See Giorgio Grassi, 'Arquitectura, realidad y vanguardia', in the records of *Primer Simposio de Arquitectura y Ciudad: Vanguardia y Continuidad*, Valencia, 1980.

15 See Giorgio Grassi 'Il rapporto analisi-projetto', in *L'analisi urbana e la progetazzione architettonica*, School of Architecture, Milan Polytechnic, contributions to the Academic Year 1968-69, CLUP, Milan, 1970.

16 See Aldo Rossi, 'Introduzzione a Boullée', *op cit*, note 4.

17 Manfredo Tafuri 'L'architecture dans le boudoir', in *La sfera e il labirinto: Avanguardie e architettura da Piranesi agli anni 70*, Einaudi, Turin, 1980.

18 See Aldo Rossi, *Scientific Autobiography*, Rizzoli, New York, 1982.

19 See AAVV, Jung*genssellenmaschinen – Les machines célibataires*, Alfieri, Venice, 1975.

20 See Giorgio Grassi, *La costruzione logica dell' architettura*, Marsillo, Padua, 1967.

———— * ————

ALDO ROSSI, CASA AURORA, TURIN, 1984-87, VIEW OF CORNER AND INTERIORS

PICTORIAL SURVEY
ABSTRACT CLASSICISM

ALDO ROSSI, *ABOVE*: MODENA CEMETRY, 1972-84, ELEVATION WITH STATUE; *BELOW L TO R*: TOWN HALL,

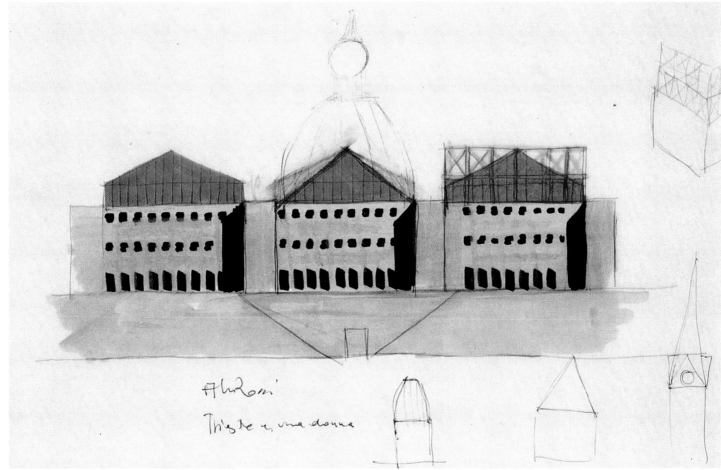

SQUARE AND MEMORIAL, SEGRATE, TOWN HALL, SCANDICCI, DESIGN ALTERNATIVE WITH DOME MOTIF

GIORGIO GRASSI, STUDENT HOUSING, CHIETI, ABRUZZO,1976-80, *ABOVE*: PERSPECTIVE OF STREET FROM STAIRCASE; *BELOW*: PERSPECTIVE OF AXIAL ARCADED STREET

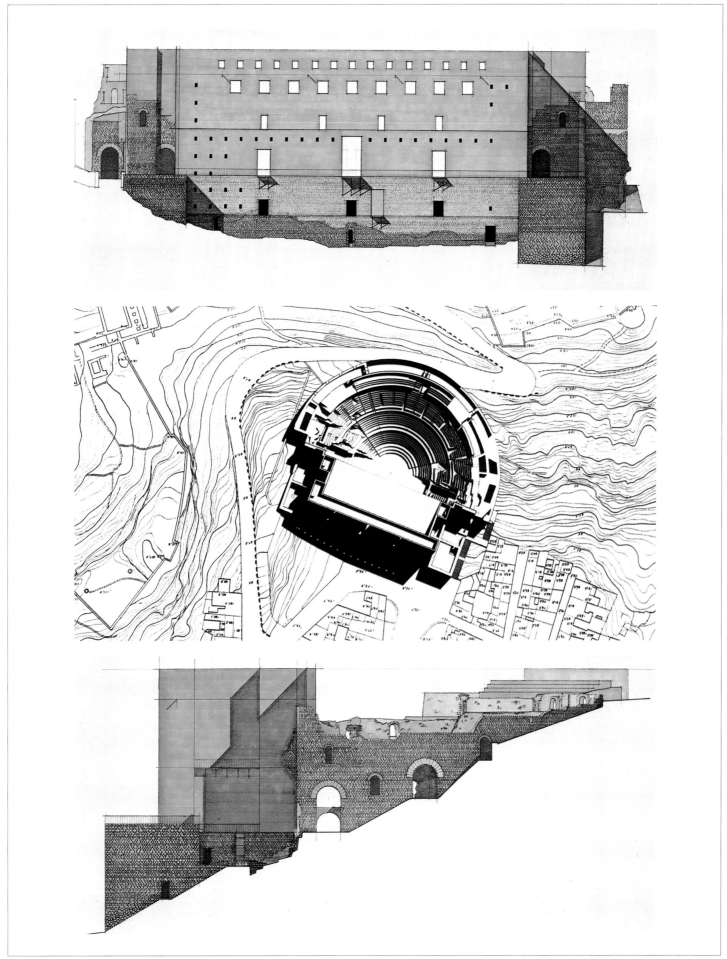

GIORGIO GRASSI, THE RESTORATION OF THE ROMAN THEATRE IN SAGUNTO, VALENCIA, 1978 *ABOVE*: LONGDITUDINAL SECTION; *CENTRE*: SITE PLAN; *BELOW*: CROSS SECTION

IÑIGUEZ & USTARROZ, RURAL CENTRE AT CORDOBILLA, BASQUE COUNTRY, 1981

IÑIGUEZ AND USTARROZ, REDEVELOPMENT OF CHÂTEAU PICHON-LONGUEVILLE, PAUILLAC, BORDEAUX, 1988, *ABOVE*: CENTRAL SQUARE; *BELOW*: OVERALL VIEW

MIGUEL GARAY, CASA MENDIOLA, ANDOIAN, BASQUE COUNTRY, 1977-78

GARAY & LINAZASORO, *ABOVE*: SCHOOL AT IKASTOLA, BASQUE COUNTRY; *BELOW*: TOWN HALL, SEGURA, 1981-3

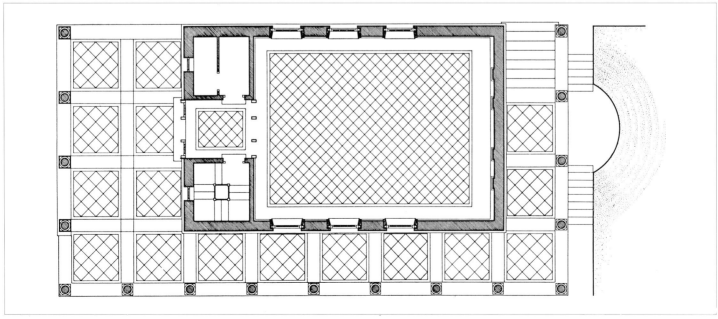

CENICACELAYA & SALOÑA, RURAL CENTRE AT LA RIGADA, MUSKIZ, 1985-87

CENICACELAYA & SALOÑA, SCHOOL OF THE SACRED FAMILY, DERIO, 1990

ALEXANDER AND CHARIS CALLIGAS, HOUSE IN MONEMVASIA, PELOPONNESE, 1975

HILMER & SATTLER, *ABOVE*: HERLICH HOUSE, 1981, KARLSRUHE; *BELOW*: FETZER HOUSE, MUNICH. 1984

MICHAEL GRAVES, DOMAINE CLOS PEGASE WINERY, CALIFORNIA, 1984

IV

POST-MODERN CLASSICISM

MICHAEL GRAVES, PORTLAND PUBLIC SERVICES BUILDING, PORTLAND, OREGON, 1980-82

FREE-STYLE CLASSICISM
CHARLES JENCKS
THE WIDER TRADITION

Many people are confused about the classical revival today, and this muddle is not confined to the general public or journalists. Architects are confused, experts are confused, classicists are confused and I hope to show there is good reason for this intellectual imbroglio. Today's classical revival is so unlike any other that it forces us to reassess the basic meaning of the term, to change the meaning of Classicism, and it would be hard to find anything more disturbing than that, for the meaning has been established for generations. In this essay Classicism is defined broadly as a tradition more than a Graeco-Roman style, a tradition which includes some periods, such as Gothic and Mannerist, which are often regarded as anti-classical. While some may consider this redefinition as too wide, it has the virtue of illuminating the ideas behind current Free-Style Classicism, and the limits of Classicism in general.

Old and New Definitions

John Summerson, in *The Classical Language of Architecture* (1963 re-edited 1980), sets out the conventional definitions which have held sway since the Renaissance. 'Classical architecture has its roots in antiquity, in the worlds of Greece and Rome. . . The aim of classical architecture has always been to achieve a demonstrable harmony of parts. . . And while we must incorporate these essentials (harmony and proportion) in our idea of what is classical we must also accept the fact that classical architecture is only recognisable as such when it contains some allusion, however slight, however vestigial, to the antique 'orders'.[1] This compound evocation (Summerson says: 'It is a mistake to try to define Classicism') seems all right and was accepted by Helen Searing as the basis of her show on the kind of architecture we are also concerned with here.(The title of her exhibition was 'Speaking a New Classicism: American Architecture Now', held at Smith College and the Clark Art Institute in Massachusetts before travelling elsewhere.) Searing expands Summerson's potentially open 'definition' in the following way: 'Thus, by the "new Classicism" we mean the presence in a given design of recognisably classical motifs (the orders, the aedicule), formats (the prostyle temple, the domed rotunda), and typologies (the Palladian villa, the Roman castra).'[2] Again this seems a commonsense way of classifying recent developments as long as we don't enquire too deeply and ask more embarrassing questions: '*who* is recognising the motifs, *how many* formats or typologies must exist before we call a building classicist?'

By contrast, Helen Searing's co-author Henry Hope Read is much more strict in his definition, confining it to straight revivalist buildings such as America's national Capitol. Reed is adamant that 'in architecture, the classical is identified not by proportions, nor by the plan, nor by materials, however important, but by ornament . . . the human figure . . . animal (lion mask and dolphin) and vegetable (acanthus and laurel) forms and . . . this ornament is not Art Nouveau, nor Arabic, nor Egyptian, nor Gothic but Classical.'[3] However quaint this view of Classicism seems, there are some architects willing to stand by it, and the implied 19th-century view is echoed by Summerson,

who says: 'The porches of Chartres Cathedral are, in distribution and proportion, just about as classical as you can get, but nobody is ever going to call them anything but Gothic.'[4] That may be quite true in a linguistic sense; we all follow conventions and the Gothic is not about to be overthrown. But, on a deeper level than social convention, don't the porches of Chartres accord with Summerson's own 'definition' – 'some allusion, however slight, however vestigial, to the antique "orders"?' They are certainly full of columns, 'harmony' and much of the animal, vegetable and human ornament which Henry Hope Reed finds necessary for the definition. If Summerson, later in his book, is going to allow Auguste Perret, Peter Behrens and Max Abramovitz into the back door of his classical pantheon, can he rightfully exclude a tradition which has so obviously evolved from the classical?[5] Indeed his own doubt is expressed in a double negative when he says of the classical and gothic: 'they are very different but they are not opposites and they are not wholly unrelated.'[6] The further we push such questions the more we explore the contradictions in thought which have become conventionalised since the 19th-century Battle of the Styles.

Other current theorists such as Demetri Porphyrios, who may be speaking for present classicists and some of the 'Rationalists', defines the tradition as strictly as Reed but with, inevitably, another set of norms. He defined Classicism in a symposium on the subject in December 1980 as 'the constructional logic of vernacular and its mimetic elaboration': for example, Doric elaborating some vernacular wooden details.[7] Again a set of 19th-century polarities – building versus architecture, necessity versus myth – are brought in to support a familiar argument. Porphyrios, like Reed, has the singular virtue in his canonic definition of excluding 95% of today's interesting Classicism, a virtue pursued with some zest since he wants to keep his tradition pure and untainted by commerce, kitsch and, we might add, the reality principle. Indeed most classical revivals, including that of Vitruvius, have been movements of exclusion, and so it should be no surprise that certain architects today wish to reassert some old taboos. They can find many precedents in the Renaissance, or with the Neo-Palladianism of Campbell or the Neo-Classicism of Laugier.

However helpful these purification rituals might be to the brotherhood of confirmed believers, they don't help us understand what Classicism was in a wider sense, or what it is today. We have to look elsewhere for enlightenment. Helen Searing and Gavin Stamp have pointed out the current interest in looking at Romantic classicists, a set of favoured architects from Ledoux to Schinkel. They have put forward various theories to explain it: if Modernism starts at this time, why not the new Classicism? Stamp avers that this manner is the easiest style to copy and the least intellectually demanding.[8] But other periods and figures are in equal favour today: the Mannerists and Hawksmoor, the generation of 1900 and Lutyens, the Early Renaissance and Alberti – even, to introduce a doubt into this discussion, Egyptian, Romanesque, Baroque and Art Deco architects are studied with interest. No theorist or architect has yet been prepared to admit what may well be the truth: all periods of architecture are being explored for their lessons and all of them have classicising elements.

Before the implications of this disarming pluralism are explored, we might consider a few well-founded definitions of the subject outside architecture. The 11th edition of the Encyclopedia Britannica (1911) speaks for the informed opinion of that time when it focuses on the twin meanings of the classic as concerning 'authority' and 'Greece and Rome':

> The term 'classic' is derived from the Latin epithet *classicus* found in a passage of Aulus Gellius (XIX.8.15) where a *scriptor classicus* is contrasted with a *scriptor proletarius*. The metaphor is taken from the division of the Roman people into classes by Servius Tullius, those in the first class being called *classici*, all the rest *infra classem*, and those in the last *proletarii*. The epithet 'classic' is accordingly applied 1) generally to an author of the first rank, and 2) more particularly to a Greek or Roman author of character.[9]

Hence in Western architecture the treatises which consider only the best of Greek and Roman architecture, or the canonic genealogies of design from Bramante to Palladio, or with

own distinctive form, belongs to a class of similar and interchangeable parts, and can be identified by name, the Miesian building consists only of rectangles – shapes that have little relation to the human body and which do not come together, in a work such as the Seagram Building, to constitute a society of members, as do the parts of the Parthenon.[10]

Here we again have the characteristic problem of definition. Certain things are taken to be essential to Classicism which are not discovered in the building at hand and so it is excluded from the canon. That the 'canon' or 'classic' is variably defined across time tends to be overlooked by the definers of each generation. In reviewing my *Post-Modern Classicism* (*Architectural Design* 5/6 1980), Nicholas Penny, a classical scholar and co-author of *Taste and the Antique,* adopts the typical essentialist position:

> From a new Classicism one has the right to expect a system of *ideal proportions,* certainly *lucidity* and *harmony* of plan and elevation, but there is less evidence of this in the buildings that are the book's subject than there was when the Modern Movement was in full swing. As for *monumentality,* which one would also expect, it is certainly

MIES VAN DER ROHE, CROWN HALL, IIT, CHICAGO, 1962

Summerson's slightly expanded set, from Michelangelo to Borromini. These genealogies of design, reserved for the highest pedigree, make sense as far as they go.

But again a certain doubt may be introduced by pushing the analysis further. Suppose the tradition which starts with Greece, in the Doric, is continued to the recent past with, say, the 'Doric' of the first rank', Mies van der Rohe and his allusions 'however slight, however vestigial', to the antique 'orders'. No one will deny that Mies produced a kind of Schinkelesque Classicism when young then transformed it into a kind of modern Doric I beam order when older, but some will dispute bitterly that this has anything of importance to do with Greek architecture or the deeper classical tradition; Norris Kelly Smith is one:

> I do not mean to suggest that the measured and impersonal style of Mies and his imitators can be regarded as a modern equivalent of the traditional Classicism that descends from the Greek temple. While it possesses something of the formal purity and objectivity of that style, it quite lacks the relationship to the *word* which is essential to the humanising significance of the ordered architecture of the past. Whereas every part of the Greek temple . . . has its

attempted at Les Arcades du Lac, the glum, pre-cast concrete new town by Ricardo Bofill . . . which includes some painfully ungainly cylinders and triangles. . . There is no evidence here of any serious desire to revive the solemnity or the grandeur of the ancient stone architecture. . .[11] (my emphasis)

The essentials Penny expects to find thus differ from those of Summerson, Searing, Porphyrios and Reed, some of the other authorities we have looked at. There may be overlap in their judgement – Greece and Rome remain as a common definer – and perhaps they might agree on some mutual view of classical and non-classical buildings, but when they come to define it they look for different essentials, and with considerably different taste and assumptions. The straight revivalism of Reed has little to do with the 'slight allusions' of Summerson and Searing, which has little in common with the severe Doric of Porphyrios, and so on. We might conclude in exasperation that the word 'classical' is even more hopeless than 'romantic', a concept which has already been subjected to historical dismemberment.[12] Should we give it up because of its permissive vagueness; or keep it for its evocative power, since it can mean something to everyone? Clearly there are choices other than these.

Before we look at them we might focus on Nicholas Penny's distaste for Post-Modern Classicism and Bofill's work in particular, because this uneasiness is shared by some other critics who have a taste for 18th-century Classicism. Basically the work of Bofill is being excluded from their canon not because it lacks their essentials (ideal proportion, harmony, monumentality and grandeur it does have), but because it is crudely done in comparison with the pre-existing canon. It is done in concrete not stone, with heavy pre-cast walls and not delicate, sculpted pilasters. In a word it is *proletarii* not *classici*, or for the 'masses not the classes' – a phrase that apparently perturbed Penny.

Another shift in the concept of Classicism which is starting to get underway is that a few architects are using new materials, outside the canonic stone, wood and stucco, like neon and stainless steel which are associated with mass culture, and they are also designing buildings for the *proletarii*. This, in a style previously used mostly by the upper class for banks, clubs, country houses and places of civic grandeur, violates a still powerful taboo. But even if we probe this we can see its arbitrary nature; after all the style was also used in that most canonic

and cultural levels. We find an aspect which has always been inherent in its claims for universality: it can modify archetypal patterns to suit local conditions, building materials and meaning. The wider tradition of Classicism, in spite of the authorities, includes Gothic.

Classicism as Tradition and Essence

Once we admit Gothic as a sub-class of this genre then along come a host of other styles for inclusion: Romanesque[13] is clearly part of the main family as are Mannerism, Baroque and Rococo because of their elaboration of some classical tropes. After this the more unpedigreed styles can be related to the main bloodline: Art Nouveau Classicism (eg, Otto Wagner), Art Deco Classicism (eg, Raymond Hood) and the current Post-Modern Classicism. Other styles may be contrasted with it: Expressionism and Constructivism. Finally it can be seen in a new historical context as a continuously changing language which has evolved from the Egyptians and Assyrians.

Here is another fundamental shift in our definition and one obviously related to the egalitarian and pluralist shifts we have just noted. Instead of Greece and Rome being the sole originators

RICARDO BOFILL AND TALLER DE ARQUITECTURA, LES ARCADES DU LAC, SAINT QUENTIN-EN-YVELINES, FRANCE, 1972-83

building of all, where Christians were slaughtered for amusement, the colosseum. If one looks more closely at Greek and Roman architecture than at their idealism, as the classical revivalists have done, a richer picture emerges than the expurgated one. Ancient Classicism was always a mixed symbolic system, partly high-minded and abstract, partly vulgar and representational, partly applied to the temples on high, and partly used in the market-place and brothel.

Classicism, as a living language of architecture today, is just as involved with the new technologies, the vulgate and *prolatarii* as the Greeks and Romans were: that is somewhat involved. When Charles Moore uses steel volutes on his capitals, his 'imitations' are no less nor more vulgar than those of Callimachus, who copied acanthus leaves in bronze. The vibrating reds and blues, the strong almost day-glo colours which some attribute to the Parthenon are mirrored by the violent colours of Thomas Gordon Smith or the rich colours of Michael Graves, colours unpalatable to many tastes developed by white Modernism and white Classicism. So we have a slight shift in meaning today as Classicism becomes more democratic and involved with the social reality of building for different tastes

of the style we can now see that most of the salient features have evolved from Egyptian architecture: a monumental building of continuous, smooth stone having several ornamented Orders based on different vegetable and animal metaphors, with much of the articulations of subsequent Classicism. Stylobate, abacus, echinus, fluting, architrave, frieze, cornice; on a supra-segmental level – anthropomorphic proportion, grid planning, simple harmonies, axes and cross axes, and elementary addition of functional units are the main classical features which the Greeks learned from the Egyptians. A future definition of classical architecture, as opposed to classical music and literature, may have to recognise this fundamental historical evolution and relatively diminish the role of Greece and Rome. At least this would be true if counting stylistic motifs and architectural ideas were all that is involved in classification. It is nevertheless more complex than this: the relative importance of ideas is basic to our definitions of Classicism and these include several notions which may act like the essence of the style.

Before we try to adjudicate between motif counting and essentialism, or take up the old philosophical argument of realists versus nominalists, the current implications of the debate should be noted. For it is these which have sparked off the need for a reassessment. Architects, as pointed out, have started to look at all classical periods of architecture, (not just Mannerism and Neo-Classicism), and thus the stylistic references may be placed in different epochs. For instance, Michael Graves' Portland Building has a black podium and arcade, which tends to be seen in America as Art Deco and Egyptian (deriving its heavy blocks from the solid square piers of the river temples); in Europe, because of other associations, it is seen as related to Neo-Classicism, the Fascist architecture of the Thirties or the work of Aldo Rossi and Leon Krier. With Graves we know that all of these references are possible, for he looks to many periods for inspiration. With Japanese designers, and even those I have characterised as Fundamentalist, the heterogeneity of reference is wide, if not equally so. Takefumi Aida uses classical fragments in his Building Block Building – square attic window, triangular pediment and central column – which might be derived equally from Eastern and Western sources (he is acquainted with both), but he recombines these elements in a fundamentalist and childlike way that is distinctly his own. Thus the precise source is lost or generalised to the classical tradition as a whole. Likewise Andrew Batey and Mark Mack summarise a heterogeneous set of classical (and other) sources which are universalised through reduction to an archetype. Their Stewart Houses derive, as other work, from Roman courtyard houses, Egyptian wall architecture, Luis Baragon and here, specifically, the Los Angeles courtyard houses of Irving Gill. The strong symmetry and central axis, as in Aida's work, is combined with very simple Renaissance harmonies and rhythms to produce an image that is, in the classical phrase, 'timeless' (although we know only certain times prefer this ascetic aesthetic).

We could multiply this heterogeneity of sources indefinitely, but the point is probably accepted that Post-Modern Classicisms may revive, or learn from, any period which has developed the classicist archetypes (arch, dome, order etc). This eclecticism of sources is a counterpart to the egalitarianism of the movement as well as a result of present day travel and scholarship which have, in a sense, equalised different periods. Perhaps the influence of current media should not be over-emphasised, but architectural magazines, excellent and inexpensive histories of architecture, and the architects' extensive and growing slide collections have, in one way, collapsed time and space, so that we may feel very familiar with Ancient Greece without being able to speak its language. The fashionable way to dismiss this as 'consumption of the image' misses the important point that the image is, in the best case, absorbed and transformed by the architect into one of his linguistic means – as we have just seen with Graves, Aida, Batey and Mack.[14]

Central to the argument for a tradition of Free-Style Classicism (rather than just a Graeco-Roman style) is one idea of a form-model or theme. We classify, at the crudest level, by counting the number of themes which can be statistically correlated with other members of a class. Thus, if a Romanesque building has ten of 15 major classical themes we might place it in the corpus. To a degree this is what biologists do with their method of 'numerical taxonomy': compute the taxons, identifiable characterisics, to see how related one species is to another.[15] On a more traditional level of building it is simply noting the concurrent

transformations of several architectural themes across time. The idea of the engaged column and its relation to the wall, floor and entablature may be traced from Egypt to the present day. If this theme persists, and if enough of them persist, we may speak of a continuous architectural tradition – Free p-Style Classicism. Furthermore, as a consequence, we may also speak of a cluster of such ideas which are greatly important and which constitute several models of the Western facade. These may be treated as *essential types,* the major themes of the tradition: the arch/dome; the street/doorway/facade; the Orders; the colosseum/palazzo; the temple/gable/aedicule.

Perhaps one reason for the present classical revival is explained simply by architects rediscovering these archetypes after they had been censored for so long. The themes amount to a type of architectural 'truth' rather like the mathematical kind, midway between invention and discovery. This is a classical notion itself and one which has led to the ideal of universality, an ideal which may have been overdone in the past as certain 'universal' forms were applied indiscriminately. But, as engineers will admit, there are only a few intelligent ways of designing the wheel. The essential types of architecture are also limited and Classicism has taken out its patent on a number of them. Furthermore we might add that the essence of Classicism, historically speaking, consists in achieving a balance between several such archetypes and the contradictory codes of architecture, so that the balance represents, if not the harmonious integration always claimed, at least the idea of including opposite elements: ornament and representation, sculptural plasticity and architectonic order, urban propriety and appropriate functional expression. The list of antitheses could go on until it reached one of the final classical polarities – truth versus beauty – the argument between the naturalism of Michelangelo and the aesthetic order of Raphael which E H Gombrich has found to characterise so much classical art.[16] Or it could be seen as a natural working out of the contradictory demands which Vitruvius and the classical tradition put on the art; that is mediating between 'firmness, commodity and delight' or in modern terms 'technic, function and form'. On the most general level we could hazard our definition: the essence of Classicism is to include opposite codes of architecture in such a way that none of its contradictory demands are altogether sacrificed. The wider tradition of Classicism *conventionally* included opposite codes: not only the Vitruvian triad, but painting, sculpture, ornament and polychromy; on other levels, political ideology, social aspirations, and urban ordering principles. In this sense much Neo-Classicism was anti-classical.

To sum up the implications of Free-Style Classicism we may say that it is a wide tradition, not confined to the Graeco-Roman alone (although that may be the heart of the tradition). It is a changing body of theory and practice which keep a set of themes developing and not, as in the case of the Straight Revivalists, an application of static formulae. It is a tradition which acknowledges the authority of precedent and the discovery of architectural truths. But it hardly regards those discovered as the final ones, and it seeks the extension of these by engaging the emergent social reality, using new materials, and developing new rhetorical tropes. In a word it is a living tradition full of faults and promise.

THE CLASSICAL SPIRIT AND THE FREE STYLE ORDERS

Now that Classicism has been revived, discussed, debated, exhibited and built for more than ten years, now that every period of Classicism from the Pure Greek to the Impure Mannerist, from the doctrinal neo-classicist to the Art Deco classicist has been reinvented, now that several new tracts have been written giving us a fresh view of the subject – those of Michael Greenhalgh and Tzonis and Lefaivre – now that there is a classical revivalist proposal for the Paternoster area and opinion polls have shown that some of the public want a traditional style for the King's Cross redevelopment – in short now that Classicism is becoming a political and public issue again after 60 years in the cultural gulag, it's important to question some fundamental assumptions and open up the debate – let it breathe the fresh air of enquiry – not close it down prematurely.

Too many people are still working with the assumption that classical architecture means the revival of a Graeco-Roman language (the assumption of several recent centuries), or that it is a dead language (the assumption of 60 years), just as others believe it refers to some essence such as certain ideal proportions or geometrical compositions. Alternatively some writers believe it is the Latin of architecture – the five Orders – while others hold that it is a specific kind of ornamental system – those languages which use mouldings and references to the human figure and animal forms such as lions and dolphins, or vegetable forms such as the laurel and acanthus. Those with a philological bent hold that Classicism refers to the best works of a period – the classics, the true blood-line of examplars from Vitruvius to Palladio – or trace this meaning to the class distinctions of Rome, the fact that the first use of the term is to a *scriptor classicus*, that is a writer who is upper class. Today there are apologists for each one of these positions here.

From this short and imperfect list at least one thing is clear. There is a disagreement among the experts, a divergence of opinion especially between those who are most convinced they know the true essence of Classicism. 'Conviction politics', the phrase of Margaret Thatcher, has its counterpart with 'Conviction Classicists', although unlike the Tory Party they haven't achieved a consensus of views. This dissensus and pluralism is enjoyable and perhaps even fruitful because it creates several competing Classicisms and forces each viewpoint to sharpen its methods – even improve its standard of building. But it leads to conceptual confusion. It has also led Sir John Summerson, with whom I have debated these notions for several years, to write judiciously, but rather hopelessly, that 'It is a mistake to try to define Classicism'. If all definitions are going to prove partial and inadequate, he suggests, it is far safer to give telling instances and principles of its practice. But even with this wiser and more modest approach there are similar problems of limitation, the tacit reduction of the field to Graeco-Roman architecture and its revivals.

From all the above it will be guessed that I favour an expansion of the discussion to a wider field, a Free-Style Classicism, which includes the supposedly non-classical architecture such as Egyptian, Gothic, Mannerist and Post-Modern modes. The reasons for such expansion are philosophical and historical.

Following Wittgenstein and set theory I would say that the classical language consists of an identifiable family resemblance of formal and thematic elements, an overlap of sets of concerns which give the wider tradition of Classicism a coherence. It's not the presence of the orders, proportion, dolphins and mouldings alone, but many overlapping sets of such concerns *and* the intention to be part of the classical tradition. There is no 'essence' of Classicism; the idea that any period or style has an essence has been refuted by Karl Popper and Ernst Gombrich, although perhaps the whole world has not yet taken note of this refutation.

The historical reasons for expanding Classicism to the wider tradition have become clearer with recent archaeology and scholarship. We now know the Greeks borrowed many constructional elements from the Egyptians and important aesthetic ideas such as smooth dressed stonework, entasis and the Proto-Doric Order. *(Pace* Quinlan Terry we know that the orders were not divinely inspired in a direct message from God to Moses circa 1600 BC, but existed in Egypt for more than one thousand years before this). We are also now more aware that Gothic architects read Vitruvius as well as making use of the Graeco-Roman language, although they gave this system new proportions and structural types. So there are convincing philosophical and historical reasons for expanding what I'd call Canonic Classicism to this wider Free-Style Classicism – as long as we continue to distinguish historical modes and intentions within this wide field.

Since this subject is very wide I would limit my remarks to a mention of the Orders – not because columns and entablatures are the essence of the tradition, but because they are a place where all the issues come to a point. The column, and its ordering role, is a kind of test point for measuring the understanding of the spirit and letter of the wider tradition. These support my case that the wider tradition and the Orders started in Egypt and that the spirit or life of the tradition comes from developing the language for its meaning, its semantic and local reference, not from dressing up with Ionic volutes, or pretending to be a member of the Doric tribe.

The wrong letter killeth, the right contextual spirit giveth life. Since the continuity of the classical language has been interrupted by 60 years of Modernism, I would argue we cannot use the orders unselfconsciously as if we were 18th-century designers in an integrated culture. But since columns are indeed universals of an architectural language, we can and should give them ornamental and symbolic expression – not leave them as Modernists did, as barren telephone poles. To avoid this cliché of a mute structure, or its opposite – the anachronistic symbol and ornament, we might once again create columns with metaphors of the body, and references to the locality and culture we inhabit: that means, for instance, British, American or European Orders, and those that celebrate today's technology and their particular function.

Free-Style Classicism and the wider classical tradition started in Egypt – with the first stone capitals at Sakkhara circa 2800 BC and the six Egyptian Orders (papyras, lotus, bird, bell, feather, head and palm) – not in Greece or the Sermon on the Mount. From Sakkhara the forms were refined so that by Hatsheput's Valley temple both proto-Doric columns and polychromy were present, both of which were taken up and perfected by the Greeks. Egyptian capitals with their abstract quality are admired by James Stirling, whose use of these wider forms today can be seen at Stuttgart's Neue Staatsgalerie, where he uses both a simplified Egyptian cornice and polychromy.

Classicism's liveliness, spirit, cultural health – or whatever metaphor one wants to use to distinguish a living Classicism from a dead pastiche – depends on both the semantic use of form, its cultural relevance today for a particular job, and its functional and structural role. Through history there have been various attempts to institute new orders, new symbolisms. Today not only Egyptian but wider references are brought in and create a contemporary symbolism – as in my use of the Hindu-Doric Order to represent the heat and cold of an Indian Summer at the Thematic House. A current symbolism and technology must inform the use of classical forms, but the problem also is to refine these necessary motifs into an aesthetic system. This is the challenge for Post-Modern Classicists and while they have gone some way towards meeting it, one cannot say that we have yet reached a canonic expression of these goals, or indeed a classic resolution of the opposite demands. The challenge is still there: let us hope the architects working on the Paternoster scheme, or those facing any building task which demands expression and symbolism, can meet the challenge. No architect today has done so entirely convincingly.

JAMES STIRLING, NEUE STAATSGALERIE, STUTTGART, 1977-84

ANUBIS' SHRINE, HATSHEPUT'S TEMPLE, EGYPT, c 1500 BC

THE TWO FACES OF POST-MODERNISM
CHRISTIAN NORBERG-SCHULZ

VENTURI, RAUCH AND SCOTT BROWN, EXTENSION TO THE NATIONAL GALLERY, LONDON, 1987, PRELIMINARY SKETCH

Post-modern architecture came about as a reaction to the limitations of Modernism, that is, to recall the words of Robert Venturi, Modernism's inability to accommodate the 'complexities and contradictions of modern experience'. We could also say that modern architecture neglected the dimension of meaning, and accordingly that the common denominator of the post-modern experiments is the quest

for a communicative, meaningful architecture. A reaction, however, is necessarily groping and uncertain; it lacks the self-assurance of a 'movement' towards a defined goal. No wonder then that post-modern works often appear superficial and arbitrary. This very fact tells us that 'meaning' is not simply something that we may recover after a period of neglect, but that it has become a problem. It is no longer a necessary property of the world, and many present-day philosophers accordingly maintain that general meanings are impossible, and that a 'form' is nothing but a transitory *simulacrum*.

Post-Modernism, therefore, appears as a Janus head with two faces. One looks 'back', hoping to find beginnings or origins on which we may again found a language of meaningful forms. The other looks 'forward' into nothingness, advocating a nihilism according to which forms come and go as parts of a game of 'seduction'. The two faces, both, however, stem from the reaction to Modernism, and therefore have a common head.

In general, Modernism was a product of the Enlightenment, although its roots go back to Plato's *idea* and to Descartes' *cogito*. With the Enlightenment, the rationalism implicit in the Cartesian approach was taken as the foundation for a whole culture. Human understanding became a recherche de la vérité, in the sense of a 'scientific' study of what is present, and the means was Kant's pure reason. What could not be understood in this way, was simply dismissed as illusion and superstition.

Voltaire's rejection of religion with the words 'écrasez l'infamé!', is characteristic. It has to be added, however, that daily life did not suddenly become rationalistic and pragmatic. Until quite recently it remained a world of qualities, to which man had a poetic rather than a scientific relationship. But pure reason became the 'official' attitude, and practical aims were given pride of place in society.

In architecture, Enlightenment meant functionalism. Here the words *écrasez l'infamé* also sounded, translated into Loos' *Ornament und Verbrechen* and Van de Velde's *mensonge des formes* (read: *historical* forms). As a consequence, architecture had to be invented anew, 'as if nothing had ever been done before'.[1] Modern architecture also shared the Enlightenment's belief in progress, that is, the possibility of creating a 'better world' by means of a scientific approach to the problems of the human environment. This belief found its definition in Hannes Meyer's well-known words from 1928: 'everything in the world is a product of the formula (function times economy). All art is composition and therefore unfunctional. All life is function and therefore unartistic.'[2] Such an extreme attitude was not, however, shared by the leading protagonists of the Modern Movement; Giedion maintained that the task of modern art and architecture was to heal the 'split of thought and feeling' brought about by Descartes. Other pioneers over and over again stressed the artistic aims of the Movement. But the means implied were 'scientific', as is proved by the analytical approach to problems of form and expression introduced at the Bauhaus.

While the *Brave New World* of enlightened man was becoming a reality, a growing scepticism about the nature and possibilities of human knowledge came to the fore. Already Kant had realised the limits of pure reason when he wrote: 'Unconditioned necessity, which we so indispensably require as the last bearer of all things, is for human reason the veritable abyss'.[3] Thus, an abyss or *Abgrund,* where the 'things themselves' fade away into limitless darkness, is what we have to face as the origin of understanding, rather than a solid foundation of necessities. As a consequence Nietzsche exclaimed: 'The biggest fable of all is the fable of knowledge. One would like to know what things in themselves are, but behold, there are no things in themselves!'[4] To start with, Nietzsche's nihilism did not shake the belief in enlightenment and progress, but after the Second World War, a whole series of philosophers, in France and Italy, have followed up his criticism, repeating that 'no accurate representation of the world as it is in itself is possible'.[5] Such a nihilism is, despite many differences, shared by Baudrillard, Lyotard, Derrida, Perniola and Vattimo, all of whom maintain that the 'postmodern condition' is characterised by a general loss of intrinsic meaning and that all knowledge is 'interpretation'.[6]

The attitudes of the nihilist philosophers certainly reflect the present state of affairs. The world we live in no longer consists of locally rooted ethnic domains, but has become an 'open' multitude of fragments of the most varied origins. The word 'pluralism' is often used to characterise the situation. The pluralist condition in society necessarily goes together with a dissolution of the traditional concept of place. Not only have numerous places been subject to disintegration in terms of spatial coherence and character, but the new *media* of information make us also experience a 'simultaneity of places', which disturbs our sense of belonging and identity. As a consequence, the *care* for the given environment which formed the basis of past cultures, is weakened. Previously 'culture' meant to cultivate the given as a particular, integrated 'here', whereas today it may at best signify a collection of separate forms and 'memories'.

Scattered bits may, however, possess a certain meaning as 'signs', and semiology has in fact become *en vogue* as a 'theory' of meaning. According to semiology, a 'sign language' is nothing but a result of habit and convention, and therefore its validity is limited to those 'users' who are able to understand the 'code'.[7] General or timeless meanings are hence abolished, and total relativism reigns. In his best-selling novel *The Name of the Rose,* semiologist Umberto Eco concludes: 'The only truths that are useful are instruments to be thrown away'.[8] Does this mean, then, that the post-modern quest for meaning has ended in nothingness, and that the Janus face which looks for origins is the victim of an illusion?

Such a conclusion is certainly not in agreement with the aims of post-modern architecture. Rather it describes the late-modern condition, that is, the dissolution of the Enlightenment in terms of nihilism. Let us therefore ask instead: is there today any line of thought which, although it realises the collapse of pure reason, opens up for a recovery of meaning, or in other words, for an authentic Post-Modernism?

The philosophy of Martin Heidegger and his followers offers such a possibility.[9] In our context, Heidegger's concept of the thing is of particular interest. Rather than the reflection of an idea (which may never be grasped as such), Heidegger understands the thing as the 'gathering of a world'.[10] The meaning of a thing, thus consists in what it 'gathers'. In order to comprehend this definition, it is necessary to take a closer look at the words 'world' and 'gathering'. For Heidegger, 'world' does not simply mean what is present, that is, the subject-matter of traditional metaphysics, but what is given together with what is 'withheld'. It is a commonplace that we can never 'have' the whole thing; when one aspect of something comes into presence, other aspects withdraw into oblivion. Therefore, any phenomenon simultaneously consists in a giving and a withholding. This basic fact was expressed by the Greeks in their concepts of *lethe* (concealment) and *a-letheia* (un-concealment), and reappeared in Kant's characterisation of the ground of things as an 'abyss'. To Heidegger, however, the abyss does not imply that there are no 'things-in-themselves'. Any thing 'is' in the world in *its* particular way, and remains the 'same' through its indefinite manifestations. To understand what that means, it is necessary to arrive at a more structured conception of 'world' and Heidegger has proposed the 'Fourfold' *(Geviert)* as an answer. The Fourfold comprises Earth, Sky, Mortals and Divinities, and on more than one occasion Heidegger defined each of the four in realistic terms.[12] It is evident that he wanted to arrive at a *concrete* understanding of the world, in accordance with the events of everyday life. Although events are temporal, the things 'remain', and can therefore be given a *name.* As examples, Heidegger 'analyses' nameable things such as the *jug* and the *bridge,* showing how each of them gathers a world. The 'saying'of the thing is possible because names form part of a *language* which 'contains' the Fourfold. Language, thus, is the 'House of Being' and serves to reveal things as they 'are'.[13] In a certain sense, any revelation (*aletheia*) is an 'interpretation', but it is an interpretation of *something,* rather than an instrument to be thrown away after use.

In Heidegger's saying of jug and bridge, as well as in his discussions of poems and works of art, language is used in a new way. Heidegger does not pretend to write poetry, and certainly he does not offer scientific analyses. What he does is rather to investigate the phenomenological properties of the thing, using language not only as a means of expression, but also as a source of information. What results is a semi-poetic saying, as in his *The Thinker as Poet (Aus Der Erfahrung des Denkens)*: Forests spread/Brooks plunge/Rocks persist/Mist diffuses/Meadows wait/Springs well/Winds dwell/Blessing muses.[14] Here Heidegger's closeness to nature and life comes forth, repudiating those who interpret his thinking as another kind of nihilism.[15] At the same time the importance of the work of art is explained. To Heidegger, art is the 'setting-into-work of truth' as *aletheia*, that is, the disclosure of something that so far had remained 'hidden'.

The word 'gathering' explains the nature of the thing. It neither denotes a 'sign' nor a 'symbol', since the function of a sign is indication, and of a symbol representation. The thing (and the work) does not represent anything (that is, something already present somewhere else), but as a gathering of a world, it is an identity in its own right, at the same time as it brings the world 'close to man'.[16] It may be considered an *image,* since it makes something 'invisible', come into presence. Any work of art, therefore, is an *imago mundi.* Poetry speaks in images, Heidegger says, and 'the nature of the image is to let something be seen.'[17] Poetry therefore serves life. It reveals things as they are, and enables man to realise the scope of his being-in-the-world: to 'dwell poetically'.[18]

Although poetry is the original art, it does not exhaust the disclosure of truth. In poetic language truth is brought 'to word', but it also has to be 'set-into-work'. Human life takes place between earth and sky, and architecture as an art is the means to make this condition 'visible'. In his *Hebel* essay Heidegger shows what that means: 'The buildings bring the inhabited landscape close to man and at the same time place the nearness of neighbourly dwelling under the expanse of the sky'.[19] Again we recognise the concrete point of departure of Heidegger's thinking, as well as his understanding of architecture as a manifestation of man's being-in-the-world. Architecture, this is not a series of arbitrary 'codes', but has an existential foundation. Man's being is temporal as well as timeless. When Heidegger characterises human beings as 'mortals', he refers to the temporal aspect, whereas his 'divinities' recall the 'measure' which remains, and which we have to take 'to our hearts'.[20]

In the thinking of Heidegger, the metaphysical split between the *a priori* and the *a posteriori* is overcome, as well as the nihilistic negation of any foundation. The world is recovered the inhabited 'between' (*Zwischen*) of Earth and Sky, and the abstract quantification which governed man's understanding the past gives way to a qualitative, poetical approach.

How, then, does this new departure in Western thinking relate to the development in architecture from Modernism to Post-Modernism? Although radical exponents, such as Hannes Meyer, wanted to abolish architecture as an art, the Modern Movement never forgot the artistic obligations. Nevertheless its rational-pragmatic methods, led to an environmental poverty which in the long run became unbearable. Already in 1954 Giedion wrote: 'In countries where modern architecture has won the battle and been entrusted with monumental tasks involving more than functional problems, one cannot but observe that something is lacking in the buildings executed.'[22] As a consequence he demanded a 'New Monumentality', saying 'Monumentality springs from the eternal need for people to create symbols for their activities and for their fate or destiny, for their religious beliefs and for their social convictions'.[23] Ten years later he added: 'Experience is slowly showing us that the rationalist and exclusively materialist attitude, upon which the latest phase of Western civilisation has been grounded, is insufficient.[24] Giedion also understood that the approach needed to overcome the impasse was *imagination*. Quoting Shakespeare's words: '. . . imagination bodies forth the forms of things unknown', he even came close to the Heideggerian concepts of thing and meaning.[25] As the spokesman of Modernism, however, he primarily intended architecture in terms (function and space) and demanded a new 'spatial imagination presenting as examples Le Corbusier's church at Ronchamp and Utzon's Opera House in Sydney.[26]

At about the same time, Louis Kahn took the decisive step towards a more comprehensive understanding of architecture in his concluding talk at the 1956 Otterlo congress of former CIAM members: '. . . what a thing wants to be is the most important act of an object. It is for the architect to derive from the very nature of things what a thing wants to be. A thing is unable to start unless it can contain all that can ever come from it.'[27] In other words, Kahn understood the work of architecture as an interpretation of the 'beginnings', intending for instance that a house has to be 'House' as well as 'a house'. The general nature of things also comes forth in his saying that 'a man who discovers things that belong to the nature of things does not own these things', and, 'it is not what you want, it is what you sense in the order of things which tells you what to design'.[28] Putting this approach into his work, Kahn not only revived archetypal kinds of space, but also introduced echoes of historical forms. Above all, he brought back to our attention the importance of light, 'the giver of all presences'.

Kahn's endeavours were carried on and developed by Robert Venturi, who in his book *Complexity and Contradiction in Architecture* (1966) advocated the use of 'conventional elements' and demonstrated the principles of architectural composition by means of historical examples. 'The architect's main work is the organisation of a unique whole through conventional parts and the judicious introduction of new parts when the old won't do'; 'The architect selects as much as he creates'.[29] With these words Venturi initiated the post-modern development in architecture. Forms that had been 'forbidden' were suddenly allowed again and architecture became part of history, rather than something

that has to be reinvented from zero. In contrast to the generation before him, Venturi realised that conventional forms already contain man's understanding of nature and himself, and that we ought to learn from past experience even if we live in a 'new' world. Present contradictions are in fact the consequence of complex 'memories', which have to be mastered by means of an architecture which is simultaneously 'new and old'.

The significance of Venturi's approach, as well as Aldo Rossi's contemporary thoughts on typology,[30] ought to be understood by now, but over and over again we find that the new approach is deprecated as nostalgic and historicist. An unbiased study of the history of the architecture of our century shows, however, that the post-modern quest for meaning offers the only true answer to the shortcomings which were realised by Modernism itself, and even more important: that it represents a creative departure from the impasse of pure reason. During the last two decades, in fact, architectural theory has left behind the 'puritanical repression' (Jencks) imposed by functionalism, with the aim of arriving at a new language of meaningful forms.

A first step was taken by the present writer with the book *Intentions in Architecture*,[31] where the need for a 'symbol-milieu' was launched as a major point, and an attempt was also made to expand the understanding of architectural form beyond the exclusive emphasis on spatial organisation favoured by Modernism. The problem of *meaning* here implied, was in spring 1966 treated in a lecture at Cambridge University, later included in the book *Meaning in Architecture*, edited by Charles Jencks and George Baird.[32] In this publication Jencks made a first attempt at defining meaning in terms of semiology, an endeavour he carried on in *The Language of Post-Modern Architecture* (1977) and 'The Architectural Sign' (1980).[33] Semiology, however, did not prove capable of solving the problem, and in his recent booklet *What is Post-Modernism?* (1986), Jencks concludes with a statement which indicates a change of position. Citing the art critic Peter Fuller, he 'calls for the equivalent of a new spirituality based on an "imaginative, yet secular, response to nature herself", that is "a shared symbolic order of the kind that a religion provides", but without religion'.[34] An echo of Voltaire's *écrasez* is still evident, but the demand for a 'response to nature herself' certainly implies a renunciation of his previous relativism. In his own house in London, Jencks has put his aim into action.[35]

'A shared symbolic order' – the term echoes statements by other architects and critics who are concerned about the problem of meaning. In the introduction to his *Buildings and Projects 1966-1981*, Michael Graves says that 'the components of architecture have not only derived from pragmatic necessity, but also evolved from symbolic sources . . . as the resonance of man and nature'. And he goes on: 'In making a case for figurative architecture, we assume that the thematic character of the work is grounded in nature and is simultaneously read in a totemic or an anthropomorphic manner'.[36] The figures here implied, were about the same time defined by Leon Krier as 'nameable objects', that is, things such as 'tower', 'gable', 'dome' and 'house'.[37] What is thus proposed by two of the protagonists of post-modern architecture, is to understand architecture in terms of language, and furthermore to recognise language as the 'House of Being'; an approach shared by Robert Stern: 'Architecture is less an issue of innovation than an act of interpretation; to be an architect is to possess an individual voice speaking a generally understood language of form. To be really articulate as an architect is to raise that voice to heights of lyricism, to make each element, each word resonate with meaning . . . Despite the chaos that rages everywhere around us, each building still presents an opportunity to affirm and re-establish the inherent order of things.'[38]

'A generally understood language of form that allows for meaningful expression of the inherent order of things' is hence the common aim of authentic Post-Modernism. It is the only alternative to the nihilistic interpretation of the present situation. In a world which no longer consists of distinct ethnic domains and traditions, language becomes our rescue.[39] In spite of many aberrations and superficial whims, the architecture of the last two decades proves that such a language of form is on the way. We may add that the thinking of Heidegger and his followers offers the necessary theoretical foundation.[40] With his conception of *thing*, Heidegger has illuminated the real nature of symbolism, and has provided insight into the meaning of 'origin' or 'beginning'. In general, the language of post-modern architecture is new as well as old. It is an expression of man's being-in-the-world, the structure of which is temporal as well as timeless. Thus Kastner wrote: 'Also those who do not any longer believe in Heaven and Hell, cannot confound the words "up" and "down".'[41] Such simple 'qualitative facts' constitute the 'resonance of man and nature', and the basis for the language of architecture.

We understand that the nihilistic face of Post-Modernism in reality represents a late-modern outlook. It poses the problem of meaning to negate meaning, and regards forms as arbitrary instruments. In other words, it reduces architecture to fashion.[42] This also holds true for the most ingenious examples of hi-tech building. Here technology is no longer understood as *techné* that is, a revelation of meaning, but becomes a play with nameless effects. Hi-tech as well as the recent neo-plasticist and Constructivist revivals are in reality the last convulsions of Utopian Modernism, that is, a current which takes a kind of science-fiction rather than man's everyday life as its point of departure.[43] Late-Modernism believes it is forward-looking, but reveals a nostalgic nature. It refuses to give up the idea that all problems may be solved by means of reason and technology, and the moralising tone of its advocates also repeats a typical attitude of the Enlightenment tradition. Like a mask, the late-modern face hides nothingness. In a pluralist society, however, what is meaningless may sometimes satisfy the human need for meaning.

The breakdown of the Enlightenment tradition does not mean that modern architecture in general was wrong. To survive, it had to *develop*, and as an *artistic* movement it contained the seeds of what is today becoming manifest. We have seen that Giedion already intuited the direction to be taken. What he wanted was a return to *imagination*, and today we realise that this presupposes the recovery of the language of architecture. I therefore agree with Charles Jencks when he considers Post-Modernism the true continuation of Modernism.[44] Imagination, however, does not imply a rejection of reason and technology. We simply have to acknowledge that meaningful forms do not follow from functions and structures, but as means serving the creation of images. In Heidegger's words: '. . . science is not an original happening of truth already opened.'[45] A domain of truth is opened by a gathering vision which is set into work as an image by means of the language of architecture. It affirms and re-establishes the inherent order of things, and creates an 'island of meaning' within the chaos that rages everywhere around us. Thus the authentic face of Post-Modernism expresses the nature and the meaning of our being between earth and sky.

Notes

1   S Giedion, *Architecture, You and Me*, Cambridge, Mass, 1958, p26.
2   *Bauhaus*, 2, Dessau, 1928.
3   I Kant, *Critique of Pure Reason*, New York, 1965, p 513.
4   F Nietzsche, *The Will to Power*, New York, 1967, p 301.
5   B Magnus, 'The End of "The End of Philosophy"', *Hermeneutics and Deconstruction*, H J Silverman and D Ihde (eds), Albany, 1985, p 7.
6   See especially J-F Lyotard, *The Post-Modern Condition*, Manchester, 1984, M Perniola, *La societa dei simulacri*, Bologna, 1983, G Vattimo, *La fine della modernita*, Milan, 1985. Perniola wants to overcome nihilism by means of simulacra and 'seduction', whereas Vatimo advocates a 'weak nihilism', that is a happy and kind nothingness. We may only ask: can anything at all be constructed with a foundation?
7   U Eco, 'The Semiotics of Architecture', *Signs, Symbols and Architecture*, G Broadbent, R Bunt, C Jencks (eds), Chichester, 1980.
8   U Eco, *The Name of the Rose*, London, 1984, p 492.
9   C Norberg-Schulz, 'Heidegger's Thinking on Art', *Perspecta* 20, Cambridge, Mass, 1983.
10 M Heidegger, 'The Thing', *Poetry, Language, Thought*, New York 1971.
11 M Heidegger, 'Aletheia', *Early Greek Thinking*, New York, 1975.
12 M Heidegger, 'Building Dwelling Thinking', *Poetry, op cit.*
13 M Heidegger, 'Language', *Poetry, op cit.*
14 *ibid*, 'The Thinker as Poet'.
15 To avoid this misunderstanding, one is recommended to read *Hebel, der Hausfreund* and *der Feldweg*.
16 H-G Gadamer, *Truth and Method*, London, 1975, p 134.
17 M Heidegger, '. . . Poetically Man Dwells', *Poetry, op cit*, p 226.
18 *ibid*.
19 M Heidegger, *Hebel, der Hausfreund*, Pfullingen, 1957, p 13.
20 M Heidegger, '. . . Poetically Man Dwells', *Poetry, op cit*, pp 226ff.
21 M Heidegger, *Hebel, op cit*, p 13.
22 S Giedion, *op cit*, p 32.
23 *ibid*, p 28.
24 *ibid*, p 141.
25 *ibid*, p 154.
26 *ibid*, pp 178ff.
27 0 Newman, *CIAM '59 in Otterlo*, Stuttgart, 1961, pp 205ff.
28 *ibid*, pp 214ff.
29 R Venturi, *Complexity and Contradiction in Archiecture*, New York, 1966, p 49.
30 A Rossi, *L'architettura della città*, Padova, 1966.
31 C Norberg-Schulz, *Intentions in Architecture*, Oslo/London, 1963.
32 C Norberg-Schulz, 'Meaning in Architecture', in *Meaning in Architecture*, C Jencks, G Baird (eds), London, 1969.
33 C Jencks, *The Language of Post-Modern Architecture*, London 1977. C Jencks, 'The Architectural Sign', *Signs, Symbols and Architecture, op cit*.
34 C Jencks, *What is Post-Modernism?*, London, 1986, 2nd ed 1988, p 4.
35 C Jencks, *Symbolic Architecture*, London, 1985.
36 *Michael Graves: Buildings and Projects 1966-1981*, KV Wheele, P Arnell, T Bickford (eds), New York, 1982, pp 11ff.
37 'Leon Krier', *Architectural Design*, Vol 54, No 7/8, 1984, London.
38 *Robert A M Stern: Buildings and Projects 1981-1986*, Luis F Rued (ed), New York, 1986, p 6.
39 C Norberg-Schulz, 'Auf dem Weg zur einer Zeitgemassen Architektursprache', *Jahrbuch für Architektur 1987-1988*, Braunschweig, 1987.
40 C Norberg-Schulz, 'Heidegger's Thinking on Art', *op cit*.
41 E Kästner, *Ölberge Weinberge*, Frankfurt, 1960.
42 See Jencks' comment on Lyotard in *What is Post-Modernism?, op cit*, p 12.
43 The works of the Archigram group from the 1960s are particularly characteristic examples of Constructivist Utopianism.
44 C Jencks, *What is Post-Modernism?, op cit*, p 7.
45 M Heidegger, 'The Origin of the Work of Art', *Poetry, op cit*, p 62

*

THE DOUBLES OF POST-MODERNISM
ROBERT A M STERN

ROBERT A M STERN, VILLA IN NEW JERSEY, 1983-87

. . . Cubism and Superrealism (Surrealism), far from being the dawn of a style, are the end of a period of self-consciousness, inbreeding and exhaustion. One thing seems clear to me: that no new style will grow out of a preoccupation with art for its own sake. It can only arise from a new interest in subject matter. We need a new myth in which the symbols are inherently pictorial.' **K Clark**[1]

What has been called modern architecture for the past 50 years is in disarray: though such leading architects as Paul Rudolph, I M Pei and Kevin Roche continue to produce major new work, the forms as well as the theories on which that work is based are systematically being questioned by a growing number of younger architects who perceive the waning of Modernism and who are questioning the prevailing philosophic basis for architecture and its form-language. The questioning sensibility has come to be described, alternately and rather imprecisely, as post-modern or post-modernist.[2]

Charles Jencks' book, *The Language of Post-Modern Architecture*, is the first to explore the new mood and to begin to erect a scaffolding of theory for Post-Modernism.[3] Jencks suggests that the term Post-Modern is at best 'negative and evasive'. Nonetheless it does enjoy some precedent in architecture.[4]

The terms 'Modernism' and 'Post-Modernism' have been used in other disciplines besides architecture, including political history, and literary and art criticism. In each of these disciplines, they suggest two different conditions resulting in related sets of what I would describe as 'doubles' – the doubles of Modernism and of Post-Modernism. Both grow out of the same two distinct but interrelated sensibilities or conditions, and both fall within the modern – that is Western humanist/post-Renaissance – period.

These conditions affect both Modernism and Post-Modernism.

Borrowing the term from Frank Kermode, I would label the first of these conditions 'schismatic'. The schismatic condition argues for a clean break with Western humanism. I would label the second condition 'traditional', borrowing the term from Stephen Spender. It argues for a recognition of the continuity of the Western humanist tradition. Traditional Modernism can be 'conceived of as a return, at once spontaneous, willed to eternal values long forgotten or buried but which a reborn or renewed historical memory makes once again present'; schismatic Modernism can be seen as a sensibility in which 'the new and the modern (are) seen in terms of a birth rather than a rebirth, not a restoration but . . . a construction of the present and future not on the foundations of the past but on the ruins of time'.[5]

The two Modernisms can be distinguished by their attitudes toward the past: 'traditional' Modernism, typified by the writings of Proust or Eliot or the paintings of Picasso, views the past as a source of order; 'schismatic' Modernism, typified by the work of Duchamp or Mondrian, views the past as a burden. Although the two kinds of Modernism are distinct, they are linked by an apocalyptic view of the future and by a recognition of Western humanism as an on-going condition. It is important to reiterate that the Modern period as a whole encompasses a continuing tradition of humanistic thought and action though some of its stylistic movements – for example Dada and Surrealism – regard humanism as a yoke.

Like the two Modernisms, the two Post-Modernisms can be distinguished by their attitudes toward the past. While the schismatic post-modern condition posits a break with both Modernism and the modern period itself, the traditional post-modern condition proposes to free new production from the rigid constraints of Modernism, especially from its most radical and nihilistic aspects (as exemplified by Dada and Surrealism) while simultaneously reintegrating itself with other strains of Western humanism, especially those which characterise its last pre-modernist phase, that of the Romanticism which flourished between 1750 and 1850.[6] Thus schismatic Post-Modernism is a sensibility that considers itself not only beyond Modernism but also outside the Modern period, one which seeks to establish the mode of thought and artistic production that is as free from the 500-year-old tradition of Western humanism as that mode was, in its turn, free from the previous Gothic era of religious scholasticism. Traditional Post-Modernism, on the other hand, is one that seeks to reintegrate or subsume Modernism within the broad category of the Modern period as a whole.

In Post-Modernism, the distinctions between traditional and schismatic conditions are useful in illuminating the distinctions between the work of John Gardner and William Gass in literature or of Peter Eisenman and Michael Graves in architecture. Though the term post-modern appears to be used to describe sensibilities and theories that share as common ground a reaction to the Modernism which has dominated much of the cultural activity of the past 125 years, the traditional and schismatic conditions serve to distinguish between distinct sensibilities within the post-modern devolution; these distinctions have at their core the question of the relationships between new work and the tradition of humanism which characterised the modern period itself.

Thus the doubles of Post-Modernism: two distinct but interrelated post-modern sensibilities: a 'schismatic' condition that argues for a *clean break* with the tradition of Western humanism and a 'traditional' condition that argues for a return to, or recognition of, the *continuity* of the cultural tradition of Western humanism of which it holds Modernism to be a part.

'Somebody should write the history of the word "modern". The OED isn't very helpful, though most of the senses the word now has have been in the air since the 16th century, and are actually older than Shakespeare's way of using it to mean "commonplace" . . . The New is to be judged by the criterion of novelty, the Modern implies or at any rate permits a serious relationship with the past, a relationship that requires criticism and indeed radical reimagining.'[7] In order to clarify what is meant by the term 'modern' in the phrase 'post-modern', it is necessary to establish clear definitions for the related terms 'modern' and 'Modernism'. Such a seemingly pedantic exercise is necessary because the distinctions between the older terms have become blurred by daily use, and they have become ineffective for discourse.

What can be called the 'modern period' begins in the 15th century with the birth of Humanism. The renaissance of Classicism in architecture is the first of the modern stylistic phases: the Baroque and the Rococo are subsequent modern styles. The International Style of c1920-60 is also a modern style, often thought to be *the* Modern Style in which the meaning of the word 'modern' is transformed and limited so as to represent only those values more properly described as 'modernist', a term which describes the urge to produce new artistic work, that eschews all known form-language and, ideally all grammar, in favour of a new self-referential (ie in architecture, functionally and technologically determined) language of form whose principal cultural responsibility is toward its moment in time. Modernism sees art as a manifestation of the *Zeitgeist*; it strives to reflect the moment of its conception. Modernism, in the most oversimplified terms, represents a moralistic application of a superior value to that which is not only new but also independent of all previous production.

Modernism views the present as a state of continuing crisis; it sees history only as a record of experiences, a body of myth, but not as objective truth, and it is apocalyptic in its relationship to the future. A person who believes in the sensibility of Modernism is a 'modernist' as well as a 'modern', the latter term being the more general one and simply referring to someone who has lived in the modern period and has contended with or at least recognised the issue of 'modernity' but who has not necessarily adopted a modernist stance.[8]

Modernism is not a style in and of itself in the sense that the Renaissance and Baroque were styles with unifying principles. It can be regarded as a succession of attempts to redefine the syntax and the grammar of artistic composition (the poems of Mallarmé, the stream of consciousness of Joyce and Woolf, the buildings of Mies van der Rohe and Le Corbusier). As a result, and rather perversely, to the extent that it has deliberately been made difficult and inaccessible, artistic production has also shown itself to be Modernist in some cases, there has been an effort to go beyond issues of syntax and grammar and to seek to establish new form-languages which, because they are not culturally based (that is, familiar), are by necessity personal or self-referential.[9]

Modernism does not accept the appearance of things as they are in nature and in the man-made world, it seeks always to take them apart in order to discover their hidden and, presumably, essential character. Modernism seeks to close and ultimately to eliminate the distance between the object perceived and the person perceiving the object. It seeks to do this in two ways: by insisting that all experience and thereby all art exists in the present – Giedion's phrase was the 'eternal present' – and by insisting that each work of art and each act of artistic production is a personal act.[10] This presentism and the self-referential aspect of artistic production are fundamental to any examination of the nature of Modernism in relationship to the issue of an on-going culture which we call the Western humanist tradition.

It has been argued that Modernism can never be a part of any tradition, that it is a thing apart, a parallel tradition to Western humanism. This issue of Modernism as a sensibility apart from the modern has resulted in that plethora of modernist styles or 'isms' which has made the history of the literature and art of the last 125 years seem so confusing and troubled.

As a term describing a style, the use of the word 'modern' opens up a veritable Pandora's box of confusion: for example, 'L'Art Nouveau', for a while known as '*Le Style Moderne*', is a style in the modern period and, more specifically, it was a modernist style in that it sought to stand free of the *historical continuum*. At the same time, insofar as it is the 'fine art' manifestation of the bohemianism of the *fin de siècle* it also represents a sensibility.

Another meaning for 'modern' is up-to-date or 'contemporary'. The term contemporary cannot be used to describe a stylistic sensibility because it signifies merely the absence of any strongly defined period features. Thus, actually all current production is modern: in fact, 'the great claim of Modernism . . . that it at last was free of style – finally and forever open to direct experience'[11] – is rendered preposterous by the history of the Modern Movement.

As Susan Sontag has observed, this 'notion of a style-less transparent art is one of the most tenacious fantasies of modern culture. Artists and critics pretend to believe that it is no more possible to get the artifice out of art than it is for a person to lose his personality. Yet the aspiration lingers – a permanent dissent from modern art with its dizzying velocity of style changes.'[12]

Harry Levin articulates what I believe to be a fundamental characteristic of the modernist era: 'Now we are all contemporaries; about that we have no option, so long as we stay alive. But we may choose whether or not we wish to be modern'[13] (by which I think Levin means modernist).

Thus one must be wary of the use of the term 'modern' in architecture, as in most of the arts and in literature. It is not really a description of a style but, as Irving Howe has observed, a term of critical placement and judgement.[14]

Contemporary historians and critics of modern architecture, perhaps even more than their counterparts in literature and the fine arts, seem to confuse the broad historical definition of the modern period with related but distinct ideas pertaining to Modernism and to use the terms interchangeably. Until the impact of Hegelian and Marxist thought came to dominate the developing discipline of art and architectural history in Germany in the second half of the 19th century, historians undertook to define modern architectural history in broad terms and to regard the Renaissance as the first of a sequence of modern styles. Even as late as 1929, Henry Russell Hitchcock in his *Modern Architecture: Romanticism and Reintegration*, embraced a chronologically broad and relatively inclusive definition of modern architecture. Nonetheless, perhaps under the impact of his subsequent collaboration with the more polemical Philip Johnson on the book *The International Style*, and perhaps as a result of his subsequent contact with European modernist historians such as Giedion and Pevsner, Hitchcock has since drawn back from his earlier and more inclusive position.

In *Modern Architecture*, Hitchcock traces the origins of the modern period to the break-up of the Gothic style, regarding each phase since that time not as an 'independent style' like the Greek or the Egyptian, but rather as a subsidiary manner of one modern style. Yet, even in *Modern Architecture*, Hitchcock was already under the sway not only of the emerging polemic of the International Style but also of the historical determinism which pervades so much German art historical writing of the period. In *Modern Architecture* Hitchcock claimed that a fundamental characteristic of the Modern style is a 'preference for formal experimentation', as if Egyptian and Greek architects in Antiquity were never interested in trying anything new.[15] In his later books, by inference, and explicitly in an essay 'Modern Architecture – A Memoir', Hitchcock has altered his original position, claiming that had he followed his initial plan to cover '... the whole range of time from the Late Gothic to the present it would have been more or less analogous to the books of the 19th-century architectural historians such as James Ferguson (who) ... dealing with the "Modern styles" ... interpreted "Modern" in the old sense as the third portion of the relevant past: "Modern times", that is the period from the Renaissance onward, in distinction to "Antiquity" and the "Middle Ages".' Hitchcock goes on to observe that: '... what is, at any given point, accepted more broadly as "Modern architecture" can have no fixed beginning – various historians and critics have set its start all the way from the early 15th century to the early 20th. Nor, even more obviously, can it have a fixed ending. What is still properly considered Modern architecture began, according to my present view, in the 1880s, not way back in 1750, nor yet in 1900 or in 1920; it will be over when we or the next generation have another name for it.'[16]

Thus Hitchcock brings us to a fundamental issue of the moment: although at first glance it seems difficult to sustain as the broadest definition of modern architecture all the production of the post-Medieval period, upon further reflection such a definition seems more workable than those later attempts to link the historical definition of the modern period in architecture too closely with specific economic, political or cultural events that

have occurred since the middle of the 18th century – that is, with the Industrial Revolution, and the political revolutions in the United States and France – or with prior positions taken on behalf of any particular manifestation of current or contemporary production that might seem more 'advanced', 'innovative' or 'progressive'. Such a broad view opens up the definition of modern architecture, enabling it to be understood not as a humanistic pursuit involving a continuous interweaving of diverse and often contradictory formal tendencies assembled, discovered, sometimes even invented through various processes, including eclecticism, Modernism, and technological as well as functional determinism. Such a view would hold out 1750 as an important marker in time, as it would also note the decisive shifts that took place in the period 1870-90 (emergence of a dominant Post-Modernism). But this view, as I hope to demonstrate later, would not see decisive reasons why any of these phases should mark the conclusions of the modern period's larger themes, or their replacement by themes not already present in the formative stages of the modern period.

It is not Hitchcock, but Giedion, Pevsner and J M Richards who have exerted the greatest influence on the profession's and the public's view of what modern architecture was and should have been during the past 40 years: much of the confusion about the character and chronology of the modern period in architecture can be attributed to their tendency to present the history of the architecture of the past 200 years as a series of morality tales involving heroic struggles between pragmatic materialism and high ideals, 'good guys' and 'bad guys', 'progressives' and 'reactionaries', 'constituent' and 'transitory' facts. Whole careers and aesthetic movements have been cut off from the so-called 'mainstream' of historical flow: Giedion's *Space, Time and Architecture* and Pevsner's *Pioneers of the Modern Movement* have been the most influential in the architectural profession and therefore the most troublesome. In these works, as Hitchcock has observed, much of the architecture of the 19th century has been treated 'as constituent premonitions of (the) Modern architecture' of the 1920s and 30s and not as legitimate artistic production in its own right.[17]

Outside the architectural profession, most educated people now in their 40s and 50s were exposed to this point of view in introductory courses in college, sometimes in the original texts of Giedion and Pevsner, but more often in such popularising work as Richard's *Introduction to Modern Architecture* in which: '... the words "Modern Architecture" are used here to mean something more particular than the contemporary architecture. They are used to mean the new kind of architect that is growing up with this century as this century's own contribution to the art of architecture; the work of those people, whose number is happily increasing, who understand that architecture is a social art related to the life of the people it serves, not an academic exercise in applied ornament. The question that immediately arises is whether there is in fact enough difference between people's lives as they are lived in this century and as they were lived in previous centuries to justify a truly "Modern" architecture being very different from that of the past – and indeed whether "Modern" architecture is quite as revolutionary as it is supposed to be . . . For whatever reason, Modern architecture has been passing through a sort of "puritan" phase, in which the negative virtues of simplicity and efficiency have been allowed to dominate, and since 1939 a concentration on the essentials has also been necessitated in most countries by the overriding need to build cheaply.'[18]

The revisionist architectural history of the 1950s and 60s, which owes a considerable debt to the example of Hitchcock's comprehensive *Architecture: Nineteenth and Twentieth Centuries*, sought to develop a broader characterisation of the Modern period which would include the stylistic revivalism of the late 18th and 19th centuries as well as the self-referential Modernism of the 20th. But despite Hitchcock's influence, the deterministic view of history typified by Giedion's *Space, Time and Architecture* seems to have prevented the revisionists, in their search for a broader view, from considering events earlier than the mid-18th century. Thus, even the very important redefinition of modern architecture which Scully offered in 1954 and refined in 1961, though the first to free the stylistic analysis of architectural production from the futurist polemic of the Modernist Movement of the 1920s, is not free from political determinism and is not, in the final analysis, sufficiently broad in its historical scope. Acknowledging a debt to Frank Lloyd Wright, Scully offered a definition of modern architecture as the 'architecture of democracy', an 'image of ourselves' emerging 'precisely at the beginning of industrialism and mass democracy (where) we find it, in terms of fragmentation, mass scale and new, unfocused continuity'.[19] In this sense Scully, seeking to reconcile the views of such early 20th-century historians as Fiske Kimball with those of Giedion and Pevsner, brings us to the threshold of our current perception of the distinctions between the modern tradition and Modernism.[20] As a result it is now possible to see the Modern Movement as an episode in the broad history of modern architecture itself.

Similarly, one can see Modernism not as style but as strategy. Though Modernism has had its period of hegemony, resulting in a univalent style whose abstraction rendered it difficult and uncommunicative from the first, it should not be seen as a style in and of itself. The International Style was the great modernist style, and Modernism itself remains a modern sensibility. Yet there are those who would argue that it is a sensibility parallel to Western humanism and thereby outside it, that is not at all part of the tradition that began with the Renaissance, and it is this issue which constitutes the crux of the current debate.

The idea of a 'Post-Modern Age' was introduced by Arnold Toynbee in his *A Study of History*[21] and has been developed by a number of historians, most notably Geoffrey Barraclough.[22] The Post-Modern Age is discussed by Toynbee and Barraclough as one in which there is increasing recognition that co-existence is the *modus vivendi* of the pluralist condition of our time. If, as Toynbee and Barraclough argue, the modern period began at the end of the 15th century, when Western European culture began to exert its hegemony over vast land areas and cultures not its own (and Western European man found himself having to deal not only with the pluralist politics of European nationalism in its formative stages but also with the pluralism brought about by encounters with the 'native' populations of the 'New World'), then it perhaps can be argued that the post-modern or contemporary phase they describe is really just another stage in modern history, a 'global' or Post-Industrial Age following a National or Industrial Age, an era of 'relativism' that at once accepts the inherent diversity of the present while seeking order and meaning through a connection with the past, especially with the Romantic era. Post-Modernism should not be seen as a reaction against Modernism; it seeks to develop Modernism's themes by attempting to examine them in relationship to the wider framework of the modern period as a whole.

The divided nature of Modernism complicates our understanding of the post-modern devolution. At the beginning of this essay, I defined two kinds of post-modern sensibilities which can now be seen as related to Modernism: a traditional one and a schismatic one. But the complex nature of Modernism itself, with its two distinct conditions or types united by an apocalyptic view of history, complicate the situation with regard to post-Modernism. As a result, it can be argued that there are not one but two sets of post-modern doubles.

The first type of traditional Post-Modernism – and the one which I would argue is the more viable of the two – argues for a break with Modernism and a reintegration with a view of Western humanism which includes Modernism among its many and sometimes conflicting conditions. The second type sees itself as a continuation of Modernism (in which Modernism is itself seen as a successor to the Baroque and Rococo), a sensibility and style that is contradictorily and inexplicably, in its presentism, a contradiction of the very notion of style.

This second type of traditional Post-Modernism is somewhat dubious: at the very least it fails to account for the stylistic complexity of the Romantic era, and it leads us to a question of whether such a Post-Modernism is really different from Modernism itself. For if traditional Modernism is a condition in which all art is seen as being in the present, though not breaking with the values and symbols of Western humanism, then where can this second type of Post-Modernism stand in time? Is there a place beyond the present?

The first type of schismatic Post-Modernism – and the one which I would argue is the more viable of the two – is the one which argues for a *continuity with* Modernism. This kind of schismatic Post-Modernism, like the second type of traditional Post-Modernism, is a continuing Modernism, but the use of the prefix 'post' has meaning because it permits the designation of a condition which is distinct from Modernism because it breaks with the Western humanist tradition. Schismatic Post-Modernism of this type marks the full flowering of a sensibility which has its origins in Modernism's aspiration toward a clean break with the Western humanist tradition.

The second type of schismatic Post-Modernism is itself seen as a *continuing* tradition. This is the so-called 'post-modern breakthrough to post-modernity',[23] in which a totally new state of consciousness is achieved that insists on the obsolescence of Modernism as well as the entire Western humanist tradition. Attractive though such an image seems to those who view the current situation as unnecessarily confusing, it is difficult to make clear just exactly how this new condition will emerge. As Richard E Palmer has written: 'Post-Modernity raises the question of a transition and transformation so radical as to change the fundamental view of language, history, truth, time and matter – so radical that "understanding" becomes a quite different process. It raises the possibility, in other words, of a "new hermeneutics" . . . The hermeneutical problem of bridging the gap between modern and post-modern sets-of-mind goes in both directions: the problem of understanding a post-modern way of thinking when the assumptions and furniture of our thinking are themselves given by modernity, and the problem of a person who, having achieved a Post-Modern, post-spatialised, post-perspectual, or holistic framework, must then communicate it to someone who has not reached it.'[24]

Thus, though there are four conditions of Post-Modernism, it would seem that in the case of two, questions of considerable complexity remain unanswered at the present moment, thereby limiting the effectiveness of these conditions for artistic production if not for discourse. The difficulties raised by the second type of traditional Post-Modernism – that is, the notion of a continuing Modernism – simultaneously claiming a position within Humanism and apart from history, seem hopelessly contradictory.

The difficulties of the second type of schismatic Post-Modernism – the post-modernist breakthrough – have already been discussed. It takes as its point of departure the work of such writers as James Joyce but, as yet, it has not found a truly convincing voice. Such critics as William Spanos and Ihab Hassan are attempting to articulate the nature of the Post-Modernist breakthrough.[25] Because this type of schismatic Post-

Modernism is only schismatic, it doubles back on itself and reaches a dead end.

Thus it becomes clear that the second type of schismatic Post-Modernism is not just a shift of emphasis within Modernism; its relationship to Modernism is not comparable to that which Post-Impressionism had to Impressionism; schismatic Post-Modernism is radical in the extreme. In an essay on 'Joyce, Beckett and the Post-Modern imagination', Ihab Hassan observes that though 'one might be inclined to conclude that Modernism is simply the earlier movement . . . and that Post-Modernism is the later movement, which began to dominate Western literature after World War II' one must finally see that: 'however jagged or ironic modernism allowed itself to be it reained its faith in art, in the imaginative act, even at the end of cultural dissolution . . . Post-Modernism on the other hand, is essentially *subversive* in form and *anarchic* in its cultural spirit. It dramatises its lack of faith in art even as it produces new works of art intended to hasten *both* cultural and artistic dissolution.'[26]

The two conditions of the post-modern that are at this moment important, and the ones I should like to consider in some detail in the remaining pages of this essay are: 1) the schismatic Post-Modernism that argues for a clean break with Western humanism and a continuity with Modernism and 2) the traditional Post-Modernism that argues for a break with Modernism and a reintegration with the broader condition of Western Humanism, especially with the Romantic tradition. These seem the only possible categories because they are the only ones that contain in them the 'double' sensibilities of continuity and change which are necessary to sustain generative cycles of creation.

The emergence of the post-modern sensibility can be seen as a logical result of the opposition between romantic and modernist sensibilities, the former revelling in diversity, the latter struggling to find a universal cultural voice. Post-Modernism is not revolutionary in either the political or artistic sense; in fact, it reinforces the effort of the technocratic and bureaucratic society in which we live – traditional Post-Modernism by accepting conditions and trying to modify them, schismatic Post-Modernism by proposing a condition *outside* Western humanism, thereby permitting Western humanist culture to proceed uninterrupted though not necessarily unaffected.

Post-Modernism, though a reaction to Modernism, is not a revolutionary movement seeking to overthrow Modernism. Modernism cannot be ignored. We cannot pretend that it never existed and that we can return to a pre-modernist condition. The post-modern condition arises out of the need to account for, and to continue to condition action in this last third of our century. Thus it must be seen that Post-Modernism is a modern sensibility that includes Modernism by virtue of its reaction to it; it is the manifestation of what Irving Howe describes as 'the radical breakdown of the Modernist impulse', which came as a result of the experience of the Holocaust, of World War II, of the use of the atomic bomb. At its root lies existentialism, an attitude toward history and the idea of time which has extended beyond our thought processes to the very mode of our consciousness.

Schismatic Post-Modernism can be seen as an outgrowth of the anti-intellectualism of the Modernism of the 1920s and 30s. In philosophy and literature it is represented by such writers as Norman Brown, Herbert Marcuse, Marshall McLuhan, Donald Barthelme, Samuel Beckett and William S Burroughs. In architecture, Peter Eisenman is its leading advocate. It rejects the Western humanist tradition and, in the realm of aesthetics, it rejects Aristotelian composition. Though very much related to Modernism, schismatic Post-Modernism is nonetheless a distinct sensibility. And it adopts the Post-Modernist label to differentiate itself from the modernist tradition.

Schismatic Post-Modernism separates itself from traditionalist Post-Modernism by suggesting that it is not simply the crises of mid-century life that have irreparably changed the relationship of men to each other and to their ideas, but that these events have rendered untenable that relationship between men, objects, nature, and the sense of the ideal (the deity) which has been accepted since the Renaissance. Schismatic Post-Modernism sees the relationship between men and objects as a competitive one, and God as dead or, at least, removed from the fray.

It is in this context that Eisenman's position can best be understood. His proposal to make architecture autonomous is anti-historical and anti-symbolic; his endeavours to produce an architecture that is autonomous and self-referential make his works virtually impenetrable. Eisenman's houses become symbolic of their own process of conception, but that process is so cut off from contemporary culture, history and pragmatism that in the end, the effectiveness of the symbolic gesture ceases to be symbolic of anything outside itself; the building runs the danger of becoming merely an object which can, at best, make its appeal on a sensuous and hedonistic level. Although it struggles to free itself from all cultural references, by its very physicality it cannot but remind the viewer of some object previously seen or experienced.

Despite his belief in an autonomous architecture, Eisenman's ideology is culturally based. It draws extensively from the linguistic theories of Noam Chomsky and from the work of such literary critics as Roland Barthes and William Gass, who has himself written about one of Eisenman's buildings, House VI.[27] In basing his argument for an autonomous architecture on theories developed in relation to others in parallel but not necessarily related artistic disciplines Eisenman seems caught up in a contradiction not unlike the one which characterised the justifications devised for Modernist architecture by historians and polemicists such as Giedion, who sought to justify architectural Modernism by connecting it with Einsteinian physics.[28] Schismatic post-modernist architecture, as represented by Eisenman (and I can think of no other architect who might be included with him in this category) buoys itself up with analogies to literary and linguistic theory.[29] But where Modernism's connection to physics was *ex post facto*, schismatic Post-Modernism's connections have been established the other way around. As a result there seems to be in Eisenman's work what John Gardner has observed in the work of such schismatic post-modernists as John Cage and William Gass: a sense of 'art which is all thought . . . art too obviously constructed to fit a theory'.[30]

To sum up: Eisenman's work, in its dazzling extremism, brings into focus the fundamental dilemma of schismatic Post-Modernism which, to paraphrase Kermode, is based on an inherent contradiction that can be seen in Modernism itself: can one reconcile a cult of self-referential form-making with a denial of the existence of form itself? Schismatic Post-Modernism leaves us little choice: with all of previous culture removed in theory, at least, we are left with an aesthetic of unparalleled abstraction and hermeticism and without, as yet, even a hope for the emergence of an atavistic mythology to help crack the code. Eisenman leaves us terribly alone, naked.

'Linguistic opacity', a phrase of Gardner's, suggests that the need to communicate is not a primary function of art. One might ask what can this seeming 'search for opacity' do for us? What are we to make of these 'linguistic sculptures' which at best make, as Gardner writes, 'only the affirmation sand-castles make, that it is pleasant to make things or look at things made, better to be alive than dead?'[31]

It may well be that the extreme position which Eisenman represents in architecture, Cage in music, and Gass in literature, marks an end part in a cycle, and that a viable Post-Modernism must be one that opens up possibilities for a new production

ROBERT A M STERN, RESIDENCE AT MARBLEHEAD, MASSACHUSETTS, 1984-87

rather than describes a situation that can be seen as ultimately futile and nihilistic.

Irving Howe has argued that although there is in modernist literature a 'major impulse' to express 'a choking nausea before the idea of culture . . .' there is also 'another in which the writer takes upon himself the enormous ambition not to reinvent the terms of reality'.[32] It is this 'realistic', 'accepting' aspect of Modernism that is carried over in the second, traditional or 'inclusive' Post-Modernist reactions.

Howe regards Saul Bellow, William Styron and Bernard Malamud as 'traditional' post-modern writers, in the sense that in their books, the action of individuals takes place in relationship to specific cultural conditions. Robert Gillespie, writing about the younger American novelists of the 1960s, states that the work of a considerable group, among them Wendell Berry, Scott Momaday, Larry McMurty, Wright Morris and the Ken Keysey of *Sometimes a Great Notion*, shares a traditional Post-Modernist point of view. These writers accept: '. . . responsibility for the world's conditions, and therefore of authority in managing it. Consciousness for them is less a curse than it is an act of conscience. They are eager to locate themselves in "a place on earth" (the title of one of Berry's novels) and to merge their lives with that place. From such felt relation comes sustenance . . . so a region has its own mythology which may offer the only sustaining relation between the past and the future.'[33]

Traditional Post-Modernism is simultaneously inside contemporary society and critically detached from it; it uses art to comment on everyday life; it is at once 'satiric' and accepting in its view of culture; in this sense it seeks to make telling interpretations of everyday life. Such a Post-Modernism begins to 'restore that state of balance between unchecked fabulation and objective social realism' necessary to prevent artistic production from degenerating into trivial self-indulgence.[34]

In painting and in architecture, traditional Post-Modernism relies increasingly on representational as opposed to abstract or conceptual modes. Rackstraw Downes equates traditional Post-Modernism with a revived realism in painting. Critical of what he describes as Modernism's 'pictorial narcissism – it became a painting capable only of admiring its own nature', Downe's argument against Modernist abstraction and in favour of pre-Modernist representation hinges on his criticism of Modernism's exclusivist principle of selectivity: 'While Old Master painting had allowed emphasis of the different aspects of form, its nature was holistic and embracing, whereas Modernist styles were partial. As were their means, so was their grasp on reality. Expressionism, Dada and Surrealism were associational styles which dealt respectively with emotions, ideas and fantasies. Hedonistic Impressionism, Cubism – a still life style – and Purism which dealt in Utopian absolutes, concentrated on particular properties of form. Modernism, then, constituted a rapid succession of specialised styles, each one supplying some deficiency of the rest; what they gained in intensity and concentration they lost in comprehensiveness and range.

'Modernism was . . . to excel in uncompromisingly personal triumphs and, likewise, fail to produce a syntax sufficiently limber and resourceful to be widely shared and passed along. In fact, that was one of its rules, that no manner should develop into an available language; because if it did so it would become transparent and the Modernist purpose would be lost.'[35]

Downes notes that while the modernist looks to the examples of the past in a search 'for lessons which it would not have known it could reach', the post-modernist looks back on history 'in a spirit of empathy for its ostensible purposes'. Nonetheless, traditional Post-Modernism does not advocate stylistic revival, though it does support the concept of emulation. Traditional Post-Modernism looks back to history to see how things were

done and to remind itself that many good ways of doing things which were cast aside for ideological reasons can be usefully rediscovered. Thus, for example, inclusive Post-Modernism can employ recognisable imagery in an abstract way – it can be at once pre-modernist and modernist.[36]

Traditional Post-Modernism opens up artistic production to a public role which Modernism, by virtue of its self-referential formal strategies, had denied itself. In painting, as William Rubin has observed: 'one characteristic of the Modern period *seems* to be ending. That is the tradition of the private picture – private in its character and subject matter as well as in its destination – that is, for the small circle of collectors and friends of the artists, who sympathise with vanguard art.'[37] In this sense, the current interest in photography should be seen as a last-gasp modernist stance.

Architecture, of course, is by definition a public art. Yet in its Modernist phase, it often spoke the private language of painting – one need only recall the arguments advanced in Henry-Russell Hitchcock's book *Painting Toward Architecture*.[38] More importantly, as Suzannah Lessard points out: '. . . between the abstract beauty of technological principles and the underpinning of intricate solutions to innumerable problems, there is a kind of middle ground which was overlooked in the exuberant rush to modernity. Between man's desire to expand his ego and the needs of man as ant – I can think of no better way to express the dual preoccupation of the age of technology – the question of what human life would be in the new world, floated unasked, unnoticed.'[39]

It is this aspect of social and cultural responsibility – not in the narrowly simplistic sense of architectural do-goodism but in a broader and more profound sense of a genuine and unsentimental humanism – that characterised traditional Post-Modernism's distinction from the abstract, self-referential schismatic Post-Modernism which we have already discussed.

Traditional Post-Modernism rejects the anti-historical biases of Modernism; influences from history are no longer seen as constraints on either personal growth or artistic excellence. Modernism looked toward the future as an escape from the past; traditional Post-Modernism struggles with the legacy of that attitude, a world filled with objects whose principle artistic impetus often came from a belief that in order to be 'modern' they must look and function as little as possible like anything that had been seen in the world before. The traditional post-modernist struggle then, is not to free itself from the past, but to relax what has been characterised as 'the stubborn grip of the values created by the rebellion against the past'.[40]

Traditional Post-Modernism rejects what Charles Moore has described as the 'obsessive normalisation of the recent past, where we have drawn our expressive elegance out of poverty . . . (and) our process out of crisis'.[41] It argues that it is proper and sufficient to struggle with the problems of the present viewed in relation to the values continuing from the past while leaving the future to those who will inherit it. Traditional Post-Modernism recognises that the public has lost confidence in architects (though it still believes in the symbolic power of architecture). Modernist architecture offered very little in the way of joy or visual pleasure; its conceptual basis was limited and disconcertingly materialistic. By once again recognising the common assumptions a culture inherits from its past, traditional Post-Modernism is not only an announcement that modern architecture has emerged from its puritan revolution, its catharsis at last behind it, but it is also an avowal of self-confidence in contemporary architecture's ability and willingness to re-establish itself on a basis which can not only deal with the past but also match it value for value, building for building.

Traditional Post-Modernism seeks to look backward in order

to go forward. It should not be regarded as a jettisoning of modern architecture itself, but as an attempt to pick up the threads of a theory and style which were cut by the pioneers of the Modern Movement, especially the concerns for architectural history and for visually comprehensible relationships between old and new buildings. In its inclusiveness, traditional Post-Modernism does not propose an independent style; it is a sensibility dependent on forms and strategies drawn from the modernist and pre-modernist work that preceded it, though it declares the obsolescence of both. It is *a* modern style but not *the* modern style. In its recognition of the transience and multiplicity of styles within the historical epoch we call modern, it rejects the emphasis on unity of expression that was so central to Modernism itself. Traditional Post-Modernism recognises both the discursive and expressive meaning of formal language. It recognises the language of form as communicating sign as well as infra-referential symbol: that is to say, it deals with both physical and associational experience, with the work of art as an act of 'presentation' and 'representation'. It rejects the idea of a single style in favour of a view that acknowledges the existence of many styles (and the likely emergence of even more) each with its own meanings, sometimes permanently established, but more often shifting in relation to other events in the culture.

In architecture, Robert Venturi and Charles Moore can be seen as the leading advocates among an older generation of traditional post-modernists; Michael Graves and myself, among others, from the point of view of age, though not from one of ideology, occupy a middle ground (that is, we are young enough to have been students of Venturi and Moore); and an even younger generation, including Stuart Cohen, Thomas Gordon Smith and the Arquitectonica group, is beginning to make its position felt.

Venturi and Moore are in many ways transitional figures: their theoretical positions are more 'advanced' in the movement toward a position which includes modernist and pre-modernist values than is their built work, which as often as not tends to be abstract and non-representational (Venturi's Oberline Museum and his Hartford Stage; Moore's own house in Los Angeles) as it is representative of ideas that are contextually based (Venturi's three Brant houses, and his Benjamin Franklin house 'restoration'; Moore's Burns House and his Piazza d'Italia). This is not surprising since their education was modernist, and until recently theirs has been a virtually solitary struggle to integrate its ideals with the wider body of architectural culture.

The work of the other traditional post-modernists who have been cited can be characterised by a struggle to use traditional languages without falling into the presumed trap of revivalism. The heritage of Modernism remains a problem for all: its impulse to 'make it new', as Ezra Pound put it 70 years ago, conflicts with the sensibility to make it legible and make it appropriate; the preoccupation with traditional languages is often at the expense of the languages of Modernism, which, no matter how abstract, have come to mean certain things in the culture at large and recognition of stylistic diversity can be viewed as *laissez-faire* permissiveness. Thus in some traditional post-modernist work the grammar of architectural composition has not been explored with the same care as have the individual elements or the overall meanings; in other words some traditional post-modernist work has become 'picturesque'.

Everywhere there are signs of an emerging cultural resynthesis. Richard Gilam sees a 'new naturalism' in the drama; John Gardner pleads for a 'moral fiction' based on a belief in an art dedicated to the 'preservation of the word of gods and men'; Daniel Bell states that the 'problem then is whether culture can regain coherence, a coherence of substance and experience not only of form'. Signs of the shift in sensibility in art and architecture abound. All this seems clear enough and I hope that what I have written has shed some light on the nature of these shifts. If what I have written has any value, it is as a reminder that all which glitters in a new or different way is not necessarily golden, that the ranks of the avant-garde may not any longer be the exclusive defenders of the holy grail of insight; that a shift in sensibility need have very little if anything to do with progress.

The fact of the matter is that the reaction to Modernism is not only a vote of 'no confidence' in its ideology but also a recognition that its forms are exhausted. As Gardner observes: 'When modes of art change, the change need not imply philosophical progress; it usually means only that the hunter has exhausted one part of the woods and has moved to a new part, or to a part exhausted earlier, to which the prey have doubled back ... Aesthetic styles – patterns for communicating feeling and thought – become dull with use, like carving knives, and since dullness is the chief enemy of art, each generation must find new ways of slicing the fat off reality.'[42]

The fundamental nature of this shift to Post-Modernism has to do with the reawakening of artists in every field to the public responsibilities of art. Once again art is being regarded as an act of communication as opposed to one of production or revelation (of the artist's ego and/or of his intentions for the building or his process of design). Though art is based on personal invention it requires public acceptance to achieve real value – to communicate meaning. An artist may choose to speak a private language, but a viewer must be willing and able to 'read' the work, whether it be a book, a painting or a building, for the work to have any kind of public life at all. To the extent that contemporary artists care about the public life of art, they are post-modernists (modernist artists make things only for themselves and/or for the gods); to the extent that an artist believes in the communicative role of form but is not willing to accept that such a role necessarily carries with it cultural meanings that are not inherent to the form, his is a schismatic Post-Modernism.

Modernism in architecture was premised on a dialectic between things as they are and things as they ought to be; Post-Modernism seeks a resolution between – or at least a recognition of – things as they were and as they are. Modernism imagined architecture to be the product of purely rational and scientific process; Post-Modernism sees it as a resolution of social and technological processes with cultural concerns.

Post-Modernism seeks to regain the public role that Modernism denied architecture. The post-modern struggle is the struggle for cultural coherence that is not falsely monolithic, as was attempted in the International Style in architecture or National Socialism in the politics of the 1920s and 30s, but one whose coherence is based on the heterogeneous substance and nature of modern society: Post-Modernism takes as its basis things as they are, *and* things as they were. Architecture is no longer an image of the world as architects wish it to be or as it will be, but as it is.

Notes

1   Kenneth Clark, 'Boredom Blamed', *Art Digest*, Vol X, November 15, 1943, 3. I am indebted to Peter Eisenman, Kenneth Frampton and Vincent Scully for reading and commenting on portions of this manuscript in a much earlier stage of development; Suzanne Stephens has read it more recently. What is written here is much the better for their advice. Nonetheless, I am sure they will be relieved to learn, I take full responsibility for the final product.

2 Portions of this text are based on material introduced by me on previous occasions. See 'Postscript at the Edge of Modernism', in my *New Directions in American Architecture*, 2nd edition revised, Braziller, New York, 1977, 117-36; 'Five Houses', *G A Houses*, 1, 1976, pp 36-41; *Architectural Design*, 47, no 4, May 1977; 'Something Borrowed, Something New', *Horizon*, 20, no 4, December 1977, pp 50-57

3 Charles Jencks, *The Language of Post-Modern Architecture*, Academy Editions, London, 1977; see also, Jencks, 'Post-Modern History', *Architectural Design*, 48, no 1, January 1978, pp 11-62.

4 The term seems to have been initiated by Joseph Hudnut in his essay 'The Post-Modern house', *Architectural Record*, 97, May 1945, pp 70-75, which was reprinted as Chapter 9 in Hudnut's *Architecture and the Spirit of Man*, Harvard, Cambridge, MA, 1949, pp 109-19. Its earliest influential use was in Arnold J Toynbee's *A Study in History*, 8, New York: Oxford, 1954-59, p 338. Eisenman and I discussed the term and its probable definitions at considerable length in the summer of 1975. I first 'went public' with a definition for the term in relationship to architecture in 1976, using it to characterise a shift in mood represented by an event – the Beaux-Arts exhibition at the Museum of Modern Art – and a shifting of alliances among the architects who constituted the 'White' and 'Grey' groups of the mid-70s. See my 'Possibly, the Beaux-Arts Exhibit means something after all (with apology to Clement Greenberg, Rosalind Kraussh and the month of October)', a paper delivered at the 'Oppositions Forum' Institute for Architecture and Urban Studies, 22 January 1976, and published in William Ellis, editor, 'Forum of the Beaux-Arts Exhibition', *Oppositions* 8, Spring 1977, pp 169-71; see also my 'Grey Architecture as Post-Modernism or Up and Down from Orthodoxy' (Grey Architecture: *Quelques Variations Post-Modernistes autour de l'Orthodoxie*), *L'Architecture d'Aujourd'hui*, 186, Sept 1976, p 83.

5 Renato Poggioli, *The Theory of the Avant Garde*, Harvard, Cambridge MA, 1968, translated by Gerald Fitzgerald, p 217; see also, Daniel Bell, *The Cultural Contradictions of Capitalism*, Basic Books, New York, 1976, p 34; Frank Kermode, *Continuities*, Routledge and Kegan Paul, London, 1968, p 8.

6 See Stephen Spender, *The Struggle of the Modern*, University of California, Berkeley, 1963, *passim*.

7 Kermode, *op cit*, pp 27-28.

8 See Kermode, *op cit*, pp 8, 13; Kermode observes that 'the fact that defining the Modern is a task that imposes itself on many distinguished scholars may be a sign that the Modern period is over'. p 28.

9 See Clement Greenberg, 'Modernist Painting' in Gregory Battcock, ed, *The New Art*, Dutton, New York, 1973, revised edition, pp 100-110; William Jordy, 'The Symbolic Essence of Modern European Architecture of the Twenties and its Continuing Influence', *JSAH*, XXII, no 3, Oct 1973, p 117.

10 David Watkin writes that 'an art historical belief in the all-dominating *Zeitgeist*, combined with a historicist emphasis on progress and the necessary superiority of novelty, has come dangerously close to undermining, on the one hand, our appreciation of the genius of the individual and, on the other, the importance of artistic tradition', *Morality and Architecture*, Oxford, London, 1977, p 115. See also, John Alford, 'Modern Architecture and the Symbolism of the Creative Process', *College Arts Journal*, XIV no 2, 1955, pp 102-33; see also, Bell, *op cit*, pp 13, 20, 46-52.

11 David Antin, 'Modernism and Post-Modernism: Approaching the Present in American Poetry', *Boundary* 2.

12 Susan Sontag, *Against Interpretation*, Delta, New York, 1966, p 17.

13 Harry Levin, 'What Was Modernism', in Levin, *Refractions: Essays in Comparative Literature*, Oxford, New York, 1966, pp 271-95.

14 Irving Howe, *Decline of the New*, Harcourt, Brace, New York, 1970, p 3.

15 Henry-Russell Hitchcock, *Modern Architecture, Romanticism and Reintegration*, Payson and Clarke, New York, 1929, p xvi.

16 Henry-Russell Hitchcock, 'Modern Architecture – A Memoir', *JSAH*, 27, no 4, December 1968, pp 227-33; the broad view was taken by Montgomery Schuyler, for example, who stated that 'modern architecture, like modern literature, had its origin in the revival of learning. The Italian Renaissance in architecture was inextricably connected with the awakening of the human spirit which was the beginning of modern civilisation'. 'Modern Architecture', *Architectural Record IV*, July-September 1894.

17 Hitchcock, 'Modern Architecture – A Memoir', *passim*; Robert Venturi and Denise Scott-Brown first used the good-guy, bad-guy analogy in their

'Learning from Lutyens or the Case of the Shifting Zeitgeist', *RIBA Journal*, 76, August 1969, pp 353-54.

18 J M Richards, *Introduction to Modern Architecture*, Penguin, Harmondsworth, 1960, pp 9, 13; see Watkin, *op cit passim* ; also Peter Collins, *Changing Ideals in Modern Architecture*, Faber and Faber, London, 1965, *passim*.

19 Vincent J Scully, 'Modern Architecture: Toward a Redefinition of Style', *College Art Journal VII*, no 2, Winter 1958, pp 140-59; see also Scully's *Modern Architecture* Braziller, New York, *passim*.

20 Fiske Kimball and George H Edgell, *A History of Architecture*, Harper, New York, 1918; Chapter XII, 'Modern Architecture' was written by Kimball; see also, James D Kornwolf, *M H Baillie Scott and the Arts and Crafts Traditions*, Johns Hopkins, Baltimore, 1972, XXLV.

21 Toynbee, *op cit* ; see also, Toynbee, *The Present Day Experiment in Western Civilization*, London: Oxford 1962, pp 26-37.

22 Geoffrey Barraclough, *An Introduction to Contemporary History*, Basic Books, New York, 1965, using.

23 Gerald Graff, 'The Myth of the Post-Modernist Breakthrough', *Tri Quarterly* no 26, Winter, 1973, pp 383-417; see also, Bell, *op cit*.

24 Richard E Palmer, 'Postmodernity and Hermeneutics', *Boundary* 22. Winter 1977, pp 363-93.

25 William Spanos. 'The Detective and the Boundary: Some Notes on the Post-Modern Literary Imagination', *Boundary* 2, 1, Fall 1972, pp 147-68.

26 Ihab Hassan, 'Joyce, Beckett, and the postmodern imagination', *Tri Quarterly*, XXXIV, Fall 1975, pp 179-200; see also Hassan, *Paracriticisms, Seven Speculations of the Times*, University of Illinois, Urbana, Illinois, 1975, pp 55-56.

27 William Gass, 'House VI', *Progressive Architecture*, 58, no 6, June 1977, pp 57-67.

28 Sigfried Giedion, *Space, Time and Architecture*, Harvard, Cambridge, MAI, 1941, *passim*.

29 Mario Gandelsonas, 'On Reading Architecture', *Progressive Architecture*, 53, no 3, March 1972, pp 68-88.

30 John Gardner, *On Moral Fiction*, Basic Books, New York, 1978-9.

31 *ibid*, pp 69, 71.

32 Howe, *op cit*, p 5.

33 Robert Gillespie, 'Beyond the Wasteland: The American Novel in the Nineteen Sixties', *Boundary* 2, III, no 2, Windsor, 1975, pp 473-481.

34 Gerald Graff, 'Babbitt at the Abyss: The Social Context of Postmodern American Fiction', *Tri Quarterly* no 33, Spring 1976, pp 307-337.

35 Rackstraw Downes, 'Post-Modernist Painting', *Tracks*, Fall 1976, pp 70-73.

36 Traditional Post-Modernism should not be confused with the neo-traditionalism of Henry Hope Reed, John Barrington Bayley, Conrad Jameson. For Bayley and Reed, see Henry Hope Reed, *The Garden City*, Doubleday, New York, 1959, *passim*.

37 Rubin is quoted by Douglas Davis' 'Post-Modern for Stories Real and Imagined/Toward a Theory', in his *Art Culture – Essays on the Postmodern*, Harper & Row, New York, 1977. See also the 'Post-Modernist Dilemma', a dialogue between David and Suzi Gablik, *Village Voice*, March 24, April 3 and April 10, 1978.

38 Henry-Russell Hitchcock, *Painting Toward Architecture*, Duell, Sloan and Pearce, New York, 1948, *passim*.

39 Suzannah Lessard, 'The Towers of Light' *The New Yorker*, 54, July 10, 1978, pp 32-36, 41-44, 49, 52, 58.

40 Lessard, *op cit* ; James D Kornwolf makes the interesting observation that 'Le Corbusier's generation was misguided not to recognise that the 19th century's struggle with the past was also its struggle, and that a new understanding of the past, not a denial of it, was what was needed'. *op cit*. p 513.

Peter Collins observes that 'the idea of an "International Style" was a product of the Renaissance. In fact, the so-called "battle of the styles" might be more reasonably and meaningfully interpreted as an attempt to refute the concept of an "International Style" rather than as a conflict between "Gothicists" and "Classicists". This was certainly the essence of the position taken by Viollet-le-Duc and Ferguson.' *op cit*, pp 171-72.

41 Charles Moore, 'Foreword', in Sam Davis, editor, *The Form of Housing*, Van Nostrand Reinhold, New York, 1977, p 6.

42 Gardner, *op cit*.

———— * ————

ROBERT A M STERN ARCHITECTS, RESIDENCE AT CALF CREEK, WATER MILL, NEW YORK, 1984-87

PICTORIAL SURVEY
POST-MODERN CLASSICISM

VENTURI, RAUCH & SCOTT BROWN, *ABOVE*: STUDIO, BLOCK ISLAND, NEW YORK, 1980-82; *BELOW*: TUCKERS TOWN HOUSE, BERMUDA, 1976

ABOVE: CHARLES JENCKS AND TERRY FARRELL, THEMATIC HOUSE, LONDON, 1982-85; *BELOW*: HANS HOLLEIN, AUSTRIAN TRAVEL BUREAU, VIENNA, 1976-78

STIRLING, WILFORD & ASSOCIATES, NEUE STAATSGALERIE, STUTTGART, 1977-84, *ABOVE*: AERIAL VIEW; *BELOW*: INTERIOR COURT

ABOVE: JONES & KIRKLAND, MISSISSAUGA CITY HALL, TORONTO, 1982-86; CHARLES VANDENHOVE, HOTEL TORRENTIUS, LIEGE, 1981-82

ABOVE: JEREMY DIXON, ROYAL OPERA HOUSE, COVENT GARDEN, LONDON, REVISED VERSION, 1989-; *BELOW*: CHARLES MOORE, CIVIC HALL EXTENSION, BEVERLY HILLS, CALIFORNIA, 1987

ABOVE: MICHAEL GRAVES, CLOS PEGASE WINERY, CALIFORNIA, 1988; *BELOW*: PHILIP JOHNSON & JOHN BURGEE, COLLEGE OF ARCHITECTURE, UNIVERSITY OF HOUSTON, TEXAS, 1983-85

ROB KRIER, REDESIGN OF THE 'VIA TRIUMPHALIS', KARLSRUHE, 1979

V

URBANISM

ROB KRIER, *PARVIS ST GERMAIN*, AMIENS, 1984

URBAN SPACE
COLIN ROWE

In the jungle-like politics of architectural self advertisement it has become a misfortune of the late Emil Kaufman's great achievement, inadvertently and considerably after his death, to have sponsored a highly edited and, often, somewhat mindless version of Neo-Classicism. Was it *Von Ledoux bis Le Corbusier* or was it *Three Revolutionary Architects* which gave the cue? And it was probably the latter, with its so desirable connotations of dynamic and anti-academic insurrection. For, when the architectural Boy Scout camps of the 1920s (La Sarraz and all the rest) could be seen as equipped with a respectable, and still revolutionary, pedigree, then the possibilites of annexation became endless. For, then, it became possible to be interested in the late 18th century without seeming to be desperately old hat, and for a series of hero figures to be observed. And so, after certain strange leaps of the mind, Ledoux-Boullée was followed by the constellation of Saint Simon, Comte and Fourier and then, after the whole panoply of the French socialist tradition became exposed, by Karl Marx and the so curious notion that a William Morris society might be constructed out of French neo-classical components; and one might abbreviate the possible process of argument by which all this may have come about:

With the nitty-gritty of the Welfare State and the appalling bureaucratic details of pseudo-Capitalist administration we will have nothing to do; instead, we will simplify, abstract and project to the degree of extravagance a highly restricted, private and not very hospitable version of what the good society might be assumed to be; we will give a nod to Kaufmann; we will give three muted cheers for the Stalinallée; we will adore the manifesto pieces of Boullée; we will (mostly) refuse to observe the built work of Soane; instead, and if necessary, we will unroll a few hundred yards of neutral Adolf Loos façade, build a lot of little towers and stand around on top of them a quantity of Ledoux villas, wave quietly but not too exuberantly to Louis Kahn (congratulations on the Trenton Bath House), insinuate a reference to the metaphysic of Giorgio de Chirico, display a conversance with Leonidov, become highly enthusiastic about the more evocative aspects of Art Deco, exhibit the intimidation of curtains waving in the wind, and, then, gently warm up the ensuing goulash in the *pastoso* of Morandi.

But, if here is displayed the solution (with all its atavistic seductions) fresh from Milano-Venezia, one might also be prompted to ask whether its Marxism is not a little too romantic and its presumption a little too premature. Apropos of the so called New York Five and their alleged intellectualistic involutions, Aldo Giurgola spoke of *the discreet charm of the bourgeoisie*; and about this other context of gestures, postures, antics which has just been abruptly summarised, where social conscience, social agony and high fashion are almost inextricably interrelated, just what is there that needs to be said? That, although the stage set is almost completely changed from that of a few years ago, the form of words which the players use is, in some way, distressingly familiar?

For, the idea that 'art stopped short at the cultivated court of the Empress Josephine' has, in one form or another, been around for a considerable time; and, recently, though in a different framework of values, it has been given fresh currency. But, of course, even in 1881, W S Gilbert's endearing, philistine and distinctly inadequate satire of the miscellaneous aesthetes who populate the pages of *Patience* disclosed a quasi-critical orientation which was in no way new.

Something went wrong in 1714, or 1750, or 1789, or 1804, with the beginning of the Georgian era or at its end, with the death of Queen Anne or the accession of Queen Victoria, with Andrew Jackson, with Ulysses S Grant, with the discovery of Pompeii, with the emergence of the Roman Empire, with the collapse of the Roman Empire, with the decline of the Middle Ages, with the appearance of Brunelleschi, or Michelangelo, or Inigo Jones, or Borromini. One can rearrange the dates, rename the style phases, reidentify the personalities which decorate this scenario but the basic structure of what, after all, must still be historical myth will remain surprisingly consistent and intact. At some moment in time there occurred a cessation of meaningful artistic production and a catastrophic decline in all sense of value. Standards of craftsmanship were abruptly terminated. Collective endeavour declined. Society became atomised and the individual alienated. Disassociation of sensibility ensued and a tragic schism between feeling and thinking was the inevitable result. But, now, *nous avons changé tout cela*. For we, the protagonists of the new, have scrutinised and discriminated. We know the evil, we have the remedy, ours is the prescription; and, as for you, just you take a good look and a good listen.

Such, in its time, was one of the primary messages of modern architecture – a primary message of Walter Gropius, Sigfried Giedion, Le Corbusier and Nikolaus Pevsner. Only believe in this: and if you will but do so, the world will become reintegrated, the joys of craftsmanship restored and the wounds of society healed. But if, contributing to the litany of this myth, there have been many of the would-be self-consciously critical names of recent Western civilisation, it must still remain a particularly savage irony that modern architecture's most favored polemic has now been enlisted against modern architecture itself. For the locus of the historical rift valley is now shifted; the bad date is now 1923 – or there-abouts; the bad gestures/propositions are those of CIAM; and the really evil guys (the Pied Pipers who lead the children in the wrong direction and finally deposited them in a Carpathian wilderness, *terribly* dangerous and ever so far from home) are rapidly coming to be the bearers of just those names which, only the other day, seemed to be so firmly respectable and so highly established among the commemorators of architectural progress.

So, perhaps, we now inhabit a somewhat desperate Transylvanian landscape of the mind, lugubriously furnished with the wreckage of reputations and the debris of good intentions. Hamelin town is far away ('in Brunswick near famous Hanover City'); but, having been brought to our present destitution by the most charming of music, the most interesting of leaders, the most curious of subterranean routes, we can only feel disquieted, abused, disturbed and, being unable to forget the Hansel and Gretel toy town from out of which we were seduced, we can now only suspect the instrument of our temptation – the notion of an impeccable and 'scientific' solution through instant 'total' design – was itself no more than a species of late Biedermayer

187

ornamental gingerbread. For, apparently, nobody – ever – was really very good, and nothing – ever – was really very true and, in the 20th century, even those few who almost approached goodness, almost embodied truth, were invariably debauched by the flagrant influence of a local grandee – a capitalist Dracula, monstrous, sadistic and perverse – who distorted the message and rendered its results utterly vain.

Or, at least something like this seems to be among the many inherently inconsistent diagnoses of modern architecture's impending collapse; and up to a point, this diagnosis is almost believable. But, it is surely not so much the credibility as it is the wholly conventional character of such argument which deserves attention. For, if in their implication that most of the cities of the world have been approximately wrecked via the agency of modern architecture the proponents of *architettura razionale* can only be entirely correct, then should it not seem strange that the style of arrangement, even the vocabulary of argument in which these judgements are delivered – bourgeois angst, apocalyptic threat, incipient world transforming event, holistic deliverance – is representative of a critical strategy of which modern architecture should have made us only too sceptical? For, again, the decorations of the stage infer something significantly avant garde, while the libretto of the opera comes over as a standardised and entirely to be anticipated plot. To repeat: the bad date is now 1923, the good date is now 1974, or '75, or '76; and it is the persistence of an old argument, transferred from context to visual context and still presented as novelty which is here the profoundly disquieting factor. For what we are here presented with is something professing to be radical chic, elegant *fa figura*, social concern; and if, in terms of the visuals, what we receive is an engaging archaeology of the future, then, in terms of the verbals, the situation is much the same. The verbals are antique; and the problem of the symbiosis of antiquity and the would-be way-out, though not insuperable, is certainly considerable. For avant garde protestation (hey, look at our acrobatics!) and the eternal creakings of old verbal machinery are, in the end, not the best of all possible bedfellows; and, simply, the combination is less than respectably athletic.

Until recently when modern architecture, in spite of its longevity, was still, universally, proclaimed as 'new', almost any architect under the age of 60 (with appropriate achievements to his credit) was likely to be saluted and advertised as 'young' and the question 'But just how old does one have to be in order to become a young architect (?)' was scarcely ever propounded. For the legend of uncorrupted, incorruptible architectural youth (youth synonymous with the only quest worthwhile – the ongoing quest for the new and the agile) persisted as one of the most fundamental of fictions; and, indeed, the collusion between Peter Pan, Jugendstil, the Boy Scouts and the early Fascist 'giovinezza, giovinezza' is likely to remain among the more observable phenomena of early 20th-century culture – perhaps part of the inevitable heritage of the art nouveau.

So it was an important idea – and a dangerous one; and, like many important – and dangerous – ideas, it has become fossilised and survives as no more than unexamined and tedious tradition: let us rather be potential than productive; let us be dynamic rather than introspective; let us condemn the unjust sophistications and special moral codes of established society; since Rousseau's noble savage (primordial energy uncontaminated by culture) is almost the same as the statue of Eros in Piccadilly Circus) then, in order to make tabula rasa, in order to disclose a primitive house and to engender a future society – redeemed, and of renewed aboriginal purity – let us proceed to mock, to injure and to destroy the existing.

Now the fiesta of destruction (one imagines broken bottles on a New Year's Eve in Naples) which has continued since the Enlightenment surely deserves to be applauded. For the most part it has been exhilarating; also it has resulted in previously undreamed of blessings; and as one attempts to imagine the condition of provincial society, circa 1770, in almost any small city in the world, then one can only say: Thank God for the ventilations which, over the last 200 years, have been made!

But, at least for the impatient, the route of what might be conceived to be progress has still taken an extremely long time: and, of course, one of the major road blocks to emancipation has now become the fantasies which the architect entertains about himself, fantasies now little more than the platitudes of criticism, but, still, fantasies which, in their own day – now a very good many years ago – were conceived of as permanent, indeed dazzling, illuminations which were for ever to make visible the surface of a glourious *autostrada* leading to a crystalline social condition of limpid authenticity.

> And I John saw the Holy City, New Jerusalem, coming down from God out of heaven . . . and the City lieth four-square, and the length is as large as the breadth: . . . and the City was pure gold like unto clear glass . . . and the City had no need of the sun, neither of the moon to shine in it: for the glory of God did lighten it, . . . and there shall in no wise enter into it anything that defileth, neither whatsoever worketh abomination or *maketh* a lie: but they which are written in the Lamb's Book of Life.

The vision of Final Judgement and Deliverance, of the Great Hallelujah, when equipped with a technological gloss, is, of course, immensely like in kind to the vision of the *ville radieuse* to be later experienced by Le Corbusier; and, if this later vision, of a world redeemed by architecture, is now severely discredited, it is still not too unreasonable to suggest that some eschatological framework of this kind still survives as the psychological underpinning of much currently fashionable architectural polemic – and particularly that of Italian origin. For this is a polemic which, professing to be coolly critical, is still, more often than not, evidently inflamed by notions of that glaring turbulent upsurge which will for ever release us from the stinking limitations of bourgeois culture and effectively initiate the millennial establishment.

And this (though to a degree, charming and of a period) is surely something of a pity. For, if the advocates of *architettura razionale* (who are in great danger of flooding the market and inspiring a counter-wave of digust) are able to make a highly apt critique of modern architecture's urbanistic failure and if this is of immense value, it does not automatically follow that all the physical achievements of modern architecture are to be condemned and that we are entirely obliged to return to a simplified and innocent world, *à la Laugier*, a species of ante-diluvian (and Marxist) *belle époque*, reminiscent more of Knossos than New York, in which strangely deserted piazzas, seemingly prepared for not yet to be anticipated rituals, in the meantime support a somewhat scanty population of mildly desperate hippies.

Indeed, it may be a rather curious commentary upon a contemporary failure of nerve that a merely abbreviated reconstitution of the 19th-century city, enticingly equipped with surrealistic overtones, is now so widely received as the most pregnant and potential of disclosures. For, though such a reconstitution is, in many ways, what is required, there are still inhibitions to be felt about the tricking out of Beaux-Arts plans with neo-primitive façades ('a poor thing but Minoan', as Sir Arthur Evans almost certainly did *not* say about his Cretan restorations) and there are still reserves of feeling (oddly Futurist and strangely technophile?) which will operate to prevent any such, immediate, dispensation.

———— * ————

ARCHITECTURE AND CITY: PAST AND PRESENT
ALDO ROSSI

ALDO ROSSI, PROJECT FOR FIERA-CATENA, MANTUA, 1982

The problem of historic centres, that is, how to build and operate in them, has revealed the inadequacies of contemporary architecture, just as much as the problem of city outskirts. Whether urban or natural setting, the question cannot be posed solely from the point of view of the relation between old and new, but from the point of view of the necessary modification which is produced with

every intervention. In any case the relation with the surrounding world *(Umwelt)* cannot be an operation of camouflage or imitation; if it is, it is a sign of inadequacy and cultural weakness, whose effects can only be negative. I am talking above all about the superficial adaptations of many modern buildings, undoubtedly worse than the historicism of romantic buildings, which found a tension *(Spannung)* which was often far from superficial. In reality, architecture is formed with all its history; it grows with its own justifications and only through this process of formation does it fit into the built or natural world which surrounds it. It works when, through its own originality, it establishes a dialectical relationship; then it shapes a situation. The ancient temples, the cathedrals, the factories and industrial installations of our time, the bridges, the roads, characterise a landscape with the same ruthlessness. If I had to cite positive examples of intervention in the countryside, I would mention the bridges of the Autostrada del Sole, in Italy, or some dams in Switzerland, or other examples of this type. It is perhaps possible that an equal courage in the historic centres might provide the odd successful example; naturally I am referring to those cases where intervention is in some way necessary.

Every operation carried out in historic centres entails a judgement, and this judgement must be given in the first place in the terms of urban analysis and architecture; situations are too various to be generalised about. When a government body

concerned with the environment, faced with the catastrophe which is destroying the ancient cities of Europe, suggests this or that stylistic touch, that note of colour or whatever, they believe that they can resolve a more general ill with some specific device, and the results are worse still. When I talk about choice, I am also referring to the courage to rebuild a destroyed building with the fidelity of an archaeologist, as happened in the historic centre of Warsaw or in the Rathaus in Leipzig. In this case it is a precise choice, a brave judgement with all the risks it entails. I mean that the worst thing is to believe that restrictions on height, or sloping roofs, can reproduce the scale of a Gothic city, or that it is enough to put on a layer of yellow plaster (except that it is often plastic!) to fit certain ugly modern houses into the 18th-century buildings of the Baroque cities. There is no clash between the various types of architecture in time, except the ridiculousness of architecture which is born of a more general cultural decline.

How does a genuine, thorough relation with the city in which we are building come to exist? It exists only insofar as it carries over the general features of the city into motifs of its own planning. In the competition for the administrative and business centre of Turin, I registered that the prevalent character of this city was the topographical one, that no architecture could place itself outside of the Cartesian mesh which is the design of the whole city; I noted how Antonelli, in building his immense

Mole, had kept it within the mesh of the traditional block, actually stressing the precise geometrical form which the block suggests in terms of height. This was the direction, I thought, for a precise relationship, a circumstantial relationship, with the reality of an urban centre. Again in the plan for Piazza della Pilotta in Parma, I tried to grasp the architectural relations typical of Emilian towns through the space of arcades, squares, the architecture of shadows; these are the clues which architecture draws from whatever surrounds it. Perhaps one of the most precise, and architectural, relationships between study and architecture is *Italian Square* by De Chirico; these spaces, which draw their reality from the observation of Ferrara, build up a different and decisive image.

In order to be able to travel this road, architects must know the city as a theoretical part of their architecture; they must verify their theoretical premises against the situation on which they are working. Even in a natural landscape, La Tourette – one of Le Corbusier's most beautiful works – uses the section of the site most skilfully, making the most of the place and defining it; but this part of the procedure, from the planning point of view, is an essentially technical fact. In every case the architect must express this relationship with the setting in the terms which are proper to him, ie through his own technique. This requires extremely precise information.

To imagine a more complex relationship with the countryside than that of the incorporation into it of a piece of architecture may be a fascinating question, but undoubtedly a dangerous one. This type of relationship, where nature or earlier buildings are fused together with new additions without any clear limits, ends with Greek and Etruscan architecture; to hope to update it is a delusion.

Faced with any undertaking we must ask: what do we want to preserve of the city and why? What does it mean to talk of the historic city and environment? These definitions are in fact very different.

I think it is necessary to reject the concept of environment as it has been handed down to us, often born of romantic criticism and Ruskin's pages on Venice (however beautifully written), it is often confused with the picturesque, with a vague sentimental taste for those parts of the city where the urban situation has often deteriorated. Sometimes it is old houses, positive ghettos, often proof of a former poverty which we would be delighted to see destroyed. This observation concerns a broader discussion of the city insofar as to be active in the historic centres means making more general decisions; decisions of a political nature and decisions of an architectural nature. As far as housing is concerned, it is vital to grasp the implications of a slum clearance programme in historic centres, or a complete change towards services, hotels and luxury living accommodation. This type of operation, which in practice entails the working class being driven from the centre, began with 19th- and 20th- century demolition, distorting the character and compactness of the urban centres. Quite apart from questions of a political and sociological nature, since in reality this operation permits large-scale speculation at the expense of the working classes who often cannot find a reasonable alternative in the outskirts of town, the end result is incredible congestion in the city centres. This is notoriously the case with the business and administrative centre of Milan and other old cities of Europe which are faced with the problem of rapid urbanisation, with phenomena which are quantitatively overwhelming. Even if much has been lost, correct analysis can still highlight whole districts which, left to their residential function, may be a positive element within the heart of historic centres. I believe one must come out boldly and state that the total conservation of an old centre, where there is a considerable amount of urbanisation, is not possible, and that all

action in this direction is often over-ambitious; I am not talking about those small centres which, for complex historical reasons, have come down to us more or less intact and which may be envisaged as museum-cities. But today even these centres, in France, in Italy, in Spain, in Greece find themselves affected by the disfiguring action of the necessary structures for mass tourism and here too the problem of conservation should be solved in the framework of regional planning. Otherwise, even if in less obvious ways, in a short time these centres too will decline, losing what is in effect their most attractive quality. Analysis must conclude what has actual value and must be untouchable; not only monuments, but those works and those complexes where action is economically and technically possible.

But action of this type, when the proposal is to conserve or transform, must bear in mind what the final result will be from the point of view of urban reality. We prefer to imagine a Venice newly consolidated amid its monuments in a landscape of meadows and water, to a delapidated Venice, or a *papier mâché* Venice. Planning may cause puzzlement, but this is less serious than witnessing destruction and decay or the implementation of tourist-bound restoration.

It is certain that the great buildings of the past, independently of their original function, may have great importance in the dynamics of a city. The historic centres, and their architectural features, like individual buildings in the region, must be catalogued and must constitute elements, often vital ones, in an overall plan. In planning, the historic element, from the single monument to the urban complex, cannot be an accident, preserved by some official from the relevant department who finds himself in constant difficulties with its upkeep, but must be considered as a positive element, one of the many with complex implications of a social, economic and cultural nature. The historic heritage seems to be protected only when it emerges on a tourist level; in reality it represents the structure of a whole region.

In my view, the joint tackling of these problems makes it possible to correctly approach two questions which are fundamental today: the use of the buildings of the past, as a unique and concrete possibility of saving our heritage; and the apposite placing of public provisions of a cultural nature. A broader conception and analysis of the so-called historic buildings is needed; we need to start from a different criterion from that of monumental and stylistic features: what is important is the presence, in the region, in the villages, in the cities, of elements which are often capable of characterising urban fabric, topographical situation and environmental values. Reference should be made to all those complexes (castles, villas, charitable institutions, convents, farms, whole nuclei of historic centres) which are of considerable importance in typology and size, and naturally not devoid of architectural interest but which, in the present situation, could not be the object of restoration and preserved as monuments without any specific use.

An indication for the use of these structures in regional plans, with criteria for priority and pointers to expense, would bring municipal planning face to face with definite obligations and would act as a vital framework of interconnection.

The problem of historic centres, and of important buildings isolated in the countryside, poses too important a problem for the countries of Europe, in the framework of a modern ordering of their towns and countryside, to be left to devotees of civic glories or excessive preservers of the old.

Only in this way does architecture challenge history, and become history. Not through some historicist assumption, nor through traditionalism, but because it is built on a general, universal experience of the very things which surround man. In this sense the artefact is closely linked to the intensile; it shows us that even function is historically determined, in the last analysis it is a cultural fact. So that invention, if disconnected from this growth of architecture upon itself, is always sterile, abstract, insubstantial.

Rationalist architecture is necessarily realistic; in this sense its relationship with history is all important. We cannot talk of the problem of restoration and of the historic centre from a combative point of view, whether pro or contra the old; each decision must spring from an overall vision of our position as architects. It must spring from our own architecture; the fact that today we are witnessing so deep a cleft between discourse on architecture and design in architecture, is a sign of the low level to which contemporary architectural culture has sunk.

The most telling example to be seen even today of continuity in architecture is undoubtedly the city of Spalato. Spalato is an extraordinary point of reference for architects and for anyone concerned with city and surrounding countryside. This example repudiates any distinction between building and city, it carries urban values into architecture and proves that the city itself is architecture. Over the millennia man has been reproducing the palace at Knossos. But within this persistence of a unique experience the answers are always different: this is the progressive character of architecture. The transformation, in Spalato, of a vestibule into a square, of a nymphaeum into a covered square, teaches us to use the old city as a formal structure, which can become part of our planning.

The architecture of the city offers numerous examples for these theoretical theses through its continuous transformation; these examples are the reality of architecture. They show us that the routes for reunion between past and present are much more complicated than is usually believed and that operating in historic centres can offer contemporary architecture a field for even the most unexpected experiment. As an architect I have never had a clearer understanding of Roman architecture than when I saw the Roman theatre and aqueduct in Budapest; where these ancient elements are set deep in a busy industrial zone, where the Roman theatre is a football field for local boys and where a crowded tramway crosses the remains of the aqueduct. Obviously these images, this use of the monument, is not generally to be advised; but it invites a compositional vision of the ancient elements within the city which is certainly not that of the city as museum. A field, therefore, not of sterile conservation but where architecture can open new lines of research and give new answers to the question of the progressive city.

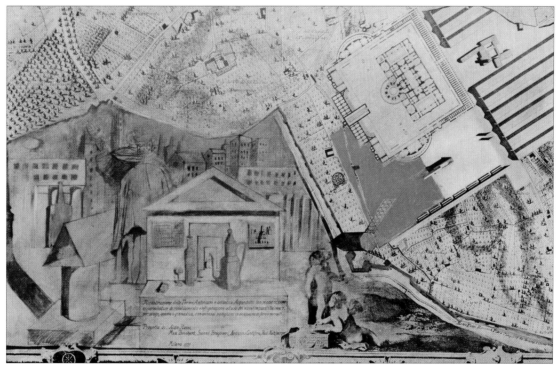

ALDO ROSSI, ROMA INTEROTTA, 1977

———— * ————

TEMPLE OF TRAJAN, PERGAMUM, THIRD CENTURY BC

CITIES OF STONE
DEMETRI PORPHYRIOS

There is an aimlessness in architecture today. It is expressed by oppositions like Modernism vs Post-Modernism, functionalism vs historicism, rationalism vs eclecticism, reconstruction vs deconstruction and so forth. Behind an endless variety of similar contrasts, however, there lies an underlying anxiety: are architecture and the city disciplines or the battleground for competing and shifting opinions? Along with the uneasiness that is provoked by these extremes, there is a growing sense that we should take stock of the 'achievements' of 20th-century architecture and urbanism. Most contemporary debates are still structured within the intellectual framework set up by the modernists of the 1920s and 30s. There is still an underlying belief that in the final analysis the only viable alternatives open to us are either some form of experimentalism or that we are led ineluctably to anachronistic historicism. The recent experience of Post-Modernism has proven – if anything – that contemporary architectural culture is not capable of 'making friends' with history. History is still seen through the spectacles of modern architecture: not as moral education but merely as the repository of stylistic frivolity. In spite of the recent attempts to exorcise history by 'wearing its clothes', architects and theoreticians alike still draw conclusions similar to those drawn in the 20s and 30s: namely that history nurtures no moral paradigms; it simply points to a value-free relativism. Whether it concerns the rationality of a city plan, the truthfulness of construction or the beauty of an architectural monument, we are told that in the final analysis all such concepts must be understood as relative to a specific form of society and life.

This incipient scepticism about foundations, methods and rational criteria governing architecture and the city appears to be characteristic of our intellectual and cultural life. We are told that it is an illusion to think that there are standards of common sense to which we can appeal in order to understand and judge the competing claims that are made everyday by architects and critics. We are told that, in our search for principles, we are limited to our historical context and to the 'Spirit of our Age'. In fact, we are told that the 'Spirit of our Age' is not only a sacred boundary we cannot trespass but that in this concept alone shines the beam of true credibility and reason. This conception of history constantly flirts with the suggestion that what we take to be true, right or beautiful is invariably arbitrary. Historicity is here confused with arbitrariness. The confusion is, therefore, that since there can be no fixed reference points, anything goes, as long as it is marked by an internal, self-regulating (and thus self-legitimating) method. Here lies the source of our demand that if an architectural project is to be judged fairly, it should be judged on the basis of *its* proclaimed aims, standards and values.

Architecture and the city are thus made adjuncts to the demands of opportunism, or at best to the conceits of agnosticism. Our predicament today can be summed up in Plato's metaphor of the 'true musicians'. To accept that architects are to fashion their own individual criteria for architecture and the city is as absurd as giving the name 'true musicians to those who would invent their own instruments and

play on them any disharmonious tune that pleases them . . . '[1]

The idea of architecture and urbanism as a discipline that is based on knowledge instead of being the endless battleground for competing and shifting opinions is surely not a new one. Its history is long and greatly nuanced. I do not intend to trace here the story of this search for an Archimedean point. Instead, I want to discuss the arguments recently rehearsed concerning this search for principles of urbanism. I will further try to show that it is within such a debate that the work of present-day classicists becomes intelligible.

To look at architecture and urbanism as a discipline based on knowledge means to accept the basic conviction that *there is* or *ought to be* some framework to which we ultimately appeal in determining the nature of the rationality of architecture and the city. The problem as stated is not just an intellectual one, nor is it confined to parochial or dated disputes about the meaning of rationality in architecture. At issue are our everyday moral and political experiences. Are we to believe that there are moral objectives of the true, the good and the beautiful and social and political objectives of the just or are we to relegate the definition of such norms to chance or individual fancy?

The rationalists – ever since Plato – have argued that relativism is self-contradictory and paradoxical since the relativist claims that though his position is true, it may also be false, given that truth is relative. In his turn, the relativist accuses the rationalist of mistaking what is at best historically or culturally stable for the eternal and permanent. When the rationalist claims that it is necessary to establish evaluative criteria for the design of architecture and the city, the relativist argues that there is something fraudulent about such claims and that, since life is complex and multifaceted, anyone striving for clarity of understanding must be, by definition, a *terrible simplificateur*.[2] But then again the rationalist argues that the fashionable varieties of relativism and the enthusiasm for an endless playfulness of interpretation that knows no rules and no limits have always led to cynicism and a growing sense of trivialisation.

It is this debate that has grown to prominence from the mid-1960s that informs the work of present-day classicists. They have been among the first to realise that indiscriminate toleration posing as the guarantor of democratic freedom had thrown architecture and the city into disarray, undermining the very discipline of architecture itself. During the last three decades or so, classicists, both through their projects and writings alike, have sought to explain the rational foundations of architecture and the city. Their criticism of the industrial city, zoning, Modernism and of building and architecture are not independent aphorisms but stages of a comprehensive critical inquiry. As long as we fail to make a rigorous distinction between *is* and the categorical *ought,* as long as we fail to realise that all attempts to ground architecture and urbanism on experimentalism and opportunism cannot possibly succeed, we are doomed to failure. In that sense, the primary aim of contemporary classicists has been to demonstrate that there is a rational certainty that informs both architecture and the city.

The search for a rational certainty in architecture and the city has been – at least recently – a repudiated conception. In many ways it has also been repellent: it offered no rewards to the experimentalist and, in the name of reason, it consorted with the grossest of our superstitions: metaphysics. Worst of all, it attacked liberal morality at its most vulnerable spot: its self-esteem as *the* age of democratic toleration.

In their search for a rational certainty, however, classicists address three main questions. First, why claim, in the first place, that there exists (or ought to exist) a universal and rational certainty about architecture and the city? Second, where are we to look for, and how are we to obtain, such a certainty? Third, even if we were to arrive at such a certainty how are we to apply its principles without lapsing into vulgar or sophisticated forms of unwarranted authoritarianism?

The *locus classicus* for the conviction that there exists a universal and rational certainty about architecture and the city has been, of course, Vitruvius, Filarete or Alberti. But whereas for the classical world this foundation of certainty was God's divinity, for the post-Enlightenment world of modernity human reason was to take the place of God. Descartes' *Meditations* stand as the great rationalist treatise of modern times and his demand that we should rely only upon the authority of reason itself has been at the very centre of modern life. And in his *Critique of Pure Reason*, Kant describes 'the domain [of pure reason] as an island, enclosed by nature itself within unalterable limits. It is the land of truth – enchanting name! – surrounded by a wide and stormy ocean, the native home of illusion . . . '

Reading the classical project as a search for a rational foundation point, we are at the same time aware that the ghost hovering in the background is the Kantian dread of madness, of the 'wide and stormy ocean, the native home of illusion', of the chaos where nothing is fixed. *Either* there exist universal, rational principles governing architecture and the city *or* the concepts of architecture and the city are vacuous. *Either* we establish a rational certainty of knowledge about architecture and the city, *or* we are left with the wayward alternatives of opportunism and agnosticism. Such is the ultimate motivation of Classicism's search for guiding principles. This search is founded neither on religious zeal nor avarice. It is neither bigotry nor power-hunting. The urge to search for certainty is a fundamental attribute of human character.

But where are we to look for and how are we to obtain such a rational certainty about the architecture of the city? The quest for a paradigm of rational certainty begins as soon as we first confront the desecrated landscape of both our cities and artistic imagination. The misery of the industrial city we witness everyday brings to mind the prescient statement by Lewis Mumford on the role of 20th-century *anti*-art: 'Anti-art . . . acclimatises modern man to the habitat that megatechnics is bringing into existence; an environment degraded by garbage dumps, auto-cemeteries, slag heaps, nuclear piles, superhighways and megastructural conglomerates – all destined to be architecturally homogenised in a planetary Megalopolis.' In a similar indictment, the classicists accuse the 20th-century Industrial State of usurping humanity by creating – in Seidelberg's terms – the 'Post-Historic Man': the ironic end product of evolution, achieved through the hypertrophy of either intelligence or mechanical power; a hypertrophy that would eventually return man to 'a state of docile somnolence'.

The almost compulsive reiteration of the same diagnosis across more than three decades shows the commitment of classicists to transcend the *mal du siècle*. The malady that has befallen industrial civilisation, that of purposeless destruction, irrationality and paranoid idiocy has to be curbed. The *is* must be transcended with a categorical *ought*.

Faced with the alienating docility of the industrial world, the city – if it is to live again – must become a *Città Felice*. What present-day classicists took from the ancients has been the essential definition of the *Città Felice* as manifested in the ideas of *disegno* and *misura*. The architect ought to enshrine the ideal in a *disegno* for reality to approximate. The *disegno* never exists as an empirical reality. It is a paradigm, an exemplar that guides and which, insofar as it is not a model to be copied, never runs the risk of trivialisation through cloning. The *disegno*, insofar as it is an exemplar, does not curtail interpretive freedom nor does it shy away from contingent reality. If anything, the *disegno* becomes a real city-plan only when it is interpreted under the stringent pressures of contingent reality. At the same time, the *Città Felice* depends also on *misura*. Measure, proportion, size (whether understood as dimensioning of a city's urban space or monument or as the finitude of the city's extent) are, in the end, the guarantors of the ultimate success of a *disegno*. A city without proper measure is like Aristotle's ill-dimensioned ship which will never sail. Yet, the paradigm of the *Città Felice* is not to be sought in the walled cities of antiquity but in the millenial history of the traditional City: for it alone shines as the embodiment of *sapientia urbanis*. Its *disegno* unfolds along the well-trod and familiar forms of the urban block, the street, the piazza and the monument. And its *misura* has since long ago become our second nature.

The re-evaluation of the traditional City by present-day classicists did not grow out of antiquarianism – though many of their findings are indebted to Sitte, Hegemann and Peets, Wagner or Saarinen. Their comparative investigations of the historical beginnings and growth of traditional cities revealed principles that were concealed in the diversity of their forms. This was no mystical or idealistic position that viewed the multiplicity of forms as mere corruptions of some abstract, *a priori* truth. Instead, the numerous traditional cities, in their historical specificity and detail, bore witness to a common and humanly satisfying *disegno* and *misura*.

To proclaim, and indeed to feel, a principal allegiance to the traditional City did not necessarily involve a patronising attitude towards some European *Heimatstil*. There have been many European architects and planners who have chosen the perilous path of the Megalopolis and the Las Vegas Strip; perhaps as a means to shed the stigmata that compromised their opportunities. One is led to conclude, however, that nobody is born a traditionalist; he/she *becomes* one only after realising that the traditional City is still today the most pleasing *Città Felice*.

Still, it took two to make the paradigm of the European City credible. Many in the audience, especially those bred in immanent cynicism, applauded the classicists for their zeal but were inclined to find their paradigm unconvincing. Why? The excuses have been as varied as the sophist's tricks. Some found the paradigm of the traditional City too sentimental for their proven sense of realism; others found it quasi-socialist and therefore prone to youthful idealism and error; many called it a utopia for they themselves had given up hope; yet others accused such a global project of siding dangerously with neo-Fascism.

The main reservation of all critics, however, was that the adoption of the traditional City as an urban paradigm was a gross setback to the idea of progress. Traditional forms of urbanisation – critics maintained – have in the past proven dangerous setbacks to the economic, political and cultural progress of civilisation. Tradition, critics repeated, considers a changeless state of order as the greatest good and, as a result, it fosters an authoritarianism that invariably stifles progress.

The classicists, of course, knew that their adversaries were calling them doctrinaire and authoritarian and they regretted the metaphors used to discredit them. To the best of their knowledge, however, they were neither powerful *podestàs* nor infallible popes. If they found themselves insisting on the truth of their findings, it was simply because the traditional City had proven to be a working and adaptable model.

What was the certainty that inspired them with such self-assurance? On a pragmatic level, there is the idea that the well-trodden and known forms of the traditional City have proven successful from the time of the ancients down to the present day. Though the world has changed enormously in the last thousand years or so, the urban structure of the traditional City has endured. There seems to exist no reason, therefore, for doubting the paradigm's validity for there have been no failures. If all available information leads one to believe that the goal of the 20th-century city – namely the well-being of its citizens – need not be different from that of previous civilisations, then it is good common sense to use a time-tested body of knowledge to cope with present-day exigencies.

But classicists were not satisfied with offering simply a pragmatic argument in support of their paradigm. The legitimation of their belief in tradition was not to be grounded merely on efficacy. It would have to stand the scrutiny of argumentation, the criterion for which was to be neither pragmatism nor historicism nor logical formalism. The ultimate criterion was to be the moral criterion of public well-being.

Let me now suggest that the apparent banality of the expression 'public well-being' shows the inadequacy of contemporary language when confronted with the essential nature of the city. And let me further suggest that the issues that come into prominence in connection with the paradigm of the traditional City open up a moral dimension in the debate about the essential nature of the city itself. To grasp the moral dimension of the expression 'public well-being' we should for a moment examine two constitutive ideas of classical thought: those of tradition and reconstruction.

Unlike the currently marketed conception of tradition as the 'peddling of antiques', the classical project does not aim at upholstering a spurious restoration. Instead, its aim has been to ferret out in existing society those traditional elements that could foster the new. But the new has never been a mere novelty. The new has always been the result of a process of transmission of knowledge and merit. The various phases of history were additive, and the storing of new experience *was* the law of mankind. The exclusive characteristic of civilised man has been his ability to record and retrieve his memory. In that sense, classicists today have been less absorbed in the dialectic between an imagined future and a nostalgic past (as many of their critics have claimed) than in the search for realistic projects. The ultimate criterion in the design of cities ought to be the public well-being of their inhabitants. By public, much the same as Leibniz, one refers here to all who acknowledge the magnificence of the *mundi civitas*. This is not a faceless universalism. On the contrary, individual cultures can and will preserve their particular character as indestructible 'monads'; that is, as individual but complete and fully grown solidarities. By definition, however, good social institutions – and by extension good city plans – are those that are best able to instil in man a social existence and 'to translate the *moi* into a *moi-commun*', a collective moral self (Jean-Jacques Rousseau, *Emile*). It is this yearning for a collective moral self that classicists make the cornerstone of their urban theory and which promises to provide justification for the *mundi civitas*.

Such is the moral content of the classical paradigm: over the centuries the traditional City has contributed to mollifying the antagonism between the *moi* and the *moi-commun* by providing a careful balance of public and private spaces and buildings as the physical framework for the life of its citizens. Here lies the root of the failure of the modern industrial city: over the last two centuries it has aggravated the antagonism between the *moi* and the *moi-commun* either by marketing the rapacity of the entrepreneur in the name of realism, or by mistaking the collective body with a mere numerical majority. The authoritarian and the democratic cities alike have tragically failed; the first by strengthening the savage instinct of omni-potent power, the second by confounding democracy with the sloppiest of all delusions: spontaneous populist egalitarianism.

Above all, and despite the tensions that might exist in their writings and projects, the classicists illuminate the fragile character of action as *reconstruction*. It is not a sentimental utopia that we confront here but a coherent and powerful 'What is to be done' that has a clear commitment and direction. When one insists that the making of the city requires the ethos of a *mundi civitas* and the shared acceptance of priorities and laws, one assumes, at least in an incipient form, that even today practical reason (reason applied in conduct) has not forsaken us totally. Despite their relentless critique of the ways in which *téchne* (craft as practical reason) has degenerated into *technique* (labour as technical reason), classicists believe that there are still solidarities of civic consciousness which could revitalise practical reason. A city is not something that can be engineered by any form of technique and by any chosen administration; to return to Plato, it would be similar to giving the name 'true musicians' to any of those 'who would invent their own instruments and play on them any disharmonious tune that pleases them . . . ' The idea that we can engineer cities by simply applying any technical know-how has been the typically modernist response to urbanism and has proven disastrous. The failures of positivist planning have been mainly due to the decision of industrial society to restrict itself to the sole horizon of technique at the expense of craft as practical reason. The chief task of urbanism today, however, is to challenge the peculiar falsehood of modern industrial consciousness and to defend practical reason against the domination of universal technique.

The idea of reconstruction as opposed to mere urban renewal points, therefore, to a practical-moral project. The aim of reconstruction, unlike that of urban renewal, is the ethical rectitude of a community and not a particular end-product. Moreover, while urban renewal is not concerned with the means that allow it to arrive at an end, this is precisely what is required in reconstruction. The meaning and task of reconstruction today is to elicit in us the will that can become a counterforce against the contemporary degeneration of practical reason.

Throughout my discussion, I have sought to elicit the central themes of is/ought, of the *Città Felice*, of tradition and reconstruction. I have stressed the practical and politico-moral consequences of these themes – for as one explores their implications, they draw us toward the goal of action and practical reason (reason applied in conduct). If we take classical thought seriously and press its own claims, they lead us beyond the sentimentalities of historicism. The world of reconstruction is not the world of the fetishism of stone and timber and of medieval guild workshops. The world of reconstruction points to the grand metaphor of the 'Cities of Stone' as a critique of the industrial city's disenchantment with culture itself. For we must not forget that culture alone 'tames the freedom of the will without stifling it'.

Notes

1 Plato, *Republic, 3:402.*   2 cf here the sophistries of Charles Jencks in his 'Abstract Representation', *Architectural Design* 7/8-1983, pp 15-16.

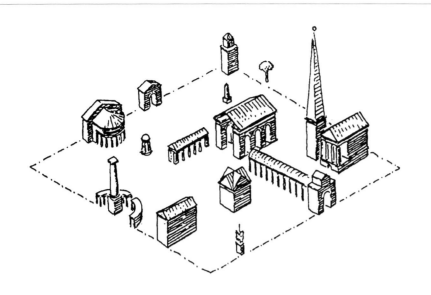

MONUMENTS
WITHOUT
STREETS AND SQUARES

RES PUBLICA

+

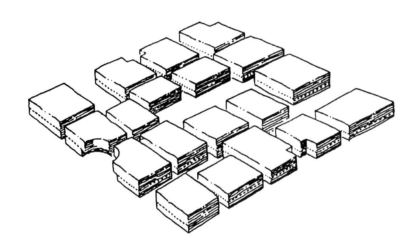

STREETS AND SQUARES
WITHOUT
MONUMENTS

RES PRIVATA

=

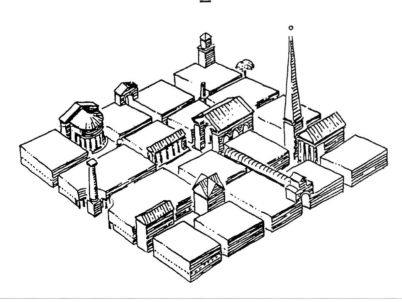

THE
TRUE
CITY

URBAN COMPONENTS
LEON KRIER

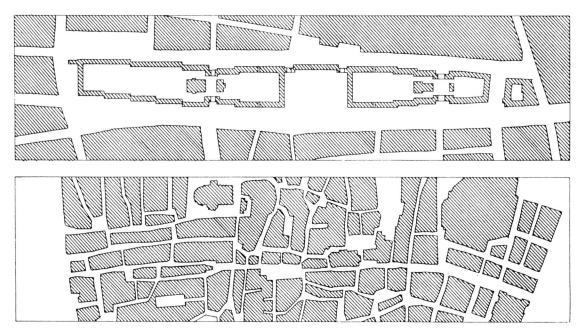

ABOVE: KARL MARX HOF; *BELOW*: HISTORIC CENTRE OF VIENNA. THIS COMPARISON AT THE SAME SCALE SHOWS HOW THE CITY BECOMES DECOMPOSED THROUGH ZONING, NOT ONLY PHYSICALLY AND FUNCTIONALLY BUT ABOVE ALL *SOCIALLY*. THE SOCIAL, CULTURAL AND ECONOMIC COMPLEXITY AND DENSITY OF PREINDUSTRIAL VIENNA COULD NOT BE CONTRASTED MORE VIOLENTLY WITH THE SOCIAL AND CULTURAL EMPTINESS OF THE 'HÖFE'. A CITY IS REDUCED TO A MERE 'ARTISTIC' GESTURE

If I talk here constantly of the European city, of the traditional urban block and street pattern, I refer to the pre-industrial city, ie to a city of mixed functions excluding the mechanical means of transport.

By 'modern' building block I refer to the 19th-century institutional and residential block as well as the 20th-century perimeter block. I exclude from the discussion all contemporary *residential* typologies like Zeilenbau and tower block. I will thus only concentrate on building forms where a precise dialectic of building type, form of property and type of public space can be detected.

General considerations

I will attempt here a cultural and morphological critique of the strange agony of the urban block. After years of discussion and reflection I am convinced that neither purely economic nor technical reasons were the main cause for the fantastic trajectory which the urban block described from being the keystone of the urban composition to its complete dissolution in the advanced industrial city.

The changing methods of production, the changing nature of urban property, the growing importance of hygienic considerations are generally accepted as the reasons affecting the typical mutations of themodern urban block and causing its final destruction. It would, however, be possible to ask why, given the conditions of production and of landownership, the Karl Marx Hof in Vienna or the vast

municipalperimeter blocks in Moscow could not just as well have been built as a multitude of small urban blocks with a familiar scale of streets and squares!

What I will try to criticise is an *historical tendency* illustrated by the fact that *larger and larger building programmes* (resulting from the concentration of economic, political and cultural power) have resulted almost *'naturally' in larger and larger building blocks!* The Palace of Justice in Brussels has the size of a medieval parish; the length of the Karl Marx Hof equals the diameter of the centre of Vienna from wall to wall: a single building gesture resulting from a single programme, executed by one architect.

My aim is, however, not just to describe an irreversible historical fatality but to establish an hypothesis: the social and cultural complexity of a city has necessarily to do with its physical and structural complexity and density. The size of an ideal urban block cannot be established more precisely than the ideal height of the human body. One can, however deduce through comparison and experience sizes of urban blocks which are more apt to form a complex urban pattern than others.

My main affirmations as regards urban design will be: *urban blocks should be as small in length and width as is typologically viable; they should form as many well-defined streets and squares as possible in the form of a multi-directional horizontal pattern of urban spaces.*

Orientation

Stübben recommends north-south orientation for rectangular blocks in order to reduce north exposure to the smallest facade and to have east-west exposure for most facades.

The most inspired contribution in relation to orientation is Cerda's 45° rotation of the Ensanche grid in Barcelona in a northeast-southwest and southeast-northwest direction, thus avoiding any north facades. Furthermore, each facade is reached by the sun both in summer and winter.

The dialectic of the building block and urban space

The building block, 'insula', 'pâté de maison' or 'ilôt', 'Häuser-Block', must be identified as the most important typological element in the composition of urban spaces, the key element of any urban pattern. It belongs to a European tradition of building cities in the form of streets and squares. As a typologically fixed element it can generate urban space but it can also remain undefined and merely result from the order of an urban pattern (of streets and squares).

The three diagrams describe the three possible dialectical connections of building block and public space. These three polemical categories have all participated in the formation of the European City, either following each other chronologically or overlaying and transforming each other in the process. They hardly ever occur as exclusive systems but complement

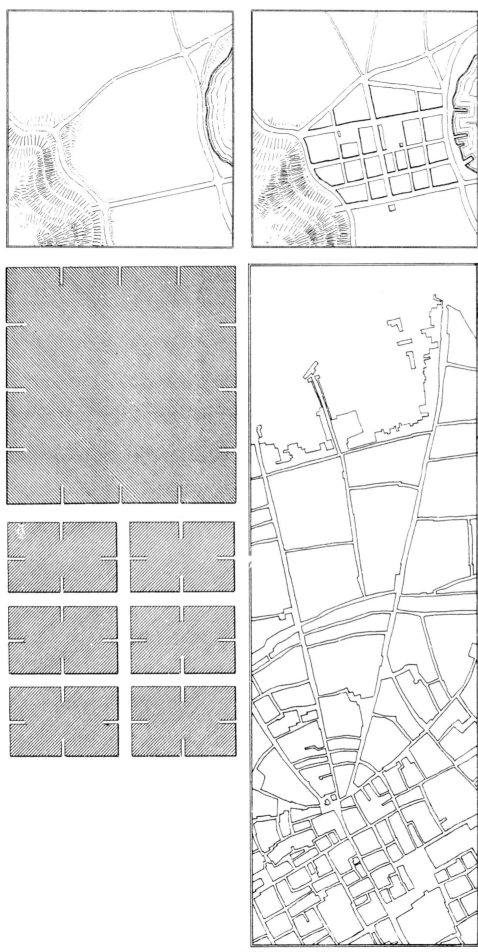

ABOVE: GEOGRAPHICAL AND URBAN BLOCKS; *CENTRE AND BELOW LEFT:* SMALL URBAN BLOCKS INCREASE PUBLIC FRONTAGE AND ACCESIBILITY; *BELOW RIGHT:* THIS ILLUSTRATION CLEARLY SHOWS THE HYPOTHESIS THAT IN URBAN CENTRES THE BLOCKS ARE SMALLEST AND THAT THEY GROW LARGER TOWARD THE PERIPHERY WHERE THEY OFTEN CONTAIN LARGE GARDENS AND FIELDS

each other to form a highly differentiated urban environment.

The building block is either the instrument to form streets and squares or it results from a pattern of streets and squares.

But before coming to specific urban characteristics, an *insula* has to be defined in a more general territorial and geographical sense.

The block is primarily a plot of land defined all around by a multitude of planned and unplanned paths, roads and streets. This is as true for the very large geographical blocks (including agricultural land, forests, mountains) as it is true for urban blocks.

Though the rural block need not be of any specific size, I want to stress that urban blocks ought to have well defined qualities of *size, volume, orientation, typology, order and complexity* in order to become *urban*. Although the size and nature of urban blocks vary enormously, I want to define a very limited range of principles not only for analysis, but as a basis of urban design philosophy.

The size of a building block

In the European city, the smallest and typologically most complex building blocks are to be found in the urban centres. They tend to grow larger and typologically simpler towards the periphery before finally dissolving into single free-standing objects. This tendency is more obvious where the sections of the centre and periphery correspond to different times of construction (pre-industrial and industrial). One can conclude that: *small blocks are the result of the maximum exploitation of urban ground caused by great density of activities, high cost of urban ground, etc; and that a great number of streets on a relatively small area correspond to the maximum length of commercial facade.*

If the main cause for small urban blocks and for a dense urban pattern is primarily economic, it is this very same reason which has created the intimate character of a highly urban environment. Such an environment is the basis of urban culture, of intense *social, cultural* and *economic* exchange. If this hypothesis is true, the opposite is also true, ie suburban or peripheral areas or city extensions are generally characterised by vast urban blocks (Berlin, Barcelona, etc). In pre-industrial cities the outer ring of urban blocks often included agricultural land, fields, large gardens. In the case of city extensions due to low cost of land, the blocks of the periphery often included large gardens, municipal parks, etc.

The high density large block

As the vast blocks of the periphery became more and more part of urban centres, the gardens were built up with residential premises or artisans' workshops. It is this internal densification and exploitation of the urban blocks which lead to their final destruction and the savage criticisms by Le Corbusier and Gropius.

The building block, form of property and form of street

The traditional *insula*, formed by an addition of urban houses, is characterised at ground level by a great number of entrances. The street is used not only as a space of distribution and orientation but as a space of economic and social exchange. There is a strict relationship between building type, form of property and the form of the public space, the street.

The 20th-century perimeter block is still able to form streets and squares but it tends more and more to become an autonomous organism with its own system of distribution, corridors, 'rues intérieures', access balconies, all competing with the streets.

The number of entrances on the street is not dependent any more on the number of residential units contained in the block. The relationship between building type and street becomes dictated purely by external legislations about fire, etc. The street is reduced purely to the function of access. The tarmac becomes more important than the public space.

The limits of the perimeter block
Perimeter blocks tend by their very nature to be very large, including gardens and even parks. However useful or beautiful they might be as isolated examples, as places of quiet green (Bahnhofstrasse, Zurich), if they are understood as a repetitive system, the street pattern they form becomes a spatial megastructure which is socially disruptive. The tendency to design these huge blocks into single architectural objects with one door is the very cause of their institutional barrack-like character (Karl Marx Hof etc). Their courts usually degenerate as they require too much servicing. The large perimeter block was only the last step in the dissolution of the urban fabric.

The street and scale of the building block
We have shown that towards the periphery of the city the blocks not only tend to grow larger but they are also generally separated by wider and longer streets; this phenomenon seems to control both the development of planned city extensions and of incremental urban growth.

It is, however, not true that in the traditional city centres wide streets are necessarily lined by large urban blocks. If a street is to be important and lively within a multidirectional urban pattern, it has to be drained by as many streets as possible. In the history of modern urban planning there seems, however, to have existed an almost 'natural' tendency to front large urban spaces with large urban blocks.

High urban density and the modern critique of the building block
High density and increased exploitation of urban ground have been wrongly identified as being responsible for the inhuman condition of the 19th-century city. Instead, the badly lit light-wells, the polluted streets and the endless corridorial spaces inside the vast blocks were in fact the result of a *wrong typological choice: the large urban block*.

One could easily demonstrate that even higher densities can be reached with smaller blocks without the disadvantage of light-wells and badly lit courts. Certain central areas of Manhattan or the 'Spanish Quarter' in Naples are good examples. The savage attacks of Le Corbusier and Gropius in the 1920s against the 19th-century block, an attack which psychologically prepared for the destruction of the traditional European city, used a global cri-

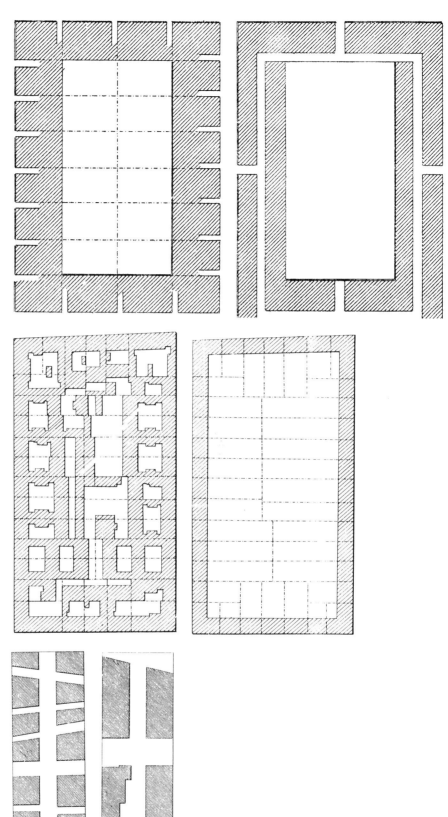

ABOVE: IN MODERN BLOCKS INTERNAL CORRIDORS COMPETE WITH THE FUNCTION OF THE STREET AS MEETING PLACE OF PUBLIC AND PRIVATE REALMS; *CENTRE*: THE BAROQUE BLOCKS OF THE 18TH CENTURY HAD LARGE GARDENS. THEY GREW INTO LABYRINTHS, WHICH MARKED THE END OF THE CULTURE OF STREETS AND SQUARES; *BELOW L TO R*: AN IMPORTANT STREET HAS TO BE DRAINED BY MANY STREETS; LARGE BUILDING BLOCKS IMPOVERISH THE URBAN PATTERN

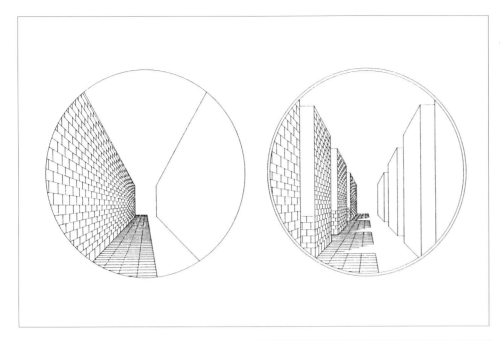

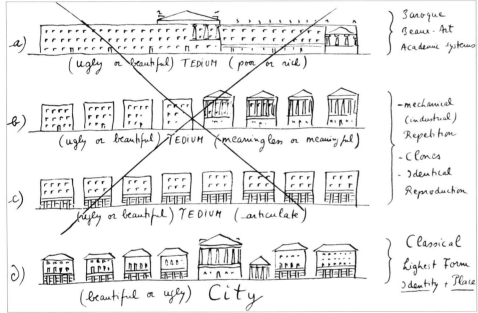

tique whereas only a technical criticism would have been necessary; a criticism which I will demonstrate in my project for west Berlin.

The 19th-century institutional building block as functional and social labyrinth

For quite different reasons from those mentioned in connection with residential blocks, the 19th-century institutional buildings formed blocks of unprecedented size. The Palace of Justice in Brussels, the Hospitals, the British Museum etc, often reach the size of a whole parish or an entire urban district. These institutional monoliths formed veritable labyrinthine islands within the fine structure of streets and squares and they contributed to the explosion of the social and physical fabric of the traditional city.

Like castles, abbeys or palaces in the pre-industrial cities, they formed secluded organisms, using their own privatised system of distribution, corridors, cloisters, balconies, courts, etc. These semi-public 'rues intérieures' became in Kafka the symbolic spaces of institutional repression, the building masses themselves became the symbols of usurped political and cultural power.

These buildings contain an alternative distributive system competing with the traditional street. The number of doors opening to the street is minimal, reducing therefore the street (the public space) to a mere access route. We find here a first and definite break in the dialectic between building type and type of public space.

In religious abbeys or royal palaces this seclusion from the city was quite conscious. Religious or aristocratic life isolated itself from the trading and manufacturing city. Instead, the design of institutional monsters was not at all a typological necessity. It had rather to do with the architectural representation of the new bourgeois power which, in the construction of extravagantly vast and overwhelming structures, symbolised its own aims.

We have shown that both the size of the 19th-century residential block and the 20th-

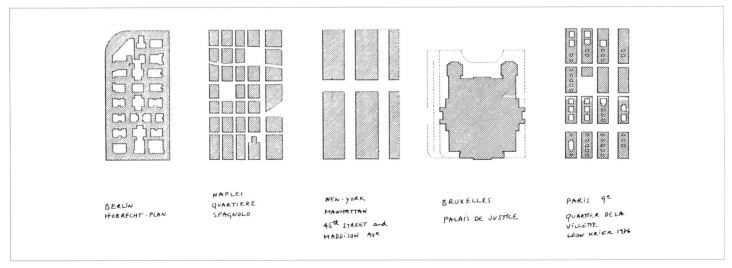

ABOVE: THE RELATION BETWEEN BLOCK AND STREET; *CENTRE*: A) AS ARCHITECTURE BECAME REDUCED TO STYLISTIC SYSTEMS IN THE 19TH CENTURY, IT WAS CAPABLE OF ARTICULATING VIRTUALLY ANY LARGE MASS OF BUILDING THAT RESULTED FROM FUNCTIONAL ZONING AND CONCENTRATION. NEITHER HOUSING NOR ADMINISTRATION OFFICES WERE SOCIALLY COMPLEX OR RICH ENOUGH TO SUGGEST HIGH ARTISTIC RESULTS OVER A LONG PERIOD OF TIME. ARCHITECTURE, AS PURELY THEATRICAL DECOR, COULD THEN BE ABANDONED ALL TOO EASILY. B) A FIRST ARTICULATION OF AN AMORPHOUS FUNCTIONAL MASS OCCURS BY REDUCING IT TO SMALLER BLOCKS. C) FUNCTIONAL MIX IS THE BASIS FOR THE ARTICULATION OF AN URBAN FABRIC INTO SEMI-PUBLIC AND PRIVATE FUNCTIONS. D) THIS PATTERN OF SOLIDS (BLOCKS) AND VOIDS (STREETS) BECOMES ARTICULATED INTO PUBLIC BUILDING (MONUMENTS) AND URBAN FABRIC; *BELOW*: PARALLEL OF BLOCK SIZES.

century perimeter blocks were not dictated by a typological necessity. The rooms of the Palace of Justice in Rome and of the Karl Marx Hof in Vienna could have been distributed without problems into a multitude of smaller urban blocks organised by public streets and squares and these could have found a close dialectical relationship with the existing city.

It is the centralisation of functions (of political and cultural power) and land which have resulted in a specific typological choice based on large building programmes. Historically, larger and larger building programmes have resulted in larger and larger buildings and this tendency reaches its apogee today in synthetic megastructures (the whole city has become one big programme, ie one building). The Berlin University, the comprehensive schools, Milton Keynes Town Centre etc, are characteristic examples of this tendency. Today we pretend that the specific typological choice of megastructural conglomerates against a multitude of building types is a stylistic one. In fact, a millenial culture of urban building types and spaces with precise measures is swept away and sacrificed to an obsession with *building systems* apparently designed to solve all the problems of the city by means of an industrialised kit of parts. The unavoidable result is the destruction of time and place, of Architecture and the City.

The size of the urban block and architectural language

The growth of the urban block had an immediate effect on architectural composition and on the architectural quality of the block. 19th-century stylistic eclecticism was able to deal successfully with the large institutional monuments, managing to articulate these enormous volumes into single and recognisable artistic gestures. However, the highly repetitive and reductive nature of purely residential blocks caused by functional zoning had neither the cultural content nor a social purpose important enough to inspire highly artistic results over a long period of time. The Karl Marx Hof, the

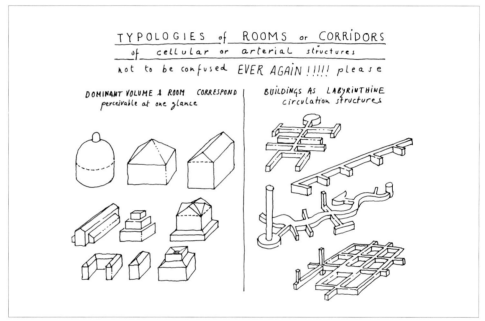

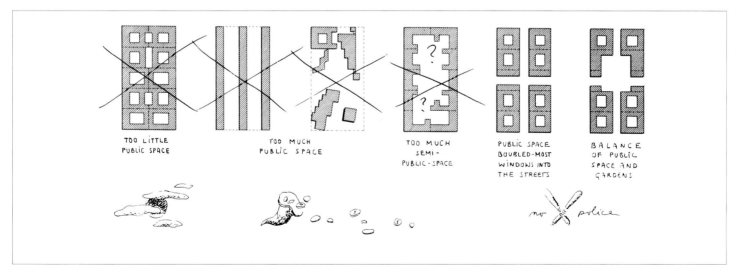

ABOVE: THE VAST INSTITUTIONAL COMPLEXES OF THE 19TH CENTURY ARE ORGANISED WITH AN AUTONOMOUS DISTRIBUTIVE SYSTEM OF CORRIDORS THAT COMPETES WITH THE PUBLIC STREETS. EXCEPT FOR REPRESENTATIONAL PURPOSES THERE EXISTED NO REASON WHY THESE VAST LABYRINTHS COULD NOT JUST AS WELL HAVE BEEN ORGANISED INTO A SERIES OF SMALLER BLOCKS SEPARATED BY PUBLIC STREETS; *CENTRE*: TYPOLOGIES OF ROOMS OR CORRIDORS OF CELLULAR OR ARTERIAL STRUCTURES. *BELOW*: THE BERLIN BLOCK WAS NOT WRONG BUT ITS MEASURES WERE WRONG. THE APARTMENT ON THE STREET WAS NOT WRONG BUT THAT ON THE COURT WAS WRONG. THE LENGTH OF THE STREET IS NOT THE PROBLEM BUT THE LENGTH OF THE BLOCK. CAR TRAFFIC SHOULD REMAIN IN THE EXISTING STREET SYSTEM. THE OVERSIZED BLOCKS SHOULD BE BROKEN DOWN INTO SMALL BLOCKS BY MEANS OF PEDESTRIAN STREETS AND SQUARES.

palatial facades of Nash's terrace buildings as well as the ones of Schushev in Moscow have to be seen as exceptional achievements in a rapid decline and extinction of formal values caused by the quick consumption of architectural styles.

The linguistic emptiness of the Modern Movement or the rhetorical kitsch of industrial Pop culture were the necessary result of the extinction of formal values.

West Berlin Centre

The study which I present here on the centre of West Berlin is the direct result of the previous reflection on the size of the urban block.

Prior to the political division of the city, what is now the centre of West Berlin was then a residential area formed by large urban blocks. The structure of vast streets and avenues was designed by the Chief of Police Hobrecht in the late 19th-century. His intention was to reduce the surface of public spaces to a minimum, thus reducing the problem of police control. One of these new blocks could measure well over 100 x 300 metres, an area approximately the size of a medieval parish. It was therefore possible to urbanise a maximum of land at a minimum of public cost in paving, sewers, etc.

The problems thus created in residential typologies were enormous. It was then generally accepted that high-density exploitation of those blocks was possible only through a system of courtyards. The best apartments would be facing the street, whereas the inferior ones would sometimes be three or four courts inside the block without any visual connection to the street. Eventually, the lack of light and orientation to the street led to the condemnation of the

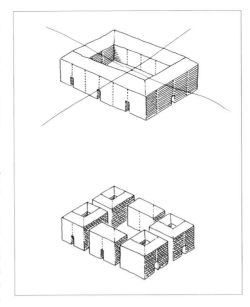

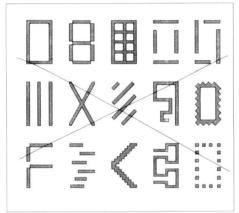

Berlin blocks by Gropius. The Zeilenbau then seemed the solution to high density housing.

Recently, the urban renewal projects of the last decades have transformed the cities into an urban wasteland, leaving much urban space to undefined and vague activities. We know now that the cost of policing – let alone of landscaping – these urban voids is too high for the community and the dereliction of most of these *espaces verts* has been the sad result.

My first intention was to keep the traffic in all existing streets and to reduce the width of the roads to a technically defendable minimum (instead of maximum, as is usually the case) and to allow parking along the streets. The project was also a critique of the vast Hobrecht blocks. The derelict interior of these vast *insulae* would be cut by a number of wide pedestrian streets resulting in four, six or eight small blocks. In that way the run-down and poorest structures (which were always situated in the heart of the block) would be rebuilt along a series of intimate pedestrian streets and small squares. In this way all the flats would now face a street or a courtyard. The urban motorways would be transformed into tree-lined boulevards and the whole tertiary sector (light industries, offices and administration) would be concentrated along these traffic routes that form the boundaries and limits of the urban quarter. These *urban quarters* would constitute real *Cities within the City* with a maximum size of 20-30 hectares – approximately 10,000 inhabitants – and with a balanced distribution of mixed functions. This equilibrium of workplaces and living quarters would allow the majority of people to reach their workplace on foot.

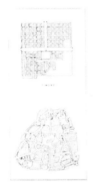

ABOVE: INSULA TEGELIENSIS; *ABOVE CENTRE*: BLOCK FORMS TO AVOID IN REPETITION; *BELOW CENTRE*: TIMGAD 110 AD; BRIVE 1280 AD; QUARTIER DES HALLES, PARIS, 1960; KARL MARX HOF, VIENNA, 1927; RUNDER PLATZ, BERLIN (A SPEER); ST DIE (LE CORBUSIER); *BELOW*: WEST BERLIN CENTRE, EXISTING STREET PATTERN; PROPOSED STREET PATTERN.

century perimeter blocks were not dictated by a typological necessity. The rooms of the Palace of Justice in Rome and of the Karl Marx Hof in Vienna could have been distributed without problems into a multitude of smaller urban blocks organised by public streets and squares and these could have found a close dialectical relationship with the existing city.

It is the centralisation of functions (of political and cultural power) and land which have resulted in a specific typological choice based on large building programmes. Historically, larger and larger building programmes have resulted in larger and larger buildings and this tendency reaches its apogee today in synthetic megastructures (the whole city has become one big programme, ie one building). The Berlin University, the comprehensive schools, Milton Keynes Town Centre etc, are characteristic examples of this tendency. Today we pretend that the specific typological choice of megastructural conglomerates against a multitude of building types is a stylistic one. In fact, a millenial culture of urban building types and spaces with precise measures is swept away and sacrificed to an obsession with *building systems* apparently designed to solve all the problems of the city by means of an industrialised kit of parts. The unavoidable result is the destruction of time and place, of Architecture and the City.

The size of the urban block and architectural language

The growth of the urban block had an immediate effect on architectural composition and on the architectural quality of the block. 19th-century stylistic eclecticism was able to deal successfully with the large institutional monuments, managing to articulate these enormous volumes into single and recognisable artistic gestures. However, the highly repetitive and reductive nature of purely residential blocks caused by functional zoning had neither the cultural content nor a social purpose important enough to inspire highly artistic results over a long period of time. The Karl Marx Hof, the

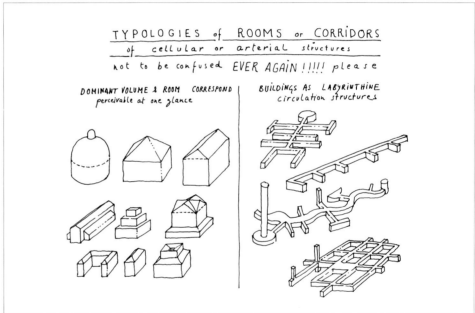

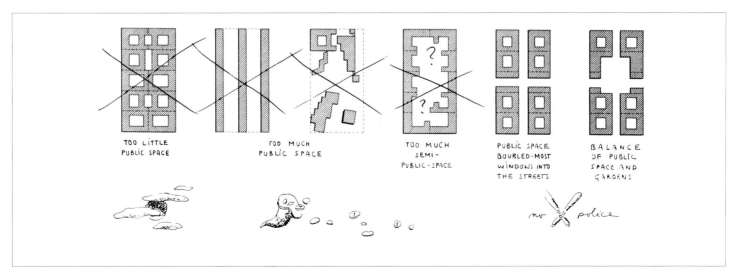

ABOVE: THE VAST INSTITUTIONAL COMPLEXES OF THE 19TH CENTURY ARE ORGANISED WITH AN AUTONOMOUS DISTRIBUTIVE SYSTEM OF CORRIDORS THAT COMPETES WITH THE PUBLIC STREETS. EXCEPT FOR REPRESENTATIONAL PURPOSES THERE EXISTED NO REASON WHY THESE VAST LABYRINTHS COULD NOT JUST AS WELL HAVE BEEN ORGANISED INTO A SERIES OF SMALLER BLOCKS SEPARATED BY PUBLIC STREETS; *CENTRE*: TYPOLOGIES OF ROOMS OR CORRIDORS OF CELLULAR OR ARTERIAL STRUCTURES. *BELOW*: THE BERLIN BLOCK WAS NOT WRONG BUT ITS MEASURES WERE WRONG. THE APARTMENT ON THE STREET WAS NOT WRONG BUT THAT ON THE COURT WAS WRONG. THE LENGTH OF THE STREET IS NOT THE PROBLEM BUT THE LENGTH OF THE BLOCK. CAR TRAFFIC SHOULD REMAIN IN THE EXISTING STREET SYSTEM. THE OVERSIZED BLOCKS SHOULD BE BROKEN DOWN INTO SMALL BLOCKS BY MEANS OF PEDESTRIAN STREETS AND SQUARES.

palatial facades of Nash's terrace buildings as well as the ones of Schushev in Moscow have to be seen as exceptional achievements in a rapid decline and extinction of formal values caused by the quick consumption of architectural styles.

The linguistic emptiness of the Modern Movement or the rhetorical kitsch of industrial Pop culture were the necessary result of the extinction of formal values.

West Berlin Centre

The study which I present here on the centre of West Berlin is the direct result of the previous reflection on the size of the urban block.

Prior to the political division of the city, what is now the centre of West Berlin was then a residential area formed by large urban blocks. The structure of vast streets and avenues was designed by the Chief of Police Hobrecht in the late 19th-century. His intention was to reduce the surface of public spaces to a minimum, thus reducing the problem of police control. One of these new blocks could measure well over 100 x 300 metres, an area approximately the size of a medieval parish. It was therefore possible to urbanise a maximum of land at a minimum of public cost in paving, sewers, etc.

The problems thus created in residential typologies were enormous. It was then generally accepted that high-density exploitation of those blocks was possible only through a system of courtyards. The best apartments would be facing the street, whereas the inferior ones would sometimes be three or four courts inside the block without any visual connection to the street. Eventually, the lack of light and orientation to the street led to the condemnation of the

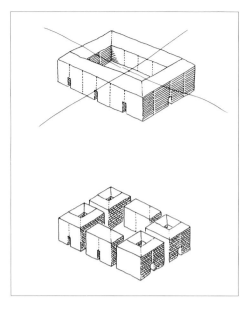

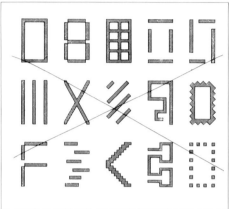

Berlin blocks by Gropius. The Zeilenbau then seemed the solution to high density housing.

Recently, the urban renewal projects of the last decades have transformed the cities into an urban wasteland, leaving much urban space to undefined and vague activities. We know now that the cost of policing – let alone of landscaping – these urban voids is too high for the community and the dereliction of most of these *espaces verts* has been the sad result.

My first intention was to keep the traffic in all existing streets and to reduce the width of the roads to a technically defendable minimum (instead of maximum, as is usually the case) and to allow parking along the streets. The project was also a critique of the vast Hobrecht blocks. The derelict interior of these vast *insulae* would be cut by a series of wide pedestrian streets resulting in four, six or eight small blocks. In that way the run-down and poorest structures (which were always situated in the heart of the block) would be rebuilt along a series of intimate pedestrian streets and small squares. In this way all the flats would now face a street or a courtyard. The urban motorways would be transformed into tree-lined boulevards and the whole tertiary sector (light industries, offices and administration) would be concentrated along these traffic routes that form the boundaries and limits of the urban quarter. These *urban quarters* would constitute real *Cities within the City* with a maximum size of 20-30 hectares – approximately 10,000 inhabitants – and with a balanced distribution of mixed functions. This equilibrium of workplaces and living quarters would allow the majority of people to reach their workplace on foot.

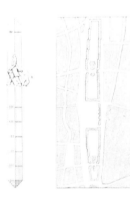
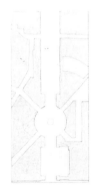

ABOVE: INSULA TEGELIENSIS; *ABOVE CENTRE*: BLOCK FORMS TO AVOID IN REPETITION; *BELOW CENTRE*: TIMGAD 110 AD; BRIVE 1280 AD; QUARTIER DES HALLES, PARIS, 1960; KARL MARX HOF, VIENNA, 1927; RUNDER PLATZ, BERLIN (A SPEER); ST DIE (LE CORBUSIER); *BELOW*: WEST BERLIN CENTRE, EXISTING STREET PATTERN; PROPOSED STREET PATTERN.

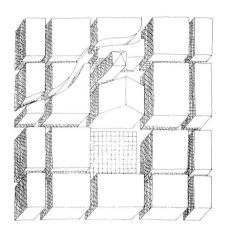
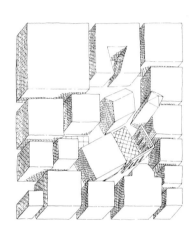
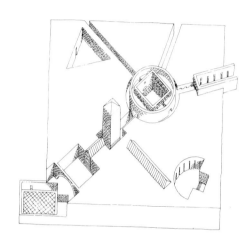

ABOVE: THREE TYPES OF URBAN SPACE, *L TO R*: THE URBAN BLOCKS ARE THE RESULT OF A PATTERN OF STREETS AND SQUARES. THE PATTERN IS TYPOLOGICALLY CLASSIFIABLE; THE PATTERN OF STREETS AND SQUARES IS THE RESULT OF THE POSITION OF THE BLOCKS. THE BLOCKS ARE TYPOLOGICALLY CLASSIFIABLE; THE STREETS AND SQUARES ARE PRECISE FORMAL TYPES. THESE PUBLIC ROOMS ARE TYPOLOGICALLY CLASSIFIABLE; *BELOW*: THE ZONING OF MODERN CITIES HAS RESULTED IN THE RANDOM DISTRIBUTION OF BOTH PUBLIC AND PRIVATE BUILDINGS. THE ARTIFICIALITY AND WASTEFULNESS OF ZONING HAS DESTROYED OUR CITIES

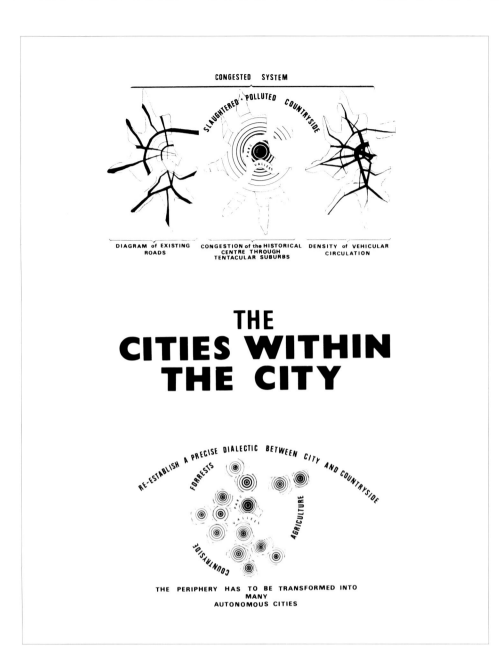

CONGESTED SYSTEM

DIAGRAM of EXISTING ROADS | CONGESTION of the HISTORICAL CENTRE THROUGH TENTACULAR SUBURBS | DENSITY of VEHICULAR CIRCULATION

THE CITIES WITHIN THE CITY

RE-ESTABLISH A PRECISE DIALECTIC BETWEEN CITY AND COUNTRYSIDE

FORRESTS
AGRICULTURE
COUNTRYSIDE

THE PERIPHERY HAS TO BE TRANSFORMED INTO MANY AUTONOMOUS CITIES

Against the global destruction of the city and countryside that we are witnessing, we propose a global philosophical, political and technical project of reconstruction. One cannot destroy the city without also destroying the countryside. City and countryside are antithetical notions. The reconsruction of the territory must be defined in a strict physical and legal separation of city and countryside. First of all we must drastically reduce the built perimeters of the city and precisely redefine rural land in order to establish clearly what is city and what is countryside. Any notion of functional zoning ought to be abol-

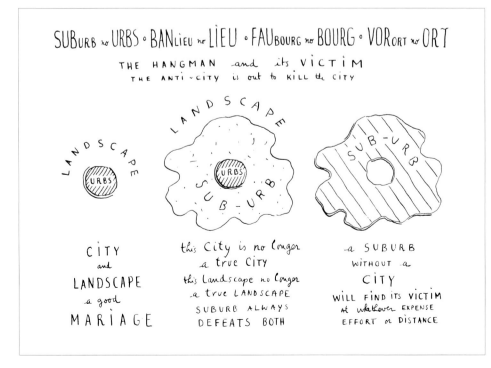

SUBurb no URBS ∘ BANlieu no LIEU ∘ FAUbourg no BOURG ∘ VORort no ORT

THE HANGMAN and its VICTIM
THE ANTI-CITY is out to kill the CITY

LANDSCAPE
URBS

CITY and LANDSCAPE a good MARIAGE

LANDSCAPE
URBS
SUB-URB

this City is no longer a true City
this Landscape no longer a true LANDSCAPE
SUBURB ALWAYS DEFEATS BOTH

SUB-URB

a SUBURB WITHOUT a CITY
WILL FIND ITS VICTIM at whatever EXPENSE EFFORT or DISTANCE

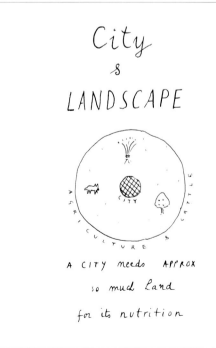

City & LANDSCAPE

AGRICULTURE
CITY
CATTLE &

A CITY needs APPROX
so much Land
for its nutrition

QUES
KRIER
COUNTRY

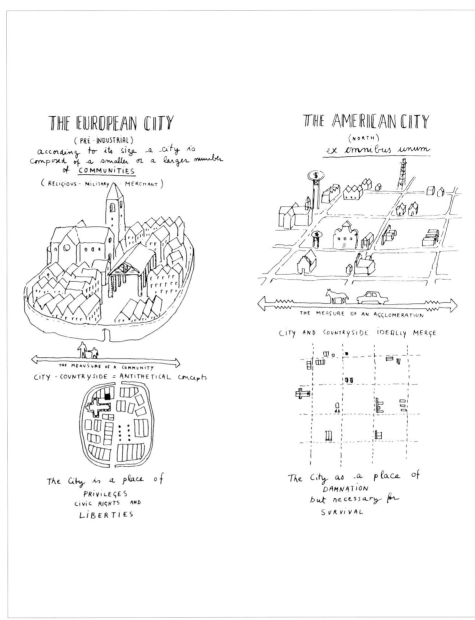

ished. *There can be no industrial zones, pedestrian zones, shopping or housing zones. There can only be urban quarters which integrate all the functions of urban life. The notions of metropolitan centre and periphery must be abolished.*

The building of new urban communities, far from restricting development and growth, will trigger a vast process of transformation, freeing for redevelopment immense expanses of residential suburbs, housing estates, redundant industrial land, depots and docks, railway and marshalling yards, administrative, commercial, cultural, educational single-use complexes.

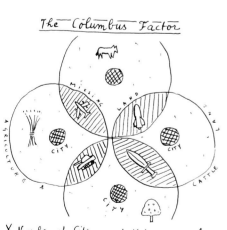

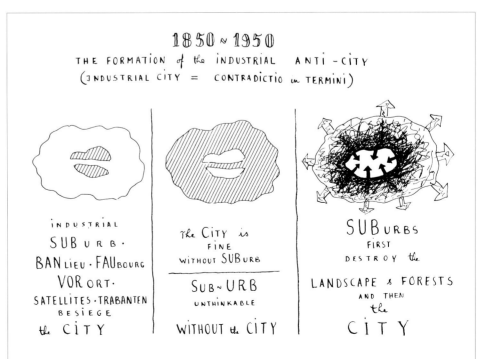

CRITIQUE

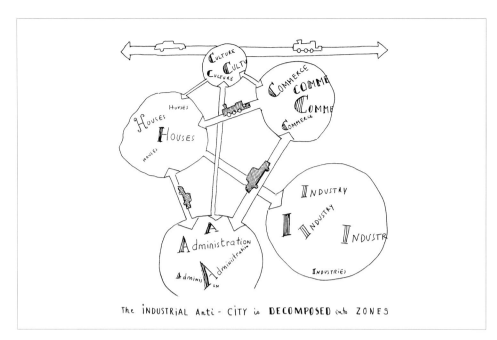

The INDUSTRIAL Anti-CITY is DECOMPOSED into ZONES

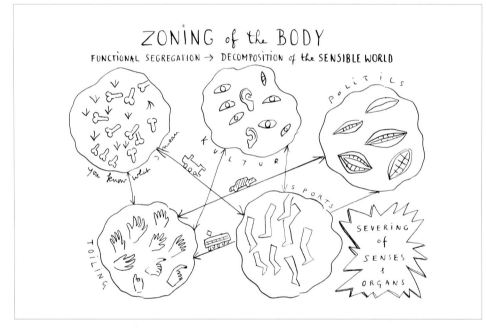

ZONING of the BODY

FUNCTIONAL SEGREGATION → DECOMPOSITION of the SENSIBLE WORLD

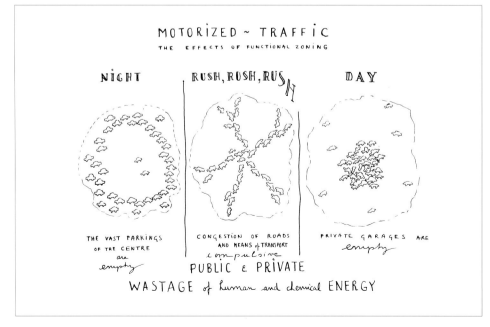

MOTORIZED ~ TRAFFIC

THE EFFECTS OF FUNCTIONAL ZONING

NIGHT   RUSH, RUSH, RUSH   DAY

THE VAST PARKINGS OF THE CENTRE are empty

CONGESTION OF ROADS AND MEANS of TRANSPORT compulsive

PRIVATE GARAGES ARE empty

PUBLIC & PRIVATE

WASTAGE of human and chemical ENERGY

The industrial project reduces the essential functions of life to three distinct categories: production, consumption and reproduction (material and intellectual, education, propaganda, health and culture). Isolation, fragmentation, separation and finally the territorial regrouping of functions encourage this process of reduction and the internal rationalisation of functions. In urban practice, this fragmentation is realised through functional zoning (administrative, cultural, industrial, commercial, residential zones, etc). The first imperative of zoning is to transform every part of the territory (city or countryside) in such a way that every citizen can finally only accomplish: only a single task; in a defined place; in a determined manner; at the exclusion of all other tasks. The second imperative of zoning is the daily and effective mobilisation of society in its en-

the cit

zonin

OF ZONING

tirety (all social classes of all ages: infants, children, adults, the elderly, the rich, the poor). The production and use of roads and means of transport become the principle activities of an industrial economy. The railroads, and the roads of concrete, asphalt and earth are the arterial system, the common gathering place and the cement of an atomised society. The means of private and public mechanical transport – trains, planes, automobiles – are the principle instrument of this mobilisation; the necessary extension of the human body. The goal of the industrial plan is to guarantee, at least for a few generations, maximum consumption of units of time and energy. Mechanical transport becomes, in other words, the principle function in the industrial metabolism of man with nature. The authorities of bridges and roads and the industries of transport and energy are sacred cows.

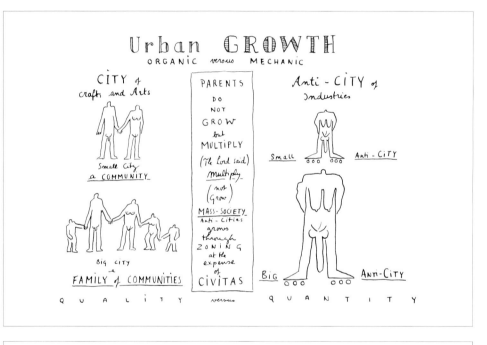

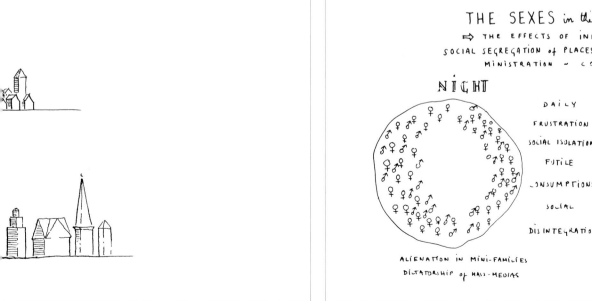

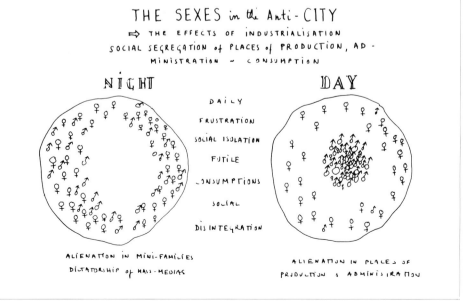

THE CITY WIT

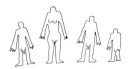

CORRECT URBAN **GROWTH**
IMMATURE QUARTERS GROW TILL MATURITY

CATASTROPHIC ANTI-URBAN **GROWTH**

MATURE PARTS DEGRADE INTO FRAGMENTS

A *city can only be reconsructed in the form of* Urban
Quarters. *A large or a small city can only be reorganised
as a large or a small number of complete urban communities; as a federation of autonomous quarters. Each quarter
must have its own centre and limit. Each quarter must be a*
CITY WITHIN A CITY.

The Quarter *must integrate all daily functions of urban
life (dwelling, working, leisure) within a territory dimen-
sioned on the basis of the comfort of a walking man; not
exceeding 35 hectares in surface and 15,000 inhabitants.
Tiredness sets a natural limit to what a human being is
prepared to walk daily and this limit has taught man all*

A FUNCTIONAL ZONE
admits
one single quality (function) of a City
at the exclusion of all others

EXCLUSIVE

All that is not specifically obligatory is strictly forbidden

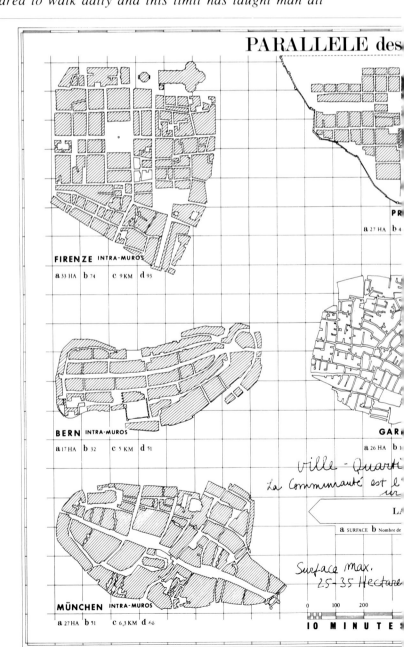

PARALLELE des

FIRENZE INTRA-MUROS
a 33 HA   b 74   c 9 KM   d 93

PR
a 27 HA   b 4

BERN INTRA-MUROS
a 17 HA   b 32   c 5 KM   d 51

GAR
a 26 HA   b 1

Ville - Quarti
La Communauté est l
u

L

a SURFACE   b Nombre de

Surface max.
25-35 Hectare

MÜNCHEN INTRA-MUROS
a 27 HA   b 51   c 6,3 KM   d 66

0   100   200

10 MINUTES

HIN THE CITY

through history the size of rural or urban communities. There seems, on the contrary, to be no natural limit to the size of a functional zone; the boredom which befalls man while driving a car makes him forget any sense of physical limit. The streets and squares must present a familiar character. Their dimensions and proportions must be those of the most beautiful pre-industrial cities. Simplicity must be the goal of the urban plan, however complex the urban geography and topography. The city must be articulated into public and domestic spaces, monuments and urban fabric, classical architecture and vernacular buildings, squares and streets, and in that hierarchy.

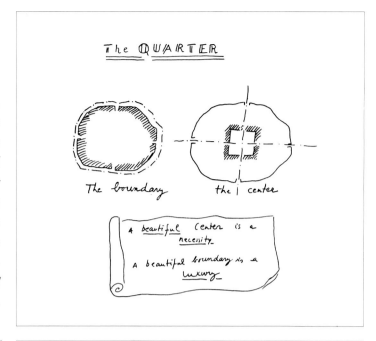

s et Quartiers

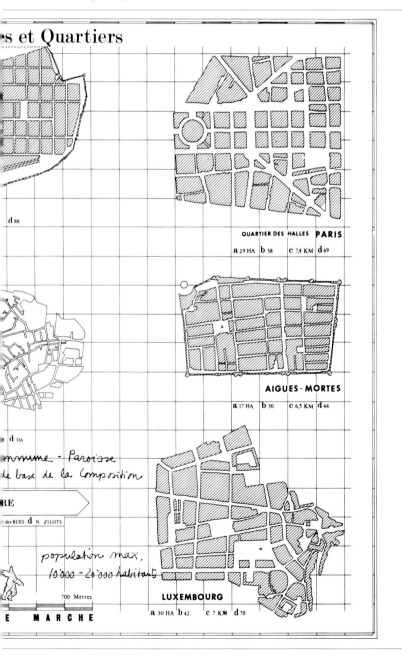

When Florence was the cultural and financial capital of the Renaissance, it contained scarcely 70,000 inhabitants. On foot, one could traverse this glorious city in 20 minutes from one side to the other. In the 15th century the most populous cities of Europe – Paris, Milan and Venice – contained no more than 100,000 people and already Leonardo da Vinci was proposing to divide his city into five autonomous riones.

Before 1800, and with the exception of Cologne, each of the most powerful and prestigious of the 150 Germanic cities had no more than 35,000 inhabitants; Nuremberg had about 20,000. If Tessenow affirmed that there was a strict relationship between the economic and cultural wealth of a city on the one hand and the limitation of its population on the other, he was advancing not a hypothesis but an historical fact. By cultural and material wealth he did not mean absolute power but the just and harmonious relationship established between the citizens of a city and its territory.

In contrast to the zones of industrialised territory, the measurements and geometric organisation of a city and of its quarters are never the result of chance or accident or simply of economic necessity. The measurements and geometric order of a city and of its quarters constitute a project which is moral and legislative, technical and aesthetic.

As the glove and the shoe are the accomplished forms used to cover hands and feet, similarly the house and the street, the palace and the square are the just types and forms to shelter and enhance civic life.

It is a fact that the city of more than 50,000 inhabitants will not succeed in living solely on the resources of its surrounding territory unless blessed by the most clement of climates. Beyond a certain size, the mere logistics of supply and distribution become the principle aim of civic life; thus the majority of citizens are employed in the branches of distribution, administration and services. Instead, we should realise that the right form of the city exists only in the right scale. There is no genuine use for trouser legs that are longer than human legs.

In violent opposition to the designers of industrial projects, in contrast to the numerous teachings of the Bauhaus, the Werkbund or the Nazi DAF (Deutsche Arbeits- Front), there is no reason to believe that the measurements of the city and its parts lie in mathematical preci-

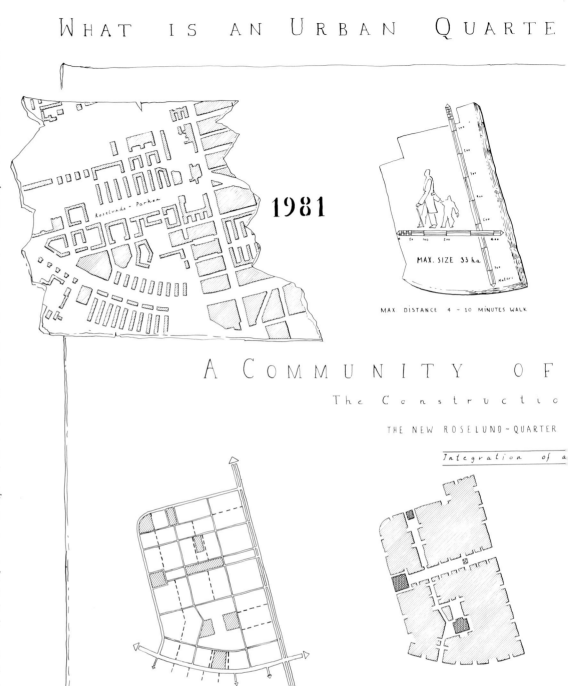

WHAT IS AN URBAN QUARTE

1981

MAX. SIZE 33 ha.

MAX DISTANCE 4 – 10 MINUTES WALK

A COMMUNITY OF

The Constructio

THE NEW ROSELUND-QUARTER

Integration of a

AUTOMOBILE TRAFFIC & GARAGES

MAIN STREETS & SQUARES

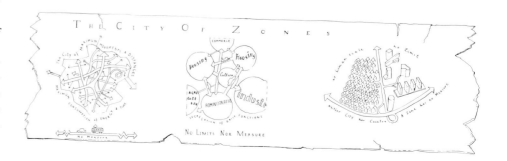

THE CITY OF ZONES

No Limits Nor Measure

? FORM & LEGISLATION

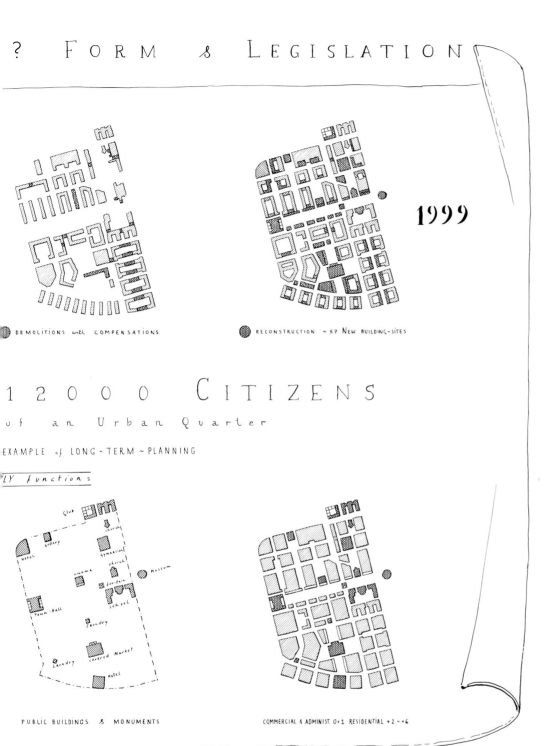

1999

DEMOLITIONS with COMPENSATIONS ◉ RECONSTRUCTION ~ 57 NEW BUILDING-SITES

12000 CITIZENS
of an Urban Quarter

EXAMPLE of LONG-TERM ~ PLANNING

LY functions

PUBLIC BUILDINGS & MONUMENTS   COMMERCIAL & ADMINIST. 0+1 RESIDENTIAL +2 ~ +6

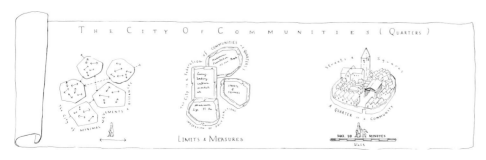

THE CITY OF COMMUNITIES (QUARTERS)

LIMITS & MEASURES

sion. We are not interested in utopias or ideal projects and we refuse to occupy ourselves with ideal and abstract measurements. Such preoccupations are characteristic of merchants and policemen; they always confuse the notions of type and standard, of normality and norm. Monsters and midgets define the limits of normality; one by excess, the other by insufficiency. In order to refine a normal measure it is thus sufficient for us to indicate limits, that is to say, the maximum and the minimum.

But measure does not only concern the geometric dimension of spaces and objects of the city and its quarters, but also the size of human communities. Like a tree or a man, a human community cannot exceed a certain dimension without becoming a monster; either a giant or a dwarf. 'To the size of cities', said Aristotle, 'there is a limit as in the case with everything, with plants, animals, tools; because none of these can retain its natural power if it is too large or too small for it then loses its nature or it is spoilt' (Aristotle, Politics).

Similarly, Galileo maintained that a man of 100 metres in height made of flesh and bone would imprison himself and would be incapable of living on this planet. The Pythagoreans taught that evil belonged to the realm of the limitless and that good belonged to that which was limited. Aristotle made this truth the foundation of everything: philosophy, ethics, and by consequence, of politics and culture.

Just as proper measure is the condition of all life, so the vitality of a community overdevelops or atrophies according to the number of its inhabitants; a city can die by an abnormal expansion, density or dispersion. And just as a family does not grow through the obese swelling of the parents' bodies but through the birth of children, so an urban civilisation cannot with impunity grow by the exaggerated expansion of human agglomerations. 'A tree grows freely,' wrote Walter Rathenau, 'that doesn't mean that it is going to decamp or for that matter grow up to the sky'.

The free and harmonious growth of an urban civilisation cannot be accomplished except by the right and judicious geographical distribution of its cities and communities, autonomous and finite. Only then will the eco-nomies of cities become eco-logical and be able to satisfy the simple and the high aspirations of the spirit.

ROB KRIER, SCHINKELPLATZ, BERLIN, 1977

TYPOLOGICAL ELEMENTS OF THE CONCEPT
OF URBAN SPACE
ROB KRIER

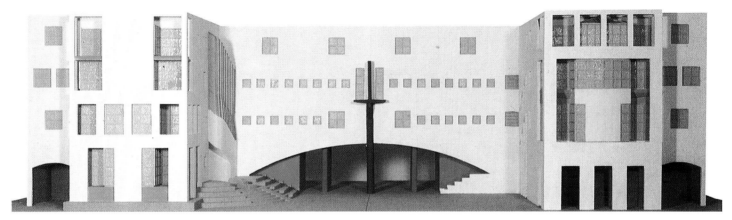

ROB KRIER, RITTERSTRASSE HOUSING, BERLIN, 1977-80

The basic premise underlying this essay is my conviction that in our modern cities we have lost sight of the traditional understanding of urban space. The cause of this loss is familiar to all city dwellers who are aware of their environment and sensitive enough to compare the town planning achievements of the present and the past and who have the strength of character to pronounce sentence on the way things have gone. This assertion alone is of no great service to town planning research. What has to be clearly defined is what should be understood by the term urban space and what meaning it holds within the urban structure, so that we can go on to examine whether the concept of urban space retains some validity in contemporary town planning and on what grounds. 'Space' in this context is a hotly disputed concept. It is not my intention here to generate a new definition but rather to bring its original meaning back into currency.

Definition of the concept 'Urban Space'

If we wish to clarify the concept of urban space without imposing aesthetic criteria, we are compelled to designate all types of space between buildings in towns and other localities as urban space.

This space is geometrically bounded by a variety of elevations. It is only the clear legibility of its geometrical characteristics and aesthetic qualities which allows us consciously to perceive external space as urban space.

The polarity of internal-external space is constantly in evidence, since both obey very similar laws not only in function but also in form. Internal space, shielded from weather and environment is an effective symbol of privacy; external space is seen as open, unobstructed space for movement in the open air, with public, semi-public and private zones.

The basic concepts underlying the aesthetic characteristics of urban space will be expounded below and systematically classified by type. In the process, an attempt will be made to draw a clear distinction between precise aesthetic and confused emotional factors. Every aesthetic analysis runs the risk of foundering on subjective questions of taste. As I have been able to observe from numerous discussions on this topic, visual and sensory habits, which vary from one individual to the next, are augmented by a vast number of socio-political and cultural attitudes, which are taken to represent aesthetic truths. Accepted styles in art history – for example, baroque town plans, revolutionary architecture etc – are both useful and necessary.

However my observations indicate that they are almost always identified with the social structure prevailing at the time in question. Certainly it can scarcely be proved that, because of the wishes of the ruling classes and their artists, the stylistic canons of the period in European art history between 1600 and 1730 appeared almost to be determined by fate. Of course for the historian every period of history forms a unit with its own internal logic, which cannot be fragmented and interchanged with elements of other periods at will.

The creative person, such as the artist, may use a completely different method of approach. The decisions he makes in deploying his aesthetic skills are not always based on assumptions which can be unequivocally explained. His artistic 'libido' is of enormous importance here. The cultural contribution of an age develops on the basis of a highly complex pattern of related phenomena, which must subsequently be the subject of laborious research on the part of historians. This example throws us right into a complex problem which appears the same in whichever period of history we consider. We must discuss this example exhaustively before we start constructing our rational system.

213

Each period in art history develops gradually out of the assimilated functional and formal elements which precede it. The more conscious a society is of its history, the more effortlessly and thoroughly it handles historical elements of style. This truism is important in as far as it legitimises the artist's relationship with the universally accepted wealth of formal vocabulary of all preceding ages – this is as applicable in the 20th as in the 17th century.

I do not wish to rally support for eclecticism, but simply to warn against an all too naive understanding of history, which has been guilty of such misjudgements as representing urban architecture amongst the Romans as markedly inferior to that of the Greeks, which from an historical point of view is simply not true. The same mistake persists today, as can be seen from attitude to the architecture of the 19th century.

Our age has a remarkably distorted sense of history, which can only be characterised as irrational. Le Corbusier's apparent battle against the 'Académie' was not so much a revolt against an exhausted, ageing school as the assumption of a pioneering stand in which he adopted its ideals and imbued them with a new and vigorous content.

This so-called 'pioneering act' was a pretended break with history, but in reality was an artistic falsehood. The facts were these: he abandoned the tradition current until then that art supported by the ruling classes enjoyed the stamp of legitimacy and, being at an advanced stage of development, materially shaped the periods which followed. It was a revolt at one remove, so to speak, for the 'Académie' lived on, and indeed came itself to share the same confused historical sense as the followers of the revolution.

I am speaking here about the modern age in general, and not about its exponents of genius who tower above the 'image of the age'. Rather than be indebted to elitist currents in art, the generation around the turn of the century sought new models. They found them in part in the folk art of other ages and continents, which had hitherto attracted little attention.

There began an unprecedented flurry of discovery of anonymous painting, sculpture, architecture, song and music of those peoples who were considered underdeveloped, and their contribution to culture was for the first time properly valued without regard to their stage of civilisation. Other artists sought their creative material in the realm of pure theory and worked with the basic elements of visual form and its potential for transformation (the 'abstracts'). Yet others found their material in social criticism and the denunciation of social injustice and carried out their mission using formally simple methods (the 'expressionists'). The break with the elitist artistic tradition was identical to the artist's struggle for emancipation from his patron – the ruling class and its cultural dictatorship – which had been brewing even before the French revolution.

The example of the baroque town layout has already been mentioned, and the question raised of the identity of form, content and meaning. We must be more exact in asking:

1 Was the resulting form the free expression of the artist?

2 Or, were the artistic wishes of the employing class imposed on the artist, and was he forced to adopt their notions of form?

3 Do contemporaneous periods exist, which on the basis of different cultural traditions in different countries or continents where similar social conditions prevail, produce the same artistic solutions ?

4 Alternatively, are there non-contemporaneous periods which led to fundamentally different artistic solutions, each being a stage in the development of the same cultural tradition in the same country under the same conditioning social factors?

In this series of permutations, the following factors are relevant: aesthetics, artist, patron, social environment, leeway given to artistic expression, formal restrictions imposed by the patron, formal restrictions imposed by the social environment, fashion, management, level of development, technology and its potential applications, general cultural conditions, scientific knowledge, enlightenment, nature, landscape, climate etc. We can conclude with a fair degree of certainty that none of these interrelated factors can be considered in isolation.

With this brief outline of the problem we should just add a word of caution about an over-simplistic undiscriminating outlook. It is certainly worth trying to establish why certain kinds of urban space were created in the 17th century which we now identify with that period. And it would be even more interesting to examine the real reasons why 20th-century town planning has been impoverished and reduced to the lowest common nominator.

The following classification does not make any value judgements. It enumerates the basic forms which constitute urban space, with a limited number of possible variations and combinations. The aesthetic quality of each element of urban space is characterised by structural interrelation of detail. I shall attempt to discern this quality wherever we are dealing with physical features: of a spatial nature. The two basic elements are the street and the square. In the category of 'interior space' we would be talking about the corridor and room. The geometrical characteristics of both spatial forms are the same. They are differentiated only by the dimensions of the walls which bound them and by the patterns of function and circulation which characterise them.

The Square
In all probability the square was the first way man discovered of using urban space. It is produced by the grouping of houses around an open space. This arrangement afforded a high degree of control of the inner space, as well as facilitating a ready defence against external aggression by minimising the external surface area liable to attack. This kind of courtyard frequently came to bear a symbolic value and was therefore chosen as the model for the construction of numerous holy places (Agora, Forum, cloister, mosque courtyard). With the invention of houses built around a central courtyard or atrium this spatial pattern became a model for the future. Here rooms were arranged around a central courtyard like single housing units around a square.

The Street
The street is a product of the spread of a settlement once houses have been built on all available space around its central square. It provides a framework for the distribution of land and gives access to individual plots. It has a more pronouncedly functional character than the square, which by virtue of its size is a more attractive place to pass the time than the street, in whose confines one is involuntarily caught up in the bustle of traffic. Its architectural backdrop is only perceived in passing. The street layouts which we have inherited in our towns were devised for quite different functional purposes. They were planned to the scale of the human being, the horse and the carriage. The street is unsuitable for the flow of motorised traffic, whilst remaining appropriate to human circulation and activity. It rarely operates as an autonomous isolated space, as for example in the case of villages built along a single street. It is mainly to be perceived as part of a network. Our historic towns have made us familiar with the inexhaustible diversity of spatial relationships produced by such a complex layout.

Typical functions of Urban Space
The activities of a town take place in public and private spheres. The behavioural patterns of people are similar in both. So, the

result is that the way in which public space has been organised has in all periods exercised a powerful influence on the design of private houses.

We might almost infer the existence of a kind of social ritual, which produces a perfect match between individual and collective. What concerns us above all here are those activities which take place in the town in the open air: i.e. actions which a person performs outside the familiar territory of his own home and for which he utilises public space, as for example travelling to work, shopping, selling goods, recreation, leisure activities, sporting events, deliveries etc. Although the asphalt carpet which serves as a channel for the movement of cars is still called a 'street', it retains no connection with the original significance of the term. Certainly the motorised transportation of people and goods is one of the primary functions of the town, but it requires no scenery in the space around it. It is different in the case of the movement of pedestrians or public transport vehicles which move at a moderate speed, like carriages. Today we have boulevard situations which apparently draw their life from the *défilé* of flashy cars and pavement cafes are visited despite the fact that the air is polluted by exhaust fumes. Looking at planning schemes of the turn of the century one can appreciate that in cosmopolitan cities such as Paris, Rome or Berlin, the air was polluted in a different way: by horse manure, stinking sewage and uncollected refuse. A problem of urban hygiene, as old as the town itself, with the only difference that people can be poisoned by carbon monoxide but scarcely by horse manure.

On medical grounds we can no longer indulge in this kind of boulevard romanticism. While the automobile in its present form continues to occupy streets, it excludes all other users.

Let us give a brief outline here of the characteristic functions of the space defined by the square and the street:

The Square
This spatial model is admirably suited to residential use. In the private sphere it corresponds to the inner courtyard or atrium. The courtyard house is the oldest type of town house. In spite of its undisputed advantages, the courtyard house has now become discredited. It is all too easily subject to ideological misinterpretation, and people are afraid that this design may imply enforced conformity to a communal lifestyle or a particular philosophy.

A certain unease about one's neighbours has undoubtedly led to the suppression of this building type. Yet in the same way as communal living has gained in popularity for a minority of young people with the disappearance of the extended family, the concept of neighbourhood and its accompanying building types will most certainly be readopted in the near future.

In the public sphere, the square has undergone the same development. Market places, parade grounds, ceremonial squares, squares in front of churches and townhalls etc all relics of the Middle Ages, have been robbed of their original functions and their symbolic content and in many places only kept up through the activities of conservationists.

The loss of symbolism in architecture was described and lamented by Giedion in *Space, Time, Architecture*. The literary torch which he carried for Le Corbusier in the 30s, and for Jorn Utzon in the 60s, expressed his hope that this loss would perhaps be compensated by a powerful impetus towards artistic expression. He hoped for the same thing from new construction techniques. I have already stressed the importance of the poetic content and aesthetic quality of space and buildings. It is not my wish to introduce into this discussion the concept of symbolism, with all its ethical and religious overtones; and I would also like to warn against the arbitrary confusion of aesthetic and symbolic categories. If I maintain that the Louvre, instead of being a museum, might equally well be housing, a castle, an office

building etc, let me make it clear that I am speaking of space or building type, not of external detailing or historical and sociopolitical factors which led to this structural solution. The aesthetic value of the different spatial types is as independent of short-lived functional concerns as it is of symbolic interpretations which may vary from one age to the next.

Another example to clarify this argument:
The multi-storeyed courtyard house, from the Middle Ages up to modern times, was the building type which acted as the starting point for the castle, the renaissance and baroque palace etc. The Berlin tenements of the 19th century are also courtyard houses, but nowhere near being palaces. Anyone familiar with the architecture of Palladio should draw the right conclusion from this. The lavish use of materials certainly does not play the decisive role here. If that were the case, Palladio would long since have fallen into oblivion. So, even in the 20th century, I can construct a building with an inner courtyard without remotely aiming to imitate the palace architecture of the 16th century and the social class which produced it. There is no reason why the building types used by extinct dynasties to design their residences and show their material wealth should not serve as a model for housing today.

The early Christians were not afraid to adopt the building type of Roman judicial and commercial buildings, the basilica, as the prototype of their religious monuments. Le Corbusier took his rows of 'redents' from baroque castles.

No contemporary public squares have been laid out which could be compared with urban squares like the Grande Place in Brussels, the Place Stanislas in Nancy, the Piazza del Campo in Siena, the Place Vendome and the Place des Vosges in Paris, the Plaza Mayor in Madrid, the Plaza Real in Barcelona etc. This spatial type awaits rediscovery. This can only occur firstly when it can be endowed with meaningful functions, and secondly is planned in the right place with the appropriate approaches within the overall town layout.

What are the functions which are appropriate to the square ?

Commercial activities certainly, such as the market, but above all activities of a cultural nature. The establishment of public administrative offices, community halls, youth centres, libraries, theatres and concert halls, cafes, bars etc. Where possible in the case of central squares, these should be functions which generate activity twenty-four hours a day. Residential use should not be excluded in any of these cases.

The Street
In purely residential areas streets are universally seen as areas for public circulation and recreation. The distances at which houses are set back from the street, as regulations demand in Germany today, are so excessive that attractive spatial situations can only be achieved by gimmickry. In most cases, there is ample space available for gardens in addition to the emergency access required for public service vehicles. This street space can only function when it is part of system in which pedestrian access leads off the street. This system can be unsettled by the following planning errors:
1 If some houses and flats cannot be approached directly from the street but only from the rear. In this way the street is deprived of a vital activity. The result is a state of competition between internal and external urban space. This characterisation of space refers to the degree of public activity which takes place in each of these two areas.
2 If the garages and parking spaces are arranged in such a way that the flow of human traffic between car and house does not impinge upon the street space.
3 If the play spaces are squeezed out into isolated areas with the sole justification of preserving the intimacy of the residential

zone. The same neurotic attitude towards neighbours is experienced in flats. The noise of cars outside the home is accepted, yet indoors children are prevented from playing noisily.

4 If no money can be invested in public open spaces, on such items as avenues of trees, paving and other such street furniture, given that the first priority is the visual appeal of space.

5 If the aesthetic quality of adjacent houses is neglected, if the facing frontages are out of harmony, if different sections of the street are inadequately demarcated or if the scale is unbalanced. These factors fulfil a precise cultural role in the functional coherence of the street and square. The need to meet the town's function of 'poetry of space' should be as self-evident as the need to meet any technical requirements. In a purely objective sense it is just as basic.

Can you imagine people no longer making music, painting, making pictures, dancing . . . ? Everybody would answer no to this. The role of architecture on the other hand is not apparently seen as so essential. 'Architecture is something tangible, useful, practical' as far as most people are concerned. In any case its role is still considered as the creation of cosiness indoors and of status symbols outdoors. Anything else is classed as icing on the cake, which one can perfectly well do without. I maintain that a stage in history when architecture is not granted its full significance shows a society in cultural crisis, the tragedy of which can scarcely be described in words. Contemporary music expresses it adequately.

The problems of the residential street touched on here apply equally to the commercial street. The separation of pedestrians and traffic carries with it the danger of the isolation of the pedestrian zone. Solutions must be carefully worked out which will keep the irritation of traffic noise and exhaust fumes away from the pedestrian, without completely distancing one zone from the other. This means an overlapping of these functions, to be achieved with considerable investment in the technological sphere, a price which the motorised society must be prepared to pay. This problem will remain much the same even when the well-known technical shortcomings and acknowledged design failings of the individual car have been ironed out. The number of cars, and their speed, remains a source of anxiety. With the way things are going at the moment, there seems little hope of either factor being corrected. On the contrary, nobody today can predict what catastrophic dimensions these problems will assume and what solutions will be needed to overcome them.

It is completely absurd to labour under the misapprehension that one day the growing need to adopt new modes of transport will leave our countryside littered with gigantic and obsolete monuments of civil engineering.

In fact, one is inclined to think that, considering the level of investment in the car and all that goes with it, a fundamental change is no longer feasible in the long term.

All this illustrates the enormous conflict of interests between investments for the demands of machine/car and investments for living creature/man; it also indicates that there is a price to be paid for the restoration of urban space, if our society is to continue to value life in its cities.

Back to the problem of the commercial street which has already been outlined. It must be fashioned differently from the purely residential street. It must be relatively narrow. The passerby must be able to cast an eye over all the goods on display in the shops opposite without perpetually having to cross from one side of the street to the other. At least, this is what the shopper and certainly the tradesman would like to see. Another spatial configuration of the shopping street is provided by the old town centre of Berne, in which pedestrians can examine the goods on display protected by arcades from the inclemency of the weather. This type of shopping street has retained its charm and also its functional efficiency up to the present day. The pedestrian is relatively untroubled by the road, which lies on a lower level. This street space can serve as an example to us.

The same can be said of the glassroofed arcades or passages which originated in the 19th century. Strangely enough, they have fallen out of favour today. From the point of view of ventilation it was obviously disadvantageous then to lead the street frontage into a passageway. With today's fully air-conditioned commercial and office buildings, however, this building type could come back into fashion. Protection against the elements is a financially justifiable amenity for shopping streets in our latitudes. The arcaded street, developed by the Romans from the colonnades which surrounded the Greek Agora, has completely died out. The remains of such formal streets can still be found at Palmyra, Perge, Apameia, Sidon, Ephesus, Leptis Magna, Timgad etc.

The appearance of this type of street is a fascinating event in the history of town planning. With the increased prosperity of Roman rule, a need arose for the uniform and schematic plan of the Greek colonial town to be modified, with emphasis being placed on arterial roads within the homogeneous network of streets, and this was achieved by marking them with particularly splendid architectural features. They certainly had important functional connotations which today can no longer be clearly surmised. Whatever these connotations were, they had an obviously commercial as well as symbolic character, in contrast to the Agora and the Forum, which were reserved primarily for political and religious purposes. Weinbrenner, with his proposed scheme for the improvement of the Kaiserstrasse in Karlsruhe, attempted to revive this idea. The Konigsbau in Stuttgart designed by Leins could be a fragment of the arcaded street of Ephesus. The Romans were astoundingly imaginative in perfecting this type of street space. So, for example, changes in the direction of streets, dictated by existing features of the urban structure, were highlighted as cardinal points by having gateways built across them. In the Galeries St. Hubert in Brussels, this problem has been solved on the same principle. By this expedient, the street space is divided up into visually manageable sections, in contrast to the seemingly infinite perspective of the remaining network of streets. It should equally be noted that in rare cases streets broaden out into squares directly without their articulation being marked by buildings. The street and the square were conceived as largely independent and autonomous spaces.

Such devices, used by Roman and Greek town planners to indicate spatial relationships, lapsed into oblivion with the decline of the Roman empire in Europe. Isolated building types such as the forum and the basilica were adopted unchanged in the Middle Ages, for example in monasteries. The forum was no longer employed as a public space. Not so in North Africa and the Near East, and to some extent in Spain, where these ancient types of urban space survived almost unchanged until the turn of the century using traditional construction methods.

Typology of Urban Space

In formulating a typology of urban space, spatial forms and their derivatives may be divided into three main groups, according to the geometrical pattern of their ground plan: these groups derive from the square, the circle or the triangle.

Without doubt the scale of an urban space is also related to its geometrical qualities. Scale can only be mentioned in passing in this typology. I wish to try and deal with the significance of proportions in external space more comprehensively in a later chapter. They do not affect the arrangement of my typology.

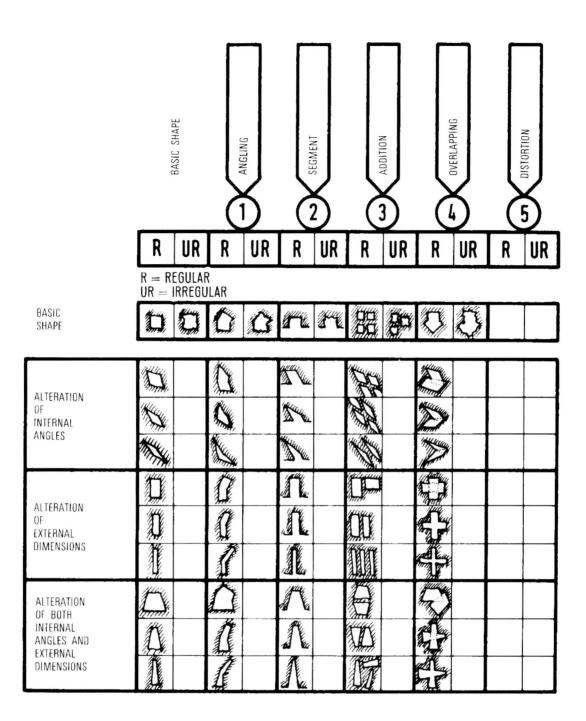

Modulation of a given spacial type

The matrix shows, reading from top to bottom:
1 The basic element.
2 The modification of the basic element resulting from the enlargement or reduction of the angles contained within it, where the external dimensions remain constant.
3 The angles remain constant and the length of two sides changes in the same proportion.
4 Angles and external dimensions are altered arbitrarily.

Reading from left to right, the matrix illustrates the following stages of modulation:
1 Angled space. This indicates a space which is a compound of two parts of the basic element with two parallel sides bent.
2 This shows only a segment of the basic element.
3 The basic element is added to.
4 The basic elements overlap or merge.
5 Under the heading 'distortion' are included spatial forms which are difficult or impossible to define. This category is intended to cover those shapes which can only with difficulty be traced back to their original geometric model. These shapes may also be described as species born out of chaos. Here the elevation of buildings may be distorted or concealed to such an extent that they can no longer be distinguished as clear demarcations of space – for example, a facade of mirror glass or one completely obscured by advertisements, so that a cuckooclock as big as a house stands next to an outsize ice-cream cone, or an advert for cigarettes or chewing gum stands in place of the usual pierced facade.

Even the dimensions of a space can have a distorting influence on its effect, to such an extent that it ceases to bear any relation to the original. The column headed 'distortion' has not been completed in this matrix, as these shapes cannot be diagrammatically expressed.

All these processes of change show regular and irregular configurations.

The basic elements can be modified by a great variety of building sections illustrate here 24 different types which substantially alter the features of urban space.

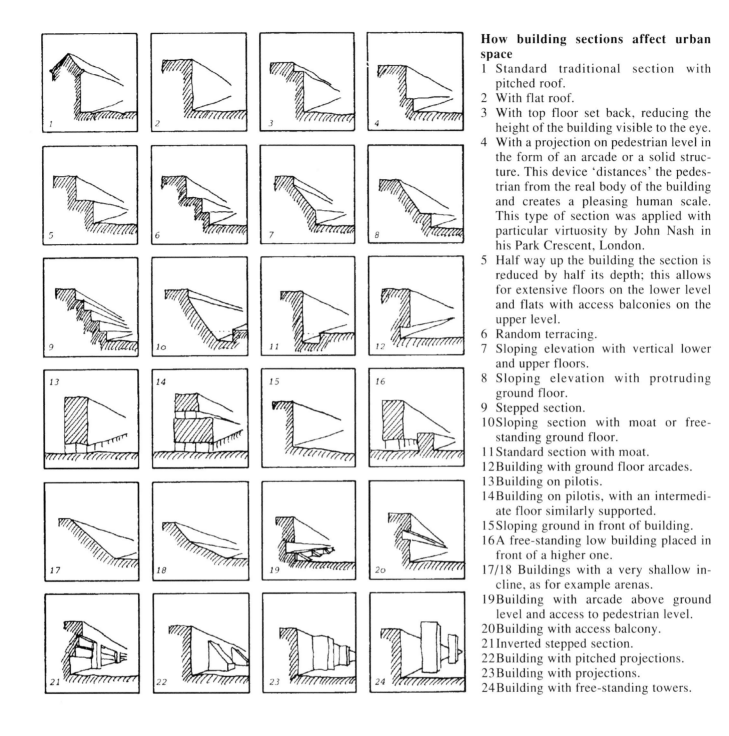

How building sections affect urban space

1 Standard traditional section with pitched roof.
2 With flat roof.
3 With top floor set back, reducing the height of the building visible to the eye.
4 With a projection on pedestrian level in the form of an arcade or a solid structure. This device 'distances' the pedestrian from the real body of the building and creates a pleasing human scale. This type of section was applied with particular virtuosity by John Nash in his Park Crescent, London.
5 Half way up the building the section is reduced by half its depth; this allows for extensive floors on the lower level and flats with access balconies on the upper level.
6 Random terracing.
7 Sloping elevation with vertical lower and upper floors.
8 Sloping elevation with protruding ground floor.
9 Stepped section.
10 Sloping section with moat or free-standing ground floor.
11 Standard section with moat.
12 Building with ground floor arcades.
13 Building on pilotis.
14 Building on pilotis, with an intermediate floor similarly supported.
15 Sloping ground in front of building.
16 A free-standing low building placed in front of a higher one.
17/18 Buildings with a very shallow incline, as for example arenas.
19 Building with arcade above ground level and access to pedestrian level.
20 Building with access balcony.
21 Inverted stepped section.
22 Building with pitched projections.
23 Building with projections.
24 Building with free-standing towers.

L TO R: GREEN OPEN SPACE SURROUNDED BY DIFFERENT KINDS OF TREES; COMBINATIONS OF DIFFERENT FACADES, OVERGROWN WITH PLANTS

Each of these building types can be given a facade appropriate to its function and method of construction.

The sketches reproduced here can only give some idea of the inexhaustible design possibilities. Each of these structures influences urban space in a particular way. It is beyond the scope of this work to describe the nature of this influence.

Elevations

1 Pierced facade: the lowest level is more generously glazed in each sketch, reducing the solid area to a simple load-bearing structure.

2 The glazed area within the load bearing structure can be modified according to taste. The following three pictures show a reverse of the design process portrayed in 1. A solid base forces the glazed area upward.

3 The window type can be modified horizontally and vertically according to the imagination of the designer.

4 Faceless modular facade as a theoretical (abstract) way in which the building might be enclosed. The modular facade can be adapted to all variations in the shape of the building. Solid sections of the building can be combined with the grid.

5 Windowless buildings: windows are placed in niches etc. and the process starts again from the beginning.

6 Exploration of different geometries; a thematic interpretation of the elevation: lowest level = heavy; middle section = smooth with various perforations; upper part = light, transparent. (One of the sketches of squares shows a variation on this theme on three sides of a square.) Arcades placed in front of houses. Different architectural styles juxtaposed.

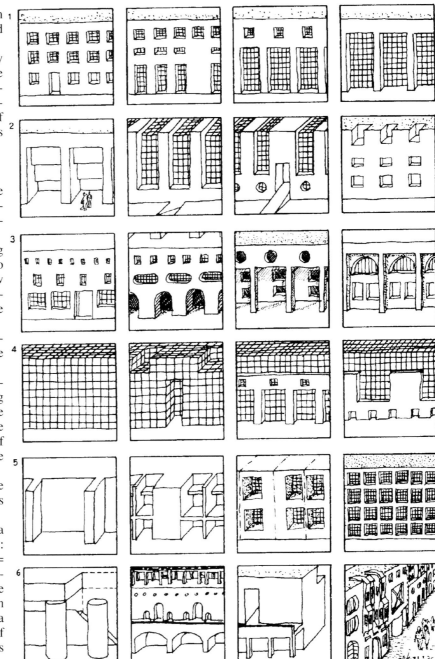

L TO R: DIALOGUE BETWEEN OLD, NEW AND GREEN; ARCADE RUNNING ROUND SQUARE

COMMENTS ON THE IBA PROPOSALS
COLIN ROWE

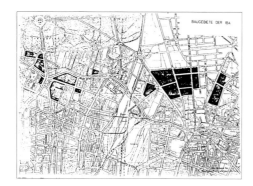
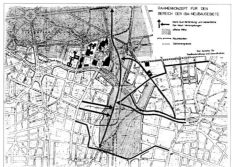

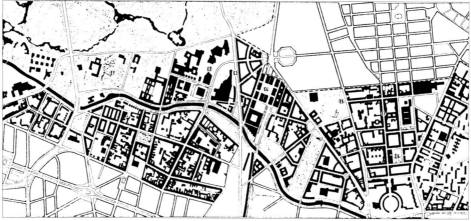

IBA BERLIN, *ABOVE*: CURRENT PLANS (1984); *BELOW*: ORIGINAL PLANS

I require a quotation in order to set in motion this memorandum; and (since I don't wish to quote from myself) I propose to make use of extracts from an article by my friend and colleague, Werner Goehner, which has come my way today. It is entitled, 'Architecture as an Integral Part of the City'; it is mostly about a number of projects for the Ballhausplatz in Vienna; and, published in *The Cornell Journal of Architecture*, Vol 1, 1981, my selection of extracts from it reads as follows:

> The scientific and analytic mind, with its tendency to break the world into ever smaller parts, has, during the past 50 years of urban and architectural development, finally succeeded in ending a long and fruitful marriage between architecture and the city. Within the modern movement, both the Neo-Positivistic view of architecture as an a-historical phenomenon, and the view of architecture as exclusively the result of political and economic conditions, dependent on technological and cultural developments (*Zeitgeist* obsession) *finally* led to the estrangement of architecture from the city... stripped of its civic dimension ... modern architecture retreated into privacy... [Therefore] in the modern city a meaningful dialogue between the *res publica* and the *res privata* is missing, leading to an impoverishment of the urban spatial morphology ... A meaningful orientation within urban

> public space has become difficult ... [and] without ... spatial articulation of the public realm, the city becomes unintelligible ...

These remarks specify the present condition of almost any major city in the world; they describe West Berlin; they are indicative of the present day concern to reconcile architecture and the city; and, particularly, they are indicative of the programme of IBA. For, I think it no exaggeration to say that IBA's principal concern is to place architecture and the city once more in a condition of fertile intercourse.

The ambition is grand; its realisation is what a large part of the world is waiting for; because it is a trial, it will not be wholly successful; but, the historical record will stipulate that it was here, in West Berlin, that a first major attempt was made to reconstitute the city.

It was several times pointed out by the *Experten* (and, most repeatedly, by Egbert Kossack) that their instruction was incomplete, that, quite simply, they didn't know whether they were supposed to be addressing their attention to *a city plan* or *an exhibition*. Nor was the information (as far as I remember) ever forthcoming; and it is in this situation of ambiguity that I now propose to address myself to these two separate conditions as the separate conditions which they are.

I The IBA Proposals as a City Plan
Again, in this context of consideration, the *Experten* were presented with the further traces

of a conflict since it is not clear whether they were supposed to be advising on a plan for a part of West Berlin or a plan for a city, at some date, to be re-united. So, here, I shall solve this problem by ignoring it. Ignoring it because I suppose that an adequate plan for a part of West Berlin immediately adjacent to the old city centre should, in no way, be compromised by reunification and that a good plan might even act to facilitate such an objective.

However, something must now be said about the prejudices induced by the boundaries of maps. For, surely, the boundaries of a map act, to a large extent, to control what one discerns within these perimeters, ie: these boundaries will encourage the reading of certain configurations; but if these perimeters are altered, maybe wholly different configurations will present themselves to the eye and to the mind.

So I make these remarks because of the documentation with which we have been presented. In the first case, as was noticed by several individuals, this documentation has tended to suppress information as to the present condition of East Berlin which, again and again, has been made to look like a large piece of water. Then the documentation which was first exhibited could only encourage my eyes, at least, to move laterally (west-east, east-west) more or less along the line of the Landwehrkanal (the result of zoning propositions made way back?). But, if one set of maps will encourage this reading, then another documentation, to which I became alerted by Professor

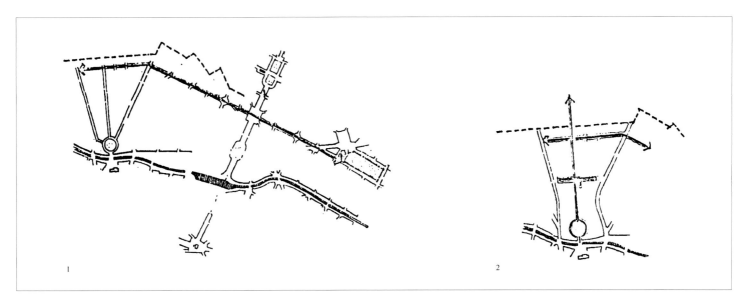

Nagel's remarks in October, could only provoke a consciousness of entirely different movements within the centre part of the same site. For, as something additional – and not contradictory – to the line of the Landwehrkanal, Professor Nagel made a very energetic illustration of the railroad tracks and yards leading to the former Potsdam and Anhalt railway stations.

However, a consideration of the possibilities suggested by north-south movement (whether visual or physical) will be reserved for later attention; and now to approach the specific proposals of IBA:

A In Kreuzberg North of the Landwehrkanal: Luisenstadt

As I recollect, though the *Experten* heard much vociferous representation from this area (and for very good reasons!), we were not called upon to make particularised commentary; and, accordingly, any remarks made here will be of the most general. So far as I can perceive this is, of all others, the section of West Berlin which possesses the most intelligible structure; and, surely, this basic structure should not be infringed or deformed in the name of necessary renewal. From what one has seen and heard, upgrading and renewal of housing *must* occur.

But may not such operations be regarded as mostly a matter of urban dentistry – of repair, replacement, and occasional extraction?

Apart from these very general remarks, there should probably be noticed the extreme importance of the line of Oranienstraße, leading from Kochstraße to the former Görlitzer railway station with its great potential for development as a place of public recreation (1).

B Friedrichstadt South of the Wall

This is an area amputated from the urban configuration of which it forms an intrinsic part and its role is then further diminished by the present format of Mehringplatz which, nowadays, merely serves as a curious appendage utterly divorced from those functions of convergence which were related to its original Baroque and Roman idea. Then, add to this that the three major north-south arteries of this area – Wilhelmstraße (Via del Babuine), Friedrichstraße (Via del Corse), and Lindenstraße (Via di Ripeta) all terminate to the north as they do; and, then, further consider that Kochstraße is not exactly the Via dei Condetti ... and, with these considerations, a sadness about this part of town becomes augmented. It is a fragment. Logically and psychologically, it belongs to the rest of Friedrichstadt; and, taken

by itself, its 18th-century infrastructure is of nothing like the decisive quality of the mid19th-century layout in adjacent Kreuzberg. Particularly, Friedrichstraße can only climax in Unter den Linden. But, if for the moment and the foreseeable future, this is impossible, then what to do?

I think, myself, that the solution is very simple; and, if the IBA plan is not absolutely congealed, I would suggest the following:
1 Somewhere approximately midway between Mehringplatz and Kochstraße, the creation of a direct east-west pedestrian promenade; and
2 At the intersection of this promenade with Friedrichstraße, the creation of a *very* small *Platz* which, in a better world (with the Wall gone), might serve as a local decoration to the line Mehringplatz – Unter den Linden (2); and I make these suggestions because of the *necessity* of finding some logical place of convergence within this area.

Apart from these issues, I listened with attention to the arguments about the location of the flower market in this not highly accessible part of the world; and I agreed with those many who think that its present site (the noise and the mess of trucks driving in and out) is more than a little mad.

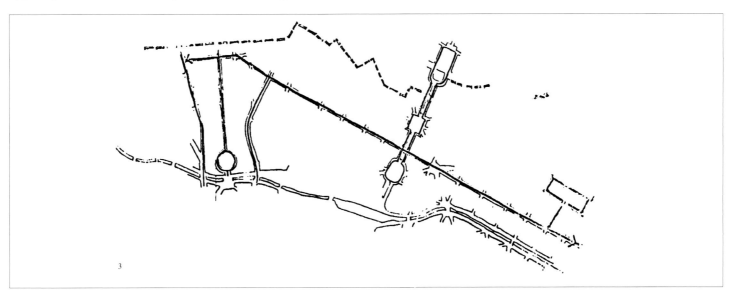

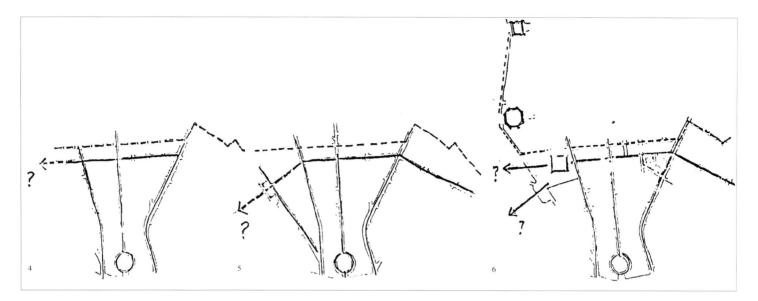

However, now to approach the controversial subject of the vanished Prinz-Albrecht-Palais and its related park. In my discussion of Luisenstadt, I have already stressed the high visibility of the connection *Kochstraße – Oranienstraße – Görlitzer Bahnhof*; and, should the flower market be shifted elsewhere, I assume that this could equally be the line *Kochstraße Junker-/Ritter-/Reichenberger Straße* – though this line would be scarcely equipped with a comparable eastward termination (3). But, whichever of these lines is assumed to predominate (one or the other of them is vital for the integration of Luisenstadt with points west), they are both, of course, approximately blocked at Wilhelmstraße; and, from then on, everything becomes confused – the prevalent condition in the Friedrichvorstadt.

But should the 'career' of a very important urban ligament (either of the lines which I have itemised) be irretrievably blocked by the horrible associations which accrue to the site of the former Prinz-Albrecht-Palais? And are there not considerations of urbanistic elegance and legibility which would urge a less abrupt solution in this vicinity?

I have seen proposals for the continuation of Kochstraße to some unspecified point further west (4); I have also seen proposals for the routing of the Kochstraße line through Askanischer Platz and Schöneberger Straße to some unspecified point further southwest (5); but, while I strongly support the examination of both of these moves, I would still like to observe another possibility – and I suggest this with diffidence.

To the north – and in East Berlin – one observes the role of Pariser Platz as entry to Unter den Linden and the comparable role of Leipziger Platz and, therefore, one wonders whether an analogue of these spaces could not be created at this point further south – as an entry to Kochstraße. The idea would, I think, have certain merits. It would imply the continuity and the intrinsic integration of the urban fabric on both sides of the Wall. It could, in itself, act as a monument. Nor need it be destructive of the present function of this site as a park. For, at this point, one does not propose building so much as an enclosure of trees through which a continuation of Koch-

straße would travel. And it is to this enclosure of trees (presumably supported by a modest architectural and sculptural apparatus) that a memorial function might then be attributed (6).

Such, I believe, might have been the solution adopted by Gilly, Schinkel and Lenné; and I suggest that it may be a solution which deserves consideration. For I do *not* think that a proper monument to the victims of the Gestapo is here to be made by simply preserving the site, by nothing more, by a pious negation; and, correspondingly, I *do* assume that a monument, *both as commemoration and release*, should be a conscious, a grand, and a positive gesture (perhaps in some very minimal and quiet way a present-day recall of those neo-classical monuments which addressed themselves to the recollection of Frederick the Great?)

I would suggest that such a development might be in the best traditions of Berlin; and I would further suggest that such a development *must* be considered vital for any future animation of Kochstraße. For, without any other entry from places west, what is Kochstraße beyond a sad and isolated street, excluded from communication, and forever rendered sad by its relationship to Checkpoint Charlie?

Which, otherwise, leaves only to be said that, in Southern Friedrichstadt, the IBA proposals represent a triumph of determination. For, although there may be some doubts about excessive use of perimeter blocks, to have secured the four projects at the intersection of Friedrichstraße and Kochstraße, which all combine respect for the existing with introduction of the new, to have combined these with the further project to the east of Lindenstraße is nothing less than a triumph and so, I am sure, this achievement will be judged.

C Around the Lützowplatz, South of the Tiergarten and along the Landwehrkanal

There is, I believe, little which should be said. The sites are separated; beyond a point the area does not presume tight coordination; and the solutions are invariably more than adequate. So, particularly within this area, one admires Stirling, who has been possibly liberated from his English inhibitions by exposure to the Germanic lands. Possibly his solution is too Wilhelminian, too Wagnerian, too Neusch-

wanstein, too Hechingen, and all the rest. But should this be a problem? And, in the present situation of Berlin, I think it should not.

So, apart from this, what else? One regrets the absence of Ungers' Hotel Berlin; and, apart from this, what other objections? Does one object to the plans of Rob Krier's *urban villas*? I think one does and, perhaps, Rob Krier should be asked to reconsider these.

D Between the 'Kulturforum', the Wall, and Stresemannstraße

This is obviously an area of maximum ambiguity, of maximum controversy, and, not unexpectedly, one in which the IBA proposals seem to be less than happy and accommodating. A comprehensive solution for this area presumably implies a variety of decisions, not all of them concerned with the area itself; and, as I see them, these are related to: the completion of the 'Kulturforum'; the role of Potsdamer Straße; the role of the Landwehrkanal; the future of the Potsdam and Anhalt railway stations; a future symbolic access to Leipziger Straße; some improved approach to Kochstraße (?); a location for the Tempodrom; and, above all, the ease of north-south vehicular movement through what, for all practical purposes, is, and will surely remain, a major traffic sluice.

Now, with these decisions apparently not made, it should not be surprising that the IBA plan seems here to be a little *ad hoc* and perfunctory. A little bit stuck together with Scotch tape. For how could matters be otherwise? And do not such decisions lie beyond IBA's mission and sphere of competence?

All the same, to surrender this territory (so central to the city both West and East) to, more or less, a naturalistic forest would surely be a gesture of defeat; and, accordingly, I add a number of notes which are not necessarily addressed to IBA but which are offered as very tentative guides for development.

1 The completion of the 'Kulturforum' and the role of Potsdamer Straße. I believe it was Alberti's advice that one should not set out to contradict what has already been begun; and this is an opinion which I share. I am only a very reserved admirer of the work of Hans

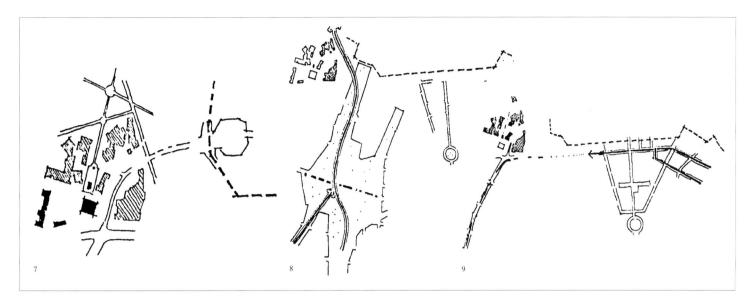

7   8   9

Scharoun; but I can see no good deriving from an interference with his intentions at this point. And, therefore, I am of the opinion that the 'Kulturforum', so far as possible, should be completed according to Scharoun's idea, with the central residential building which he intended and the axis from the Matthäikirche to a *rondell* on the Bellevuestraße which is an extremely important part of his proposals (7).

Also, though I can just *begin* to understand why Scharoun chose to use the Staatsbibliothek so as to block the route of Potsdamer Straße, I can scarcely believe that he had in mind any six lane highway which would fatally separate this Staatsbibliothek from the Philharmonie and from Mies van der Rohe's Nationalgalerie on the other side. Scharoun's concept was evidently a version of the Museumsinsel, of that cultural complex which, across the Lustgarten, not so long ago faced the Stadtschloß. Which is to intimate that, in default of a better, the least controversial policy in this territory is to accept Scharoun and to press for the Kulturforum as he presumably intended it to be – traffic-free except for local access.

2 The Landwehrkanal is a major asset in the area of the city which the *Experten* were assembled to hear about and to discuss; and, quite rapidly, one became convinced that it is the *principal* asset. For what *else is* there to compare with it?

So one believes that the Landwehrkanal is an important and idiosyncratic component of the *idea* of the city; and one also believes that it is 'very special' and much loved. Further, one has noticed that, of its nature, it is equipped with a pronounced *genius loci*. Potentially, it is a linear collection of picturesque episodes; and, if the buildings along its bank are by no means of the quality of Amsterdam (or anything like it), still, they often comprise highly respectable *ensembles* and, in general, must be considered very much worthy of conservation.

For reasons such as these, the Landwehrkanal surely deserves – and will surely reward – the most sensitive attention. Potentially, it is rich in surprises; and, as one of the few remaining urban episodes which approach the intimate-spectacular, this potential should cer-

tainly be augmented. For the Landwehrkanal presumes a close relationship (perhaps an almost Chinese involvement); and, if along with the late Louis Kahn, one thinks it possible to speak about 'what something wants to become', then one might be tempted to suggest that the most appropriate destiny of this waterway is that of somewhat reserved *enclave*, highly accessible but a little private, by no means – in any accepted sense – a park, but still a place of recreation and, sometimes, meditation.

To me, it seems that many persons spoke to this effect; and it even seems that, maybe, there is something of a consensus of opinion that the Landwehrkanal, during most of its length, should become a place a little difficult of vehicular access and should never be degraded to the status of a high speed west-east artery.

To repeat: a linear sequence which requires the most intelligent and careful response.

To observe: if the Landwehrkanal is not to be a major artery, a better access to Kochstraße becomes of even greater importance.

3 The Potsdam and Anhalt Railway Stations are two sites protruding into the area which was initially exposed to the attention of the *Experten* from a context which the 'preferred' maps did not reveal; and, personally, I am enormously indebted to the presentation of Professor Nagel for his revelation of the southern hinterland of this enormous, former railroad complex. Indeed, while Professor Nagel spoke, I myself was vividly reminded of that statement of the Abbé Laugier that he who can design a park can design a city. For, from all this huge territory (involving Gneisenaustraße and Bülowstraße, with also points further south), does there not exist the very great potential both for a park and an entry such as no other European city possesses? (8)

So, I am thinking neither of an *Autobahn* nor a *boulevard* but of a *parkway,* of a medium speed drive within a landscape from which both close and distant views of buildings may be available. Now the concept *parkway,* I suspect, is not fully understood in Berlin; and, therefore, I feel obliged to enlarge upon it. The concept *parkway* was, probably, an invention of Frederick Law Olmsted; and, as an idea, it

has probably existed within the United States for approximately a hundred years. In Boston, it is represented by the Fenway; in New York, by Riverside Drive and by the approaches to the city via the Merritt and Palisades Parkways; and, in Houston, the same strategy is illustrated by Memorial Drive.

To repeat: the *parkway* is not high speed. It is, rather, a *corso* or a *passeggiata* for the automobile; and, as an idea, it is evidently related to late 19th-century fantasies about the movement of carriages. But, for these reasons, should it be any less accessible to us? And I think not. For the *parkway* – apart from its intrinsic amenity – is also a mediation between two important interests – the ecology lobby and *the move vehicles quicker enthusiasm.*

But to qualify these remarks: though one thinks of the *parkway* as an American invention, this cannot be wholly true – since, already in the 1860s, it does occur in Florence. For, in the days of *Firenze Capitale,* what else are Poggi's two elegant drives up to Piazzale Michelangelo – the extended drive from Porta Romana and the more compacted ascent from the river – if they are not to be regarded as *parkways*? And, therefore, with the great possibilities of a *parkway* in mind, I am more than a little surprised that IBA proposes to leave the site of the Anhalt railway station vacant and *then* indicates a building over the Potsdam railway station site.

Simply, I would have imagined that this was contrary to common sense. The *Experten* were told (I do not know on what authority) that 60,000 vehicles travel through this area every day; and, therefore, to compound this problem, with what amounts to a restoration of an earlier distribution of streets (in the case of Potsdamer Straße already interrupted by Scharoun), can only appear to be an ill-advised strategy.

4 A Future Symbolic Access to Leipziger Straße is surely a polemical and a conciliatory gesture which West Berlin *must* make. It would be a representational gesture; and, in this area, its building would be equivalent to a symbolic version of the Brandenburg Gate. It would be a gesture which revealed *the potential of communication.* Nor need it be elaborate. It could be no more than a hotel, an apartment

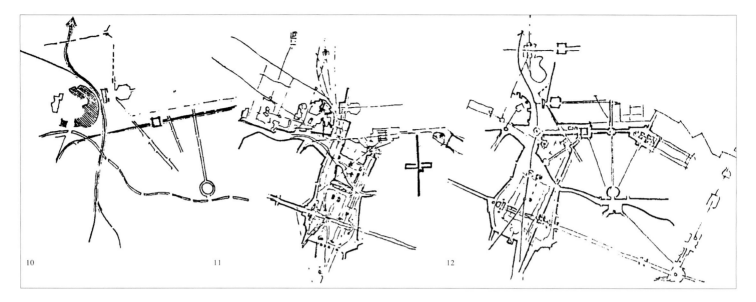

10   11   12

house or an office building; but it *could* be arranged – with a *little* rhetoric, to appear as a city gate. So why not?

5 *Some Improved Access to Kochstraße* which I also associate with a destination for Potsdamer Straße remains a topic about which I still continue to think. That is: if the associations of the Prinz-Albrecht-Palais are not allowed to become obsessive, then could not Potsdamer Straße and Kochstraße be seen as connected? (9)

6 *A Location for the Tempodrom*[1] *should not* be a problem. For, without dismay, could not the Tempodrom be placed to points either north or south of its present situation?

7 *The Ease of North-South Vehicular Move*ment is surely a major problem in this area, which is a part of what one might call the north-south corridor; and it is as a part of this corridor (as I have already said) that I feel it vital to retain the site of the Potsdam railway station as an open space connected to a larger park, further south, on the site of the former railroad yards (10, 11, 12).

Such a park, which would relieve the density of Kreuzberg and Schoneberg (so often a subject of discussion), might be intersected by the line of Gneisenau- and Bülowstraße and, somewhere in the middle of it, one might then expect to find a version of that Waterlooplatz which was originally projected for this terrain.

So the perimeters of this park are not, immediately, easy to imagine; but one does conceive that, surrounding it, there might be the equivalent of the Nash terraces which, in London, comprise the enclosure of Regent's Park; and then, projecting into this park from the north, attached to existing urban fabric, but also accessible from the 'Waterlooplatz', one might also think about the possibility of that new Rathaus (town hall) for Berlin which is often said to be so necessary.

But, meanwhile, to return to the *parkway*. It is to be thought about as travelling through this Potsdamer-Anhalter Park (not to its detriment), as moving through the site of the Potsdam railway station, as swirling around the Potsdam Gate, as extensively screened from the 'Kul-

turforum', to cross the Tiergarten as a sunken road (the image is here derived from Olmsted's sunken transverse roads in Central Park, New York), to arrive in a reconstructed version of the former Alsenplatz which might act to give the Reichstag something of the built support which it so badly needs.

So, from there on, one imagines the *parkway* (or the north-south corridor) leading on in the general direction of Tegel. But not to make comments upon unknown terrain. For one now wishes to return to the Tiergarten and to a sequence of north-south 'decorations' which might be considered auxiliary to the idea of north-south corridor.

So *can* one think about the Russian monument, at the intersection of Charlottenburger Chaussee and Siegesallee, as something in any way positive? And I say this for deliberate reasons. Meaning that the Russian monument is a useful component of the scene which I propose. For why could one not imagine the reconstitution of the Siegesallee as a canal? And, beyond this point, I will say nothing further except to suggest that, in terms of the north-south corridor, which it *must* address, the city of Berlin is presented with a major problem, available to elegant solution, with which the city has obligation to be concerned.

So, to repeat, these remarks are *not* addressed to IBA. They are addressed to the city; and, with these remarks made, I am suggesting that the city should sponsor a competition for the north-south corridor.

II The IBA Proposals as an Exhibition

It has been traditional that an important exhibition be something segregated from the fabric of the city. Such were the buildings for London 1851, Paris 1867, and Paris 1889. After Chicago 1893, it became practice that an exhibition might suggest *the model for a city*; but, all the same, this was a model which could in no way be contaminated by any intercourse with the existing city in which it might be located. The model city was to be framed, isolated (preferably by trees) from any local, empirical infringement; and this is a general exhibition strategy which seems to have persisted more or less down to our own day. The ideal city is to be something aloof and critical; it is to be

something *au dessus de la melée,* it is to be Weißenhof-Siedlung or Hansaviertel, and, in choosing to discard this almost one hundred year old tradition, IBA surely deserves the most prolonged applause. For, while the concept of *exhibition as special enclave* (exhibition as campus) was, for a long time, productive of stimulating results, it now begins to seem that it did serve to promote unnecessary abstraction – the abstraction of Paris 1900 no less than the abstraction of the Hansaviertel.

So, IBA has abandoned the high pedestal on which former promoters of exhibitions habitually placed themselves. It has chosen to embroil itself with the existing city in all its empirical density; and this conscientious and lucid decision must be emphasised because, quite often, it seems not to be observed. But, to repeat: with the idea of an unsegregated exhibition, the parts of which are to be found scattered around the city, IBA has propounded a significant novelty – an innovation which, in some parts of the world, is already acclaimed, and an innovation which promises to provide a model which no future promoters of exhibitions will be able to ignore. For it is such a model that the Berlin Building Exhibition of 1984 *will* present; and, while IBA is, ostensibly, addressing itself to problems which are local, in reality these problems are world-wide and among the more pressing architectural issues of today.

I am here thinking of the double disasters of war and of modern architecture which have both been inflicted upon the European city within the last 40 years and which (almost looking like the effect of bombs) have also been inflicted upon the American city – in terms of the slightly contrary designations of 'free enterprise' and 'urban renewal'. For the joint action of *war and modern architecture* has been so fundamentally destructive that society now reels under their impact; and, if Berlin still remains the most damaged city then, correspondingly, it is – perhaps – to Berlin that the world looks for some solution.

So it is in this context of anticipation that I would like to place Berlin 1984; but, sitting around as I have done, listening for five, long days, mostly to 'protest' disguised as 'participation', I have also wondered why the programme and the strategy of IBA is not more evident and more visible. Indeed, what I have heard has often caused me to think about London 1851; and, while thinking along these lines, for the predicament of IBA I have frequently substituted the position of Albert of Saxe-Coburg-Gotha in 1849-50. For Prince Albert, promoting the Crystal Palace, was equally under attack. The whole project seemed strange, bizarre, and foreign; and, on this occasion, the objections came from the conservatives with their endless refrain of: *this will never, never do.*

But then the triumphant inauguration of the Crystal Palace and Queen Victoria's effusive remarks:

> The sight as we came to the centre where the steps and chair (on which I did *not* sit) was placed, facing the beautiful crystal fountain, was magic and impressive. The tremendous cheering, the joy expressed in every face – the vastness of the building – the sound of the organ – and my beloved husband, the creator of this peace festival 'uniting the industry and the art of all the nations of the earth', all this was indeed moving, and a day to live forever. God bless my dearest Albert, and my dear country, which has shown itself so great today.

Victoria's English remarks are irrepressibly Biedermeier; but, if the situation, nowadays, is somewhat different, is it for all that so very different? IBA is not exactly the consort of Queen Victoria, nor are the professional 'participators' of West Berlin exactly the same as the English conservatives of the mid-19th century. But something of similarity remains; and how is one to describe it? Or should one try?

I myself do not propose to try. I propose, instead, to comment upon the abundance of IBA's problems and firstly, upon a problem of communication.

The enmeshing of the concepts *city plan* and *exhibition* is not new; but the enmeshing of these concepts *within the context of the existing city* is so innovative that the promise of a *great exhibition in Berlin* has come to be obscured. It seems to me that the 'participators' (and here I think, again, of the critics of Prince Albert) have addressed themselves to almost every other topic except this one which is so pressing and immediate. An exhibition, apart from its didactic purposes and apart from its values as paradigm, is also an occasion of public festivity – of fireworks, balloon ascents, acrobatics dramatics, subsidiary exhibitions, convergence of admiring foreigners, symposia, spectacular concerts, and all the traditional apparatus which it is so easy to imagine. But none of this – all so necessary for any major international event – has ever intruded itself as an issue for discussion; and I suggest that this

inhibition of *any* thought about pleasure (whether vulgar or refined) begins to imply serious consequences.

So, is this inhibition the effect of a socio-economic climate or is it something endemic to the city? And, again, these are questions to which I cannot attempt to respond. I notice, instead, that the topic *exemplary exhibition of historical and international significance* does threaten to become reduced to a very local and provincial affair – and mostly an affair of passion related to the intimate format of social housing.

Which remarks may now allow me to suggest that, perhaps, IBA has been too defensive and has not sufficiently loudly advertised what one presumes to be its *dual* mission. By which I mean that it is high time that the topic *model housing* should cease to occupy the centre of attention and that the topic *exhibition* should be allowed to assume the prominence which it deserves. Because, though project after project may be separately discussed and analysed, obviously and in the end, it is the *ensemble* of these projects which is going to count.

But, here again, IBA runs into problems which are scarcely of its own making. For how to make an exhibition, let alone the model for a city, out of nothing else but social housing? And, if social housing (or, indeed, any kind of housing) is to be inflated to bear such a burden, is not this to defeat its purpose which is, partly at least, to serve as background for more public urban phenomena? And, just what about *these*?

I understand exceptionally little of IBA's finances, though I am led to believe that there is little available for what should be considered *the essentials of a great city*; and, by *the essentials*, I understand not simply the details of the *res privata* but, also, the celebration of the *res publica* without which the extended affairs of the *res privata* are apt to become very little more than fatiguing. And the *res publica,* or so I assume, is *not* something to be represented by an infinite multiplication of *kindergarten* and retreats for battered women.

Serious and necessary, of course, these must be; but an appropriate expression of the public

realm, I assume, will absorb and accommodate such details as these. However, with such a remark made, in West Berlin, apart from the still incomplete 'Kulturforum' what attempts have there ever been made to project any images related to notions of the state, of the city, of society in general? I think of the equivalent of such pieces of urban furniture as, in London, the screen at Hyde Park Corner, in Paris of the *chevaux de Marly,* in Munich of he Propyläen, here of the Brandenburg Gate – all of them, judged by the criteria of the scientific and analytical mind, patently superfluous; but, all of them, intimately related to the *idea* and the *myth* of the cities where they are to be found. And is it not the absence of such reassuring fragments of urban theatre which is, at least, *one* of the causes of that somewhat interminable theatre of 'participation' which it has been part of my recent education to have observed? For, in default of a built and reliable urban theatre, of a theatre equipped with traditions and style, are we not endlessly obliged to improvise the public realm, to invent it and to re-invent it, via a series of personal and dramatic interventions? *I am speaking in public and, therefore, the public realm exists... ?*

Whether this is good or bad, I don't know. It expands debate; it contributes to vivacity; but I am, also, compelled to doubt whether it contributes to achievement. For, in the absence of a *built* public realm – that convergence of fantasy, idea, and myth – it seems that consensus, the necessary basis of *any* achievement, is impossible. And, therefore, I think yet again about the problems of IBA.

IBA is being expected to do too much with too little. And, if IBA's proposals may frequently appear to be a little stretched and a little strained, this is the cause. It is the absence of the public realm. For, as a consequence of the pragmatic state of mind and the double inheritance of both war and modern architecture, the concept of the public realm disappeared. The idea became *Existenzminimum*; and, as a result, the *res publica* became reduced to little more than a retarded and unconvincing display of diminished Baroque and neo-classical precedent. Which is to designate a universal problem and, more particularly, a problem of IBA, attempting to transform the *res privata* into something which it can never be. We have talked about kitchens and bathrooms; but have we *ever* talked – been *allowed* to talk – about the equivalent of the Brandenburg Gate? And to ask this question, is to illustrate the greatest problem confronting Berlin 1984 (13).

Note

1 The Tempodrom is an alternative organisation for the performing arts housed within a marquee during summertime and located at the vacant site of the former Potsdam railway station.

13

ROB KRIER, THE ARCHITECT'S REINTERPRETATION, RESIDENTIAL AND OFFICE BLOCK, HAMBURG ALTONA-NORD, 1978

TEN THESES ON ARCHITECTURE
ROB KRIER

The following guidelines have been valid ever since man began to plan buildings rationally and aspired to architecture as an aesthetic product – in other words, to create buildings that are more than just an answer to programmatic problems.

Function, Construction and Form
are factors of equal significance and jointly determine architecture. No single factor should dominate.

Function and Construction
are 'useful' elements whose rules always need to be acknowledged as a matter of course. However, a building can only be raised to the status of architecture through the additional fulfilment of aesthetic requirements.

The Fulfilment of Aesthetic Requirements
depends on the following factors: Proportion, Structure, Material and colour, and their artistic interpretation.

Aesthetics
The sense of beauty in architecture is rooted in man's desire to bestow everyday objects with poetic content that will convey the spirit of his epoch to future generations. ('. . . it is useful, because it is beautiful . . .' *A de Saint-Exupéry*)

Geometry
is the basis for all forms of architectural expression. As organised geometry, architecture draws its strength from opposing rather than adopting the laws of nature. Geometry is the creation of man.

Scale
in architecture is not solely determined by technical, structural and economic factors; the dimensions of the human body as well as man's perceptions, behavioural patterns and emotions must also be taken into consideration.

Architecture in the City
All new planning should submit to the overall order of the city. Its form should respond to existing spatial patterns.

The Urban Space
as a concept has been ignored in 20th-century town planning. Our new cities are a conglomeration of free-standing buildings. Five thousand years of city planning history has taught us that the complex matrixes of streets and squares are successful communication networks and means of identification and orientation. Traditional concepts of urban space are still valid today.

History
The proper evaluation of our historical inheritance crystallises our understanding of the past and teaches us how to plan for the future.

The Architect's Responsibilities
The architect alone is responsible for what leaves his drawing-board and carries his signature. No politician or developer will bear the architect's cultural guilt for a botched environment. Our universities are responsible for preparing the next generation of architects for this almost insuperable ethical and moral duty.

No one of these factors must be neglected or over-emphasised during the design process. A one-sided solution would result in a 'deformed' architecture. However, it can be the architect's intention – depending on the problem and specific situation – deliberately to over-emphasise a certain form to create a special effect. Recent architectural history bears witness to a multitude of tendencies that are a result of far too narrow a vision: eg Functionalism, Constructivism, Formalism, New Brutalism etc.
I work from the principle that the harmony of form, function and construction leads to the right solution. Since the function and construction of a building are always visible, the built form is obviously inseparable from them and is characterised by mutual dependencies and influences.
There is a wealth of formal possibilities that – whilst meeting functional and constructional requirements – can be composed into architectural form. The true form of a building is the sum of its perceivable elements. In addition, colours, surface textures, materials, light and the quality of technical details play an enormously important role.

MOUNT AIRY, VIRGINIA, SITE PLAN, 1758

THE HOUSE AS THE CITY
JAQUELIN T ROBERTSON

FITZ HUGH LANE, ENTRANCE OF SOAMES SOUND FROM SOUTHWEST HARBOUR, 1852

Our view of the City and of Nature have, for some time, intrigued and frustrated me.[1] That there was, and is, an American order of things different from that of Europe, I know. But precisely what these differences are I am less clear about. While much has been written about the history of American towns, it seems to me that we are still having a hard time with our urban genealogy, both real and

mythical, and that in order to better understand what we want our towns and cities and countrysides to be, we need to look more closely at the kinds of early towns we have built and idealised. For I am convinced that in the initial residential *esquisse* lie truths and convictions in which we still believe . . . around which we can continue to fashion strategies for the development of our precious continent.

To advance the discourse, I have put forward below an over-simplified snapshot view of certain Ideal American Cities; a sustaining mythology, if you will, which I believe to be relevant today. It is not, in any sense, a complete picture nor does it deal with the evolution of the commercial/manufacturing town, so important in other ways, to our urban history.[2] Nonetheless, certain recognitions seem inescapable.

I am convinced that the fact (and fiction) of the continent – its presence, size, variety, mystery, and vacuum – has shaped, to an exaggerated degree, our attitudes of habitat in what was literally a new world; specifically, that in the dialogue between architecture and urbanism, which was shaped here by an unusual dynamic of accelerated *growth* and *emptiness*, we became more concerned with the *individual* house, the part, than with the *communal* city – giving to it our civic allegiance and marshalling our *polis* and our institutional buildings around it. And in a land of great distances, travel and the travel machine were given

exaggerated significance.

It is not that Americans were anti-urban, but that the cities they sought and imagined were different. Very simply, their houses *were* their cities . . . which accounts for much of what is right, and wrong, today in contemporary urbanism.

The Little House on the Prairie
One does not look initially to either Texas or television for a better understanding of American urbanism. Yet in the imagery of the long-running show *Dallas,* the mythology value system associated with two of our quintessential settings – the single-family house and the high-rise office tower are given telling expression. These American places are two of the central characters – along with JR, Miss Ellie, Bobby, Ellen, and the rest – that help determine the symbolic terrain in one of our culture's more enduring popular landscapes. Like the stereotypes in a Medieval morality play, or a Western, the skyscraper and the house wear values on their sleeve, and say as much about the way Americans idealise their cities, and their communal ideals, as most texts on American urban history.

Recall, for a moment, the opening shots. The camera pans in from the air – your basic bird's-eye view now mechanised and moving – over a sinuous network of highspeed roadways to a cluster of new towers, growing out of a pile of indistinguishable, lower background stuff – the visual rubble of the 'old' city. The aerie is clearly a Magical Kingdom of thrust, hustle, excitement, and, for the lucky few, gold. 'Big-D' – the emblematic high-place of Big Deal – glimmering, abstract, minimalist; a place of surfaces, free of the nagging incidents of life and human detail.

As seen from the air, or looking up from the ground, these heights appear first as daunting; they must be scaled, wrested, won if one is to experience the thrill of risk and reward. At the same time, they are obtainable, purchasable, as in a catalogue ready for shipment. (There is the reassuring feeling that this now-familiar international skyline, like the four-square Roman camp, is our Empire's most legitimate stamp.)

Of course, The City of Dallas, presented here in aerial strike sequence, is not a specific place, in Texas, but rather the generic locus of all the drives and promises of our peculiarly dynamic (and richly empty) consumer civilisation. We are addicted to its siren call, continue to build it and worship at its secular altars. Yet, in some fundamental way, we have not yet given it our final (*Good Housekeeping*) seal of approval . . . or our loyalty. In this version of an ageless morality play, the character of the City, while undeniably seductive, is also tainted; symbolic of some of the darker traits of human character: greed, lust, ambition, ruthlessness, betrayal.

But we are not given time to think about this in these opening thematic montages; for no sooner do we start to try to pick out specific and identifiable features in the face of the City, than the camera cuts away to another world. We are now at a much lower level of attack (closer to the face of the continent) – gliding in across a vast green lawn – a domesticated prairie unsullied by urban detritus, towards a white, porticoed, gabled . . . house. South Fork is a large cabin, the home of a proud, individualistic, modern (typical but rich) American Frontier Family. (The name and essential architectural iconography suggests kinship with older Colonial orders, to a legitimate and sustaining past somewhere back East; but the unframed horizontal plane of the setting, as in so many 19th-century paintings, is clearly of the great heartland.) Again, as before, we have no trouble identifying the character of the house or its implied value system. If Dallas, the city of disembodied towers, is a secular precinct, surely this homestead is one of our very few sacred places. South Fork stands as a retreat from the moral ambiguities of urban life, detoxified, as it were, of the poisons of the City of Commerce. The single-family house, standing alone on its own piece of ground surrounded by nature, is the centre of gravity of American sensibility. We feel grounded here as we have never felt downtown.

The seemingly contradictory yet coexistent nature of these two quite different settings of American life, presented here in rapid sequence, do not seem to trouble us . . . perhaps because they give us two kinds of moral arenas in which to operate, allowing for convenient double standards. (Europeans, not surprisingly, are as addicted to *Dallas*, the contemporary Western, as we, appreciating perhaps even more than we, the clear demarcation of idealised worlds, where two building types say most of what there is to say.) What is arresting about the contrasts in these opening scenes is that they have nothing to do with race, or political ideology, with real poverty or social upheaval, or even environmental pollution. No, *Dallas* sets up a caricatured backdrop for American life – as if *all* Americans aspired to, and will ultimately inhabit, this world — in which obvious physical aspects represent more subtle, but less well understood, ethical and emotional surroundings; a McLuhanesque variation in which the setting is the message, and style, the content. Like plywood veneer, all the depth there is is on the surface. The producers of *Dallas* have grasped the totemic power of our two most important building types and, in their juxtaposition of the house and the skyscraper, have offered

up, yet again, one of the simplest truths of American identity: that our houses are not only the only reliable places of anchorage on the sea of our vast continent, but symbolically, the first building block of our loosely-structured and changing communities; and that for us, the City, devoid of these single houses, can never be our *home* – no matter what other riches it offers us.

Without stretching this analogy from popular culture too far, it is worth lingering, if only a moment longer, on this presentation of the American stage of life.

The Ewings' homestead is smallish, and like Monticello, one-storey in appearance. The house is white and made of wood, a natural material. It is surrounded by grass, with a long straight drive leading to the front door and a fenced entrance court – big enough to dock a flotilla of opulent cars and trucks. The private yard is differentiated from the more public world of the road and from the rolling prairie, by fences – another essential American set piece. Somewhere to the side (so as not to be too obvious) is the pool, tennis court, breakfast terrace with umbrella – that miniaturised country club now so much a requirement of domestic luxury. The working outbuildings of the ranch – the outskirts of our city – are at a distance from the main house, an undefined edge and link to the fabled frontier. Importantly, South Fork is the domain of the wise and kindly matriarch, Miss Ellie, the Good Witch of the play, whose powers, as long as she is at home, are more than a match for those of the wily J R, less menacing and potent in his own back yard. Most of the camera work around South Fork puts the characters against the friendly backdrop of small-scale architecture and outside terraces, occasionally panning, as if seeking sustenance, to sweeping panoramas of land – a part of the continent, which the story implies, is the Ewings' (and every American's) birthright. This tamed landscape only becomes unfriendly when others want it (Indians and home-steaders having been replaced by poaching oil barons, and real estate speculators).

In contrast, downtown; the other place – where the men go each morning after their hearty breakfast with the family, to make deals, drink whiskey (each office scene in 'Dallas' seems to open with a move to the bar) and carry on various *liasons dangereuses*– is a kind of ethical no-man's land where everyone is on the move and on guard. Clearly, the City is where we can encounter fortune, failure, and moral laxity. Its lower regions – streets, sidewalks, plazas – are treated fleetingly; intended primarily to bring one to the foot of the great monoliths. Here the camera slides lovingly up scaleless (and scaly) walls to the abode of the archangels. In the high towers above God's prairie with its white homes, all moral codes are cast down (thus most illicit sex takes place in apartments, not houses); this is JR's world of power and intrigue, sell-out and betrayal. And here his satanic appeal is Miltonesque. There's no end to the trouble that can be planned from on high in Dallas.

Why is it that this popular television serial posits a moral landscape of high and low, pitting the mysterious and cosy powers of the vernacular white house against the legion forces of a modernistic netherworld of towers? And why are the same visual themes so pervasive in the rival serial, *Dynasty*, where Joan Collins, the seductive bitch/witch, works *and* lives high above the ground? Why this struggle between high and low, between the house and the city in American culture?

That we have no trouble in drawing or recognising such a landscape in which good and evil, safety and threat, fidelity and betrayal are so clearly associated with certain building types, says much about the continued mythic setting of American urbanism, and helps suggest why our ideal cities, essentially about the freestanding house, are different from those of other cultures.

Ideal New World Villages

Settlers came to North America for a variety of reasons, but among them was a belief that in the New World they would be able to establish new kinds of free communities which would be different from the cities they'd left behind. But the *ideal* communities would have to come later; one had first to survive and multiply.

Our earliest settlements were clusters of huts near water or a path – the escape/supply routes – with little else in the way of companions, other than our travel machines and nature. Because the land was so large and and our number so few, the setting and lifestyle of the camp, with its proliferation of small buildings, became a way of life over our 400-year nomadic history, even up until today, and can be said to be imprinted on our psyche. The hut, cabin, house, shack and trailer became, during the course of our slow trek across the continent, institutionalised set-pieces of an extended impermanency with the open road, river or harbour the major connecting public thread. Loneliness, emptiness and the need to be on the move have been, from the start, ever-present aspects of our urban sensibility. The iconography and feeling of these early archetypal outpost cities is tellingly presented in Fitz Hugh Lane's *Entrance of Soames Sound from Southwest Harbor* – a serene yet highly charged view of life at the edge. Mt Desert Island, like a piece of the continent's backbone, stakes out the horizon and is a sentinel reminder of the limits – the city limits – of civilisation in this part of the new world. (This same bread loaf, or headland, shape pushes itself up again and again through the surface of 19th-century canvases like a beaching sperm whale – in Church, and Gifford, and Kensett, and Heade. It is a part of the skeleton and flesh of the giant Land on whose body we have settled. Lacking the exaggerated drama and scale of Beirstadt's towering Western peaks, its low silhouette is nonetheless a dormant, bony, aboriginal presence which frames and establishes the limits of our activity here and our relative distance from infinity – marking off *our* piece of the continent from all the rest out there, from what beckons but is beyond us. It stands also as a reminder of the forces, obligations, and mores of Nature, and remains as a powerfully retained image on the retina of our perception. For me, at least, these outcroppings and long rounded hills are seminal to notions of urban location and composition in North America – from Chattanooga to Newport, Charlottesville to New Haven. Lookout Mountain, Beacon Rock, Lewis and Buck Mountains, and East Rock are as essential to the design of their fledgling cities as any buildings or streets. They are, in a palpable way, our real continental companions. And, because they represent our greatest asset and gift, yet do not *belong* to us, they are as *sacred* as our own Colonial graveyards. If Vincent Scully is correct, and I believe he is, then North America set out equally clear markers as did Greece – clues which did not escape Jefferson, and other founders of our early settlements.[3]

At the centre of Lane's *Soames Sound* composition lies a lucid and immutable anchorage – the ultimate archaic parking lot where one of our great magical travel machines sleeps: immaculate, white-masted, powerfully delicate, beautiful. Visually, it is a surrogate church to this primitive cluster of small shacks and few men. Yet, also, we know that it is ready to fly away, our umbilical cord, back to an outside world. With uncanny prescience, Lane catches our wonder at the resolving promise of travel and escape and our love for the detail of our travel machines (on which we have lavished more attention than on any of the nearby buildings). The surrounding cityscape here, is of marginal interest, the harbour being the true *agora* of this vernacular settlement, and its resident sea chariot, the town's most cherished possession and artifact. Yet one is also drawn in the canvas to the notion of a clean, unencumbered life (no

'entangling alliances'); to the idea of staying in Arcadia as well as having the freedom to fly away from it.

Our earliest villages and towns then were made up of individual houses, freestanding on their own piece of raw land, in which an essential juxtaposition was of small buildings set against an enormous panorama of Nature and striking natural phenomena. The front door faced the horizon; the house was against the route (be it path, road, river or harbour) which led on to, or back from, some other place; and the travel machine was at centre stage – all bespeaking the fundamental transiency of our situation. Later, after we had become more confident in our new home, these features of composition were more subtly digested and rendered; and became *canonised* in what I have chosen to identify as ideal city villages.

Plantation and Farming Villages

The plantation villages in the South and the farming/fishing communities of New England were our first steps towards a more established urban building pattern. In the tidewater of the Virginia Colony the towns were large houses and their surrounding precinct of scattered outbuildings, dependencies, gardens, fields and yards. Here were organised education, defense, entertainment, animal husbandry, agriculture and the production of goods. In the house one was born, baptised, educated, trained, apprenticed and married. It was in the precinct of the home that one raised one's children, met one's fellow settlers; lived, planned, and partied with relatives and friends; received and harbored travellers; worked in one's fields; shaped politics and meted out justice (or injustice); fought, aged and died. One set out from and came back to one's house as if to one's city. It was the very centre of one's loyalty, and the vessel of one's values. Whether William Byrd's grand brick Georgian river plantation, Westover, or William Howard Payne's shingled saltbox, Home Sweet Home, the single-family house was the centre of life for early Americans. In New England, there were other similar houses nearby, as well as communal buildings and spaces; nonetheless, the house was *the* essential urban component, expressive of the individual life.

A French tutor coming up the James River and seeing Westover for the first time, rising up, high-chimneyed, out of the forests, exclaimed that he had encountered his first American City. The great house was indeed an elegant if provincial reminder of European culture fronting a wilderness river highway. If one mounts that lawn today and passes through the screen of giant tulip poplars ('the 12 apostles') to the finely-wrought, pedimented front door, one can experience, for a moment, with stunning recognition, the suspended balance of our two worlds, which like opposite magnetic poles have given our culture its peculiar dual vanishing points. Facing the door one sees all the appurtenances of Anglo-European culture. The house, especially the broach-like pediment, is decked out in imported finery and seems to say 'I am someone who counts; someone of lineage and connections; I *come from somewhere* . . .' And you know that to enter is to go back to something known; Westover's facade is the face of continuity with the past.

And then one turns 180 degrees, and faces back across the lawn and river, to an endless, open, unbuilt horizon . . . to the 'fresh, green breast of the new world' that 'flowered once for Dutch sailors' eyes'.[4] And one gasps inwardly at the *nothingness* that was there for us; the vast emptiness and promise of our arcadia. Europe and the frontier, the house and the continent, meeting on our own doorstep, are two powerful draws on allegiance, interests and energies. And this pairing of open and closed axes reoccurs in various forms in our building patterns, again and again, and is profoundly important to how we have conceived and put down our imprint.

231

The river at Westover was the supply line to one's own kind. Books, dresses, china and furniture came in; tobacco went out. Tidewater planters lived off its connecting thread and were part of an international economy. They went to England to school, to barter, and often to marry; they came back to work and prosper: a dual life.

As the plantation villages became more sophisticated, so also became the layout of their extended realm. At Mount Airy (1758), one of the first great Georgian/Palladian houses in the colonies (situated on a hill above the Chikahominy River), one encounters a formal garden plan which can also be read as a map of the city. There is a central public square in front of a palace, street/paths, and block/planting beds, city walls and gates – a pattern of organised spaces set down not just for gardening and ostentatious show, but, perhaps unconsciously, as a miniature surrogate for places of assembly in the cities left behind. Like the ornamented facade of Westover, Mount Airy's garden is an assertive call in the wilderness to the parent culture . . . and the Gods: 'I am here. See. I have marked the ground with our sign. Do not overlook or foresake me!' (This attempt to give exaggerated presence – either by giving them miniature city plan

America an exaggerated significance, starting as a necessity but becoming, over time, a national preoccupation. Dealing with distance meant organising our settlements, our schedules, and much of our inventive genius on all aspects of travel and travel machinery. And it is not coincidental that some of our most refined artifacts, from the Clipper ship to the F-16, reflect this obsession.

The extended precincts of Westover and Mount Airy can be seen then as miniature surrogate towns. Their lawns, paths, service yards, paddocks, walled gardens, and scattered dependencies are the DNA in our genetic city code; the routes connecting them a crude national skeleton.

If these two plantation precincts were both private and at the same time part of an imagined international public realm, the village green at East Hampton was more limited, local and communal. Here small wooden houses face a public space around which are also located a church, a meeting house, a windmill (part of the local public infrastructure system), and a graveyard. Behind the houses are private farms (our first backyards) which stretch in thin bacon strips of land back to the ocean. New Englanders, perhaps because they are largely

L TO R: SHIRWOOD FOREST, CHARLES CITY, VIRGINIA; GEORGE WYTHE HOUSE, WILLIAMSBURG, VIRGINIA

settings or through the use of a classical language which is often overscaled – to what, in fact, were relatively tiny buildings in a vast continental landscape, is a touching and reoccurring aspect of our ongoing efforts to make our mark on the new world. Jefferson, in particular, both in his siting and overscaling of certain details – in Richmond on Capitol Hill, at Monticello, Barboursville, Farmington, and Edgemont, and finally at the University of Virginia – seems intent upon drawing the Gods' and the Ancients' attention to his distant wilderness endeavours. The same can be said of Latrobe's United States Capitol, which, in early engravings, stands out monumentally against its surrounding Arcadia, reaffirming the timeless authority of the Classical Old World in the New.)

Since the plantation villages were separated from one another and from other colonial settlements, often by considerable distances, travel in the New World, not to mention travel back and forth to Europe, was a time-consuming activity, which became institutionalised. For early settlers, being on the road – or the river or high seas – whether for purposes of business, politics, exploration, or merely social intercourse, became a way of life. The travel machine and the route assumed in North

dissenters, even outcasts, tended to turn away from their European connection. Almost everything was here – and the structure of the town reflected more accurately their inward-turning sense of self-sufficiency. Low fences demarcated 'your' from 'their' space and one did not have to travel far to encounter one's neighbours. These little villages, where much was accomplished by joint agreement and effort, gave to New England a nascent sense of urbanity, however primitive, that the South never really achieved. (It also fostered a sense of local self-satisfaction and intolerance.) Later, of course, these same farming/fishing villages threw out an extensive net of international commerce over the world's shipping lanes which far exceeded that of the plantation villages. And whether in whaling, slaves or rum, New England fortunes remained on the rise long after the exchange economy of tobacco had begun to die. Yet in both cases it was the freestanding house which best symbolised the course of colonial life and individual fortune.

The Capitol Village
The most refined and clearly structured town plan of this early period was the Capitol Village of Williamsburg – the first of our

mixed-use, Main Street towns. The layout is deceptively simple, yet also rich, complex, and flexible. A wide east/west street (given appropriate importance by its name, the Duke of Gloucester), provides a spinal structure to the plan and is sensibly laid out along the ridge which separates the drainage basins of the York and the James Rivers, respectively. The street, however, is not open-ended (that was to come later), but plugged at each end by important institutions: to the east by the House of Burgesses, the seat of international government, a touchstone of the Empire; to the west by the College of William and Mary, the place wherein Colonials were transformed and sent out into the world. (Tellingly, the axis of the village passes directly through the college, from the confines of the city on the one side to the limitless frontier on the other. While one building ties us to our European past, the other opens a door to our future. Both are at the scale of large plantation houses, our equivalent of palaces.) A third large institutional building lies at the end of a wide north/south residential boulevard which marks the village's major cross-axis (the 'number one' corner of town): it is the Governor's Palace, the house of parent England, and has an extensive garden which, on occasions, hosts public events, ceremonies, and

reappears in our towns, a precursor to the longer and grander avenues which become the important residential addresses of leading colonial cities (Commonwealth Avenue in Boston, Monument Avenue in Richmond), and establishes the primacy of *the street of important houses* to our urbanism. The intersection of this landscaped way with the village main street is marked by a church, a common, a county court house (local versus international government) and a powderhorn, all practical modes of authority, recourse, and citizen self-defense; a pattern not difficult to read and with a commonly agreed-upon hierarchy.

But, of course, the most arresting feature of Williamsburg is not these institutional buoys but the corridor they mark. This is the real centre of the town: a wide mixed-use street of houses, shops, taverns, and light industrial service uses which can be appreciated both individually and collectively. Here on the Duke of Gloucester Street are small buildings of brick and timber, that stand free but close together on their own lots, that are similar, but *not* identical, in scale and architectural character, as in their front door stoops and uniform setbacks. While they advertise their various uses, they are all essentially variations of small single houses, which contrast a certain Sunday-dress formality

THOMAS JEFFERSON, UNIVERSITY OF VIRGINIA, *L TO R*: PAVILION X AND PAVILION IV

entertainments; the village's only formal park. Along the flanks of this up-market residential street live some of the colony's most influential citizens. Their houses, sometimes in brick, are pared-down versions of river plantations, the most important constituency for the Capitol Village.

One of the most paradigmatic of these first urban villas belonged to George Wythe, a leading lawyer of the Virginia colony who happened also to be Jefferson's patron and teacher (indeed it was Wythe's library that the young man from the piedmont up-country had his first exposure to Palladio and other seminal architectural treatises, an acknowledged leap forward for our country's most significant statesman/builder). At the Wythe House one encounters most of the characteristics of an emerging American urban order. The house – a shrunken version of the plantation house now come to town – is tied to the street system by a low permeable fence, which sets off the private yard from the public way, in this case a boulevard with a wide median in which there are large native trees planted (almost) regularly. Hitching posts (for travel machines – horses, coaches, wagons) and lamp-posts complete the inventory of necessary street furniture. It is a composite of urban design elements which

and communal regularity along their frontage, with highly irregular and varied private side and back yards well suited to the changing requirements and less formal activities of their users (as in the New England villages). The street itself is characterised by wide sidewalks, with large trees dividing the vehicular from the pedestrian rights-of-way, and acts as a linear park as well as a movement corridor and public forum – a wondrous place.

The gardens (which have been restored to a level of refinement and tidiness unknown in colonial times) form a world unto themselves, expressive of the idiosyncracy of individual American life. Taken together they are among our greatest achievements in urban landscape.[5] Scattered throughout their maze of domesticated nature are a progeny of vernacular outbuildings of all types – well house, smoke house, ice house, summer house – which have been brought in from the plantations to assist us in their daily tasks. These friendly anthropomorphic companions, like the giant overscaled chimneys of the buildings along the street, are at the same time part of the alphabet of an emerging architectural language and powerful totems of a virile, archaic period. They embody an accumulating knowledge and love of vernacular detailing and provide us with a variety of small elements with which we can later fashion a practical and humane cityscape.

A third kind of vernacular open space, characteristic of most American towns, appears in Williamsburg in the form of a shallow ravine system which interrupts the built pattern of yards and gardens as if to proclaim the easy coexistence of the continent and the city in our daily life. These green fingers are home to a great variety of wildlife and allow children and adults to experience nature in the heart of town in a way rarely found in Europe.

Thus, Williamsburg gives us a clear American order of things, elegantly canonising the format of our public buildings, streets, houses, trees, yards and natural terrain, a town pattern which can adapt and move westward. We have to go to Georgia to find a more complex city order, which can accommodate number and can expand without losing its structure.

The Urban Village

Savannah is, I believe, our ideal *urban* pattern. Founded in 1733 by Colonel Oglethorpe, on a high bluff overlooking a navigable, working river, it remains today the supreme achievement of

core. This produces a palette of mixed-use, semi-sufficient blocks which can be joined together like so many squares in an American quilt (our version of the Persian carpet garden plan); a cover which is theoretically infinitely expandable. (Sadly, when the original repetitious layout was abandoned after the Civil War, city structure and city quality were lost. There is nothing memorable about new Savannah!)

Oglethorpe's quilt of squares is not, however, relentless; it does not attempt to deal with the edge of the river bluff where use and topography require a change of pattern, but is drawn up to a long multi-level strip of land which acts as a zone of commercial transition between a working waterfront and the city above. The town's main commercial street, running parallel to the river along this seam, highlights a functional shift of the plan and provides appropriate sites for larger buildings. Within the linear precinct a number of practical problems are dealt with vertically, taking advantage of the three-storey grade change between river and bluff. At the bottom, goods which have come in by boat are unloaded and stored in the ground floor of long multipurpose structures; at a middle level they are sorted and put out for vehicular delivery into a suppressed service street which

L TO R: FACTORS WALK, SAVANNAH, GEORGIA; WILLIAMSBURG DEPENDENCY, VIRGINIA

American gridiron planning.[6] The layout, an amalgram of European models, is rational and healthy (more subtle and efficient in its organisation than Jefferson's checkerboard plan for Richmond), and allowed for an orderly and predictable expansion for over a hundred years. (I am reminded, when looking at Savannah's growth, of Kundera's comment that 'happiness is the longing for repetition.')[7] Savannah, unlike Williamsburg, is an aggregation of building blocks, or Wards, each with an open landscaped square at its centre which can be taken as a trapped piece of the continent. Its multi-directional pattern can expand easily through and around the exigencies of natural terrain and accommodate larger public precincts when required (for graveyards, public parks, ravines, and so on).

In the hierarchy, quality, clarity and practicality of its open space skeleton, Savannah is pre-eminent. Each block has its own internal local circulation system, including necessary service mews, and is bounded by city-wide streets, thus sorting out local from through traffic and more private from more public areas in the most direct (and cost-effective) way. Four public lots on the opposite sides of each square are given over to institutional use, while single houses, both grand and small, wrap the central open

runs like a moat along the upland face of the waterfront; at a third level, the grade of the city proper, are commercial frontages: offices, shops, banks, the cotton exchange which, in turn, serve as the ground floor for two to three storeys of supporting uses including inns, restaurants, and walk-up offices. This extraordinary, vertically integrated megastructure (called Factor's Walk), is one of the most sophisticated building complexes in the world; revealing of both the pragmatism and art of American urban design.

Adjacent to this high-activity area and similarly a part of the extended riverfront esplanade is Emmet Park, a composition of stunning simplicity and richness. Here one enters a double *allée* of live oaks, along two parallel walks which cut through a thick carpet of ground cover. Here one finds dappled shade, Spanish moss, elegant lamp standards; the city on one side, the river on the other; another model of how relatively easy it is to do simple things well. (In the mind's eye I cannot escape imagining how this same park would be designed today: tiresome changes of level and paving pattern; a disparate variety of materials, plants, shrubs, ornamental trees; aggressive metal equipment, trash bins, decorative lights, concrete pyramids, sunken sand pits,

DEMETRI PORPHYRIOS, BELVEDERE PARK FARM, ASCOT, 1990-

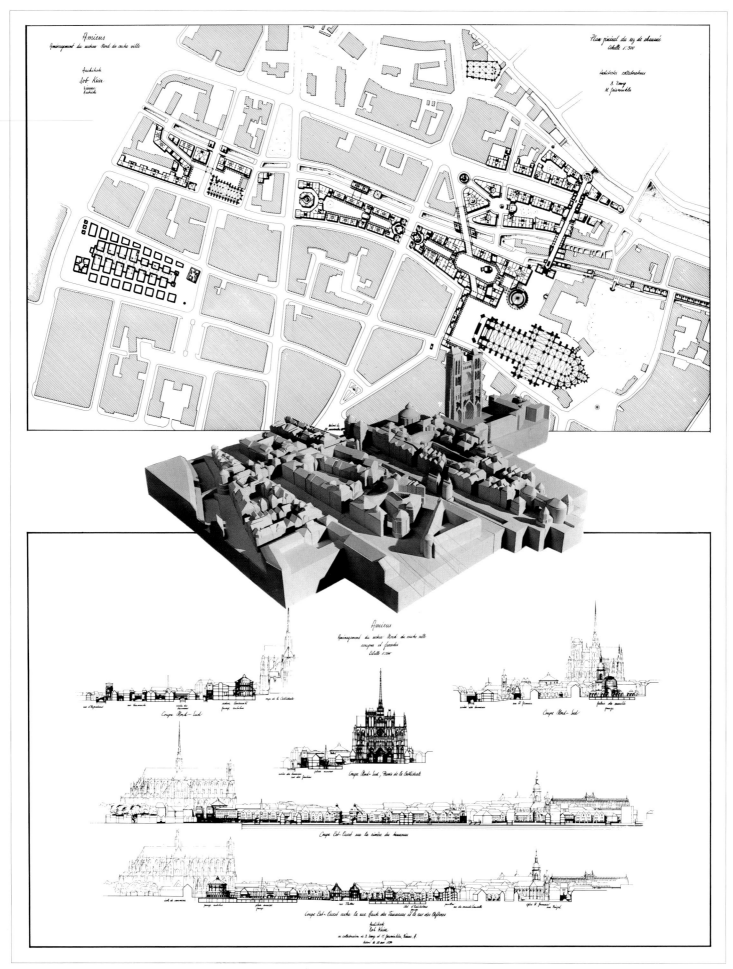

ROB KRIER, DEVELOPMENT OF NORTH OF CITY CENTRE, AMIENS, 1984-, *ABOVE*: GENERAL PLAN; *CENTRE*: MODEL; *BELOW*: SECTIONS AND FAÇADES

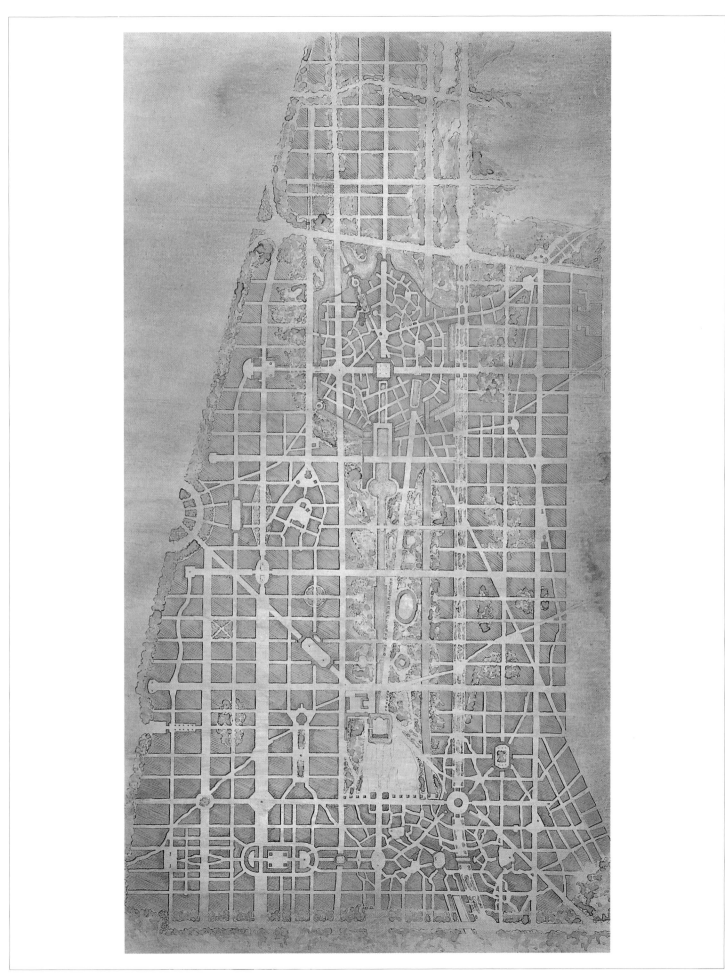

ROB KRIER, GENERAL PLAN FOR CITY OF 25,000 INHABITANTS, MARNE LA VALLÉE, PARIS, 1988

ROB KRIER, BREITENFURTERSTRASSE, VIENNA, 1984-88, *ABOVE*: THE SQUARE; *BELOW*: SOUTH PORTICO OF THE SQUARE

ANDRES DUANY & ELIZABETH PLATER-ZYBERK, CRAB CREEK, FLORIDA, 1988

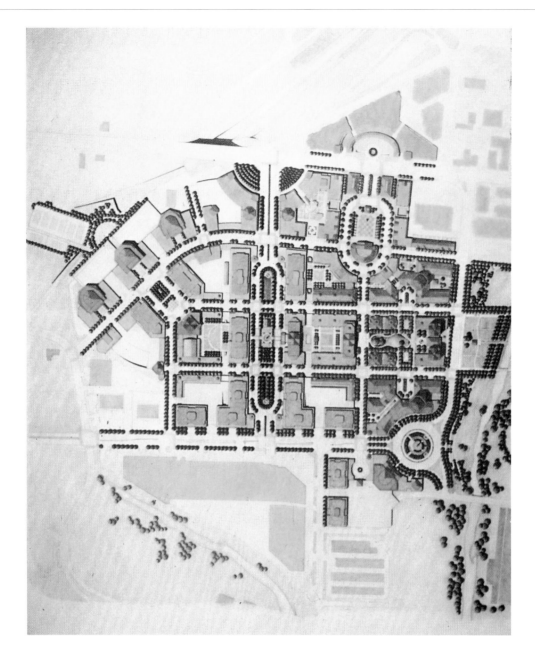

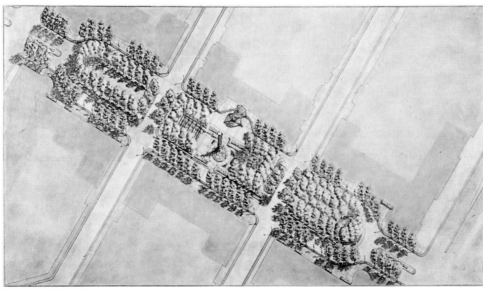

COOPER ROBERTSON & PARTNERS, REGENT'S CENTER, ALEXANDRIA, VIRGINIA, 1990, *ABOVE*: MASTERPLAN: *BELOW*: AXONOMETRIC OF PASSIVE OPEN SPACE

ABDEL WAHED EL-WAKIL, MIQAT MOSQUE, MEDINA, 1990, *ABOVE*: OVERALL VIEW; *CENTRE L TO R*: PLAN AND AXONOMETRIC; *BELOW*: ELEVATION

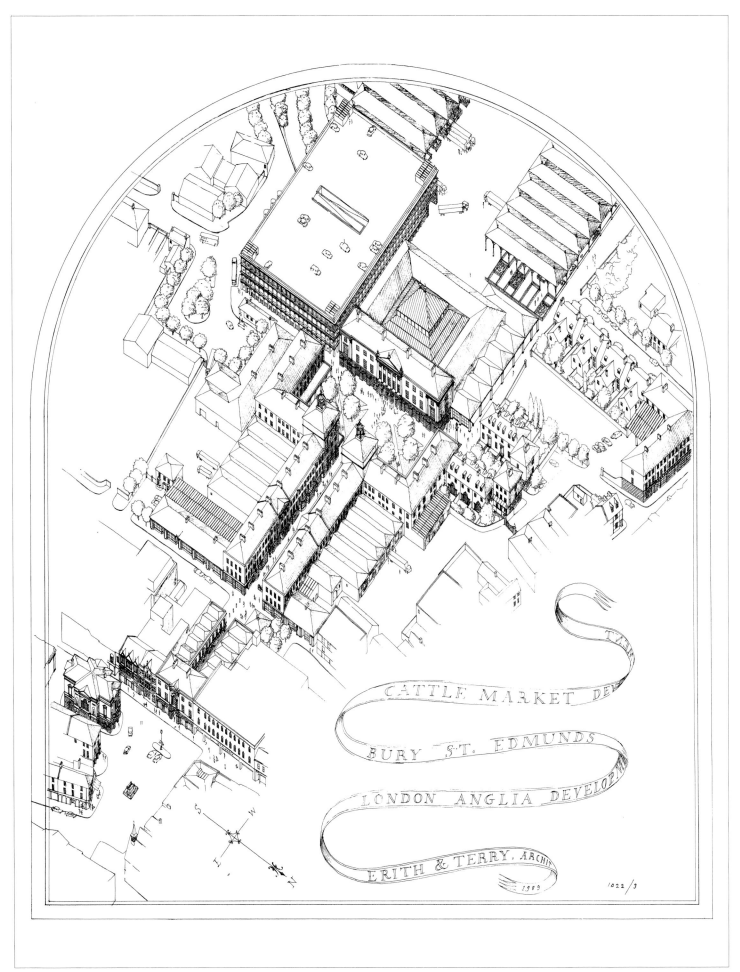

QUINLAN TERRY, REDEVELOPMENT OF THE CATTLE MARKET, BURY ST EDMUNDS, 1989

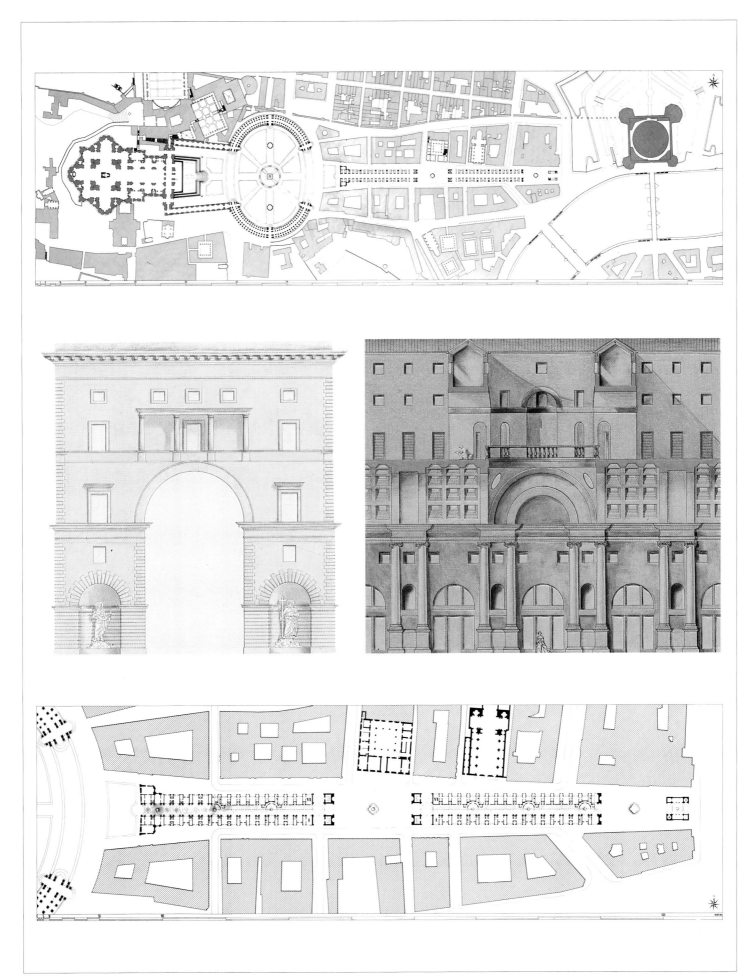

HELMUT PEUKER, RECONSTRUCTION OF THE BORGO QUARTER, ROME, 1989, MASTERPLAN WITH GALLERY FAÇADE AND ROTUNDA

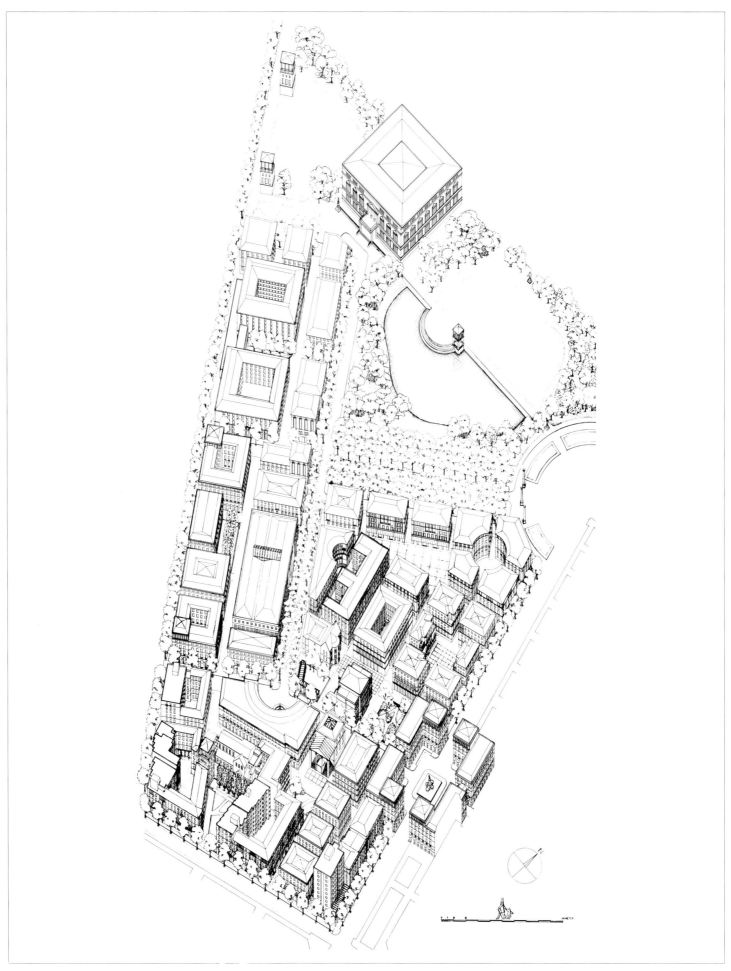

M CULOT, L KRIER, C LANGLOIS, L STEIL, M GARAY AND J-I LINAZASORO, PROJECT FOR RECONSTRUCTION OF THE FRIEDRICHSTADT-SUD QUARTER, BERLIN, BLOC 9, 1986

ACKNOWLEDGEMENTS

The Publishers acknowledge the generous help of architects, authors and artists who have provided work featured in this volume. We are particularly grateful to Demetri Porphyrios for providing many photographs, which include those on pages 3, 14, 17-19, 22, 29, 32, 53, 57-8, 60-65, 67, 84-5, 99, 100, 146-9, 192, 232 (left), 233 (left), 234 (right); likewise to Rita Wolff for a number of paintings and watercolours. Unless otherwise stated illustrations accompanying articles have been provided by the authors and architects. All illustrations provided from other sources are as follows:

COVER, PRELIMS & CONTENTS PAGES
The cover and frontis are by Rita Wolff. The photograph on p 42 is by Richard Cheek. The photograph on p 154 is by Otto Baitz

LEON KRIER: FOREWORD, pp 6-13
This essay has been specially written for this volume.

JOHN SUMMERSON: CLASSICAL ARCHITECTURE, pp 16-17
This paper was given at the Academy Forum's Symposium on New Classicism on Art and Architecture at the Tate Gallery, July 1988.

DEMETRI PORPHYRIOS: CLASSICISM IS NOT A STYLE, pp 18-21
This article originally appeared in *Architectural Design*, Vol 52, 5/6 1982, *Classicism is Not a Style*.

ALDO ROSSI: THE GREEK ORDER, pp 22-23
This article is an extract from 'L'ordine greco', first published in 1959. It appeared in its present form in *Architectural Design*, Vol 52, 5/6 1982, *Classicism is Not a Style*.

MANFREDO TAFURI & GEORGES TEYSSOT: CLASSICAL MELANCHOLIES, pp 24-28
This article originally appeared in *Architectural Design*, Vol 52, 5/6 1982, *Classicism is Not a Style*. Painting of p 24 courtesy of Fondazione Giorgio e Isa de Chirico, Rome.

MICHAEL GREENHALGH: THE CLASSICAL TRADITION, pp 29-30
This article is an extract from a paper entitled 'Classicism in the 19th and 20th Centuries' given at the Academy Forum's Symposium on New Classicism.

ROBERT A M STERN: WHAT THE CLASSICAL CAN DO FOR THE MODERN, pp 31-32
This article has been specially written for the forthcoming *Architectural Monograph* on Robert Stern.

LEON KRIER: 'THE BLIND SPOT', pp 33-35
This is a shortened version of an article which originally appeared in *Architectural Design*, Vol 48, No 4, 1978, 'Urban Transformations'.

LUDWIG LOHDE: THE CONCEPT AND ESSENTIAL FUNCTION OF ARCHITECTURAL DECORATION, pp 36-38
This article originally appeared in *Die Architektonischen Ordungen der Griechen und Romer* by J M Mauch, 1872. Translated from the original German by Eileen Martin.

OLIVER TAPLIN: GREEK FIRE, pp 39-41
This article is a series of extracts from Oliver Taplin's *Greek Fire*, published in the UK by Jonathan Cape, 32 Bedford Square, London, Copyright Oliver Taplin 1989, price £14.95; and in the USA excerpted from *Greek Fire* by Dr Oliver Taplin. Copyright © 1990 by Dr Oliver Taplin. Reprinted by arrangement with Atheneum, an Imprint of Macmillan Publishing Company. The illustration on p 47 is by M Korres, published with permission of the Greek Cultural Attaché in London and the Committee for the Preservation of the Acropolis Monuments.

LEON KRIER: CLASSICAL ARCHITECTURE AND VERNACULAR BUILDING, pp 44-45
This is a revised version of an article which originally appeared in *Architectural Design*, Vol 52, 5/6 1982, *Classicism is Not a Style*. POLICY STATEMENT – THE FIRST *SOMAI* PROPOSAL is the full text of Leon Krier's proposal for SOM Architecture Institute.

DEMETRI PORPHYRIOS: THE RELEVANCE OF CLASSICAL ARCHITECTURE, pp 52-67
'Building and Architecture' originally appeared in *Architectural Design*, Vol 54, 5/6 1984, *Building and Rational Architecture*; 'Imitation and Innovation' originally appeared in *Architectural Design*, Vol 58, 1/2 1988, *The New Classicism*; 'The Relevance of Classical Architecture' is a paper given at the Academy Forum's Symposium on New Classicism and originally appeared in *Architectural Design*, Vol 59, 9/10 1989, *Reconstruction/Decon-struction*. Photograph on p 59 is by Andreas Papadakis

ALLAN GREENBERG: THE ARCHITECTURE OF DEMOCRACY, pp 68-72
This article has been specially written for this volume. The photograph p 68 is by Richard Cheek, that on p 70 by Thomas V Noble.

CARROLL WESTFALL: CLASSICAL AMERICAN URBANISM, pp 73-75
Versions of parts of the article were presented

at the Design Committee Conference, American Institute of Architects, Los Angeles in 1988, in a Smithsonian Associates Programme in Washington, at Amherst College, and at the Universidad Francesco Marraquin in Guetamala in 1989.

QUINLAN TERRY: THE AUTHORITY FOR ARCHITECTURE, pp 76-81
'One Wonders Why...The Seven Wonders of the Modern World' originally appeared in *Architectural Design News Supplement* March 1981, marking Quinlan Terry's first exhibition at the *Architectural Design* Gallery; 'The Authority for Architecture and how it should develop in the Future' is an edited version of a speech given at the Jan Hus Educational Foundation, Czechoslovakia, October 1989; 'That this House Would build Traditional Buildings' is an edited version of a speech given at the Cambridge Union Debate, January 1990.

ROBERT ADAM: THE RADIANCE OF THE PAST, pp 82-87
This article has been specially written for this volume.

GUILIO ARGAN: ON THE TYPOLOGY OF ARCHITECTURE, pp 116-118
This article originally appeared in *Architectural Design*, Vol 33, December 1963, and is reproduced here by kind permission of the author. Translated from the Italian by Joseph Rykwert.

ALAN COLQUHOUN: VERNACULAR CLASSICISM, pp 119-121
This article originally appeared in *Architectural Design*, Vol 54, 5/6 1984, *Building and Rational Architecture*.

JOSÉ-IGNACIO LINAZASORO: ORNAMENT AND CLASSICAL ORDER, pp 122-125
This is an extract from *El proyecto clasico en arquitectura*, Gili, Barcelona, 1981, and was first published in *Architectural Design*, Vol 54, 5/6 1984, *Building and Rational Architecture*. The illustration on p 125-26 is from Heinrich Tessenow, Hausbau und Dergleichen, 1953.

GIORGIO GRASSI: THE QUESTION OF DECORATION, pp 126-131
This article originally appeared in *Architectural Design*, Vol 54, 5/6 1984, *Building and Rational Architecture*.

ALDO ROSSI: AN ANALOGICAL ARCHITECTURE, pp 132-135
This article is reproduced from *Aldo Rossi, Selected Writings and Projects*, AD, 1983.

Translated from the original Italian by David Stewart.

IGNASI SOLÀ-MORALES: NEO-RATION-ALISM AND FIGURATION, pp 136-139
This article originally appeared in *Architectural Design*, Vol 54, 5/6 1984, *Building and Rational Architecture*. Illustrations on p 136 courtesy of Aldo Rossi and Giorgio Grassi.

CHARLES JENCKS: FREE-STYLE CLASSICISM, pp 156-162
'The Wider Tradition' is an extract from 'Free-Style Classicism – The Wider Tradition' first published in *Architectural Design*, Vol 52, 1/2 1982, *Free-Style Classicism*. 'The Classical Spirit and the Free-Style Orders' is a paper given at the Academy Forum's Symposium on New Classicism. All photographs by Charles Jencks.

CHRISTIAN NORBERG-SCHULZ: THE TWO FACES OF POST-MODERNISM, pp 163-166
This article originally appeared in *Architectural Design*, Vol 58, 7/8 1988, *Contemporary Architecture*.

ROBERT A M STERN: THE DOUBLES OF POST-MODERNISM, pp 167-175 This article first appeared in the *Harvard Architectural Review*, No IV, 1980. It is also published in the forthcoming *Robert Stern Monograph*. Photographs on p 170 and 172 are by Whitney Cox.

COLIN ROWE: URBAN SPACE, pp 186-188
This is an extract from the Foreword to *Urban Space* by Rob Krier, first published in English by Academy Editions, 1979.

ALDO ROSSI: ARCHITECTURE AND THE CITY: PAST AND PRESENT, pp 189-191
This article is reproduced from *Aldo Rossi, Selected Writings and Projects, AD*, 1983. Translated from the original Italian by Judith Landry.

DEMETRI PORPHYRIOS: CITIES OF STONE, pp 192-195
This is a revised version of an article which originally appeared in *Architectural Design*, Vol 54, 7/8 1984, *Leon Krier: Houses, Palaces, Cities*.

LEON KRIER: URBAN COMPONENTS pp 196-203
This article originally appeared in *Architectural Design*, Vol 54, 7/8 1984, *Leon Krier: Houses, Palaces, Cities*.

LEON KRIER: CRITIQUES, pp 204-211
These critiques originally appeared in *Architectural Design*, Vol 54, 7/8 1984, *Leon Krier: Houses, Palaces, Cities*.

ROB KRIER: TYPOLOGICAL ELEMENTS OF THE CONCEPT OF URBAN SPACE, pp 212-219
This article is an extract from *Urban Space*, Academy Editions, 1979.

COLIN ROWE: COMMENTS ON THE IBA PROPOSAL, pp 220-225 This article originally appeared in *Architectural Design*, Vol 53, 1/2 1983, *Architecture in Progress*.

ROB KRIER: TEN THESES ON ARCHITECTURE, pp 226-227
This is an extract from Rob Krier's *Architectural Composition*, Academy Editions, 1988, p 10.

JAQUELIN T ROBERTSON: THE HOUSE AS THE CITY, pp 228-237
This article was first published as 'In Search of an American Order Part II', *Modulus 19*, 1989. Photograph on p 233 (right) is by C W Westfall; Photographs on p 234 (left) is by Jac Robertson; Photograph on p 235 is by K Train; Photograph on p 237 is by W Fensbach.

ANDRES DUANY, ELIZABETH PLATER-ZYBERK & CHESTER E CHELLMAN: NEW TOWN ORDINANCES AND CODES, pp 238-243
This article originally appeared in *Architectural Design*, Vol 59, 5/6 1989, *Prince Charles and the Architectural Debate*. Photograph on p 238 by Frank Martinez. Photograph on p 239 is by Steven Brooke.

ALBERTO USTARROZ: THE CITY AND THE CLASSICAL TRADITION, pp 244-245
This article is a revised version of a lecture given at Liverpool Polytechnic Student symposium, 1989, and originally appeared in *Architectural Design*, Vol 59, 9/10 1989, *Reconstruction/Deconstruction*.

PICTORIAL SURVEYS
We would like to thank the many architects who provided material for the surveys. All illustrations from other sources are as follows:

FIGURATIVE CLASSICISM pp 88-113
p 88, 90: Photographs by Matt Wargo
p 91: Paintings by Carl Laubin
p 92: Photographs by Peter Mauss, Esto
p 93 above: Photograph, Alan Greenberg; below: Photograph by Richard Cheek
p 94: Photograph by Steven Brooke
p 96: Painting by Carl Laubin
p 97 above: Photograph by Andreas Papadakis; below: Photograph by Charles Shoup
p 98: Photographs by Otto Austwick
p 99: Photograph by Tom Leighton; Project Team – D Porphyrios, A Sagharchi, I Sutherland, N Cox, L O'Connor.
p 100: Photograph by Mark Fiennes; Project Team – D Porphyrios, A Sagharchi, I Fleetwood, N Cox, M Bradbury, I Sutherland.
p 103: Courtesy of Mr Thody of Haslemere Estates and Chris Parkinson of Richard Ellis
p 105: Photographs, Hammond Beeby & Babka
p 106: Photograph by Langdon Clay
p 107 above: Photograph by Jaquelin Robertson; below: Photograph by Langdon Clay
p 108 Projects for reconstruction of Rue de Laeken supplied by Maurice Culot and *Archives d'Architecture Moderne*.
p 109 All three photographs by Dominique Delaunay
p 110 above: Photograph, Julian Bicknell; below: Photograph, Charles Warren
p 112 above: Photograph, Chapman Taylor Partnership; below: Photograph, James Gorst & Associates
p 113: above: photograph by Andreas Papadakis, centre: Drawings from The Acropolis at Athens, published with permission of the Greek Cultural Attaché in London and the Ministry of Culture Committee for the Preservation of the Acropolis Monuments. Below: Photograph by D Porphyrios.

ABSTRACT CLASSICISM pp 140-153
p 140 Photographs by Luigi Ghirri, courtesy of GFT Gruppo Finanziaro Tesseli, Turin
p 142-3 Photographs supplied by the German Architecture Museum in Frankfurt
p 145 Drawings reproduced from Restauració i Rehabilitació del Teatre Roma de Sagunt, Ganeralitat Valencia, Consilleria de Cultura, Educació i Ciécia.
p 150-1: Photographs, Cenicacelaya & Saloña.
p 152: Photographs, Alexander & Charis Calligas.
p 153: Photographs, Hilmer and Sattler.

POST-MODERN CLASSICISM pp176-183
p 176: Photograph by William Choi
p 178 above: Photograph, Venturi, Rauch & Scott-Brown; below: Photograph by Tom Bernard
p 179 above: photograph by Richard Bryant, below: Photograph by J Surwillo
p 180 above: Photograph by Charles Jencks; below: Photograph by Andreas Papadakis
p 181 above: Photograph by Robert Burley Photography; below: Photograph by Charles Vandenhove.
p 182 above: Painting by Carl Laubin; below: Photograph by Leon Krier.
p 183 above: Photograph by Otto Baitz; below: Photograph by Philip Johnson.

URBANISM pp 246-260
p 251 Project team – D Porphyrios, N Cox, V Duepi, C Britton, P Lorenzoni
p 260 Plan reproduced by courtesy of Maurice Culot and *Archives d'Architecture Moderne*.

———— * ————

INDEX

QUINLAN TERRY, FULHAM FOOTBALL GROUND, 1990 (PAINTING BY CARL LAUBIN)

LIAM O'CONNOR, PROJECT FOR COUNTRY HOUSE